THE SECRET
ARCHIVES OF THE
VATICAN

THE SECRET ARCHIVES OF THE VATICAN

by MARIA LUISA AMBROSINI

with MARY WILLIS

with illustrations

LITTLE, BROWN AND COMPANY · BOSTON · TORONTO

Published simultaneously in Canada
by Little, Brown & Company (Canada) Limited

PRINTED IN THE UNITED STATES OF AMERICA

To Vivina and Stefania

Approach

IN the time that I have been working on this book, friends who are historians have asked me — sometimes in a spirit of amused incredulity — just how I went about researching such an extensive subject. With twenty-five miles of documents, partly explored and partly unexplored, where does one begin? I had to answer that I had begun by following the method of trial and error.

On my first visit to a large museum or archaeological site, I seldom take a guidebook, but wander for a while, led by curiosity and random interest. It is only later that I use a systematic approach. I began this study of the Secret Archives in the same way. I examined the indexes in the index room — or rather, those more easily deciphered — and made a long list, following a generally chronological plan, of documents that caught my interest. As time went on, the nature and structure of the Archives that lay behind the long shelves of indexes absorbed me more and more. The hundreds of documents that I had studied seemed like a few leaves fallen from the forest.

I now did what a professional historian would have done in the first place, and examined what has been written on the Secret Archives and on their separate *fondi*. There are excellent works by Fink, Brom, Giusti, Battelli, Mercati, and Macfarlane, among others. Now and then, in these highly technical studies for the use of archivists and historians, there were glimpses of the history of the Secret Archives, glimpses that I found fascinating. I came to realize that the history of the Secret Archives was the history of the papacy, of the Church; that the Archives were a dark mirror of the world. The plan of my work finally began to take shape — it was to be an overview of the development of the Archives as part of history, illustrated by close-ups of individual events and documents. With the example of medieval manuscripts before me, I have not hesitated to decorate my margins.

A book of this length cannot be inclusive, and I have tried to emphasize the periods most closely related to the history of the Secret Archives and the events that illuminate their times. Many subjects that would be part of a work on general history have been omitted.

Most of my research has been done in the Secret Archives and in the Vatican Library. In the Secret Archives particular use has been made of the papal registers, the Archivum Arcis (the archives of Castel Sant' Angelo), and the Miscellanea and Instrumenta Miscellanea *fondi,* which contain individual ancient documents. Since the indexes are incomplete, I have often found, in the large bound volumes that were brought to me, manuscripts not listed in the indexes, such as the legend of the repentance and death of Judas, which is quoted in Chapter 13.

The Vatican Library was used for background, for examination of documents which in the past were part of the Secret Archives, and for published studies and translations by various historical institutes and by individual scholars. In background reading, and especially for the early historical periods, English and American as well as continental references have been used.

Only selected notes are given. Complete documentation would greatly lengthen the book, and some references, such as works on the Secret Archives in general and works on Rome, run throughout the period covered. Also, some paragraphs, particularly those relating to the history of the Archives, have been built up from many fragmentary references and from personal inquiry. To simplify the matter I am giving a selected bibliography and, in the notes, pointing out some of the sources used. For Archives documents I have normally indicated the *fondo* or other source from which they were drawn, but have not always given the "Archivistic collocation," roughly corresponding to a call number, since this book is not intended for the specialist.

In some cases my collaborator, Mary Willis, and I have used material already in English, such as that quoted from Fremantle's collections, but in large part the English translations are our own. They have been done freely, and are often greatly summarized. We have not used dots to indicate ellipses except when necessary to retain the meaning. Space was a consideration, and the number of ellipses required for these often verbose documents would have impeded the flow of thought and given a granulated appearance to the pages.

My grateful acknowledgments are offered to the Secret Archives and to the Vatican Library, which have allowed me so many years of study in an atmosphere of perfect freedom. I also extend my thanks to all who have helped me to locate material, and who, in informal conversations, have helped me to understand both the structure and the spirit of these institutions. The staff of the State Archives of Rome have been helpful in my study of the transition of these archives from Church to state control.

I want, too, to thank the linguists who have helped me with Greek and Latin documents, and scholars who have given me of their experience and knowledge. Among them are some whose names I do not know: students working in the Secret Archives and in the Vatican Library, who sat with me in the little garden and told me of their own illuminating experiences in research.

I should also like to thank my unusually permissive publishers, especially my editor, Llewellyn Howland III, for generous encouragement and for compelling me to limit the extent of this study; Allison G. Selfridge, copy editor, for valuable criticism and assistance; and Alan D. Williams, now of Viking Press, who introduced me to Little, Brown nearly a decade ago.

Contents

*Illustrations appear between
pages 178 and 179*

THE SECRET
ARCHIVES OF THE
VATICAN

THIS book is an attempt to give readers some idea of the treasure that humanity — not only the Church, but all mankind — possesses in the Secret Archives of the Vatican, and to tell a little of how this vast collection of knowledge came into being, how the letters of Saint Peter and Saint Paul grew into twenty-five miles of shelved documents.

I am not an archivist; I am not a historian. I have not attempted to write the history of the Church nor to explain in detail the contents and structure of the Secret Archives. My plan has been to follow their story, so often like the Sisyphus legend, and to give a glimpse of what they contain, or may have contained, in the light of the times that produced them. Books must follow their own logic, and the interest I have taken in historical personages is not always proportional to their importance or to the strength of their ties to the Archives.

While I am most grateful, in the human sense, for the discreet hospitality that has been offered me for so long in the Secret Archives, I must state that no official help was given to me and that what I have written is based on my own individual impressions and conclusions. In my research in the Archives I was left completely free. No information was refused me when I had technical difficulties to overcome, and no question was ever put to me, after the initial interview, as to the purpose of my study.

I began this work with a certain boldness, and I am finishing it with a sense of humility, realizing the greatness of the task. At least I can say that it has been done with love.

The Caves of the Time-Stream

M Y acquaintance with the Secret Archives of the Vatican came about almost by chance; I was looking for a sculptor three centuries dead.

In the Sacred Wood of Bomarzo, within a hundred miles of Rome, onormous Oriental statues of elephants, tigers, goddesses, lie in a valley of the Italian countryside. Their origin is a mystery. In writing an article on them for an American magazine, it occurred to me that some clue might be found in the archives of the Burghese family, the last private owners of this monstrous sculpture garden. These archives had been purchased by the Vatican and were lodged in the Secret Archives.

I had no clear idea of what the Secret Archives were. I had been acquainted with the Vatican, from the outside, for many years. I had attended the great ceremonies at Saint Peter's, and small private audiences where the pope speaks from a human heart of our personal griefs and hopes. But I had heard of the Secret Archives only vaguely, in casual conversation and in the footnotes of historical works. In fact I had never cared for archives. They seemed like tombs of the past, tombs of ideas that no longer mattered. I felt for them the physical distaste that one feels for dusty old papers.

Wondering how quickly I could get through with the Burghese archives, I crossed the great square of Saint Peter's, that place of stone and water, fountains and obelisk. I passed the Leonine walls, a last defense against the Saracens, and went through the Gate of Saint Anne into Vatican City. An arched road leads past the *Osservatore Romano* building to the Court of the Belvedere, where the Secret Archives are housed next to the Vatican Library. Three successive Swiss Guards asked to see my pass before I reached the stairway to the Library and the Archives.

At the foot of the stairway was a statue of the third-century antipope Hippolytus robed and throned. I had read of its discovery among the rubbish of a basement, and that Pope John XXIII, with the courtesy of a winner to a loser, had ordered it installed at the entrance to the Vatican Library. I noticed that the identifying inscription referred to Hippolytus not as antipope but as a learned doctor and philosopher of the early Church. John's kindness and generosity had reached back to a man of ancient Rome. The feeling began to grow on me that this was a place where the world appeared *sub specie aeternitatis,* where one saw the centuries from a high place.

I had brought with me a letter from the prince who is head of the Borghese family; but I also needed the permission of the Prefect of the Archives and, on paper at least, the permission of the Pope himself. I found Monsignor Giusti, the prefect, very courteous, but with a serene detachment. Deeply cultured, he has written essays on the Secret Archives and on Archives documents, and his mental discipline is apparent in the clarity of his explanations. He wears the priest's robe with a simple elegance. In him one can see the difference between being a modest person and being a humble one.

At last admitted to the Borghese Archives, I found no conclusive answer to the puzzle of the massive Oriental statues half buried in the soil of an Italian valley, but I found certain clues that made one answer seem more probable than the others. The dead sculptor was a little clearer to me now — a lonely young prisoner of war, turning to the art of his Asian homeland in an alien country. And I found allusions that raised further mysteries. (Where, for example, is the mausoleum that Hannibal Caro, a writer of the time, said Prince Vicino Orsini was building in that Etruscan country?)

In the detailed documents of the Archives, the little sixteenth-century principality, the country kingdom, came to life for me. I could see Prince Vicino with his "immense, almost fatal physical beauty"; I knew the names of the horses. I read the letters of friends, written in a time when friendship had an intellectual meaning — letters of brilliant men who wrote to each other of art and archaeology and ideas. And I found documents that led me far away from the field of my research. Here were the stories of Pauline Borghese, Napoleon's sister, whose selfish extravagances humiliated her husband until illness made her gentle and aware of human kindness. Here were the records of the investigation into an Orsini prince's alleged strangling of his wife, Isabella, in her marriage bed, a sixteenth-century murder story with the last chapter unwritten. And here were the legends of a Borghese princess, Guendalina, whose last act of charity was done after her death, when a poor woman kneeling at her grave suddenly discovered on her own finger the diamond ring that the princess had worn to her burial.

The ancient documents had already worked their spell on me when I was given a chance — a rare one, as I later learned — to visit almost all of the Secret Archives of the Vatican. It was four o'clock on a foggy November day; except for a few employees the rooms were deserted.

Besides the area next to the Library, the Secret Archives have taken over the Tower of the Winds and two long corridors, each of them containing bookshelves that, end to end, would reach seven and a half miles. One corridor leads like an aqueduct from the top of the tower to the Borgia apartments; the other, on the ground floor, leads from the administrative offices to a small chapel, then in temporary use as a photostating room, directly under the frescoed private chapel of Pope Borgia, where Saint Catherine (Lucrezia Borgia?) argues with the philosophers, her blond hair less a saint's than a nymph's.

In a large room called the Hall of the Parchments there were thousands of documents relating to the rights of the papal state, turned purple because of a violet-colored fungus that scientists have so far been unable to control. They will eventually become illegible.

Next is the room of the inventories and indexes. These are not card files, as in British or American libraries, but enormous handwritten volumes, some of them so heavy that I was unable to lift them.

The ground-floor corridor, without windows, was dark by now. This is the most modern part of the Secret Archives, equipped with electric lights and with great steel bookshelves from America, so large that they have two levels; little stairways lead to the second level, where there is a labyrinth of small passages. The long, straight corridor was deserted at this hour, and the lights, which one turns on as he progresses through it, go off automatically within a few minutes, so that one moves in a small island of light, with darkness behind him and in front of him, as consciousness moves along the time-stream. Always there is the illusion of being in an underground world.

Here in the ground-floor corridor are the records of the Consistory, the ecclesiastical senate of cardinals that once, acting as a body, advised the popes on important matters. I opened two volumes at random; in the first I read of the appointment of theologians to confute the theses of Luther; in the second, Adrian VI received the nuncio from Denmark, who brought news of the bloodbath in which Christian II had executed two bishops and many Danish aristocrats. With the Consistory records are the records of the conclaves for the election of popes from the fifteenth century onward. Besides the bare official tallies of the votes, there are richly detailed memoirs of the pontifical masters of ceremony, full of passion and politics.

Here is the series of indulgences, the sales slips of long-ago sins, of broken promises, of special exemptions from ecclesiastical law. The payment was not always in money; sometimes it was in acts of humility, hardship, or courage. And here are the registers of petitions, one of the largest series in the Secret Archives — over seven thousand heavy volumes of requests for every kind of ecclesiastical grace and favor. In these one finds the supplications of kings, of the literary lions Petrarch and Boccaccio, and of poor country churchmen.

More personal still are the records of the Sacred Rota, one of the ecclesiastical courts, named for the circular bench on which its judges sat. This very old tribunal once had wide powers but now deals mainly with annulments of marriage. Its records contain details of the personal and physical lives of the supplicants, given in answer to questions more searching than a psychiatrist would venture. Except for the very earliest volumes, these records are inaccessible.

On this lower floor, and also difficult of access, are some of the family archives of the historic Roman families, from which many of the popes and cardinals have come, and the private archives of the cardinals, which reverted to the Church on their deaths or were purchased from their heirs. Here in the uniform bindings was all that was left of Cardinal Ferrata, whom I knew from family tradition as a witty old man of the world, who delighted in escaping his secretaries and stealing fruit from his own fruit trees. He had been appointed papal Secretary of State and his villa had been stripped, its furniture sent to the Vatican, when he was stricken with pneumonia. He died on a mattress on the bare floor, muttering something about *vanitas*.

Near the end of the corridor is a large dark door, closed. The key to it never leaves the possession of the prefect, for behind it are the rooms where the very sensitive documents are kept: recent records, highly classified since they concern persons now living and still-existing political situations.

There is a great safe in the corridor; in its drawers the most precious of all the Archives documents are kept like jewels in a giant jewelcase. Some documents have a drawer to themselves; there are never more than a few in each. They seem like fragments of history:

The ratification of the abdication of Queen Christina of Sweden, four sheets of yellowed parchment bearing the signatures of the members of the Swedish Parliament and their three hundred and five seals of wax like red stars, each with its coat of arms. It is signed simply *"Christina."* I remembered a phrase of hers —"The heart is made for love and the soul has no sex." Christina, who took as much care for her white death-dress as for the dress worn at her abdication, and whose body, exposed on a bier, was followed to its grave by the poor of Rome, their arms full of narcissus and hyacinths gathered from the hills surrounding the city. . . .

The last letter of Mary Stuart to the pope, written a few days before she fell under the axe of Elizabeth. The letter is in French, in a handwriting at first fine and firm, but becoming irregular toward the end. It is signed "*Marie Royne d'Escosse douayriere de France*" — a letter very humble in regard to God, very queenlike in regard to men. "I, born of kings, I alone have remained, of the blood of England and Scotland, to profess this faith. . . . Today I have had a message, in the name of the Queen, that I must prepare myself to receive death. I would be quite willing to lose the title and all royal privileges if only the court would end the persecution of Catholics. I have no more wish to live in this world. And as the last of my earthly requests I commend to you my son, that he may be a worthy son of Catholic kings. Bidding you my last adieu . . . please take care that after my death the enemies of the Church do not calumniate me. . . ."

A letter from a Ming empress, written in 1655 on a sheet of ivory silk, on one side the address in red characters, on the other an embroidered golden dragon. The empress asked that more Jesuit missionaries be sent to China. She had taken the name Helena at her baptism and her little nephew, the crown prince, had been given the name of Constantine — a suggestion that the Chinese empire, like ancient Rome, might become Christian. But the empress had been dead for four years when the pope's answer arrived, and the Jesuits' enemies were plotting to destroy them . . .

The fruitless petition of seventy-five lords of England, with their seventy-five wax seals as large as saucers, asking the pope to grant an annulment of the marriage between Henry VIII and Catherine of Aragon; an appeal based, ostensibly, on theological arguments. But other documents had already reached the Vatican — love letters of Henry to Anne Boleyn, perhaps stolen from her rooms, signed "*Henry* (AB) *Roy*" and "*Henry autre* (AB) *ne cherche*" — tender, respectful letters, presenting a king entirely different from the vulgar lout who has come down to us through history . . .

Seventy-eight seals in gold and silver, the world's foremost collection, the second being that of the British Museum. Particularly remarkable are the heavy golden seals of the Spanish kings Philip II and Philip III. Each of them weighs nearly two pounds. The one of Philip II shows the sovereign bearded, crowned, with armor under his mantle, enthroned against an architectural background of columns that give a feeling of great distance. The seal of Philip III is an equestrian portrait; there is a sense of movement in the armored horse, seen against a golden plain . . .

The "Greek diplomas" between the popes and the Comnenus emperors of Byzantium, a dynasty of handsome men of great strength and courage. One diploma, dated 1146, deals with the protection of the crusaders, a protection that ended in slaughter. It is a scroll over thirteen feet long and fifteen inches wide, on purple parchment with an intricately decorated border. The writing, of great beauty, is in gold. The imperial signature, placed between the Latin and the Greek versions, is blood-red. When Constantinople fell, the Comnenus family became part of the Diaspora of aristocrats and scholars that enriched the cultural life of Italy. Some of them settled in Corsica; there, according to the memoirs of the Duchess d'Abrantès, they contributed one of the bloodlines that made Napoleon . . .

And finally the dogma of the Immaculate Conception, illuminated in delicate colors and bound in pale blue velvet.

Facing the exit from the ground-floor corridor is the home of the prefect. Even at night he is not far from the Archives and their problems.

A small twisting circular stair leads to the oldest sections of the Archives, which open off the Tower of the Winds, built as an astronomical observatory in the scientific enthusiasm of the early baroque period. There is an ancient lift that goes as high as the third floor, but it was out of order during my visit. The stairway is steep and difficult, but no other passage to the uppermost floors exists; even John XXIII, when he inspected the Secret Archives shortly after his election, was forced to climb it. One is surprised at the great number of telephones short distances apart on the stairway, for use in calling employees — the equivalent of a modern institution's speaker system.

In this oldest part of the Secret Archives most of the ancient and precious documents and records are kept. It was here that Paul V Borghese set up the centralized Archives early in the seventeenth century, gathering together the various collections of records that had been stored in different places. They were welcomed as guests of honor in rooms that had been prepared for them, rooms frescoed with pictures of those who had donated greatly to the Church — Charlemagne, John Lackland, Matilda of Tuscany. Their poplar cabinets were made by the great cabinetmakers of the time; they still bear the coat of arms of the Borghese pope.

These cabinets now hold the oldest series of documents in the Secret Archives, nearly five thousand papal registers. The registers are collections of handwritten copies (the medieval approximation of carbon copies) of the official letters of the popes, with a few incoming and personal letters as intruders. The oldest and most important of the three series, called the Vatican registers, starts its regular flow with the letters of Innocent III in the year 1198, though three stray earlier volumes exist. The letters, written on parchment, are artistically bound in volumes of a size that one now sees only in world atlases. Their ink, with the passing of time, has turned a warm yellow, so that they seem to be written in gold. Rather curiously, on many pages there are small humorous drawings, very modern in conception. A cow, for instance; a pushcart; a countryside. I opened the register of Innocent III, and at the bottom of the page were scattered nightmare drawings, Draculas, women with bestial anatomical features — the work of a twelfth-century Hieronymus Bosch. Each section ended with a design shaped like a star, in which was written the first word of the next section, a device also used by the first newspapers to make it easier to connect the different sections. The papal letters and bulls were written by officials of the papal Chancellery, often, especially in the Renaissance, leading authors. They used to boast that they had in their hands the most important world affairs — that they were admired and marveled at by kings and princes and peoples, and were dependent on no one but the pope.

In all there are 4857 registers, including a few duplicates but not counting those lost in the wars, upheavals, and lootings of the times. The last raid on the Secret Archives was made by Napoleon. Following his dream of a European library, a world brain, he took nearly all of the Secret Archives to France. In the period that followed the breaking of the empire, nearly two thousand of the registers were lost. Many of them were sold as wastepaper to groceries and drugstores, where sheets torn from them were used for wrapping parcels.

In the same section are the archives of Castel Sant'Angelo, the fortress that was able to defend its contents from the Sack of Rome. Here are the imperial diplomas, the seventy-eight "sovereign documents," from Barbarossa's time to Napoleon's, from Armenia to Spain, and transcriptions of very ancient documents that have been lost, such as trial records, old inventories of books, and thirteenth-century reports on the Mongols.

Perhaps the most intriguing of all the collections in the Secret Archives is the Miscellanea, which fills fifteen enormous closets. This *fondo* (roughly, archive) is closed in the sense that it is complete — no documents are being added. It contains material relating to political and religious history, such as reports of nuncios before the permanent nunciatures began. There is a vast documentation on Luther and Calvin; there are monographs on the condition of the Church in various periods of history; there are reports on Ethiopia and on Oriental religions — and intriguing fragments of trials for sorcery. Much of the Miscellanea is in code and only partly explored.

There is also a live Miscellanea *fondo*, the Instrumenta Miscellanea. Documents that cannot be filed in any of the other *fondi* are put into this one. Among them are summaries of acts of inquisition of the fourteenth century, secret letters of the popes, especially of the Avignon period, documents relating to the early banking companies that served the popes, an autographed letter of Melanchthon. Both these *fondi* are particularly interesting grab-bags for research.

In time the Archives spread like weeds through the adjoining rooms, into the old attics running along the western wall of the Court of the Belvedere and over the new picture gallery, till they invaded the Tower of the Winds itself. The attic corridor, parallel to the one on the ground floor that I had already seen, resembles it except for being less modern and having the slanted ceiling of the succession of garrets from which it was made. From its windows one can see the fresh green of the Vatican gardens. Here are the diplomatic archives of the Church, that include the correspondence with the nuncios. Between the nuncios and the Secretary of State there took place an exchange of letters amazingly frequent for the time, often on a weekly basis. Many of them are in code.

The reports of the nuncios have contributed to one of the Secret Archives' interesting minor collections, the hundred and fifty volumes of *avvisi* from Rome, Antwerp, Cologne, Venice, London, Naples, Paris, Versailles. These bulletins of information, like small newspapers in their content, were sent to the Curia as supplementary reports by nuncios and other papal officials. The nuncios gathered this information from various sources — conversations with ambassadors and princes, reports from secret agents, news from merchants and sailors. All this was added to the formal reports on a separate sheet, or *foglio di avvisi*. These dispatches were often augmented en route by agents in other cities, who added their own reports. This multiple authorship explains the discrepancies in handwriting and the variety of content, ranging from political information to the petty gossip of a court.

At the very top of the Tower of the Winds is the airy, empty Room of the Meridian. Two of its walls are covered with frescoes portraying the winds as godlike figures with blowing garments; on the other two are peaceful scenes showing ancient Roman life in the four seasons of the year. This room was built as an astronomical observatory — a fact that might have been of some comfort to Galileo, whose signed confession is stored below. On the floor is a zodiacal diagram oriented to the sun's rays, which enter through a slit in the frescoed wall — it was in this room that the Gregorian calendar was worked out. On the ceiling is a moving pointer to indicate the direction of the wind.

As a precaution against fire and thieves, the Tower of the Winds has no lighting system. It is thought that since no artificial light is ever seen there, any flicker of illumination would draw immediate attention to the presence of intruders. As we came down from the tower at six o'clock, my guide did not use even a flashlight. So complete was his knowledge of all the turns and corners of the passageways that he moved easily and surely in the dark.

L' Archivio Segreto Vaticano

L' *Archivio Segreto Vaticano,* perhaps the most important archives of
the world, contains about twenty-five miles of bookshelves laden
with parchment and paper manuscripts of great historical value. The
Secret Archives are not simply a repository of records of the past, but a
functioning organ of the Church, dealing with every human concern;
with art and science as well as with theology and politics. They began
with records of the struggle against imperial Rome; they continue with
records of the work of the Church in the lands where "The East is Red,"
and in the agnostic, alienated cities of the West.

In some ways the papal archives are like those of secular princes, particularly for the times of the imperialist popes. But they also reflect the
Church's spiritual rule of that part of humanity which recognizes its authority, and its concern for all of humanity. It is this universal coverage
that makes the papal archives far more inclusive than those of the national states.

For some parts of history, such as the Middle Ages, they are the key
(the Key of Saint Peter, they have been called); for other parts they
offer only a few master documents or valuable supplementary material.
Just as the city of Rome shows the student of art masterpieces and other
works in all styles — Romanesque, Renaissance, baroque, modern — so
the Secret Archives have major and supplementary records for more
than a thousand years of history. In addition to the main groupings —
the *fondi* — that are the archstones of the Archives, there are the hundreds of thousands of little incidental documents that often tell us more
about the life of man in the past than we can learn from more official
records. Yet most of us have only a vague knowledge of the existence of
these archives, let alone of their nature and extent. They are often con-

fused with the Vatican Library, and are sometimes wrongly referred to as the Secret Library of the Vatican. Even the Lateran Agreement of 1929, between Mussolini and the Church, spoke of the Secret Archives' School of Paleography as belonging to the Library.

The Secret Archives and the Vatican Library are separate institutions. The Archives are the papal Curia's working files: correspondence relating to diplomatic matters and to the internal life of the Church. They are functional in their origin; their first purpose is to serve the Curia. But, as the prefect says, "Little by little, as the documents of an archive age, they leave the realm of administration for the realm of history."

The Vatican Library is, like other libraries, primarily a collection of individual works. Its contents emphasize religious subjects and allied fields such as philosophy and art history. It also contains some material that, according to the normal distinction between an archive and a library, should have remained in the Archives. When the Library and the Secret Archives were separated, the Library got more than its share of the community property. Its intellectual opulence is incredible. I realized it faintly when I asked to see Michelangelo's letters, in the original, and was told apologetically that I couldn't have them right now — the Pope had them out and they couldn't press him to return them.

Though the Secret Archives and the Vatican Library are separate organizations, they are twin — and sometimes rival — organizations. In the past they were closely connected; part of the Archives was once a secret section of the Vatican Library. Great interchanges of material have taken place between the two, and shifting is still going on.

There is a back-and-forth flow of students between the Library and the Archives. Researchers often do their spadework in the Library and then follow up clues in the Archives. A door is kept open between the Archives and the Library, and one sees Archives officials — the prefect, the scriptors — as well as Archives students in the Library. But two separate permits, granted by different authorities, are required for reciprocal access.

The name "Secret Archives" and the fact that the Archives are off limits to journalists and photographers has given them an atmosphere of mystery that has excited curiosity and encouraged speculation. Various rumors circulate as to their nature. One says that they contain an authoritative collection of "naughty and lascivious" documents and books like those in *L'Enfer* of the National Library of Paris or the Private Case of the British Museum. Another suggests that they are made up of material of explosive political significance. The idea that the Archives contain quantities of sexually exciting works seems to derive mainly from human hopefulness. Certainly, in the miles and centuries of documents one can find instances of such writing, but those which I have seen are factual in their intent and no more pornographic than medical case histories or court proceedings.

The existence of a *Riserva,* formerly called the closed section, may have contributed to this idea, since it contains books and documents that can be examined only with the permission of the prefect. But this is a repository not of questionable but of particularly valuable material, such as the record of Galileo's trial and Napoleon's Treaty of Tolentino. Occasionally books, documents, or seals from the *Riserva* are put on exhibition as treasures of art or history. As far as I have been able to discover, the *Riserva* contains nothing withheld because of its subject matter. Nor did I, in the two years that I worked in the Secret Archives, see any attempt to censor material. As it happens, the section of the Archives most thoroughly gleaned by historians and writers is that dealing with humanism and the Renaissance — the time when popes were kings and politicians, and sometimes also artists, warriors, and lovers. When the historian Pastor discovered a group of personal letters of Pope Alexander Borgia, including letters from the women surrounding him — Lucrezia, Vanozza Catanei, and Julia Farnese — it was a monsignor of the Vatican who helped him translate and publish them, even though they worked against the attempt to rehabilitate the reputations of Pope Alexander and Lucrezia. In this collection of letters Julia Farnese writes, "I kiss the desired feet, for where my treasure is, my heart is also," to a pope who eventually calls her *"Julia ingrata et perfida."* The Vatican even permitted them to be printed with the facsimile signature of Pope Borgia.

Then why are the Archives called Secret? As the personal archives of the popes, they were truly *Segreto* for centuries of their existence. Leakage sometimes occurred, but it was heavily punishable. Only a few scholars were allowed, by special permission, to have access to some limited sections. Officially the Archives were opened in 1881 by Pope Leo XIII. "The Church," he said, "needs nothing but the truth."

But the name is not only an echo of the past; they still retain strong elements of secrecy. First there is the "hundred years' rule" that makes documents of most of the past century inaccessible. Time limits are set by other archives as well, but the period is usually shorter. For example, the State Archives of Rome are closed only for material of the last thirty or fifty years, depending on the subject.

Besides the documents too recent to be consulted, some other contents of the Archives are inaccessible. The *fondi* which have been deposited in the Secret Archives by the Congregations must be considered barred, unless special permission, hard to obtain, is given by the prefect of the Congregation concerned or by the prefect of the Archives. In addition to the records of the Sacred Rota, which include annulment proceedings, there are the closed archives of the Congregation of Rites, dealing with the processes for beatification and canonization. In these the "devil's advocate" brings forward all the less creditable incidents in the life of the "Servant of God," and the witnesses who testify for or against him tell their own lives in detail.

The Archives are open to the public, but only to a very limited section of the public. The opportunity to do research in them is regarded as a favor, not as a right. They are still a feudal territory of the Church. Ordinarily, in order to use them, an Italian layman must have a letter of introduction from some important cultural organization or from the head of a major library or private archives. A priest must have a letter from his bishop. A foreign layman must have a letter from a high-ranking diplomat, his consul, or a well-known cultural organization. (This introduction may be waived in the case of eminent scholars.)

After the presentation of such a letter, you have a conference with the prefect, in which you discuss your project and your reasons for consulting the Archives, which operate on a need-to-know basis. You are then given a form addressed to the pope as "*Beatissimo Padre.*" In due time you receive a permit bearing your photograph and good for a certain period. No matter how well the staff comes to know you, you must still give them your permit each time you enter the Archives, to be kept until you leave. You must also sign yourself in and out as one does at a closed military installation or a government office under strict security.

Permits are granted only after careful screening; about two hundred may be given in the course of a year. One reason for this is the necessity of guarding against the use and abuse of documents by sensationalist writers. Even writers of solid reputation sometimes cannot resist the temptation to publish material that, in a modern courtroom, would be discussed only in a closed hearing. For example, the author Mazzuchelli, working in the archives of the Archbishopric of Milan, with the special permission of Cardinal Montini (later Paul VI), found in a safe the original records of the trial of the Monaca di Monza, that dramatic and pathetic figure of *I Promessi Sposi.* When he published them he discussed them mainly from the legal point of view, but the records gave the most intimate details of the life of the Nun of Monza and other nuns of the convent. The effect of the book was explosive and Mazzuchelli was attacked by the conformist press.

Another reason for limiting the number of researchers is the practical consideration that many of the documents are fragile, and heavy use would mean danger of damage. There is also the fear of theft, since some of them, particularly the illuminated books, might arouse the illicit love of collectors.

Then, too, students carrying on research in the Archives are very much dependent on the personnel, who bring them the volumes and *buste* (folders) that may contain the material needed. Permission to use the Archives does not include browsing privileges. And the Archives have a limited number of attendants. Even more limited is the professional staff. There are the prefect, appointed for life by the pope himself, the vice-prefect, three archivists, and four *scrittori*. The archivists and the *scrittori* do the same kind of work in organizing the *fondi* — the difference is a matter of rank. These seven persons make up the entire professional staff of this large and complex institution.

But perhaps the main reason for considering the Archives as secret is that, in spite of the great quantity of material that has been inventoried, vast sections remain unexplored. The Secret Archives of the Vatican are an extensive buried city, a Herculaneum inundated by the lava of time, and they are secret as an archaeological dig is secret. No one, not even their staff, knows all that is in them.

To understand the jumble of the Archives one must know something of their unsettled history. Documents had been accumulating for centuries, but the Archives were not established in their present form until 1612, when Paul V Borghese ordered all the records of the Church to be channeled to the part of the Vatican where they are now kept. Before this, they had been stored in several places in the Vatican and throughout Rome. Some had never returned from the captivity at Avignon.

The *Trésor de Chartes* of the Church was transferred from Castel Sant' Angelo; its documents still bear their original classification mark: "A.A." for Archivum Arcis. Other archives flowed in like tributary rivers. Some came from departments or organs of the pontifical Curia; some from other Italian cities and from monasteries that were being closed. Diplomatic and political archives came in from nunciatures abroad. Then there were archives that were not strictly connected with the Curia but were related to the history of the Roman Church.

Often the incoming archives were themselves a confused combination of other archives, some of them long dead, belonging to organizations that no longer existed. Such are the archives of the nunciature of Venice, which came to the Secret Archives in 1835 after the Republic of Venice had fallen. This is a very rich and complex *fondo,* since the nunciature of

Venice had also been the place of deposit for the archives of three religious institutions that had been suppressed in the seventeenth century — one of them San Giorgio in Alga, so called because the island on which the church was built was covered with algae pushed there by the sea.

It was impossible to inventory and organize such a flood of documents. Many collections were simply given broad general classifications and then neatly stored to await a time when they could be examined more thoroughly. Seeing these carefully labeled collections one would not suspect that their contents are a mélange and a mystery.

After the Secret Archives were opened to research, various countries — England, Spain, Norway, France, even Eastern nations — sent commissions to Rome or established national historical institutes there to search for and publish documents relating to world history and the history of their own nations. Aside from this government-financed work, academies and societies have sent scientific missions, and many private researchers have carried out individual studies.

But the research has been fragmentary and uncoordinated. Scattered shafts have been sunk into the buried city, but none of the archaeological expeditions knows of the findings of all the others. In spite of the amount of work that has been done, we still do not know how many *fondi* there are. Fink lists 75, another authority 130. We do not know just what exploration has been done. The national institutes have published their findings, but aside from these only a fraction of the thousands of books and articles relating to Archives documents have been sent to the Archives as is required by regulation. Much of the Archives is *terra incognita*, but we do not even know how much. An enormous quantity, the experts say.

Some *fondi*, especially the older ones, have been rather thoroughly excavated; others only in sections. Then there are the thousands of *buste* or folders of loose documents. It is especially in the folders that one hopes to make discoveries.

An attempt is being made to bring modern methods to bear on the problem. Since 1955 an international committee with headquarters at the Vatican has been preparing a bibliography of books and articles which publish or mention Archives documents. Four volumes of this have already been issued on printed works that have appeared since the opening of the Archives to the public in 1881. The committee's program is ambitious, and it may cover earlier years as well. Experts say that this bibliography, while extremely useful, shares the fault of other inventories in not being all-inclusive. One might consult it for information on what he hopes is a new document, and, finding no mention of it, be happy at having made a new discovery. Instead, it may already have been exploited by another writer, in a work that the bibliography failed to include.

Besides the work of such organizations, there is the silent invisible work of the staff archivists who, at their lonely desks among the documents, prepare new inventories and indexes. But the problem sometimes seems to be beyond human capability. I have seen rooms full of documents that are virgin in terms of research. Often the folders of documents have been carefully gathered into volumes and filed by year. But what they contain no one knows. Opening off the Meridian Room in the Tower of the Winds, I saw a small square room where, in a single great bookcase, there were nine thousand packages of unexplored documents. These packages were not large — about the size of a small magazine. I was told that in order to inventory — not study, but simply inventory in chronological order — one package, two experts would need a week of steady work. To do all of the nine thousand packages in this single bookcase, they would need a hundred and eighty years. It is hard to say what will be the outcome on this particular sector of the war between order and entropy.

The student quickly finds that working in the Archives is quite different from working in a library. In a library it is enough to know the name of the author of a book or to keep in mind the subject one is interested in. Then, with the help of card catalogues arranged by name and by subject, one can find the work he wants. But in the Archives a great deal of preliminary reading on one's subject and on the Archives itself is necessary before the real research problem can be attacked.

The Archives is not a collection of documents in the way that a library is a collection of books. Instead it contains an interdependent documentation that has arisen from the functioning of various offices. In order to orient oneself in an archive one has to know the purpose for which the office originating it was established, and how it functioned. In the Vatican Secret Archives the student cannot look for documents on a personage — even on an ecclesiastic working in the pontifical Curia — without knowing exactly the Congregation and the office for which he worked, or his relationship with the Holy See. For instance, did he have a consistorial benefice, or did he work in a nunciature? The archivist or the scriptor of the Secret Archives may help the student by telling him the offices for which archives exist. But they cannot help him in searching for such documents unless the student himself first knows in which *fondo* he intends to start his research. The Archives staff gives students a general orientation and indicates the indexes or inventories to be consulted, but they are expected to carry out most of the research for themselves.

There are 684 indexes or inventories compiled by different authors. Nearly all of them are handwritten. For most of the *fondi* that were in the Archives by the eighteenth century, there are summaries, inventories, chronological indexes, or onomastic (by name) indexes. But to assume that they are complete is misleading. A person may find nothing in them on a certain person or subject, even though interesting and important information is actually available. The index most likely to be used by the occasional student — the many volumes of Cardinal Garampi — is not only incomplete but uses symbols and abbreviations that can be deciphered only with the help of a handbook available in the study room. For example, in the indexes for the documents in the *armadi* (closets) of the Miscellanea, Garampi uses the letters of the Greek alphabet, but in a handwriting so inexact and variable that most of the time one cannot decipher it.

In searching for documents bearing on a given subject, it is not enough to look in a *fondo* where an index says that there are documents. One must also look in other *fondi* that he suspects may contain documents somehow related to the subject. Suppose, for example, that you are searching for information on the trial of the Templars. Some documents may be found in the registers of Clement V, some in the few scattered records of the Council of Vienne, some in the Miscellanea or the Instrumenta Miscellanea, some in the archives of Castel Sant'Angelo, some in other collections that may contain documents on Philip the Fair. In each *fondo* or collection you must look up all the names connected with the trial of the Templars, and the years in which the trial occurred. And you may still miss important information.

The difficulties of research are so great that sometimes a student, having enthusiastically gone through the complicated procedure of getting permission to work in the Archives, disappears after a few days' work and never shows up again. But for persons with greater frustration tolerance, work there is rather pleasant, and I found it far more interesting than library research. These ancient papers, these writings of men dead for centuries but still alive in their words and thoughts, make history seem no longer history but humanity. And there is the spirit of the chase, the intellectual thrill of the hunt. There is always the gambler's chance of finding some very important document — an unknown and perfect poem written on the back of an official document, or a map more accurate than a map of its time has any business to be.

I came to feel at home in the study room, so like an old scriptorium with its big black desks that have slanted lecterns to hold the heavy volumes brought by the attendants. There is a raised throne, like a bishop's throne except for its black color and severe style, for the prefect, though he seldom sits there more than a moment. Instead, late in the morning, he makes a quick tour through the study room, answering kindly the questions that are put to him.

The Archives personnel, attendants as well as staff, are dignified and discreet. I have seen them excited only twice. Once was when news came that white smoke had announced the election of a new pope, and we all rushed to a crowded Saint Peter's to hear his name — Cardinal Montini. The second time was when, at the closing of the Archives for the summer, buses arrived in the Court of the Belvedere to take the employees to the country for an office picnic.

The students who work in the Archives — most of them foreigners, most of them priests, very few of them women — are as serious as the personnel. They seem to be chain workers as some people are chain smokers. They were there when I reached the Archives in the morning; at closing time they were still there. I came to regard taking a coffee break as a weakness of the flesh. Work in the Archives can be a way of life, as it is to a Polish woman, always dressed in clerical black, who came to Rome as a refugee and plunged into Archives research. She has published two books on ancient Archives documents relating to Poland; copies of them, bound in white silk, were presented to the Pope.

Opening off the study room is a patio or courtyard like that of a monastery. From it one sees only a rectangle of sky, walled in by gray stone buildings and the Tower of the Winds. In spring there are white daisies, and two great rosebushes bloom up to January. Then come the perfumes of the orange trees in blossom, and in summer the red oleanders. In a cold winter I have seen the courtyard covered with snow, and on the snow there were fallen oranges, like flowers. And there are pigeons that look like the Dove of the Holy Ghost.

It is very seldom that one sees the students or personnel of the Archives there, but the people from the Library come to smoke or for little snacks. I could hear the most interesting conversations going on — the shoptalk of students from all over the world. And there were other conversations that I could not understand, that were not in the languages of Europe.

It was in the courtyard, rather than in the study room where I had to struggle with almost indecipherable documents, that questions rose in my mind about the Archives and their history. What was hidden on the miles of shelves — why do the Archives seem to begin abruptly in the late Middle Ages — what happened to the hundreds of thousands of

Between Legend and History

O N the Tiberine Island, which lies in the river like the hull of a gray stone ship, there stood, in the time of the Emperor Claudius, the luxurious palace of a Jew who had tried to buy with gold and precious stones the thaumaturgic powers of the Apostles. With him was his beautiful friend Helena, whom he had elevated from the status of a courtesan to the dignity of a primordial idea of God.

Dedicated once to Aesculapius, the island today has two hospitals, one of them large and modern, the other a small Jewish hospital on the first floor of a dilapidated building. Near the waterline, on small natural terraces, are the houses of fishermen and boatmen, as there were in ancient times. Two arched bridges still connect the island to the city; one of them leads toward the Palatine Hill and what is left of the palaces of the emperors; the other to Trastevere, "across the Tiber" from the empire's government buildings.

In Trastevere of today the roof gardens of the rich are a fringe of green on the top of the old slum buildings. Italian aristocrats and "crazy Americans" have fitted up magnificent apartments in the ancient shells of brick and concrete. But the narrow streets, which smell in summertime of the basil and mint on the balconies, the little squares, are much as they were in the time of Augustus.

Here in Trastevere, very likely, was the first archive of the popes. Trastevere was a Jewish section, a settlement of the Diaspora. The Jews were working people — boatmen, tanners, makers of copper pails, men engaged in trade and moneylending. They lived in rooms next to their shops, as they have in the ghettos of all ages.

Among the working people of Trastevere there were some who had known Christ and who in the days after Calvary and the Pentecost had documents that must have belonged to the early Church — what were these vanished documents?

Trying to imagine what the papal archives were like in the early centuries, before they became the Vatican Secret Archives, is a little like trying to reconstitute the Library of Alexandria, though it has the same fascination. The archives were repeatedly destroyed, by fire and feud and time itself, so that almost nothing is left of their early documentation, in a physical form that could be subjected to Carbon 14 dating. But things of the mind have an existence beyond their physical form, and documents survive in their copies. Some documents, or copies of documents, were fortunate enough to be elsewhere than in Rome, like the letters of Pope Leo that had been sent to the provincial cities. Others ceased to be archives and became literature or history, like the writings of Augustine and Ambrose. Some we know about because of references to them by contemporary writers — they are in Eusebius' bibliography, or an irritated pope asks why such-and-such a report has not come in from Alexandria. And for the very first germination of the archives of the Church we can turn to Scripture itself.

listened to Peter. The first Christians of Rome were Jews, and lived un-
observed in the shadow of Judaism.

The community of converted Jews and Gentiles must have been fairly
strong at the time Paul wrote his letter to the Romans, for in it he praises
their devotion, as strongly as he had rebuked the Christians of Corinth
for continuing the pagan *dolce vita* among too many theological arguments. His letter must have been treasured when it arrived in Trastevere (letters of praise are usually kept), and Paul had added many personal greetings at the end of the long theological discussion that he had
dictated to his physician and secretary, Luke.

Accompanied by his "dear doctor," Paul came to Rome in the spring of
the year 61. When news of his arrival spread in Trastevere, some of the
Christians traveled by cart along the Appian Way to welcome him. The
meeting took place in the commercial clatter of the Appian Forum,
among the "perfidious tavern-keepers" and "boatmen and servants insulting each other" of Horace's poems. When Paul saw that the Christians
had come to meet him he "thanked God and took courage." Then the
carts turned back to Rome, through the green of the spring fields and
orchards, along the Appian Way that was not yet lined with the tombs of
the martyrs.

A little later another apostle arrived among the Christian Jews and the
Gentiles who, once the requirement of ritual mutilation had been removed, were being baptized in increasing numbers. It was the rough,
white-haired fisherman Simon Peter, who leaned on his collaborator and
secretary, Mark. The first pope was illiterate. He may have lived for a
time in the rooms behind the shop of Aquila and Priscilla, who had
already shared bread, work, and prayer with Paul in Corinth. Later he
may have accepted the use of a palace offered him by a Christian convert, Senator Pudens. (Recent excavations under the Church of Santa
Pudenziana have revealed an ancient palace of the Neronian period with
a mosaic of an enthroned Christ.)

At this time Nero was emperor, and the imperial orgies were held
publicly in the streets and squares. Nero's subjects could see the young
sovereign, carried in procession in a cage, covered with skins and taking
the part of a lioness, while the robust Doriferus took the part of a male
lion. Peter thought that he had plunged into the most sinful of Babylons,
and "from Babylon" dates the first of the papal encyclicals, warning that
Christians must respect the public peace and the established order. Sylvanus, the first papal legate, was charged with carrying the encyclical to
"the elect of the wisdom of God" in Pontus and Cappadocia, in the hot
sun and stones of Anatolia. It may be that a fisherman's basket of papers
was the very first of the papal secret archives.

Then Rome was in flames, and Nero, "the unbelievable lover of pleasure," rushed to the city from his palace down the coast at Anzio, perhaps as a king going to help his people, perhaps as a pyromaniac hurrying to a fire. There were rumors that he had planned the holocaust to clear the way for a new city, for the "sacred eternal Neronia." Tacitus says that it was to kill this rumor that he fixed the blame on the Christians. This may have been easy to do. Aubrey Menen has suggested that the Christians may have been persecuted because they looked forward so happily to the destruction of the world by fire. The Romans might easily have regarded them as we would regard a secret organization that favored Death of Earth. In any event, the Christians were put to death in ways that showed a good deal of criminal imagination: used as torches to light Nero's gardens, charged by infuriated bulls, raffled off for raping.

The first violent, destructive attack on the Roman Church's documents must have come with the Neronian persecutions. In any such time, ancient or modern, compromising papers are made to disappear. What the imperial police wanted was lists of names, and the Church was already sufficiently organized to have them; there were baptismal records and membership rosters, the names of people on home relief, the receipts for money given to widows, orphans, and the poor. The deaconate system of dispensing charity had already come to Rome from the Church in Jerusalem, and organized relief requires records.

It may be, too, that far more important documents were destroyed. It was in this period that the writing of the Gospels had begun, and the number of sources used was extremely limited, though Christ had been dead for only a generation.

Ancient writers say that Peter was crucified head downward in Nero's gardens, among treasures of nature and art, and buried nearby at a place already known by the Etruscan name of Vatican Hill. Part of the Vatican area, infected with malaria and infested with large snakes, was given over to the burial of the dead.

That Peter was buried on Vatican Hill appears to be confirmed by recent excavations and by recently found inscriptions. One, in Greek, dating from about the year 160, reads "Peter is in here." Another is a prayer addressed to the Apostle on behalf of the Christians buried near him. It is accompanied by a primitive, ingenuous portrait of a profiled head, with a forehead allowing for a remarkable development of the frontal lobes. Here too were found the bones of a sturdy old man, wrapped in crimson cloth, now thought by Paul VI to be those of Peter.

Not far from these inscribed stones, with their confidence in a day beyond death, was the tomb of the very pagan Flavius Agricola, with an epitaph celebrating wine and easy love. "Friends who read this, I'll give you some advice: drink a toast to Bacchus, with a crown of flowers on your head, and drink it a long way from here. And never say no to coitus with a good-looking girl. When you die, dirt and the funeral pyre will get what's left of you." The stone bearing this epitaph, one of the crudest of all paganism, was discovered by Bernini when he was excavating the area around Saint Peter's tomb to lay the foundations for the great altar of the new Saint Peter's. The pope ordered it made into lime, but some humanist copied it first.

Nero died in a bungled suicide, helped by the hand of a freedman. Perhaps he had foreseen his own death as an enemy of the state; there are rumors in Anzio that subterranean passages connected his palace here with Rome thirty miles to the north, and I have talked to men who say that in their boyhood they explored these tunnels up to the point where they were blocked by earthfalls. Whatever his escape routes were, he had no chance to use them. But he is still present in the Italian countryside: the men of Anzio are derisively called "the sons of Nero" by the men of nearby towns. One often sees the Nero face in the streets and shops of Anzio — oddly, more often on the women than on the men. It is dark, regularly featured, rather handsome, and utterly closed.

In the reconstruction period that followed Nero's reign even his Golden House, the *Domus Aurea,* was condemned. Part of it was remodeled into public baths with murals that inspired Michelangelo; Nero's "pool like unto a sea," with miniature cities around it, was filled in and became the site of the Colosseum. A third section became a private mansion for the emperor's cousins, Flavius Clemens and his wife Flavia Domitilla, who, according to an unverified tradition, donated it to Pope Clement for use as the *Domus Ecclesiae,* the home of the Church.

This house, called the Christian Palace, is now the lowest level of Saint Clement's Church. The way to it leads through a Mithraic area, once part of a Roman *insula* or apartment house. The arched ceiling of the cavelike room was painted with the constellations, for Mithraism was a cosmic religion of earth and sky, and this grotto represented the universe. Its altar is carved with a bas-relief of Mithras slaying the lunar bull; bull and god together, antagonists as they are, forming a triangular group of great unity and vigor.

The interface of religions here is shown by a memorial stone with a pagan inscription, handsomely carved, on one side and a Christian inscription in irregular letters on the other. The Christian inscription reads "To Surus resting in peace. Erected by his brother." The pagan one is the tribute of grieving parents to a boy nicknamed "the little rover," and his "life incomparably sweet."

Next to the Mithraic area is the legendary *Domus Ecclesiae*. There is none of the silence of ancient places here; the walls of this underground building are alive with the sound of water pouring from some lost spring or stream, or from some broken aqueduct. The great courtyard of the palace is rimmed on two sides by many small rooms; if this really was the Christian Palace, one of them may have been used for the storage of documents. Very little remains of the white stucco with festoons of flowers that have not seen the sun for so many centuries.

If the documents were here, they could not have been for very long. Flavius Clemens and Flavia Domitilla were accused and convicted of atheism and Jewish manners, and according to one legend Pope Clement himself was sent to a concentration camp in the Crimea, where he carried on missionary work so effectively that the Romans tied him to an anchor and threw him into the Black Sea. There the angels built him a tomb under water.

But not even legend tells us where the popes lived, or where the archives were kept, in the following years. The administrative center of the Church, with its archives, may have moved to Church property in Trastevere. Early in the third century Pope Zephyrinus, in claiming ownership of a Trastevere building near the veterans' hospital known as the Taberna Meritoria, was able to produce documents showing that it had been in the possession of the Christians since ancient times. A few years later Pope Calixtus is said to have been attacked by a mob and thrown out the window of a Trastevere house, then dragged, dying, into the well. This well is now in the cellar of the Osteria della Cisterna, and is proudly exhibited by waiters costumed as in Pinelli's engravings.

Persecution always meant danger to the Church's archives. The flight or arrest of the pope, or of any Church official, meant the flight or confiscation of documents, and the germinating archives of the Church must often have been shifted from place to place. But for the latter part of the third century, and for the fourth century, we have a very likely location for the archives — at the site of the present-day Apostolic Chancellery. As one goes along the Corso Vittorio toward the Vatican and sees this building, majestic in its Renaissance aspect, its white marble slowly dusting away with the centuries, he knows that he is walking on ancient ground. Directly under it is one of those great channels of clear water that served Rome's domestic uses and provided motive power for her factories. Like the sewers of Victor Hugo's Paris and of Warsaw in World War II, like the water-tunnels of defeated Jerusalem, such channels and the sewers running near them could have served the Christians as escape routes or hiding places. It may be significant that water still runs in the walls of the Christian Palace.

That at least part of the archives were here in the fourth century was told us by a pope, Damasus, who was born during the persecutions of Diocletian and whose father was an archives official. The fact that the church adjoining the Chancellery, dedicated to Saint Lawrence in Damasus, was originally built by Damasus himself, and that the chapel in the Chancellery courtyard is also dedicated to Saint Lawrence in Damasus, gives a certain support to the tradition that archives were here in the third century when Saint Lawrence the Librarian underwent torture to defend the treasure and the records of the Church. The nature of the documents in his care, and the presence of the Pope, suggest that this was also the Church's administrative center.

It was during the persecutions that followed the Valerian edicts of 257 and 258 that the imperial guard appeared at the door of the archives to confiscate them in the name of the emperor. Old Pope Sixtus had already been arrested. The guards searched in vain for the administrative records, and for the gold and silver that should have been in the safe. All had disappeared. Lawrence had sent the Church's documents, with their incriminating lists of names, into hiding, and had distributed the gold and silver in its treasury to the poor. The guards put him to the fire torture on a gridiron — a method commonly used in ancient times to discover the whereabouts of treasure. But the librarian died without talking. His charred body was claimed by the Christians, and his mummified skull is still in the care of the popes. At the Vatican on the tenth of August every year they expose in its golden reliquary the head of Saint Lawrence that still, in the distorted mouth, in the burned bone of the skull, shows the agony he suffered to defend the archives of the popes.

It is rather surprising that the Church should have had a more or less permanent location for at least some of its archives at a time when the threat of persecution was always present, as it has been for the Jews in Christian Europe. But persecution was not continuous and it varied in strength. The antagonism of the government was often interrupted by practical arrangements — the Christians were a bloc vote — and by periods of real tolerance, either ideological or resulting from personal relationships.

The great thinker and writer Hippolytus the antipope apparently had free access to the court of Alexander Severus. He dedicated his *The Resurrection* to the Empress Mamaea, and the Emperor decided to erect a statue of Christ in the imperial palace, near those of the ancient gods and of giants of human thought such as Homer, Socrates, and Plato.

Christianity had even infiltrated the court of the Emperor Commodus, the spoiled and dissolute son of the philosopher Marcus Aurelius. Commodus had three hundred concubines, the most beautiful women of the Roman aristocracy, and three hundred boys, all of whom shared the same banquet table and the same baths. The "lover of his heart," the unbaptized Christian Marcia, widow of a man that he had killed, successfully carried out what modern security agencies call a black-lace-blouse assignment by taking the list of convicted Christians, brought her by the priest Jacinth, and inserting some of the names into a list of pardons. One of those set free was the Deacon Calixtus, later the sixteenth pope of the Church.

But the archives lost heavily in the persecutions, and even the leaders of the Church sometimes collaborated and yielded up Church books and documents. Some of them managed to substitute heretic books and false documents; others were compelled to deliver sacred books and genuine archival documents. These traitors, the *traditores,* or handers-over, were the most despised of the lapsed Christians, because they had compromised all Christians and the organization of the Church itself.

The damage done to the archives in these earlier persecutions was lessened by the fact that they were local rather than general, and the lost books could be replaced by making copies from those belonging to churches in other regions. The sending of books to other churches seems to have been a regular practice, for in Hermas' *The Shepherd,* probably written early in the second century, the Sibyl says, "When I have finished, it shall be made known by thy means to all the elect. Thou shalt therefore write two little books, and shalt send one to Clement, and one to Grapte. So Clement shall send to the foreign cities, for this is his duty . . ." The Clement referred to may have been Pope Clement, who died in the year 97.

At this time the Church's library and archives were probably a single institution. Thus Saint Lawrence the Librarian was, according to tradition, also in charge of the working records of the Church. The collection of books, records, and documents came to be called the *Chartarium,* the *Scrinium Sanctae Romanae Ecclesiae,* or the Holy Scrinium. The Christians seem to have taken over their archival system from the culture that surrounded them, and the Romans called their archives the *scrinium* — something that had to be screened apart from ordinary things. The closets that held them were even made of a special wood, *lignum scrinarium.* In the Holy Scrinium the Church kept its administrative and financial documents, the acts of its martyrs, its judicial decisions, the decisions of its councils. Since it was needed for carrying on the administrative work of the Church, it usually followed the pope to his place of residence.

Besides their function as working files, the Church's documents were already being used for research. Disputes were settled — or exacerbated

— by reference to documents of past times. Historical research had already begun: Irenaeus drew up a "list of the bishops of Rome" from which historians derive much of their knowledge of the popes between Linus, the Etruscan pope who followed Peter, and Eleutherius, who died in 189. In outlining the papal succession, he in all probability used the Church's own documents.

The persecutions and the later invasions have left us only a little definite evidence of what the Church's archives and library contained. First, of course, there were the books of the Bible and their commentaries, and perhaps the lost *Logia* in which some follower of Christ had taken down his words, as the words of Mohammed were taken down on the shoulder bone of a camel.

We can be certain that they contained administrative documents of a practical nature. In the middle of the third century Pope Cornelius was able to give figures on the number of priests, deacons, acolytes, and supported widows, so detailed that they must have been based on statistical data.

By this time the businessman pope, Calixtus, who had been trained in his youth as bookkeeper for a rich exporter, would have brought current business methods into the Church, if it did not have them before. The Church's acquisition through donations of extensive real estate would have been reflected in deeds and tax records. Calixtus himself, before becoming pope, had been in charge of the administration of cemeteries, and had dealt with the cadastral acts (roughly, records of real estate transactions) of the farms near Rome that were being made into burial grounds, as well as with all documents and funds relating to the construction of churches, catacombs, chapels, and tombs.

Like the present day Mormons, the Church looked after its own. Among the financial records would have been the inventories of the warehouses of supplies for needy families, where — along with grain for bread — cheese and olives were given with the ancient benediction: "Sanctify, O Lord, these curds, uniting us also in your love, and let this fruit of the olive never lose its flavor, that is the symbol of the abundance you have made flow from the tree of the Cross, for those who hope in You."

Copies of papal letters must have accumulated in the archives, along with incoming letters and reports, as it came to be recognized that the relationship of the Roman Church to the other churches was that of a home office to its branch offices. Even before the year 100 Clement had asserted the Roman Church's claim to the leadership of the Christian world, in a very long letter remarkable for its literary quality. Here he also writes of Paul's death, as one might write of Arthur and Avalon:

". . . having taught righteousness unto the whole world and having reached the farthest bounds of the West; when he had borne his testimony before the rulers, he departed from the world and went unto the holy place." And Clement answers a question that did not face the Church till fourteen hundred years later when he says: "The ocean which is impassable for men, and the worlds beyond it, are directed by the same ordinances of the Master." This letter appears in fourth-century Greek manuscripts now in the British Museum. That it survives only by fortunate chance is shown by the fact that no other certainly authentic papal letter exists for the next century and a half.

Rome was receiving reports from the foreign churches in the middle of the third century. A letter of Saint Cyprian to Pope Cornelius says apologetically, ". . . the matter was not one which must at once and in haste be brought to your notice, as though it were very great or serious . . ."

Besides the papal letters and incoming letters and reports there would have been the records of the councils, where important decisions were made that were regarded as ecclesiastical law. The contents of the Archives were used to prove the authority of the Church from the time of Saint Peter onward, and to settle controversies of theology and ecclesiastical practice.

Then there were the records of the persecutions and of the heroism of the martyrs. These stories gave a sense of identity to the Christians, as stories of the concentration camps and of the Arab war do to the Israel of today. Their value was recognized by the Church, and one pope himself achieved martyrdom as a result of commissioning seven notaries to collect the tales of the martyrs. Some of the stories were in the form of stenographic reports of trials; in these one can sense the irritated compassion of the proconsul who is trying to give the Christian an out that he refuses to take.

Saint Irenaeus in 177 brought to the pope from France reports of the martyrs of Lyons and Vienne. There the Christians had been charged with incest, infanticide, and, apparently because of the wording of the eucharistic ritual, with cannibalism: "Certain slaves, in fear of the tortures which they saw the saints suffering, falsely charged us with Thyestean banquets and Oedipodean unions." One sees the glamor that the martyrs had for Christians of the time in Irenaeus' description of those who "advanced full of joy, having in their looks a mingling of majesty and of great beauty, so that even their chains were worn by them as a comely ornament, as for a bride adorned with fringed raiment of gold richly wrought."

A copy of the story of the martyrdom of Saint Polycarp (69?–155?)

was made by the Roman ecclesiastic Gaius, which suggests that the original text was in the papal archives. When the mobs began shouting for him, the old man, "the much-admired Polycarp," was persuaded to leave the city and go into hiding at a small farm. "Afterward, feeling that those who were searching for him were nearby, he went to another farm." Here one of the servants, under torture, gave him away. About dinnertime the guards from Smyrna arrived, "at a late hour, while Polycarp was asleep in a small room above the stable. He could have escaped but would not, saying, 'God's will be done.'" He ordered food and drink prepared for them, and prayed for an hour before he was taken to town for trial and martyrdom. The mob shouted, "Polycarp to the lions!" but the asiarch Philip said that the games with the lions were over. Then the mob shouted "Polycarp to be burned alive!" and took firewood and kindling from the kitchens as fuel for the pyre. The old man took off his clothing, but had difficulty with a shoe because his foot had been hurt. "And as a great flame flared up, we saw a wonder. The fire, taking the shape of an arched vault, or of a sail filled with wind, surrounded the body of the martyr who was there in the middle of it, not like meat that was being burnt, but like bread that was being baked, like gold or silver melted in the crucible. And we smelled a great perfume, as of incense or other balsams."

Christian literature even included fiction. In *The Shepherd*, that strange romance, half adventure and half apocalyptic, we can glimpse the daily lives of some of the small Christian bourgeoisie: dissolute youngsters, sons of Christians, who informed on their parents for a reward; a Christian domestic who planned to marry his employer to improve his standard of living; and adulterous wives, for whom the writer recommended eviction, but with the way left open for future repentance.

The Scrinium must also have contained material on the organization and personnel problems of the Church. One such work was the *Didaché*, or, The Doctrine of The Twelve Apostles, perhaps written when the last of the Apostles were still alive. It probably came from Syria or Palestine, but books and treatises had high mobility in the early Christian world: the empire's magnificent communications system was as much of a convenience to the Church as to the government. In any case some of the *Didaché* had the qualities required for an ecclesiastical best seller. One passage in it suggests that the theme of Sinclair Lewis's *Elmer Gantry* is a timeless one. Christians are warned against the teachers of false doctrine, but the authentic preacher is to be welcomed — for a limited time. "If he teaches justice and the knowledge of God, then welcome him as if he were God himself. He may stay as your guest one day, and two if need be. But if he stays three days, then he is a false prophet." They are warned against unauthorized fund-raisers: "When he goes, the true apostle will not accept anything but food for the trip. If he asks for money instead, he is not a true prophet."

There is a suggestion that the generous communal hospitality of the early Church was sometimes abused by traveling lay Christians as well as by preachers. "If one of your brothers in the spirit comes to your city, help him as much as you can. But he must not stay with you more than three days." If the traveler wanted to marry and settle down he was to get a job, and Christians were enjoined to help him in finding it. "If he cannot find work, help him to, so that you will not have an idle Christian living with you. And if this person will not work, then he is making use of the faith for his own purposes. Watch out for such trash."

More serious than the problem of freeloading travelers was that of the *lapsi,* or lapsed Christians — the weaker souls who had declined martyrdom. Some advocated readmitting them to the Church, others were willing to allow readmission on a second-class-citizenship basis; others wanted them kept out entirely. In our time, French and Italian communities were split in the same way after the end of the Occupation: what was to be done with collaborators? The Church faced the same question in regard to ordinary sinners, such as murderers and adulterers, and those who wanted to return to it after joining a heretic sect. As decisions were made on the basis of individual records, some sort of dossiers must have been kept. And since the popes at times acted as magistrates within the Christian community, the archives would have held records relating to this judicial activity.

The controversy over readmission brought the Church to schism between the antipope Hippolytus, who favored a rigid policy, and the legitimate popes, who offered forgiveness to the penitent. The presence of these antagonistic Christian groups offered Rome the spectacle of repeated fights and appeals, and the imperial police finally chose a radical solution. They arrested both pope and antipope and sent them into exile together, to the labor camps of Sardinia. In the harsh reality of the mines the two men were able to resolve — or forget — their doctrinal differences, and before dying they became friends. The bodies of Pope Pontianus and of Antipope Hippolytus were brought back to Rome by a peaceful and united Church, in a procession resembling a triumph. The strength of the group supporting Hippolytus is shown by the fact that, while we have no portrait of the legitimate popes of the time, there is the magnificent statue of Hippolytus that is now at the foot of the stairs leading to the Vatican Library.

The archives must have had many records and treatises dealing with the heresies, since so many writings on this subject have come down to us through copies. This was a time when Christian philosophy was still fluid, and good minds wrestling with eternal problems came to different conclusions. The heresies differed with the Church of Rome on the great questions — the nature of Christ, the Christian's relation to the natural world and to sex, the existence of evil under an omnipotent God, the problem of death. That these were eternal questions is shown by their resurgence in the heresies of the medieval and modern period, that have left massive documentation in the present Secret Archives.

Some of the heresies of the early Christian period differed from the Roman faith in only one or two doctrinal points; others were a confused mixture of sensuality and mysticism, like that reflected in an almost unknown inscription from a tombstone of the Valentinian sect: "Ardently wishing to see the splendor of the Father, you, my wise Flavia, companion of my blood and of my bed . . . have hurried away to contemplate the divine features of the Eoni . . . the sun of Truth. She came to the nuptial alcove, she rushed to the nuptial bed of the Father . . . She lives for those who live, she died for those who are truly dead. Substance, why do you wonder that this kind of dead is different from you?"

The reaction of the Church against the heresies, when they were identified as such, was one of active condemnation. Unlike Islam, which has no central organization and therefore no means of rejecting spiritual mutations such as the cult of the Black Moslems, early Christianity had a central organization and used it vigorously to maintain the homogeneity of the faith.

There must have been a great deal of material on the doctrinal controversies of the time, for it was in this period that the philosophy of the Church was expanded and defined. The question of the date of Easter engaged some of the best minds; but it was at this time too that the doctrine of the resurrection of the body took its present form. Its opponents argued — as they did in the nineteenth century — that a burned or decayed body is utterly destroyed. But the patristic philosophers seem to have sensed by intuition one of the findings of modern genetics — that the body is not substance but pattern. A half-believing friend of mine commented to me recently that the discovery of the DNA code makes the destruction of the dead body irrelevant — physically, we are our formulas, and if our formulas are on file somewhere in the Eternal Mind, then the resurrection of the body is truly possible.

But it was in this period too that the Church took on an enemy that has become stronger rather than weaker through the years — the sexual instinct of man. The patristic writers had so little to say in favor of sex that it was with obvious relief that the recent Ecumenical Council rediscovered the phrase "And they twain shall be one flesh." It was not that the Fathers neglected the subject; in fact it fascinated them, and the patristic literature is aphrodisiac in its effect. But even "chaste and legitimate unions" were regarded as shameful.

From knowledge of the secular documents of the time one can make some guess at the physical appearance of the material in the Church's archives. The very early writings were on papyrus. Some of the Church's books would have been in scroll form and some in codex form. Codices had certain practical advantages. Finding a particular text on a scroll is as difficult as finding a particular article in a microfilmed newspaper, and, whether for purposes of teaching or for purposes of disputation, early churchmen did a good deal of locating texts. For books in frequent use, the material on which the book was written would have undergone less wear and tear in a codex than in a scroll that had to be rolled and unrolled frequently. Then, too, codices were more portable and more easily stored. And there was another advantage that must have had some weight in times of persecution: books can be more easily concealed. As every surreptitious reader knows, a pocket book is much better than a newspaper for office reading. The tiny Armed Services editions, particularly good for this, remained in use for years after World War II.

Of all the persecutions, the most tragic for the Church and for its documents was that of Diocletian at the beginning of the fourth century. Eusebius, who lived through it, writes: "I saw with my own eyes the places of worship thrown down from top to bottom, to the very foundations, and the inspired holy scriptures committed to the flames in the middle of the public square."

Churches, books, and cult objects were destroyed throughout the empire. Especially in Africa, sacred books were handed over to the authorities by unfaithful custodians. The papal archives and the library of the Roman Church were destroyed. Even Pope Marcellinus, old and sick, is said to have handed over some documents and books, and to have burned incense at the pagan altars.

Chaos and *sede vacante* followed, and the next pope, Marcellus, was condemned to work as a hostler in one of the imperial relay-posts on the road that led to the Via Flaminia and the north of Europe. Today the Church of San Marcello stands on the site of the stables that once, according to the *Liber Pontificalis,* were cleaned by a pope. But these acts of persecution were stones thrown at the rising sun.

"Thus Constantine, an emperor and son of an emperor, a religious man and son of a most religious man, most prudent in every way." Constantine, marching toward Rome from the north by the Via Flaminia, at the head of Celtic and German infantry and African archers, laid down the banner of Jove for the Chrismon, the mandala of the Christians.

To the Church, these days were what the days of liberation near the end of the Second World War were to the men and women of the Underground. Eusebius writes: "Men had now lost all fear of their former oppressors; day after day they kept dazzling festival; light was everywhere, and men who once dared not look up greeted each other with smiling faces and shining eyes."

The archives no longer had to be secret because of fear. But the damage had been done. The destruction had been so general that many of the lost books and documents could never be replaced; there was nothing left to make copies from.

The Church of the Firstborn

CONSTANTINE was an army brat; he had grown up knowing the Mithraic religion, harsh and pure as the code of military justice. We are not certain how much of a Christian he was; he was baptized only on his deathbed, and he once referred to himself as "a bishop of those outside the Church" (the bishop of unbelievers?). But when he wrote to Pope Miltiades (311–314) in a letter fortunately preserved by Eusebius, and addressed him as "Your Diligence," he referred to himself as "My Dedicatedness."

He may have been a reverent skeptic of the type familiar to modern churches. Or he may have been mainly a pragmatist. The imperial ordinance that proclaimed freedom of worship and ordered the Christians' property returned to them ends with the comment: "For by this provision the divine care for us of which we have been aware on many earlier occasions will remain with us unalterably forever."

Certainly his gifts to the Church indicate dedication — a palace and three large basilicas, one (the Lateran) on the Caelian Hill, one on Vatican Hill, and one, dedicated to Saint Paul, outside the walls.

The first of these gifts, the Lateran Palace, had a history of violence and murder. Nero had executed its owners, the Laterani, who for centuries had lived on the shady Caelian Hill, in this Etruscan area of Rome. It later became "the Palace of Fausta," the second wife of Constantine. According to Zosimus, Fausta accused her stepson Crispus of incest; Constantine had him killed. Hearing that his son was innocent, he had his wife strangled. He gave the Palace of Fausta — or Phaedra — to Pope Sylvester, and probably had him as a house guest while his official residence was being prepared. Even before that, in the time of Pope

Miltiades, the palace had been used for a conference on what was to be done about Christians who had abjured during the persecutions. Rebuilt for the Church, it probably had several stories, the topmost one being used for official purposes such as receptions and conferences. Its great door was bronze and magnificent; during the day silk curtains like those in the palaces of princes hung in the doorway.

The Lateran Palace, the *Episcopium Lateranense,* was the papal seat for nearly a thousand years, and the main site of the archives. It and the Lateran Square, the *Campus Lateranensis,* were the stage setting for much of the drama of the Middle Ages. Some of the popes preferred the Roman-pink palaces of the Caesars on the Palatine; some the episcopal residences on the Vatican Hill; but the Lateran remained their official residence. Even today a newly elected pope must take ceremonial possession of the Lateran, though the mounted processions of other days have been replaced by simple lines of limousines.

Nearby, Constantine built the basilica dedicated to Saint John, with its gold-shingled roof and its seven silver altars. The green columns, the great colored mosaic of the Christ, the gold and silver candelabra beside the altar, all the rich gifts of an emperor in search of immortality, brought it the name of the *Basilica Aurea,* the Golden Basilica, "the mother and head of the city and of the world." A small city grew up around the Lateran — oratories, hospices, cloisters, residences for those who carried out the duties of the faith and the administrative work of the Church.

At the same time, at the other end of town, he built Saint Peter's, the largest of the basilicas, with its silver altar studded with four hundred precious stones. The building site was poor, on a steep hillside; part of the hill had to be sliced away and part of it built up to make a level place for the basilica over the tomb of the apostle. The strains of the site may have contributed to the weakening of fabric that led to the replacement of Saint Peter's at the time of the Reformation. But even so it stood for twelve centuries, and it was a building of honesty and elegance. The old Saint Peter's was literally a barn of a place — one can still see barns built on similar lines here in the *agro Romano,* the Roman field, the agricultural district that feeds Rome. It was decorated with mosaics of the earthly paradise, of cedars and palm trees, of harts drinking at the water-brooks; it had a fountain of purification in its courtyard, and it was a place where the soul even of a modern man could feel at home.

Behind the silver altar was the Chair of Saint Peter; in front of it the choir with six columns from the Temple at Jerusalem, of alabaster twined with vine leaves, brought here because Christ was said to have leaned against them when he was teaching at the synagogue. Saint Peter's still has one of these columns, and shows it near the *Pietà*. Looking at it I have thought of Christ as a young instructor talking to his students between classes, and had the feeling one sometimes has in the Holy Land, of astonished realization that these things really happened.

Constantine found that building basilicas for the Christians was easier than governing them. He had the typical army officer's approach to the problem — do a thorough staff study, choose a solution, then carry it through. He allowed a surprising amount of democracy and self-determination to the Christians, but he wanted them to make up their minds. After that, "such is the regard I pay to the lawful Catholic Church that I desire you to leave no schism or division of any kind anywhere." As he said, if men were united in regard to religion, "the conduct of public affairs would be considerably eased." Instead councils were held, decisions were made, and the dissidents continued to dissent. Constantine complains "they refuse to accept the decision already reached." The emperor himself seems to have been something of a Unitarian — "I had proposed to lead back to a single form the ideas which all people conceive of the Deity"— though he had no objection to the Christians' adopting an intricate theology if they would only agree on it. His polite letters and ordinances do not conceal his conviction that the quarrels of the Christians were a lot of damn' nonsense.

On one occasion he did succeed in dazzling them into virtual agreement for a time, when a Council met in the year 325 at Nicaea, at his summer palace in a fortified village near the Sea of Marmora, to deal with the Arian heresy and to formulate the Nicene creed. Arius held that the Son was not coterminous in time with the Father, but came into existence after him. Oddly, this idea is still reflected in a line of the Church's Christmas ritual, inspired by the Psalms of David but with overtones of Velikovsky: "Amid the brightness of the saints, before the Day-star was made, I have created Thee."

The conference room was the hall of the palace; Constantine acted as chairman and host, in the absence of the aged Pope Sylvester. "The flower of flowers of the bishops" were there from all parts of the empire. Many of them carried on their bodies the scars of the persecutions. The Egyptian bishop Paphnutius wore a bandage over the socket of an eye that had been torn out in the time of the Emperor Maximin. And old Paul, bishop of New Caesarea on the Euphrates, had to be supported by his armpits: his hands were paralyzed, their tendons having been burned out with red-hot pincers. Constantine's manner toward the bishops was courteous and friendly, and at the banquet that closed the Council the fathers remarked that they seemed already to be in the kingdom of God.

We know what was said in the discussions of the Council of Nicaea, but only from theological treatises and historical narratives. The reports that the papal delegates Vitus and Vincent brought home to Pope Sylvester — and to the archives — have been lost along with the great mass of documentation that accumulated in the Church's era of prosperity before the barbarian invasions.

The papal archives and treasury in these years received as gifts or "Acts of Devotion" not only chalices of gold and lamps encrusted with pearls, rubies and emeralds, but deeds to palaces, estates, and mines. From the time of Pope Julius I (337 – 352) when the Holy Scrinium was constituted an official place of record, it was swelled with an added mass of financial documentation. Every document relating to the clergy or the Church was to be registered in the Church records by the chief notary. This included down payments, deeds, donations, barter deals, sales, wills, liberation of *servi*. When we remember the information about social history that has been distilled from the Archives' financial records of the Medieval Age and Renaissance Church, we realize what has been lost in the destruction of even this utilitarian section of the ancient archives.

The Church's administrative records must have had a similar growth, for the popes expected to be told of important problems of the Church throughout the empire. Pope Julius I wrote in a letter to delinquent bishops: "Why were we not written to especially about the church of the Alexandrians? Are you ignorant that the custom was first to write to us, and then for justice to be determined from here? If then the bishop was at all suspect, it should have been reported in writing to the church here."

We do not know how much had been saved from the persecutions of Diocletian, when churches and scriptures were burned throughout the empire. Eusebius quotes or summarizes from over a hundred sources, though it is possible that Eusebius had an excellent memory that to some extent took the place of reference works. But historians agree that the Holy Scrinium must still have contained literary and theological writings, including the biblical writings and the Acts of the Martyrs. Master copies kept in the archives were used to check the accuracy of texts that had deteriorated with repeated copying, and new copies were made for the new churches.

We find various contemporary references to the archives, but they do not mention where they were located. After the sixth century they are known to have been at the Lateran, and it is likely that at least a part of them were there long before. The pope's personal archives and the live files relating to administration normally accompanied him to his residence and to the nearby administrative offices. But it is very possible that part of the archives, those not in current use, or the library section, remained at that archives building near the present Apostolic Chancellery where Saint Lawrence had worked. Here Pope Damasus, who died in 384 at the age of eighty, and who was born when the last persecutions were raging, erected a memorial stone to commemorate his father who, coming to Italy as a stranger from Spain, had advanced through the various ranks from employee to priest. The Pope says, in his own verses:

> *Here my father, employee, reader, levite, priest,*
> *Advanced in merit and in deeds.*
> *Here Christ honoured me with the supreme power*
> *   of the Apostolic Seat.*
> *I have built new roofs for the archives,*
> *And added columns at the left and right*
> *That the name of Damasus may live through the*
> *   centuries.*

Though we do not know what archives were here, we can assume that the building was large, since one would hardly mention on a commemoration stone that he had repaired the roof of a small building. In thinking of this fragment of archives life in the century of Constantine one has a mental picture of a pillared white building surrounded by palm trees, like the government buildings of Egypt where the scribes worked. Here the young Spaniard was promoted through the ranks of the Church's civil service, and the child who was to be Pope Damasus grew up among the codices. The existence of such children, "born in the house of intellect," is the price the Church has had to pay for the single-hearted devotion of her celibate priests.

Damasus, a great pope in his own right, a poet and an archaeologist, apparently took a particular interest in the archives. He wrote his epistles in characters that he himself had designed. A reading man, he is credited with having begun the papal library. But his greatest service to learning was his sponsorship of Jerome, who left his desert study to become the Pope's secretary and the translator of the Vulgate.

This was the age of the desert saints. Paul had found his hidden valley with its date palms and its "spring of shining water," and so many idealists had followed him into the desert that the older hermits had begun to complain that the place was overpopulated.

Their desert society had an Essene innocence. In the little huts with their irrigated gardens and their windowsill bookcases, men who had been princes and men who had been casual laborers lived together in a frontier democracy. Race was of little importance; one of the most honored of the hermits was the Abbot Moses, a black man. And for once in the history of Christianity the animal creation was accepted as part of the household of God. A hermit who had renounced clothing slept warm because he snuggled up to a lion; another offered tin cups of water from his well to the desert beasts.

The date palms and the little gardens gave them food; they braided mats to sell in town for walk-around money; they copied ancient manuscripts and taught their illiterate comrades to read; they found their way from place to place by astral navigation, watching the stars of the desert night; and they thought about God and tried not to think about women. To control their thoughts they punished the body with brutal hardships. But this was a time of experiment, and in experiment even negative results are valuable. Their excesses of asceticism, observed and reported by John Cassian, made it possible for him and for Cassiodorus to avoid the same error in their own monasteries, and for moderation to become part of the Benedictine Rule.

The hermits talked to God as King David did, person to person, and the stories written of them have a beauty that makes even the modern reader want to leave his office and find the hidden valley, the date palm, and the spring.

Jerome had been one of an Oxford reading-party of young men — Jerome, Innocent, Heliodorus — staying at a country house near Antioch, discussing manuscripts, writing poetry, and talking about the desert road to eternal life. A little later he was "the comrade of scorpions," fighting the dual temptations of lust and literature — he had taken his library into the desert with him. To get his mind off the flesh and Cicero, he flung himself into the study of Hebrew as Saint Benedict, a century later, flung himself into a thicket of thorns.

He was a good Hebrew scholar by the time he emerged from the desert and went to Rome, a young man still, but already "the most bilious and ill-tempered of saints." There Pope Damasus, the poet, the bridegroom priest, recognized his abilities across the gulfs of personality and made him papal secretary, charging him with the additional task of translating and editing the New Testament. The Gospels had been translated into Latin at least as early as the second century, but in the continuous copying and recopying by scribes "more asleep than awake" they had come to be full of error and doubtful passages. "There are almost as many versions as there are copies."

Jerome's reasons for hesitation must sound all too familiar to modern translators of the Bible. He wrote to Pope Damasus: "The labor is both perilous and presumptuous; for in judging others, I must be judged by all; and how can I dare to change the language of the world in its hoary old age, and carry it back to the early days of its infancy? Is there a man, learned or unlearned, who will not break out immediately into violent language, and call me a forger and a profane person for having the audacity to add anything to the ancient books, or to make any changes or correction therein?"

His misgivings about the public reception of any new translation were later proved right by a rather catty letter from Saint Augustine: "A certain bishop, one of our brethren, having introduced in the church over which he presides the reading of your version, came upon a word in the book of the prophet Jonah, of which you have given a very different rendering from that which had been of old familiar to the senses and memory of all the worshipers, and had been chanted for so many generations in the church. Thereupon rose such a tumult in the congregation, especially among the Greeks, correcting what had been read, and denouncing the translation as false, that the bishop was compelled to ask the testimony of the Jewish residents. These, whether from ignorance or from spite, answered that the words in the Hebrew manuscripts were correctly rendered in the Greek version, and in the Latin one taken from it. What further need I say? The man was compelled to correct your version in that passage as if it had been falsely translated, as he desired not to be left without a congregation — a calamity which he narrowly escaped. From this case we also are led to think that you may be occasionally mistaken."

Jerome's office as papal editor may have been near the old archives building where, according to tradition, Lawrence the Librarian and the young Spaniard Damasus had worked. Here the master copies and the variant copies of the Scriptures stored in the archives would have been available to him. The patrician Paula is said to have lent him a palace nearby, on the site of the present Church of Saint Jerome. All these clues — Damasus' commemoration stone, the location of the chapel and the Church of Saint Lawrence in Damasus, the location of the Church of Saint Jerome, and the tradition of Paula's palace — seem to point to the conclusion that an important archival or library area of the ancient church existed near the present site of the Apostolic Chancellery. It may be that occupational groups, like ethnic groups, tend to maintain the same geographic location. After all, there are two hospitals on the island outside my window in Rome — an island that once held the temple-hospital dedicated to Aesculapius.

Part of Roman society took to Jerome as Parisian society, much later, took to the supposedly rough frontiersman Benjamin Franklin, and he used this popularity to advocate the meditative reading of the Bible. As a result, the libraries of the aristocratic palaces of Rome came to have new collections of biblical literature in Latin and Greek, next to the old collections of pagan authors. To provide such literature Jerome, in addition to carrying out the revision of the Gospels that the Pope had ordered, also translated into Latin the Septuagint Psalter, which had been translated into Greek in Alexandria two centuries before Christ. In three days he translated the Song of Songs, the Proverbs, and Ecclesiastes. In one night, "and very unwillingly," he translated the Book of Judith and in a day that of Tobias. A scrupulous scholar, he searched for the "Hebraic verity" and called on the collaboration of the rabbis. He was a natural stylist, and the roughness of Hebrew and the roughness of his own personality gave strength to the graceful Latin of the late empire.

In Jerome's letters there are frequent references to the Holy Scrinium, which he called the *Chartarium*. In writing to his friend Senator Pammachius, Jerome advises him to consult the Roman Christian libraries for commentaries on the First Letter to the Corinthians. He also found the archives and library very useful in his I-said-you-said controversies with other scholars. In his long feud with Rufinus, a man he had once loved, he writes, "If you suspect me of writing such a letter, why can't you ask for it in the *Chartarium* of the Roman Church?" which seems to imply that the *Chartarium* was rather inclusive in its contents.

A running controversy with Augustine contains the dialogue, scattered through many letters. Augustine: "I heard that some brethren have told Your Charity that I have written a book against you and have sent it to Rome. Be assured that this is false." Jerome: "The letter of Your Grace has arrived, in which you clear yourself of the charge of having sent to Rome a book written against your humble servant. I had not heard that charge . . . I had almost forgotten your letter, or, more correctly, the letter written in your name . . . Therefore, if it is your letter, write me frankly that it is so . . ." And, again: "As to your calling God to witness that you had not written a book against me, and of course had not sent to Rome what you had never written, how comes Italy to possess a treatise of yours which you did not write?"

A circle of aristocratic women had gathered around Jerome in the palace that Paula had lent him; he called it his House of Ladies. There were matrons of the aristocracy, there were young girls who had vowed themselves to virginity, and there were young girls who married, against his advice. With Jerome as seminar leader they discussed problems of religion and sex — the early Christians had not heard the French proverb that equates talking about love with making love. When one of the girls who had been following Jerome's ascetic practices in order to be "pale of face and thin with fasting" died, he was blamed for her death. Even more serious for him was the death of Pope Damasus, whose powerful protection had made it possible for him to live in Rome while insulting its citizens. The new pope did not renew his appointment, and Jerome decided to abandon the city that he, like Peter, referred to as Babylon. He went to Bethlehem with the patrician Paula and her daughter, established a monastery and a convent, and fitted up a cave as a study. There he continued writing his magnificent translations and his letters to the people he loved and hated.

Jerome was prickly as a desert plant; yet we can remember his free school for children, his gentle account of the lions that helped bury the hermit Saint Paul in his hidden valley, and his long years of inspired, laborious scholarship. Aquinas said that at death we all become thirty-three — the age at which Christ died, the age at which humans are at the height of their powers. We do not know the exact date of Jerome's birth, but he must have been about thirty-three at the country house near Antioch, in the house party of young men who wrote poems to God and to each other.

Of all the works of Jerome, what has come down to us? Nothing in its original, physical form, from the tragic fifth century.

However, copies, or copies of copies, have survived, as colonies sometimes survive when the motherland is destroyed. Transcripts were immediately made of Jerome's translations, especially in Italy and Spain, and later in Ireland.

We happen to know the history of one such book. Sent from Rome as a master copy, from which others could be made, it came by about the sixth century to the monastery of Vivarium in the south of Italy. There the Abbot Cassiodorus had new copies made because of the deterioration of the original, already used for two centuries. One of these copies was brought to England by a monk. A hundred years later, that is, between the seventh and eighth centuries, the abbot Ceolfrid in his turn decided to have other copies made to distribute throughout England. But in order to have papal approval of the genuineness of the text, he had a particularly fine copy made to send to Rome, and entrusted it to a British monk who was to check it against Jerome's original, which the abbot thought was still to be found in the papal archives. The English monk with his precious luggage came to Italy, but when he arrived at the isolated monastery of San Salvatore, on savage Mount Amiata, he died. The very beautiful Bible was hidden away by the shrewd Tuscan abbot of the monastery, who did not carry on the project of his English colleague. In his defense, one could say that he very possibly knew that it was useless to seek Jerome's original text in Rome; that everything had been destroyed by the barbarians. In the Benedictine library of San Salvatore this beautiful codex remained for centuries, up to the moment when, at the destruction of the abbey, it went to the Biblioteca Laurenziana of Florence, where it is now treasured as "The Amiatino Gospel."

V

The White Barbarians

THE century of peace was over and the age of invasions had begun; in 410 the Goth Alaric was marching on Rome, impelled by his daemon: "There is always someone behind me that torments me, pushes me, and cries to me, 'Go on, go on, destroy Rome!'" Rome was a city of many ethnic elements, and it had its fifth column. At night German slaves opened the Porta Salaria, in one of the slum areas. Alaric and his army set fire to the buildings and the flames spread rapidly along the narrow twisted streets. For three days Rome was ravaged by fire and looting.

Alaric had promised Pope Innocent to respect the persons and property that were gathered in the basilicas of Saints Peter and Paul, and to order that churches not be sacked. Even though the basilicas and the buildings around them were crowded beyond capacity, most of the population and treasure had to remain outside. The basilicas of Saints Peter and Paul were respected — Alaric said he didn't want to quarrel with the apostles — but the Lateran was sacked and partly destroyed. And the Lateran held much of the archives.

Again in 452, the Hun Attila erupted into the breadbasket plain of the Po Valley and headed toward Rome, the goal and dream of every barbarian king. Pope Leo and two senators met him at the confluence of the Po and Mincio rivers; Attila turned back from Rome. No one knows what happened; the historians say that he had logistical troubles; tradition says that he saw the swords of Peter and Paul playing around the head of the Pope. Perhaps the aid of the Etruscan haruspices, refused at the time of the first invasion, may finally have been accepted. Visions were something that they might have been able to arrange.

Not even Pope Leo on the road to Ostia could avert the next invasion.

The Vandals had been plundering the shores of the Mediterranean for years, with their cavalry carried on shipboard. (The "horse marines" mentioned as an impossible military unit in a nineteenth-century song were a reality then.) They landed at Ostia and plundered Rome. Probably the basilicas of Saints Peter and Paul, and the Lateran, were spared. But they liberated the seven-branched golden candlestick that the Romans had looted from the Temple of Solomon, and even took away part of the copper roof of the Temple of Jove. Files of Romans were led into slavery, and other Romans watched incredulously as the Vandal ships sailed, loaded with prisoners and treasure. One ship heavy with statues sank on its way to Carthage; other treasures looted from Rome were kept by the Vandal cities until the Byzantines took them away to the East. There they disappear from history.

The invasions shocked and bewildered the Christian world. Why had God permitted them? Jerome, who had roused himself from scholarship to carry out relief work among the Roman refugees, wrote: "Who would have believed that in holy Bethlehem, each day there would come begging for life men and women who not long ago shone for their wealth and high birth?" He had despised Rome in its great days, but now "the bright light of all the world was quenched, the universe had perished in one city."

Alaric's troops sacked Rome for only three days and the Vandals for fourteen, but the first invasion was accompanied by fire. Besides the danger of book-burning that is present in all riots and invasions, there is some sense that written material represents the soul of a people. And the books of the fifth century were vulnerable in another way too: their wooden covers were often set with jewels. We can guess at the extent of the destruction of important documents in the first invasion by the fact that Pope Zosimus in 417 quoted the papal decrees of the Council of Sardica as if they had been those of the Council of Nicaea. Apparently the needed records were still lacking, seven years after the fire.

The texts of some fifth-century documents have come down to us because they had been sent as messages to other cities, and so were preserved in the archives of the local bishops. For centuries the search for them has been a passionate adventure of papal archivists and historians. About a hundred and fifty of Pope Leo's letters have now been recovered. But the *Liber Pontificalis* says: "There are only fifty-one letters of Pope Leo preserved in the archives. Twelve to the Emperor Marcian, thirteen to the Emperor Leo, eight to the Bishop Flavian, eighteen to various Oriental bishops." No register of Leo I has survived, but one was kept in the Church's archives, since Pope Pelagius II mentions it in a letter of the year 585. It was in *polyptycha* format — tablets bound together. For the first time since Clement, three centuries earlier, we have enough surviving documents to form some idea of the character and personality of a pope.

When it seemed that the sound principle of authority that had been represented by the imperial government had vanished in the West, Pope Leo, as bishop of Christian Rome, demonstrated this power and this dignity. Though he humbly stated that "the pope is more happy to serve than to occupy the Chair of Saint Peter," he also claimed the title of "custodian of the traditional doctrine," and proclaimed his "solicitude for all churches," implying the supremacy of the Roman Church. Most of all, he fought victoriously against heresy.

One of his "sermons," which reflects both his constant concern for this problem and his excellent juridical background, is the account of his inquiry into the "perverted and magic sexualism" of the Manichaeans. Many of this sect had fled to Italy from the Vandal invasions in North Africa, and Rome had a Manichaean community of considerable size. This papal document, which the Vatican would now call an "official discourse," deals with Pope Leo's investigation into a charge of contributing to the delinquency of a minor. In a rite designed to demonstrate that the soul is not stained by the actions of the body, two children still sexually innocent had been placed together until copulation occurred. The Pope relates: "There were with me, as judges, bishops and priests and also the laymen of the aristocracy. We ordered that the 'elect' men and women of these Manichaeans be brought to us. There came to judgment, in fact, all the persons who had perpetrated the infamous crimes, that is, a young girl not more than twelve years of age, and two women who were her governesses and had arranged the crime. Also asked to come were the boy who had raped the girl, and a Manichaean bishop who had planned the crime." The confessions of these persons were identical. The Pope continues: "In order not to offend your chaste feelings by speaking openly, we refer you to the documents of their actions, which show that in their sect there is only lying, a demonic cult, and rites of turpitude."

Transcriptions of this trial of the Manichaeans were sent to the bishops of Italy and the rest of the Christian world, and the Manichaean books were burned, as those of the Arians had been.

Somewhere in these troubled centuries the Acts of the Martyrs, except for one small book, disappeared. Pope Gregory the Great (590 – 604) explicitly says that in his time the Acts of the Martyrs no longer existed "except for a very few in a single book." Private enterprise seems to have provided substitute reading matter, for at the end of the fifth century a "List of Books to be Accepted and Not to be Accepted" was drawn up. This list, possibly a private compilation, is usually called by historians the Decretum Gelasianum. It has survived through a contemporary copy made by an Italian or Provençal priest. A forerunner of the Index of Prohibited Books, it forbids the reading of certain stories of the Roman martyrs, because the names and characters of their authors were not known Also prohibited were apocryphal books, and all heretical and superstitious writings.

Among the books condemned as apocryphal were the Gospels supposedly by Matthew, Barnabas, James, Peter, and Thomas, used by the Manichaeans; *The Book of the Nativity of the Savior and of Mary*, or *The Book of the Obstetrician;* the book about the daughters of Ada, called *Genesis;* the *Cento* of Christ, composed of the verses of Vergil; *Ogia,* a book about the Biblical giant who fought with a dragon after the Deluge, (unacceptable because Ogia had survived the Deluge outside the Ark); *The Physiologist,* written by the heretics and attributed to the Blessed Ambrose, the pamphlets of Tertullian, and the writings of Simon the Magician. All of these were declared "damned for eternity," along with their authors and the followers of their authors.

Papyrus scrolls of the Gospels of Thomas and Peter were rediscovered in Egypt in the past century, and seem to be written from the viewpoint of the Gnostic and Docetist heresies. But one can regret the loss of any such books, not only because their titles would make one reach for them on a rack of paperbacks — and gaudy covers some of them would have — but because modern scholarship can learn facts even from false books, as a psychiatrist can learn the truth from the lying stories of his patients.

One of the earliest documents in the Secret Archives to come down to us in its physical form is an act of donation to the pope by a Romanized Goth, which escaped destruction because it was hidden in a very small church near Tivoli. Its date is 471, but its story begins in the previous century. In the year 359 there had died a great gentleman of this Rome that was going down to its tragic sunset: the consul Junius Bassus, prefect of the city. He was only forty-two years of age, and he was buried in a sarcophagus that is a masterpiece of the time. Now in the Vatican grotto, it is covered with bas-relief scenes from the Scriptures; the central one shows Christ between the apostles Peter and Paul. At first one thinks that the scene has been misinterpreted and that it actually represents the boy Jesus in the Temple, for on it the Christ appears as a very young adolescent, a large fair child. Then one notices another scene, of the Palm Sunday episode; here again the Christ is shown as a young boy;

and one realizes that the artist has seen him not as a historical figure but as the divine child of Deity.

The very rich Junius Bassus had built, at his own expense, at what is now the Piazza di Santa Maria Maggiore, the last secular basilica of Roman times as an auditorium for public meetings and political ceremonies. Fifty years later the invading Goths requisitioned the basilica, and in the aristocratic palace of Junius Bassus a barbarian chief — whose name we do not know — installed himself after killing or evicting the owners. Here the son of the usurper grew up, the young Flavius Vatila, called Theodoric, Roman in tastes and in spirit, but with the Germanic love of arms. He was "head of the two armies," Gothic and Roman, and called himself "illustrious consul and count of the palace."

All this wealth and magnificence, acquired by violence, may have weighed on his conscience, or he may have feared another barbarian invasion in which he himself might be killed or evicted from his property. Whatever the reason, he decided in 471 to donate his property to Pope Simplicius, and to retire to a villa near Tivoli — also taken by force from the Bassus family — keeping for life the usufruct of his lands near Tivoli.

Like many financial documents, his Act of Donation gives a picture of the life of its times: "So that those who offer divine services may have a local source of support, and the temple of the divine religion be adorned with chandeliers, and for the repair of the roof, with our wealth we will pay all expenses. May our homage serve as a propitiation to God." He therefore deeds to the church on the Cornutia estate, "ours by right and by myself established," a group of farms, which apparently included their human livestock: "the Farm of Paternus Maranus, the Farm of Mount Paternus, the Farm of the House of Mars, the Farm of Green Things, and the Basilian Farm, with the exception of Sigillosa, daughter of Anastasius and of Pica, farmers, whom we keep and will keep in our own right." He also gives the Church the land it is built on and an adjoining lot for orchards and a residence for priests and custodians. He then offers farms in the Tivoli area, "reserving to myself the usufruct during my lifetime and giving the property to the said Catholic Church." There follows a list of objects in silver and gold: chalices, lusters, censers, vases, two small silver doors for the confessional, with their little keys, a lamp in the shape of a great vase decorated with eighteen dolphins. All these silver objects were to be weighed on a public scale.

He also gave the following books: four Gospels, the Acts of the Apostles, the psalter, and a lectionary. The paucity of books, in comparison with the abundance of farms and of gold and silver objects, can be explained by the fact that books, at that time, were rare and precious treasures. The Babylonians had used the earth itself to write on, and they wrote with a stylus and a system that made possible rapid transcription free from the inaccuracies of individual handwriting. The West had adopted materials and methods that made the wide dissemination of documents so expensive as to be almost impossible until the invention of paper and printing.

This document, in the original version belonging to the Secret Archives, could still be read in the twelfth century, when a transcription was made. The original itself is now like sand.

Perhaps for the same reason that people expecting to become refugees turn their property into diamonds, the popes of the late fifth and early sixth centuries sponsored the compilation of summaries: the *Liber Canonum* and the *Liber Pontificalis*. The first is in the Secret Archives; the latter has been transferred to the Vatican Library.

The monk Dionysius Exiguus — "little old Dionysius" — was one of the leading intellectuals of Rome, a friend of Cassiodorus and of Boethius, members of the barbarian king Theodoric's brain trust. He compiled the *Liber Canonum,* a collection of Church law based on the acts of the Eastern synods. To it he added a collection of papal decrees later called the *Liber Decretorum.* Pope Adrian revised and extended it in the eighth century, and as the *Collectio Dionysio-Hadriana* it was accepted by Charlemagne, became part of Carolingian law, and for centuries was the primary legal source in Italy, in Gaul, and in Christian Africa.

The *Liber Pontificalis* is the Book of the Popes — a series of short papal biographies from Saint Peter on. Compiled by an anonymous cleric about the middle of the sixth century, it drew on the accounts of earlier authors such as Egisippus and Irenaeus. It was carried forward by other writers through the Avignon period, with an eclipse for the dark ninth century. The first biography runs: "Blessed Peter, apostle and prince of apostles, man of Antioch, son of John, of the province of Galilee, in the vicinity of Bethsaida, brother of Andrew, first sat in the episcopal chair in Antioch seven years. Then Peter entered into the City of Rome, Nero being Caesar, where he sat in the episcopal chair twenty-five years, three months, and three days. It was he who transmitted the power to bind and to loose."

These biographies of the popes, with their interesting, curious information, sometimes legend-like, sometimes partisan, are an important source for the history of Rome in the Middle Ages. In them we read of the rise of the deaconates, which distributed to the poor the goods offered to the Church, of Calixtus building the first basilica in Trastevere, long before it was illuminated with Cavallini's mosaics, of gifts such as a golden cross for Saint Peter's tomb with the inscription "*Constantinus augustus et Helena augusta* have adorned this royal house," a golden crown "stormed (*tempestata*) with precious stones" from an Ostrogoth king, and Justinian's cross containing splinters of the Cross of Christ, the only jewel from these early centuries that is still in the possession of the Vatican. There are itineraries of pilgrimages, descriptions of hospices. We see something of the building that was always going on in Christian Rome, the erection of the Vatican Palace, the construction of tricliniums at the Lateran as the Church turned to luxury. And in the *Liber Pontificalis* we learn something of the documents contained in the Scrinium of the Church. At the time when its first editors were at work, the papal archives still showed the wounds of the barbarian invasions — the references to archives documents are limited to a very small number of original texts.

The Vatican Library has a ninth-century volume of the *Liber Pontificalis,* bound in red leather and written in the clear efficient Carolingian script, its ink still iridescently black. On its cover, in gold, are two coats of arms, those of Queen Christina of Sweden and those of Pope Alexander VIII, who bought her library.

Also in the Secret Archives is still another compendium, the *Liber Diurnus.* Kept in a separate case, it is written on parchment in a beautiful Lombard script. It was compiled some time before the ninth century, and contains documents going back to the fourth.

The *Liber Diurnus,* or Daily Book, so called because it was needed every day, was a book of formulas or models for the Chancellery to use in composing papal acts and messages. I have seen a similar book of model letters that was used by American army officers in the nineteenth century. One of them, apparently going back to the Seminole war, shows the proper method of writing to the family of a soldier who has been eaten by an alligator.

Like these "Letters for all Occasions" books of the nineteenth century, the *Liber Diurnus* included examples. And this is its interest for the historian, since the hundred and seventeen documents that it quotes as models give a lively picture of the life and thinking of the Lateran patriarchate, especially for the century of Saint Benedict.

We find a list of the furnishings, human and otherwise, of a sixth-century Roman hospital — doctors, beds, mattresses, linen, thermal baths, olive oil, fats, meat dishes. We learn that boy slaves were habitually used for the service of the sick, and that the doctors of the time anticipated the modern treatment of "tender loving care" by ordering attendants not to wait for the sick to ask for help, but to give it before it was asked.

Some of the documents deal, though in a humanitarian vein, with slavery in the Church — the monasteries used slaves for agricultural and domestic work. There are various formularies for the donation of slaves, for their exchange between monasteries, and for their manumission, sometimes done in a church ceremony. In one of the model documents, the abbot of a monastery informs the pope that a serf of his monastery intends to marry a slave woman attached to the pontifical patrimony, and asks the pope if he may give him another slave as a substitute. Permission is granted.

One of the formularies given in the *Liber Diurnus* is still in use: the prayer said by bishops in dedicating new churches, which reflects the time when monasteries and churches had a *Xenodochium* — a place for strangers — where pilgrims were sheltered. "May you always abundantly enjoy this happiness of quiet, this grace of hospitality."

The Infrastructure

THE old governess had broken a dish and she was crying, because it wasn't her dish and it wasn't her house. The young boy Benedict took the pieces from her and pressed their broken edges together; they joined so that no crack was left. Pope Gregory tells the story of this miracle, a little domestic miracle like that of the wine at Cana. The young boy was Benedict of Nursia, and he had just quit school.

Brought up in a lost village in the Apennines, Benedict (480?–543?) was a provincial but of great family, and his parents had sent him to Rome to prepare him for a public career as ambassador and then governor in some place where the imperial power still had status. Shocked by Roman corruption or by his own experiences in it, the boy fled Rome and returned to the countryside near Subiaco. He did not go home. Perhaps he had a call from God; perhaps the stories of the hermits in the desert had enchanted him; perhaps he was afraid to present himself to his family as a dropout.

He spent over twenty years in the Subiaco area, as a hermit and as an abbot, though his imagination made solitary life difficult for him and as an abbot he was so strict that his monks tried to poison him. After each traumatic incident he went to a new place. But he was so successful in establishing an island of order in the confusion of the age of invasions that Roman patrician parents brought their sons out to him to be educated. Then on a hot August day an envious priest sent twelve nude harlots to dance in a field in sight of the students, and his monks made another attempt to poison him. Once more he followed the personality pattern of flight, and this time it took him to Monte Cassino, where he and his work have stood forever after.

Monte Cassino was a *castrum,* where a fortress, a pagan temple, and a sacred grove overlooked the green valley of the Iri. Here Benedict built his monastery and his sister Scholastica her convent, where she ruled as abbess until her death — "Brother, do not leave me alone this night; go on talking to me about eternal life."

The same year that saw the founding of the monastery saw the establishment of Benedict's even greater monument, the Holy Rule, a sensible and workable constitution for communal living, under which men could survive and be useful instead of torturing themselves as had some of the desert saints. "We have, therefore, to establish a school of the Lord's service, in the institution of which we hope to ordain nothing that is harsh or difficult." This moderation may not have been an original idea of Benedict's. He may have evolved it partly by trial and error — his monks had twice tried to poison him. But word of the Essene communities had drifted down through the vertical gossip of history, and there had been other monasteries run on the principle of moderation — Basil's in the Eastern Church; John Cassian's in the West. Cassian had visited the desert and had conducted interviews in depth with the desert saints; what they told him convinced him that too much solitude was a danger to sanity.

The practicality, the detail, and the foresight of Benedict's Rule are apparent in the paragraphs dealing with sleeping arrangements: "Let each one sleep in a separate bed. If possible let all sleep in one place; but if the number does not permit this, let them sleep in tens or twenties with the seniors who have charge of them. A lamp shall burn constantly in the cell until morning." He guarded against sloth as well: "Let them sleep clothed and girded with cinctures or cords; being thus always ready, the monks shall rise without delay when the signal is given. And when the brethren rise for the work of God, let them gently encourage one another because of the excuses of those who are given to sleep."

As far as possible the Benedictine monasteries were to be economically self-sufficient; sealed cities capable of withstanding the siege of the world. The City of God was to be an enclave. "The monastery should be built in such a way that within its walls are all that is necessary to life, that is, water, meal, an orchard, the oven, the shops of different kinds of artisans." Within Benedict's lifetime this list was expanded to include "the library for the books to be read and studied; the scriptorium for the transcription of the books necessary for spiritual culture."

The Benedictine Rule did not particularly stress the transcription of books, but by requiring their use in a time when they were expensive and hard to come by, it made such transcription necessary. "Laziness is the enemy of the soul; therefore the monks must perform manual labor at certain hours, and at certain other hours they must read the sacred books." Reading was equated with fasting, and some monks apparently resorted to skipping, or to what we would now call rapid-reading techniques: "During fasting periods, each one must take a book from the library, and read it in an orderly manner, beginning at the beginning."

The Benedictine Rule must have had at least the approval of the Holy See. Some historians have seen a closer connection: Benedict was part of the Establishment, and the Rule is authoritative in tone and contains provisions for adaptation to varying geographical conditions. The rules regarding monasteries given in the *Liber Diurnus* show that in the seventh century the thinking of the Chancellery was exactly in line with the Rule of Saint Benedict.

The copy of the *Regula Sancta* that was sent to Rome has been lost, but we can follow the story of the holographic copy that was kept by the monks of Monte Cassino. When the monastery was looted by the Lombards its monks fled to Rome, taking with them this original copy of the Rule, written by the saint himself, the sandals of Benedict and his sister Scholastica, a pound weight (each adult monk was to have a full pound of bread daily) and a standard measure for wine. The Rule was placed in the papal archives, where it remained up to the year 742 when Pope Zachary gave it back to Monte Cassino. In 883 the monks again fled before invasion, Saracen this time, and took the manuscript with them to Teano on the way to Naples. There they underwent a surprise attack and the manuscript was burned to ashes; only a single fragment of it was saved. This was revered as a relic and brought back to Monte Cassino when peace was established. But in the Napoleonic Wars even this very last fragment of parchment written by the hand of Benedict was lost.

Benedict shares with another Roman, his contemporary Cassiodorus, the honor of establishing monastic scriptoria. The aristocrat Marcus Aurelius Cassiodorus (490 – 585?) had built his life around the concept of *civilitas*. The Roman Empire had fallen but what it stood for could still survive — the roads, the aqueducts, the rule of law. He served Theodoric as *quaestor,* in almost the position of a secretary of state, and nearly made a civilized ruler out of him; Theodoric's coins bore the motto *Civilitas*.

When Theodoric's dynasty fell, Cassiodorus returned to his family estates at Squillace in southern Italy, an aging man with a distinguished career behind him and apparently nothing ahead of him but the life of a retired civil servant. His peasants must have thought that he had come home to die. But the dream of *civilitas* was still with him, and he remembered one of his projects that had failed — the attempt to start a university in Rome

Instead he founded two monasteries, Vivarium and Castellum. They were unusual monasteries; he could write to his monks, "You have therefore been given a city of your own; you already enjoy a prefiguration of your heavenly home." A small river ran through Vivarium, to irrigate its gardens and turn its mills. The monastery was near the ocean, and Cassiodorus remarks that the fishing is good. "And, when it pleases you, a fish once caught may be shut up in the fish ponds. For there, with the help of the Lord, we have made pleasant ponds, where a multitude of fish may drift beneath the monastery: the situation so much resembles the caves in mountains that the fish in no way realizes that it is a captive. We have also ordered baths to be built of a sort suitable for sick bodies in a place where fitly flows limpid water, which is most pleasant for drinking and for bathing "

He then hastily adds that all these are only present delights, and that Christians have more important things to think about. For those who had already "made the ascent in their hearts" and wanted something higher than monastic life, there was "the solitary sweetness of Castellum's hill, where you may live happily as anchorites. For there you will find places secluded and like a desert, shut in by ancient walls."

The old diplomat may have had a practical purpose in making Vivarium into an ecclesiastical summer resort. "Consequently, your monastery is sought by other people rather than other places by you." Cassiodorus the administrator knew what it means to have a happy staff and a low turnover when a difficult and important project is under way. For what he had in mind was nothing less than saving pagan literature and science for the Christian world.

The legalization of Christianity, and the fact that it had become the state religion, had brought into the Church men of deep culture. The patristic writings have class; they make most of the religious writing of later periods look, in a literary sense, like trash. Cassiodorus realized that the Church was living on its intellectual capital, and that much of this capital had been inherited from the pagan world. He set his monks to copying both pagan and Christian manuscripts. (That is, the monks in the monastery of pleasant ponds and limpid baths; the ones in the ascetic monastery he left to their prayers.)

In his encyclopedic textbook *Institutiones* he taught the practical usefulness to Christianity of the study of pagan literature, and adapted the *trivium* and *quadrivium* curricula to Christian education. The theological student was to be taught many disciplines — not only theology and knowledge of the Bible, but grammar, rhetoric, pagan literature, world history, mathematics, astronomy, music. In modern academic terms, Cassiodorus succeeded in slipping literature and science into the vocational-school curriculum.

While Benedict and Cassiodorus were preserving literacy in Italy — Cassiodorus intentionally — the monks of the Irish church were performing the same service for civilization. Ireland's dark ages had not yet begun; they would come when the Northmen attacked, and even the ghost of Saint Kieran, wielding its crozier, would rise to fight against them. But in these days the Irish Church was wealthy and learned, and could draw on rich intellectual reserves.

According to tradition the Irish culture had been founded by two aristocratic couples from Sidon — one of the women was the pharaoh's daughter — who brought with them Greek and Egyptian colonists and the system of writing that was later to develop into the Greek calligraphy. Ireland became, to the Tyrian sailors, "the Temple of the Setting Sun," and the high throne at Tara faced to the West. Here at Ireland's capital were a university, a state hospital, and a national archives, where the kings kept the records of legislation and the genealogies of the tribes.

It was a civilization that worshiped excellence of body and mind. No man of imperfect body or ugly face could become a king or a bard. Even the fairies, a legendary race of a little less than human size, were famed for their horse-breeding, and the bogs of Ireland have yielded the bones of prehistoric cattle that must have been fine agricultural animals.

Though there was a national archives, the Irish culture depended largely on oral transmission. The chroniclers told and retold the nation's traditions, and bards, who were allowed to wear nearly as many colors as the king, molded public opinion by eulogy and satire. Yet this oral culture developed the ogham writing, made by cuts on the edge of a staff or stone, a system so rational, so simple, and so easily learned that perhaps the only reason it has never been adapted for the use of the blind is that no one has thought of trying it.

Ireland's religion was a mixture of scientific sophistication and human sacrifice. Firstborn children belonged to the god, but the "new fire" given every three years to all the homes of the island was kindled by a concave bronze lens similar to the solar stoves that have recently been invented for use in the undeveloped countries.

Into this remnant of the great megalithic culture came Saint Patrick, with the drive, the skill in public relations, and the staff of a modern mass evangelist. He traveled the country with a hundred and fifty assistants, he used a choir of harpers to draw crowds, and when he had Christianized a place he left staff members behind to see that it stayed Christian. We are told that he bought the press by decreeing that if a bard mentioned in one of his songs that a certain piece of land belonged to him, the claim was to be recognized as constituting title to the land. Censorship was imposed on the bards, the chroniclers, and the judges by the "men of the white language."

By the end of the sixth century Ireland had become Christian, and it brought to the Church a genetic and cultural wealth that was not spent for many generations, along with a joyous enthusiasm that expressed itself in action as well as in prayer.

The only wheels that have been found among the artifacts of pre-Columbian America are those on a few little toy animals. Were they made for a child of an alien race by a man who would never see a white child again? In Ireland's Age of Saints, monks made themselves coracles of oxhide stretched over a wooden frame, provisioned them for a certain number of days, and, in a suicidal splendor of faith, launched themselves on the ocean currents to be taken anywhere on earth. God would decide the destination.

Ireland's social structure had been based on the tribe and the clan; perhaps for this reason it did not develop a hierarchy connected with particular areas. Instead there was a more personal hierarchy of abbots who gathered monks around them in monasteries that they had often founded with their own money. Ireland had always valued the arts, and the monks of these idiosyncratic monasteries spent much of their time in transcribing and illuminating codices, using the patterns that had once been used on pagan weapons and jewelry. Their workmanship was such that Irish books and art teachers were valued in continental Europe. And in the Irish monasteries Greek was kept alive as a learned language during the centuries when knowledge of it almost disappeared from western Europe. Irish medical treatises embodied Greek knowledge, and it was from Ireland as well as from Byzantium and Spain that continental Europe caught the first rays of Renaissance.

The monasteries, whether Italian or Irish, provided special workrooms called scriptoria for the copying of manuscripts and codices. A typical scriptorium is described as having a large table in the middle, with the copyists sitting at comfortable bookracks near the windows. Their tools were a reed or quill pen (the Romans had had slit steel pens), a knife to sharpen it, a *punctorium* to get lines an even distance apart, a sponge, an instrument for erasing, and an inkhorn.

Such scriptoria were nothing new; the Romans had carried on mass copying, with a reader dictating material to a roomful of scribes, and there had been bookshops on the Forum between the Basilica Emilia and the Curia. The early Church, even before the time of Constantine, had produced books for circulation through the Christian community. The Clement whom Hermas speaks of as having the duty of sending books to the foreign churches must have had some sort of scriptorium to copy them. And popular writers had private scriptoria. (Jerome says sourly that it is no wonder that Origen was so productive, since Ambrose supplied him with "parchment, money, and copyists, and thus enabled our man of brass and adamant to bring out his innumerable books.")

The establishment of monasteries, with their duties of regular prayer (four hours a day was standard) and teaching, as well as of compulsory reading, increased the demand for books. According to the Benedictine Rule, each monastery had to have a library, though the number of books was small — seldom over a hundred. It was likely to contain Biblical commentary, some of the patristic writings, including those of Pope Gregory, religious and sometimes recent history, lives of the saints and martyrs, textbooks, Christian poetry, and a few pagan classics. The expansion of the Church to northern and eastern Europe, as the pagan tribes were converted and as the frontier areas were settled, must have meant a continual demand for new books.

And books were very expensive. Their value and scarcity are shown by the fact that the property inventories of the monasteries list codices along with such things as jewels, golden reliquaries, and liturgical garments — and there were more of these luxury objects than there were of codices. Tombstones of the time sometimes mention that the deceased was the donor of a codex.

The laboriousness of hand copying is usually given as the reason for the scarcity of books in the Middle Ages. Yet books were plentiful in imperial Rome, in Byzantium, and in Islam — and in all these cultures they were copied by hand. If the labor of hand copying was not the reason for the scarcity of books, what was? The expense of materials? Or simply that people in a nonreading society didn't care enough to copy them? (Petrarch did — he copied so much of Cicero that when the manuscript fell over it injured his leg.) Possibly one reason for the scarcity of books was the inefficiency of some of the copyists. Jerome complains of them — though Jerome complains of nearly everything. But a sculptured plaque showing Saint Gregory and three of his scribes suggests that the scriptoria may sometimes have lacked convenient working equipment. Gregory himself is writing in a book held on a lectern, but the three scribes have no lectern, desk, or table to write on. One of them seems to be writing on a lapboard, but is holding a cornucopia-shaped (probably horn) container of ink in one hand while he writes with the other. The other two have nothing to support the books in which they are writing;

not even the tight skirts that Egyptian scribes used to take the place of a desk.

Another reason must have been that the codices were often regarded as works of art rather than as means of communication. Illuminating a missal with pictures in color and gold leaf could take almost any amount of time that one was willing to give. Elaborate bindings added to the expense; books were often bound in gold, silver, or ivory plates, studded with precious stones. The parchment, expensive in itself, might be dyed purple; the ink was sometimes, especially in Charlemagne's time, made of gold. Such codices were less books than works of art, to ornament a church or monastery. Even in more modest transcriptions, it may be that more attention was paid to regularity of lettering than was necessary for the sake of readability.

The high cost made purchase impractical; the monasteries and the most important bishops' seats copied their own books just as they baked their own bread. Books were exchanged; rare copies were lent for transcribing. In time some of the scriptoria became the medieval equivalent of publishing houses. Monte Cassino, through its work in copying and disseminating manuscripts, became an intellectual center. Here Paul the Deacon wrote his *History of the Lombards,* and Alberic wrote his *Vision* of hell, heaven, and purgatory — an early *Divine Comedy.* Monks from Monte Cassino became bishops, abbots, and popes. In times of unrest in Rome, when the popes had to flee the city, they sometimes sent documents to Monte Cassino for safekeeping; the monastery became host to part of the papal archives.

Monte Cassino's calligraphy, called Beneventana, spread throughout the scriptoria of southern Italy. But in general each of the great monasteries tended to have its own style of writing. In this way codices can be identified as to their place of origin, and often as to their time of origin. Carbon 14 dating is inadequate; it can tell when the sheep lived but not when the parchment was written on. But the varying styles of calligraphy follow a fairly regular and known pattern. The first Latin writing was in capitals, either straight or inclined. From the straight letters the so-called librarians' writing developed; this was used for the codices. From the inclined letters came the cursive scripts used for documents. Various calligraphies were developed — uncial, (large rounded letters), semi-uncial, Merovingian, pre-Carolingian, Beneventana, Visigothic, Carolingian, Gothic, humanist. (At this point printing took over.) The various writings are characteristic of a country and of a time.

In general, the scriptoria produced codices and the Chancellery produced current documents. The Chancellery, made up of notaries and *scrinarii,* headed by a *primicerius,* goes back to the time of imperial

Rome. In the Chancellery the papal letters and other communications were prepared, the registers, which served as records of outgoing correspondence, were made up, and incoming correspondence was filed. The Chancellery is the major source of the material in the papal archives.

That the Chancellery produced a large volume of written materials is suggested by the fact that it, like the publishing-house monasteries, had its own distinctive calligraphy — *cancellaresca*. This varied from one age to another — the *curiale romana*, the smaller, more rounded, more cursive *curiale nova*, the light, airy, smart *minuscula cancellaresca*.

Because of the importance of calligraphy in the identifying and dating of documents, a School of Diplomatica (study of documents) and Paleography is attached to the Vatican Secret Archives.

VII

Gregory the Great

THE grounds of the Church of San Gregorio Magno on the Caelian Hill are one of the vertical parks by which Rome, in an unconscious inspiration of city planning, provides thousands of square yards of natural terrain in return for the loss of far fewer yards of building area. The church has been rebuilt through the centuries, but some parts of it go back to Gregory's time (590–604). Its gray façade and stairway face the pink skeleton of the Palatine and the green pines that surround it. On this hill stood Gregory's monastery, which had once been his family palace. A *frater minor* attached to the church shows the visitor the faded frescoes of Gregory seeing the "bright-beautied people" of England waiting to be sold in the slave market, of Gregory blessing his monks as they prepare to leave Rome, and of the missionaries arriving in the green land that they were to make Christian. And he shows two pieces of furniture that have survived the centuries: Gregory's marble throne of meditation, large enough only for a fasting man, and a marble table, that from its combination of fine with less fine supports seems to have been a good table relegated to humbler use. Here Gregory served the poor, twelve at a time, but once the head count came out wrong, because an angel was eating with them. And there is the place where the Virgin Mary chided him, "Gregory, when you were a monk, you always used to come to pray to me; now that you are Pope you are forgetting me."

We know too little about Gregory to be able to understand this complex man with the soft-fleshed face, the hard Roman words, and the subtle psychological insights. But we know much more about him than about his predecessors, or indeed about any pope for the next five hundred years, for we have more of his letters. Eight hundred and fifty-four of them have survived, even though the register in its physical form has disappeared. It was Adrian I, pope from 772 to 795, who began the collection by extracting six hundred and eighty-six letters from Gregory's original voluminous register. (There are over a hundred manuscripts containing Gregory's letters, though they all belong to a later time: Monte Cassino has one of the eleventh century; others ranging from the tenth to the fifteenth century are now in the Vatican Library.) Part of the register must have been secret — the letters in which Gregory tries to break the ties between the Gauls and the Lombards, and his very personal exchanges with the emperor at Byzantium.

This register, when it no longer served as the active files, would have been placed in the papal archives at the Lateran where Gregory himself mentions having placed his sermons. Both register and sermons were still there in the ninth century, along with a very large volume listing the name, age, and sex of the persons helped by the Church in Gregory's pontificate. The register was in the form of fourteen rolls of papyrus that corresponded to Gregory's fourteen years as pope.

We know that the archives were at the Lateran in the century of Gregory's death, from a seventh-century document in the *Liber Diurnus* which speaks of a certain decree as being "*in archivo dominae nostrae sanctae Romanae ecclesiae, scilicet in sacro Lateranensi scrinio*" ("in the archives of our lady the holy Roman church, in the sacred scrinium of the Lateran"). This scrinium was very likely under the chapel of the Sancta Sanctorum and the Holy Stairs, the steps of Tyrian marble that Constantine's mother had brought from Pilate's house. The chapel was originally dedicated to Saint Lawrence the Librarian, and it was well guarded both because of the stair, up which Christ had dragged himself bleeding, and because of its contents, which may have included the heads of the saints Peter and Paul. In 1900, during excavations under the chapel, a large library room with a fresco of Saint Augustine was discovered.

The young patrician Gregory was the son of a noble house that had already given two popes, and would give three saints, to the Church. He had begun a brilliant career in the hierarchy of the empire; promoted from one office to another he finally became Prefect of the City. But his life, like Rome's, was shadowed by the Lombard invasion. Pushed on by overpopulation, the barbarians were claiming what the United Nations, by the end of our century, will probably be calling the right of Freedom of Residence. "As a sword drawn from the scabbard, these hordes of savages throw themselves on us, and men everywhere are falling like mown grass. The cities have been depopulated, villages destroyed, churches set on fire, convents of monks and nuns razed to the ground. The fields have become a desert; the squalid land is in mourning because there is no one to cultivate it."

Gregory and his family, like many Christians of these years, thought that the world was coming to an end. "I do not know what is happening in other parts of this world: what I know is that in this land in which we live, the end of the world has announced itself openly."

Gregory left politics, tore off the pallium of silk and gold, the high boots of red leather with moon-shaped buckles. He became a monk and retired into a part of his palace — emptied now of furniture, of comfort, and of servants — and there he prayed and fasted to expiate the sins of the consuls that had conquered the world. His old father, the lord of Gordiano, giving his vast fortune to the Church and the poor, became a priest, and his mother, Lady Sylvia, entered a convent. Every day about noon the people could see, along the narrow streets linking the Aventine and the Caelian hills, the old Lady Sylvia dressed in shoddy, bringing to Gregory a small silver dish of vegetables that she had prepared with her thin white hands. For five years they waited for the last day. Instead there arrived news of the massacres carried out by the king of the Lombards, and of the death of relatives and friends, as the great Italian families were systematically destroyed.

It was a German, Pope Pelagius II (579–590), son of an Ostrogoth captain, who found the strength to fight against the Germans. He loved Rome passionately, as happens today also to men of German blood. Perhaps he hoped to awaken the Roman quirite in the monk Gregory when he sent him as ambassador — in modern terms, nuncio — to the court of Constantinople, to ask for help against the Lombards. But Gregory fasted at official banquets, spent much of his time writing a book on Job, and returned as soon as possible to his monastery. He was routed out from the religious life by the death of Pope Pelagius in the plague, and his election by acclamation as Pope Gregory I.

It was a time of flood: the Tiber was even washing away the Church's granaries where wheat to feed the poor was kept. It was a time of plague: Gregory commented that one could see the celestial arrows striking the Romans. It was a time of war: the absence of the emperor left a power vacuum that only the Church could fill, and the new pope, both a priest and a ruler, was caught in the pacifist dilemma. He met the situation by holding a march, not of protest but of penitence. The secular city was to disown herself, to be born again as a holy city. On a Lenten morning in the year 590 all the men assembled in one basilica, the women in another, the widows in a third, and the children in a fourth. In the same way the nuns, the monks, and the clergy assembled separately. At a signal of bells the seven lines turned toward the Basilica of Santa Maria Maggiore, in a collective expiation for the triumphal processions that had once ascended the Campidoglio. As they neared Saint Peter's, tradition says that the Archangel Michael appeared above Hadrian's tomb, sheathing his sword to show that the plague was over. Thus the great tomb, with its memories of Hadrian and the boy, became the Castle of the Angel — Castel Sant'Angelo — that would later hold the most precious of the archives.

But the Lombards were still advancing, little by little, sure of final victory. "Why not come to terms with them?" Gregory suggested to the emperor. "The soldiers are not being paid and are abandoning the defense, except for guarding the walls. Resistance is impossible. We make peace or the city is destroyed." But the imperial government delayed, and Gregory again wrote to the emperor. "Rome has been abandoned to save Perugia. With my own eyes I saw Italians with ropes around their necks like dogs, taken away by the Lombards to be sold as slaves in France."

The emperor, offended by Gregory's direct negotiations with the invader, accused him of having changed from a priest to a foolish diplomat. Gregory answered, "I have been called foolish. It is true. If I were not a fool I would not have accepted this job of Pontifex, or have put up with all I have had to put up with in consequence."

A determined effort might have evicted the Lombards, but Pope Gregory had resolved the pacifist dilemma by limiting himself to defensive warfare. The war hawks of the time proposed a Sicilian Vespers, a sudden massacre of all the Lombards, at a fixed time and on a given signal. Gregory refused. In a diplomatic dispatch to the papal representative in Constantinople he writes: "If I had wanted to involve myself in the death of the Lombards, the Lombard nation would no longer have a king, nor dukes, nor counts, but would be divided and plunged in confusion. But as I fear God, I am afraid to involve myself in the death of any person whatsoever." The modern mind compares this with General Belisarius' magnificent plea for the first faint glimmer of the concept of the open city.

But if Gregory was a Hamlet pope where warfare was concerned, he was a vigorous administrator in areas where he had no conflict of conscience. Refugees from the Lombard war were everywhere, and the Church had the means for large-scale charity. The popes were the most important owners of land and mines in Italy. Sardinia was practically a papal property. So was Sicily, a grain-producing area not yet eroded by the destruction of its forests. The coast of the Tyrrhenian Sea, with its silver and iron mines, was largely in the hands of the Church.

Gregory, who had founded six monasteries in Sicily, sent many letters to the pontifical administrator there, urging him to help people in need. "I asked you, in our previous letter, most of all to take care of the poor. And if you knew of people in poverty, you should have pointed them out to me immediately, but you did this unwillingly and only for a few. I desire that you give the woman Pateria, immediately, as soon as you have received this order, forty *soldi* for the children's shoes and forty bushels of grain . . ." The letters reflect the problems of an absentee landlord: the Pope had great estates in Sicily, but how much came to Rome? "You have sent us a miserable horse and five good donkeys. I can't ride the horse because it is a real nag, and I can't ride the donkeys because they are donkeys. Therefore we ask you to send us something more decorous."

There are also letters to the barbarians. The Lombard civilization was flourishing, and Gregory hoped to bring the Lombards, already Arian, into the Roman Church. Their queen was Theodolinda, a Catholic, beloved by her people, and a woman certain of her power and charm: widowed, she had chosen a husband by saying to one of her warrior nobles, "You need not kiss my hand when you can kiss my mouth." Gregory writes to Theodolinda on her decision to educate the Crown Prince Adulovald as a Roman Catholic: "You have given your son the armor of the Catholic faith." In this letter he mentions gifts that he is sending to Adulovald — a golden cross to wear around his neck, containing a splinter of the Cross of Christ, along with a small box of Persian wood containing a New Testament, and for the little princesses, three rings. "I ask you as a favor to give the children these little gifts with your own hands, so that our love towards them may be presented by Your Excellency."

And as Theodolinda had asked for some relics of the Roman martyrs for the chapel of her palace at Monza, the old Pope sent her some ampoules filled with the oil of the lamps that burned before the tombs of the martyrs in the Roman basilicas. For the student of the papal archives this last gift is the most interesting, for Gregory had attached to each ampoule a strip of papyrus telling where it had come from. These little strips of papyrus were preserved in a wooden box up to 1042. After the destruction of the Lombard palace the box was kept in a marble urn behind the great altar of Saint John the Baptist in Monza. Lost and then rediscovered in the year 1881, they are now in the cathedral treasury. These minuscule fragments of writing are all that is left of the thousands and thousands of words that came from the pens of Pope Gregory and his Chancellery. The pectoral cross sent for the baptism of the young prince, with its splinter of the True Cross, has also survived history in the treasury at Monza; Pope Paul VI asked that it be lent him to wear on his visit to Jerusalem.

The nuns had a new chapel, dedicated to Our Lady of Light, but when they moved into it they discovered that the builders had forgotten to install a stairway to the choir loft of the eighty-five-foot-high room. Recalled to supply one, the builders pointed out that there was no room for it, and suggested a ladder. The nuns rejected this as unseemly.

Next morning a gray-haired man came with his donkey; tied to its saddle was a small tool chest that contained only three old tools — a T-square, a saw, and a hammer. He offered to install a circular stairway for them, and, eight months later, when it was finished — of wood without nails, beautifully wrought, and ascending in two 360-degree curves that seemed to have no means of support — he tied his tool chest on the donkey's back again and disappeared. When the Mother Superior went to the lumber merchant to pay for the wood, she was told that there was no bill because no wood had been bought. On examination the wood proved to be of a kind that grew far to the north. And the nuns remembered Saint Joseph the Carpenter.

This happened, if it happened, in New Mexico in the nineteenth century. If the story had arisen in sixth-century Italy, Pope Gregory would have annexed it happily for his collection of Golden Legends. Some skeptical historians have wondered whether Gregory himself believed these charming, credulous tales that were so popular in the Middle Ages, and suggest that the legends may have been written as a public-relations project to get and keep customers for the faith. They are said to have had great appeal for the Lombards. The unsympathetic historian Michelet thinks that such legends arose from the hallucinative effects of hunger and solitude. But another possibility is that people were ready to believe because they had already seen things that were hard to believe — that parapsychological phenomena which are now very rare may then have been commoner. The clairvoyant Saint Wulfric kept a small boy running here and there in the community giving people advice on better ways to do their work. The woman whose mistake in sewing had been corrected by this meddlesome saint would have been ready to believe Gregory's legends.

Actually the Pope seems to have made an effort, unusual for that time, to establish the authenticity of his tales. The staff assisting him in his writing included notaries, theologians, and Benedictine monks from his monastery, among them Augustine and Melitus, the future apostles to

England. He took great care to give his sources and the testimony supporting the legends, and often had his assistants make on-the-spot investigations. He was so scrupulous that he burned many of his works without publishing them. Others remained in the archives, still unpublished, in the ninth century.

Gregory the lawyer, the administrator, the ruler, seems to have seen the injustice of condemning a soul to eternal torment for temporal sin, and elaborated Augustine's idea of purgatory. But hell he pictured in all its medieval horror. With Gregory the North African light leaves the Church and the European winter begins.

Yet the Pope, in his work on the Gregorian chant and in his sponsorship of the Schola Cantorum, brought beauty to that winter and to ours. The Christian liturgical service, from the time of the clandestine church, had been accompanied by the songs of the faithful. Responsive singing of the Psalms and other passages from the Old Testament and the Gospel resounded in the dusk of the catacombs, at the tombs of the most venerated martyrs, bringing to life what would otherwise have been only a cold dominion of death. Pope Damasus introduced alleluia melodies, Saint Hilary of Poitiers wrote Latin hymns to the rhythm of the legions' marching songs, and Saint Ambrose brought antiphonal singing to the West. One tradition says that the *Te Deum* was composed extemporaneously while Saint Augustine of Hippo was being baptized by Ambrose, each singing alternate lines — an interesting elaboration of the technique of the Happening, if the participants are geniuses.

Gregory revised the liturgy and collected and amended those of the Church's chants that he wanted to preserve, assigning different chants to the various services throughout the Christian year. "He brought all the music of the Western Church for the first time into a systematic and well-proportioned whole." The original copy of this collection, the *Antiphonarius Cento*, that must have been in the archives-library along with his other works, has been lost. A probably complete illuminated copy is in the Monastery of Saint Gall in Switzerland, a musical center of the Middle Ages.

Besides compiling this large collection of sacred songs, Gregory reorganized and strengthened the Schola Cantorum, providing economic support and a dual physical plant at the Lateran and at Saint Peter's. (He also provided personal encouragement, the little *flagellum* which he used to motivate the boys' singing was kept by the Lateran until about the ninth century.) This school gathered in young boys, especially orphans, but the training sometimes lasted a lifetime. It had great cultural influence throughout the Middle Ages, since it taught not only singing but grammar, rhetoric and ecclesiastical administration. Music welded together the various elements of the curriculum and was the stimulating force in the study of religious disciplines.

The Schola Cantorum gave music a status that exotic abuses had compromised; Roman singers had often been chosen as much for their physical beauty as for their voices, and had exhibited themselves in varicolored clothing and with long hair equivocally loose on their shoulders. In place of this the new Gregorian discipline had a moral integrity beyond question.

In one of his letters to the Bishop of Palermo, Gregory directed him to gather and melt all the old bronze belonging to the Sicilian churches; the supplies of tin needed to make new bronze were no longer arriving from England. The island that had furnished tin to the Greeks, the Etruscans, and the Romans had gone back, after its splendid imperial flourishing, into such a state of barbarian degradation that savage men wandered on the coast of Sussex.

According to one legend Joseph of Arimathea was the uncle of Christ, and after the crucifixion brought the faith to England. Some said that Christ himself had spent a few years there, as a boy in the company of his trader uncle. The inner shrine of Glastonbury Cathedral was a small Neolithic house of basketwork covered with clay, in which they were supposed to have lived, and one wonders whether the boy who questioned the doctors in the Temple may also have questioned the Druids. But British Christianity, strong in the fourth and fifth centuries, had been almost destroyed by the Anglo-Saxon invasions, and Christian civilization survived only in the western regions.

Gregory, a lover of books, must have read Saint Gildas' "Book of Tears." Gildas, a poor British monk who had escaped to France, describes the Britons as a population mild and unwarlike, who even in Roman times "stretched out their hands like women to be chained" so that they "never were strong in war nor faithful in peace." With the imperial power withdrawn and the invasion of the Scots, the Picts, and the Saxons, "the most cruel massacres took place. The population came to blows among themselves, and to the carnage was added accusation among people of the same family." There was a general moral breakdown, and Gildas denounced "that kind of perversion against nature which turned to evil that which instead should be turned to good." The Britons asked Rome to intervene: "To Aetius, thrice consul: The barbarians push us toward the sea, the sea drives us back toward the barbarians. All we have is a choice between two kinds of death; either we are slaughtered or we are drowned."

The mission to England was Gregory's most personal project, and the

men who were to take part in it were Benedictine monks trained in his
own monastery. But when they reached France what they heard about
conditions in England-–very like Gildas' reports—dismayed them.
They wanted to return to Rome, and continued only because of Gregory's orders: "It would have been better not to start a good work at all
than to turn back from it." To tighten discipline the Pope made Augustine abbot. Canterbury was chosen as the place of settlement because, at
its royal court, the queen was French and Catholic. Her husband, Ethelbert, dominated the other tribal chiefs and had taken the title Bretwalda
—a barbaric translation of *Dux Britannorum.* Augustine sent him a
message telling him that he had come to offer him a kingdom that would
never come to an end. Ethelbert was skeptical as to the unending kingdom, but he met the monks in the field in front of his castle, enjoyed
their processions and their litanies, and allowed them to remain and to
preach.

This meeting and its outcome were typical of many such meetings that
were to take place in the coming centuries between missionaries and
native rulers. Ethelbert was finally christened, and the Pope wrote to
him: "Be quick to spread the Christian faith among the peoples subject
to you. Persecute the worship of idols, destroy the temples of the sacred
wood. Elevate the customs of your subjects, exhorting, frightening, correcting, and showing examples of good works."

The text of this letter was preserved for centuries as an English official
document. More important is the text that describes the king's christening, since it is thought to be the first literary document in the new English language.

Gregory also planned to build up a corps of young English clergy (the
"native preachers" of modern missionary work) to take the place of Roman and French missionaries and avoid eventual nationalistic conflict.
His method of recruiting them was very direct: he wrote to the presbyter
Candidus, "Going as you are to administer the patrimony of the Roman
church in Gaul, we desire that with the money you receive from it you
buy English boys seventeen or eighteen years of age, so that they can
offer themselves to God in the monasteries. But since these little slaves
that you will find may be pagans, I want you to send a priest along with
them, so that if, during the journey, they should get sick, he can christen
them before they die."

Gregory's missionaries had come to an island in which a Christian
church was already functioning. Celtic Christianity, like the Britons, had
been pushed back into the western part of the island, where it had literally taken to the hills. There, like the bronze-age chieftain Arthur, it organized its resistance. At the same time Celtic activity extended to the

islands west of Scotland. Iona, under the royal and gentle Columba, became a holy place, so much a domain of God that even now professional men, college students, and laborers spend their vacations there, rebuilding its ancient beauty by heavy manual labor, for no pay but its peace. From Iona and Lindisfarne the Celtic faith spread to Scotland and northern England.

The Celtic Church had always been Roman in its major allegiance. It recognized the authority of the pope but preferred its own way of doing things. Perhaps one could say that the Celtic Church was Catholic in the separate and slightly superior way that the American Episcopal Church is Protestant. It had inherited an aristocracy of intelligence from the Druids, its learned men knew Greek, and its Latin was uncontaminated by a surrounding Latin vernacular. The Celtic clergy felt for the Roman liturgies the same distaste that people accustomed to the King James version of the Bible feel for the Revised Standard Version. And there were other differences; the date of Easter now seems of minor ecclesiastical importance, but these men were too near to the time of the astronomer-priests to take such things lightly. Actually the date-of-Easter controversy was an inheritance from the early Church Fathers, who had left a set of instructions capable of being interpreted in at least four different ways.

And one almost feels that some degree of separateness can be condoned, when it produces such a charming culture, so learned yet so close to poverty and the soil. Saint Columba on his deathday inspected the granary to make sure that his monks had enough grain to last the year, and Saint Cuthbert's description of the three loaves of bread brought him by a young-boy angel suggests a homelike Heaven. It was a world where sea otters warmed the feet of saints with their breath, and where the abbots took off now and then, as the Druid priests had done, to visit "God's paradise over the sea"; their garments were fragrant for forty days after their return. It was a brief and beautiful culture, vanished as that of the seven-foot blond kings of the Canary Isles.

Augustine was unable to win the collaboration of the Celtic Church, which refused to give up its traditional rites and customs. He met their bishops and doctors in a synod, but it started off badly because he failed to rise from his seat at their entrance. He offered to recognize the supremacy of their Archbishop of Saint David's in Wales, but demanded that they accept Roman discipline, conform to Roman customs in such matters as the date of Easter and style of haircut, and integrate with the Anglo-Saxons, who had recently been killing their relatives. The Celtic Church remained separate until the major confrontation between Celtic and Roman Christianity sixty years later, when the Synod of Whitby decided for the Roman date of Easter, on the ground that Saint Peter outranked Saint Columba. But it was hundreds of years before all of the recalcitrant Irish and British clergy submitted to Rome in regard to all the details of the faith.

Meanwhile the Roman clergy continued their Christianization of the pagans. Boniface V himself worked for the conversion of Edwin, King of Northumbria, who had a Christian wife. The Pope, a Neapolitan, wrote to the queen: "We send you a silver mirror and an ivory comb, decorated with gold . . . but because a part of your body (your husband) has remained alien to the Trinity, how is it possible to say that true union takes place if the king remains alien to the splendor of your faith? The consummation of carnal affection makes you seem one body, but after passage from this life it is unity of faith that preserves you in perpetual togetherness. You must insist therefore, O glorious daughter, in softening with every effort the hardness of the king's heart, implanting in his senses how splendid is the mystery that you have learned by believing." The king was baptized, and asked for a Roman bishop for his court.

As the Christianization of England continued, the traveling preachers were replaced by missionaries in many permanent residences scattered through the island. These monasteries functioned as a permanent Peace Corps, supported by the most intelligent and progressive people at the native courts.

As Lewis Mumford has pointed out, the bells of the monasteries, ringing at fixed hours, gave the newly emerging peoples the sense of time that barbarians lack. And perhaps the Christian year as it was finally elaborated, with its recurrent festivals and saints' days, gave them a more accurate sense of time than we get from our modern calendars. ("It is two years ago today that you went to America, madam." "But how can you remember? *I* don't remember." "Because the next day was Saint Rita's day, and I took red roses to the church for you.")

The monks reclaimed the swampy plains and taught agriculture to the English hunters; they showed the men of the island that had once built Stonehenge the techniques of cutting and squaring stones, of erecting walls, arches, and towers. Many of the young men of the tribes gave their allegiance to new tribes, the monasteries. They learned to read and write from the New Testament and from missals, and to decorate parchment with colored figures. The monks of the Roman Catholic monasteries, like those of the Celtic, produced illuminated manuscripts of great beauty.

England reached its intellectual takeoff point very rapidly, and poetry of permanent worth was produced by men only a generation or two away from barbarism. Much of it was deeply Christian in its nature and inspiration. Some, like *Beowulf,* had its roots in Scandinavian folklore, but both pagan and Christian elements are apparent. Grendel the mist-walker was still of the kraken kind, but he was sired by Cain. There is the same mixture of pagan and Christian elements in *The Dream of the Rood,* where Christ appears as a Germanic *Held:* "Then the young warrior, God, the All-Wielder . . ." And perhaps more significant than the creations of Caedmon, since genius can occur anywhere, is the fact that the making of music and poetry was one of the usual recreations in his monastery.

Documents relating to the missions accumulated in the archives — directive letters from Rome and anxious questions from the missionaries in the field. The archives were even used as source material by an English historian, the Venerable Bede (673?–735), in writing his *Ecclesiastical History of the English Nation.* Though he never left England, he was able to use material from the papal archives. Not only did the missionary fathers leave Rome with documents in their luggage (they would be talking with kings who were likely to ask for proof) but they kept up a continuous and intimate correspondence with the Holy See. Papal letters were carefully preserved; they were regarded as relics and ecclesiastical treasures. But many of the sources Bede used were brought to England through intentional research and transcription. Nothelm, later archbishop, traveled to Rome and collected official letters from Gregory and other popes to the missions in England. That he was able to do this is further evidence that copies of papal letters were made and were kept for reference. Thus Bede, on the backwoods border of a vanished empire, was able to use the archives both of Rome and of England. At about the same time, Saint Wilfrid appealed to Rome in a conflict about territory that tested the powers of the secular princes over the Church — the first recorded instance of an English prelate appealing to the Holy See. He won the appeal but his enemies refused to accept the decision — in fact the queen took the relics Wilfrid had collected in Rome and made a necklace of them, which she "wore both at home in her chamber and when she rode forth in her chariot." She gave them back when she was taken ill "with the muscles of her limbs all contracted and screwed up," but Wilfrid found it necessary to go to Rome again. Here the reported comments of Pope John VI show one of the major uses of the archives: "Members of this holy synod, it is our duty first of all to go through the canons of our holy predecessors, and examine the documents treating of these injuries and wrongs sent by either party up to now. We must bear in mind and carefully weigh what blessed Agatho and Benedict and my holy predecessor Sergius thought of the matter, and what orders they gave the kings and archbishops. After that we shall be in a better position to stamp out falsehood and perceive the light of truth when we have both sides before us in the presence of our brethren contesting against each other. We shall follow the canons and judge according to the rules laid down by our predecessors."

In giving his judgment the Pope said: "We had the parties debate the matter for some days before an assembly of reverend priests and prelates. Every document, old or new, adduced by either side, all their verbal statements, together with any relevant matter we could find in our archives — all this has been most carefully sifted and the findings made known to us." Wilfrid made another collection of relics and returned home with "the text of the papal bull properly stamped and sealed."

In time the flowering of culture among the Irish and among the descendants of the Anglo-Saxon raiders was ended by new raids. The Viking invaders, who could pick their time and their place, broke through the islands' defenses again and again. The beautiful books in the monasteries were destroyed, but the Vikings themselves eventually became Christian. Missions were sent to the pagan countries bordering the North Sea not only to save souls but to bring the raiders under some degree of control. The policy slowly succeeded. In England a few years ago the imprint of a disintegrated ship was found in the earth. In it, among other artifacts, was a spoon bearing on one side the name Saul, on the other the name Paul — a suitable baptismal gift for a converted king.

The Archives at the Tomb

THE Church was a de facto government, and the seat of government was at the Lateran, in the palaces next to the Basilica of Constantine. Like today's Vatican, the Lateran was a small city. Building was always going on somewhere. One of the builder popes was the eighth-century Zachary, who, the *Liber Pontificalis* tells us, erected a portico and a tower opposite the Lateran scrinium — "*ante scrinium Lateranense porticum atque turrem.*" That the scrinium could be used as a point of reference seems to imply that it was rather prominent in the geography of the Lateran.

After the open days of the empire had ended, most Italian towns had built walls and towers, but Zachary's tower was for pleasure rather than for defense. At its top was an aerial triclinium — a dining room with reclining couches — luxuriously furnished and frescoed with the map of the world that so impressed Charlemagne. A little later Pope Leo III built an even more magnificent triclinium with marble walls, a porphyry fountain, and a flight of columns decorated with the lilies that were to be the crest of France. Here the popes received emperors and princes, and here they pronounced the excommunications that shook Europe. But here too Leo celebrated the *Cena* on Easter Day. The table was laid for eleven and the *primicerius* — head of the Chancellery and archives — took the part of Judas. The Pope held out a piece of lamb to him, saying " 'What you have in mind to do, do it quickly.' As he received it for his damnation, you are receiving it for your forgiveness."

A later pope, Gregory IV, built a new triclinium with walls of white marble thirty inches thick, and added heated rooms and apartments of rest where he and his clergy could relax after the dawn-singing of Lauds.

But the meals for the pope and the poor were cooked in the same kitchen.

The Lateran was the residence of the pope, the center of government of the Church, the site of the scrinium. But there was another stage for religious and political drama, and another depository for the Church's archives — Saint Peter's Basilica, the cult center of the Prince of Apostles. Like the Lateran, Saint Peter's had an accretion of buildings. Among them were two episcopal palaces, built by Pope Symmachus when he was kept out of the Lateran by schism — the beginning of the Vatican of today.

Saint Peter's was richly decorated; perhaps overdecorated. In the seventh century Honorius plated the altar and the main door with silver, and covered the roof with golden-bronze tiles from the Temple of Venus. In its atrium was the statue of Saint Peter that legend said had been cast from the bronze of the Capitoline Jove; when the Byzantine emperor forbade the use of images, and threatened to send troops to destroy it, its foot was already worn with the kisses of the faithful.

In an apse at the end of the raftered nave was the Confession — the Tomb — of Saint Peter. It was much changed from the little *aedicula* that the early Christians had built on Peter's grave. The pavement had been raised, so that the top of the tomb could be used as an altar; a balustrade separated it from the public, and first one, then two rows of spiral columns gave it the look of a shrine. Above it was a mosaic, on a rounded surface like half of a planetarium dome, in which Christ and the apostles Peter and Paul, under a sun like a great flower, were surrounded by the lambs and palm trees of a Mediterranean paradise.

It was the Christian world's first place of pilgrimage. Emperors camped in the fields around Saint Peter's, to pray and leave votive gifts before going to the Lateran, and poorer pilgrims left little offerings in the varied coinages of Europe. Councils were held there and anathemas pronounced in darkly dramatic rites. When Pope Theodore denounced the heretic bishop Pyrrhus, he went to the tomb and mixed "a drop of the blood of Christ" with the ink that he used to sign the anathema.

The Confession of Saint Peter was regarded as being more than holy. It was a sensitive spot where the barriers between the seen and unseen worlds were very thin, a place where psychic power was believed to be concentrated, a place of divine witness. Here adversaries of the pope deposited their accusations against him, their armed men slaughtering the *mansionarii Scholae confessionis Sancti Petri* who guarded the tomb, in order to lay their complaints on the body of Saint Peter.

A document left at the tomb constituted a most sacred oath. Here the

bishops laid their holographic oaths of fidelity to the Church's teachings
— the *promissio fidei* — and the *cautio,* in which the bishop obliged
himself to follow certain rules in governing his diocese. Even the popes
deposited professions of faith at the Confession. Records of the Church
councils were placed here, to serve as foundation for Church law. Here
the sovereigns presented their imperial and royal insignia, their magnificent gifts, their purple diplomas, and the deeds of donation of land and
power. The Confession became a storage place for the most valuable
material, a special and select archive. Sooner or later some of these documents must have been transferred to the scrinium at the Lateran or to
other places in Saint Peter's Basilica, since storage space at the Confession was limited, but others remained there, entrusted to Peter. It may
have been, in part, this custom of storing valuable things near the high
altar that made the Avignon pope John XXII, in his insistence on the
idea that souls do not immediately enter Heaven, say that they were
stored "beneath the altar."

It was at the *Confessio Beati Petri Apostoli* that the emissary of Pepin,
king of the Franks, in the year 756, laid his donation of central
Italy and the keys of the Lombard cities he had conquered. For protection against the Lombards, who had developed an alarmingly good government in the north of Italy, the popes had cultivated their enemies the
Franks. The Merovingian line of Frankish kings was biologically played
out, and the Franks were being governed by the mayors of the palace, in
an arrangement foreshadowing the modern city-manager system. When
the Mayor of the Palace Pepin posed a question to Pope Zachary: "Who
should be called king, the man who actually has the power or the one
who has the appearance of power?" the Pope gave the desired answer.

In the winter of the year 753 Zachary's successor, Stephen II, traveled
over the Saint Bernard pass to a meeting with Pepin, described in the
"*Vita Stephani*" of the *Liber Pontificalis.* Pepin went three miles to meet
the Pope, prostrated himself on the ground, and led the Pope's horse to
the palace. (A good deal of medieval history hinges on the matter of who
led whose horse.) The next summer the Pope consecrated Pepin as king,
and with him consecrated his two sons. One of the children was to become Charlemagne; a specimen of *homo superior* had been born into the
backwoods culture of the Franks. By an agreement of the same year, the
Lombard realm was to be divided between Pepin and the Pope. The
Secret Archives has no contemporary copy of this agreement, but historians such as Baronius, a papal historian of the Renaissance, write as if
they had seen it.

Early in 756 the Lombards attacked Rome, and the Pope wrote to

Pepin for help: "They have destroyed all the villages around Rome, setting fire to the houses and burning the holy images. And they threw the Host into the niches they have profaned and call savings banks. Often after rich banquets of meat they have eaten the sacrament. And they have used the draperies of the altars for their corporal necessities. Nuns who have been in seclusion since infancy and puberty have been soiled and some of them killed during the contamination . . ."

The same day the Pope sent a second letter to Pepin, to the princes Charles and Carloman, and to the Frankish people, written as if by Saint Peter himself: "I, Peter, Apostle of God, that consider you as adopted sons for the defense of Rome and the people entrusted to me by God, implore you for help. Hasten to help me before the life-source from which you have been born a second time dries up." The Frankish response was swift and energetic; their invasion of Italy gave the papacy the Donation of Pepin, presented at the tomb of Saint Peter. Later Pepin's son Charles confirmed and extended it by another diploma, also deposited at the Confession, a copy of which is in the Secret Archives. The original donations of Pepin and Charles have disappeared.

When Charles had come to Rome the Pope had gone thirty miles to meet him at the gray lake of Bracciano. The papal procession, singing psalms and praises of the king, had included not only children bearing palms and olive branches, but the Roman army. The papacy had sought and accepted the dangerous gift of temporal power.

Charlemagne, who reigned from 784 to 814, lived in a time when kingship still had a biological basis. He was six feet four inches tall, a man of strength and energy. The best representation of him that we have — a small equestrian statue probably done in the century of his death — shows him as heavily built, with a barbarian warrior's moustache. Both horse and rider have something faintly Mongol in their appearance. His contemporary biographer Einhard wrote of him, "There emanated from his body a virile charm."

He loved horses and hunting; he swam with his sons, his nobles, his bodyguards, so that sometimes a hundred men went into the water with him. The king's family life was devoted though somewhat extensive; he had several wives and concubines. "He took such great care of his children that when he was at home he never went to table without them, nor did he take a trip without their company. The sons rode near him and the daughters after him; a certain number of bodyguards were expressly commanded to look after them. As these daughters were very beautiful indeed, and he very much loved them, he never gave any of them in marriage (very strange indeed) neither to any of the Franks, nor to strangers. He kept them near him, in his home, up to his death, saying that he could not do without their company."

His poet Theodulf called him "the sword of the popes." In return, Charles had papal sanction for his kingship, but he also had something equally important to him — glimpses of civilization. Like Cassiodorus, who had been brought up to it, this disadvantaged sovereign loved *civilitas.* He was very much influenced by Augustine's *City of God,* but the realist in him knew that there would have to be many intermediate gradations of improvement before the City of God could be built in his stockaded towns. He codified the laws, reformed the administrative system, and provided a stable currency and good roads.

He loved beauty and wanted to possess it. Everywhere he collected statues, paintings, mosaics, jewels, though unlike those later collectors, Napoleon and Hitler, he always asked permission to take the things he wanted. Sometimes his requests were extensive; when he built the basilica at Aquisgrane (Aix-la-Chapelle or Aachen), he took the columns and the marble he needed from Rome and from Ravenna. Today at Ravenna's Church of Santo Apollinare Nuovo one can see mosaics of the royal palace of Theodoric; the colonnades, the loggias, the draperies of silk embroidered in gold. But in its barren garden only the scanty ruins of the palace of the Lombard kings remain. In return, Charlemagne sent the pope a gift of blooded horses, and although the pope said they were quite good for size, and suitable in build and musculature, their value must have been much less than that of the marble. And from his trips to Rome he brought back armfuls of books from Saint Peter's library: one imagines the librarians hiding their favorite volumes when they heard the emperor was coming.

He collected people as he collected art objects, and brought to his court Paul the Deacon, the Lombard scholar, and the learned English monk Alcuin. His association with Alcuin was one of those close friendships that one sometimes sees between extremely able leaders and contemplative scholars, men who are the best of their separate kinds, and are able to admire each other generously because they are too different for rivalry.

The king had come to learning late; he could have said with Augustine, "*Sero te amavi.*" But like the Roman general Lucius Emilius Paulus, he was humble enough to attend classes with his own children. Reading was always difficult for him; a fact that turned out to be fortunate for the cause of learning. And he never quite learned to write, although he kept tablets and sheets of parchment under his pillow to work on during the night. But in Alcuin's talk he found a liberal education. The English monk was "a well of sciences"; what C. P. Snow would call a man of both cultures. He knew everything from mathematics to classical poetry, from history to astronomy, a subject that particularly interested the king, who "loved so much to study the way of the stars." With the confidence that Charles sometimes mingled with his intellectual humility — as if fundamentally he knew his own stature — he gave more realistic names to the constellations (in England the Great Bear still is Charles's Wain), and replaced the localized nomenclature of the winds with one that can be used anywhere, on any planet.

To provide for all the children in his realm the instruction that had not been given him in his palace childhood, Charles set up a system of general education in which schools were to be established in all monasteries and cathedrals. No tuition was charged and no distinction made between the children of serfs and of freemen; he noted regretfully that the children of the common people worked harder than his own.

Besides the schools, libraries and scriptoria were established all over France. He instituted large-scale copying programs, and the books that he begged from the papal library and the books Alcuin borrowed from his friends in the British Isles were copied and multiplied. Jerome's Vulgate, the patristic writings, and surviving Latin classics were copied in the Carolingian monasteries. While the Vikings were destroying the intellectual wealth of the Christian coasts, the Carolingian monasteries were replacing the text, if not the art, of the lost codices.

It may have been Charlemagne's difficulty with reading, as much as the shortage of writing materials, that led to the adoption of the Carolingian minuscule system of lettering, in which the letters were small and separate. Since many of Europe's small literate class were, like Charlemagne, marginal readers, the introduction of more legible letters must have been enormously effective in facilitating the spread of learning by books.

As the king learned his sense of history developed; the history of Israel and of Rome fascinated him. And he had seen the papal archives in the patriarchal palace at the Lateran. In his own country, which still had so little history, he established the *Codex Carolinus*, which was intended to contain a copy of every document received from the Holy See. With the loss of most of the papal archives in successive waves of destruction, the documents in Charlemagne's archives are sometimes the only source of knowledge for some points of papal history.

It was Alcuin who helped the king to see that history was something more than a series of battles and biographies, and to realize his own place in it. Alcuin called him David, after another king from an emerging nation, and was ambitious for the extension of the king's power. Charlemagne's coronation in the year 800 remains a mystery; his biographer

Einhard says he would not have gone to Saint Peter's if he had known it was to take place. But on Christmas night in the year 800, "the venerable priest with his own hands put on the head of the king a very precious crown, and all the Roman faithful shouted, 'Duke Charles, pious and august, crowned by God, great and pacific emperor, life and victory!'"

It is from the *Song of Roland* that most of us know Charlemagne now; it is ironic that such a man should have come down to us as an aged emperor with a beard "white as any flower of spring," instead of as the horseman in full strength, the unlearned man in love with learning, the symmetrically superior human that he was.

Disasters of This Night

THE papacy had hoped for too much from its alliance with the empire. Charlemagne's casual marriages had produced no offspring that bred true. His sons and grandsons, some pious and some profligate, spent their energies in quarreling with each other, and Europe was upset by the love affairs of the grandchildren of Charlemagne.

The papacy and the empire were interdependent but antagonistic, like rival siblings quarreling, like eclipsing binaries wobbling around each other. The Vikings were attacking from the north, and the Saracens from the sea that was no longer *mare nostrum*. It was a time when, for practical security, people relied less on either emperor or pope than on good walls and a good water supply.

Then came the dark age of the papacy, the time of the iron popes, when the Chair of Peter was controlled by warring Roman families and by the demands of the Roman crowds, the time of the great popes and their conflicts with the emperors, and the time of revolution when Rome rose against the papacy, carrying on its red-and-gold banners the SPQR of the Senate and people of Rome.

In this age of disorder most of the papal archives were to disappear, perhaps in the Norman and Saracen invasions, perhaps by political theft, perhaps by intentional destruction in times of schism or by the unintentional destruction of war. From this period between Charlemagne's time and that of Innocent III in the late twelfth century, only a few important documents have survived - the registers of John VIII and Gregory VII, and the diploma of Otto I. The registers of the many other popes have vanished, and with them the rest of their official documentation.

The register of John VIII (872–882) is called Vatican Register I, since, while we have many letters of Leo I and many more of Gregory I, they are collections made later from various sources. The register of John VIII opens one of the main series of the Vatican Secret Archives — that of the nearly five thousand papal registers. These volumes, a major historical source, have been compared to a river that sometimes disappears underground for a time, and does not flow steadily aboveground until the regular sequence starts with the register of Innocent III.

The first Vatican register is about the size of a missal. It is bound in deep-red leather with a rosy cloud of patina over it. The pages are of parchment that has become yellow with time; as one turns them the light filters through the places that have worn thin, as it does through the colored windows of a cathedral. The ink on the two-columned pages is very black and still shining. No space is left between the documents copied into the volume. The initial of the first word of each communication is usually elaborated with curious little drawings, such as the head of a dragon, with eyes extremely alive — perhaps the caricature of a person?

The writing is Beneventana, the calligraphy of Monte Cassino, for the register is not an original but an eleventh-century copy. A little note, almost unreadable, on the first page says, "This volume, that was once the property of the monks of Monte Cassino, has been entrusted to Lord Pope by Berardo, canon of the Basilica of Saint Peter." This inscription is thought to go back to the thirteenth century. If so, "Lord Pope" was Clement IV. The volume is carefully described — though it was bound in white leather then — in 1311, and it later traveled to Avignon.

It contains the letters written by John VIII during the last six years of his pontificate; not in the exact form in which they were sent, but in the form of the Chancellery's draft copies. Some columns, and even some pages, are left blank, and there are several erasures and corrections. The copyist apparently had difficulty with the original text, which may have been in a deteriorated state and in a handwriting already antiquated. Proper names are sometimes a wild guess, but he often omits a word he has been unable to decipher, leaving a white space of the same length.

In addition to this register, part of the correspondence of John VIII has been retrieved from extracts from the papal register included in various canonical compilations, especially Deusdedit's *Collectio Canonum*, compiled under Pope Victor III (1086–1087), and the twelfth-century Britannic Collection. Other letters have been found at their place of destination.

Pope John VIII was elected in December of the year 872. The papacy, like hereditary monarchy, sometimes gives unusual opportunities to the aged, and this sick old man became a warrior pope. He was still very much a part of his times. The first letter of the register is an order for an organ from Bavaria, one of those that a Venetian priest, who had learned how to make organs from the Byzantines, had just taught the Bavarians how to manufacture. In another letter he asks King Alfonso of Spain for Arabian horses. These light, fast horses were guarded by the Saracens in the same way that a new model fighter plane is guarded by modern nations, and were killed to keep them from falling into the hands of the enemy.

Perhaps in a reflected light from the Carolingian Renaissance, the papal court had elements of culture, for John had in his entourage two noted intellectuals, Anastasius the Librarian and John Immonide. Anastasius was one of the most brilliant men of his time, a master of law, theology, and Greek (useful in diplomatic negotiations with the Eastern Empire), and author of the *Chronographia Tripartita*. Like so many humanists of the Renaissance, he was ambitious, and had once, before John's time, tried to seize the papacy by a *coup d'etat* backed by imperial power. He might have succeeded if he had not made the mistake of slapping the Pope's face and throwing him into prison; at this many of the clergy rebelled. To please the emperor he was given a position corresponding to that of the present Cardinal Secretary of State; he was called Anastasius the Librarian, and under Adrian II (867–872) he became the most brilliant editor of the papal Chancellery, making successful political use of the papal archives that were entrusted to him. He had almost reached the summit of political power — Adrian was old and bedridden — when his brother kidnapped the Pope's daughter and her mother, and later murdered them both. Tried for connivance, Anastasius was accused in the course of the trial of having destroyed the decrees in the papal archives condemning him for his attempted coup as antipope. Put on probation, he later rebounded to power.

The papal court had another prominent literary figure in John Immonide, "John the Deacon." John Immonide was one of those who kept Latin culture alive in a time when there was ignorance everywhere, even among the clergy, when the schools were decaying and the monasteries decadent, when papyrus no longer came from Egypt and the old parchment codices were being erased to provide writing materials.

Immonide's *Life of Gregory*, which has come down to us, was written from Gregory's own letters and documents kept in the "scrinium of the holy apostolic seat." Immonide suggests that critical readers who doubt the truthfulness of his writing can check it by referring to his source material. He probably had unusual opportunities of access to the scrinium, since he is thought to have assisted Anastasius in the editing of

John VIII's letters. But his assumption that his readers could check his work by referring to scrinium documents seems to imply that, as at the time of Jerome, at least part of the archives were open to the use of qualified persons.

A rather surprising work by John Immonide that has survived in five manuscripts, the oldest going back to the tenth century, is his *Supper of John the Deacon,* dedicated to Pope John and played in his presence in the Lateran Square. This was a poetical rewrite of the *Caena Cypriani,* the *Supper of Cyprian* the third-century Bishop of Carthage, but the symbolic stage settings are those of the very modern theater. A banquet is given by an Eastern king at Cana in Galilee to personages of the Old and New Testaments. Eve sits on an enormous fig leaf and Samson on a column; Jesus chooses a wine called the *passito,* in reference to the Passion.

Immonide introduced allusions to contemporary political figures, so that the performance had something of the quality of a Gridiron Club dinner in official Washington. He also reinforced the crudity of certain of the Biblical skits. In a scene where a young girl defends her virtue against two dignified personages, one of whom is pouring water and the other undressing, the Roman deacon adds stage directions: *"Plangebant cuncti recisa palpantes preputia . . ."*

The *Caena Cypriani* had a great success in the Middle Ages and was apparently used as a mnemonic device for the study of the Scriptures, even in the Schola Cantorum. It is hard to explain why this parody of the holy books had the enthusiastic consent of the Christian milieu, was given in the papal presence, and was copied so often by the monks of the Middle Ages. Perhaps the people of that time were more familiar with Biblical characters and therefore less awed by them. Or John the Deacon's version may have been put on in the Lateran in the same way that avant-garde plays are sometimes put on in American churches, as a gesture of contact between the religious and secular worlds. Modern church theater groups might find this ancient script, as far as I know unpublished, well worth examining.

Like another old pope eleven centuries later, John VIII had to face the question of a vernacular liturgy. This arose through the work of the missionaries Cyril and Methodius in Czechoslovakia. Cyril was a protegé of the Dowager Empress Theodora and her eunuchs; he had spent his youth in the shade of the golden plane tree, with golden birds on its branches, that spread over the throne. Methodius had been a government magistrate in one of the Slavic districts, where he had learned the Slavic language and customs. Like Cyril, he had escaped from worldly honors and fled to a monastery. When these two men were sent to Moravia, in about 860, in answer to Prince Rotislav's request for missionaries, Cyril devised a Slavonic alphabet and script and translated the gospels and liturgical texts into Slavonic. The Cyrillic alphabet later became the basis of the Russian written language. With these characters Methodius transcribed the prayers of the Mass. The mission was extremely successful; churches rose one after the other, and in them the Moravians listened to the divine mysteries and sang hymns not in an incomprehensible foreign language but in the language of their own country.

But opponents objected that only three languages — Hebrew, Greek, and Latin — could be used in prayer because the sign "Jesus of Nazareth, King of the Jews" that had been affixed to the Cross had been written only in these languages. This argument convinced even the Pope, who in 879 wrote reproachfully to Methodius: "We hear that you are singing the Mass in barbarian Slavic, though we forbade you to celebrate Mass in this language. You are allowed only to preach and to pronounce homilies to the people in the Slavic language, because the Psalmist admonishes all peoples to praise God, and the apostle Saint Peter writes, 'Every language confesses that Jesus is in the glory of God the Father.'"

But Methodius persisted in his defense of the Slavic liturgy, came to Rome, and brought the Pope around to his own point of view. A copy of the confirming letter that John VIII personally handed to him is in the Secret Archives register. Not only preaching and certain prayers may be in Slavic, but all the offices, the hours, the lessons, the mass — the entire Christian liturgy. The historian Lapôtre speaks of this letter as "a certificate of the equality of all languages before God."

This part of the register was removed from the scrinium by political opponents, and a few years later Stephen V (885–891) prohibited the new Slavic Christians from using their mother language in the liturgy. The removal of John's letter permitting the use of the vernacular made it possible for Stephen to state that Methodius had violated the vow he had made to John VIII. Except for the evidence of this surviving register, we would not know that a pope had decided to allow the use of a vernacular liturgy long before the Second Vatican Council.

John's pontificate was torn by civil strife and threatened by Saracen attack. The Moslems had established themselves in Naples and were raiding up to the gates of Rome; the city was filled with hungry refugees. A letter written by the Pope in 877 to the Emperor Charles the Bald describes the situation: "Within the walls of Rome the refugees are poor and utterly miserable. Everything in the country is completely and maliciously devastated. There is nothing to wait for — may God have mercy on us — but the destruction of Rome." Three days later he asked the emperor for help that he knew would not be given for nothing — "and here we send to you the *bravio* of very green palms. We implore you to fight for Christ's church, so that your conquering right hand may wear the *bravio* and your head the crown of glory . . ." But the imperial army did not come, and never came; the emperor's towns were being burned by the Northmen, and he himself, abandoned by his people while crossing the snowy Moncenisio Pass, died in a hut that was lent him by a compassionate herdsman.

In this crisis the Pope himself took action, and left Rome to rally the dukes of southern Italy, a task so difficult that he wrote bitterly: "Since I had sowed the seed of the word of God, I thought I deserved not the fluttering leaves of words but the fruits of work. What more could I have done for the Vineyard? And why did I expect the Vineyard to bring forth grapes when instead it brought the wild, sour, bitter wine?"

Returning to Rome by sea, John encountered an Arab fleet. He immediately gave orders to attack, and the Arabs fled, leaving eighteen ships in the hands of the Pope. In them were six hundred Christian slaves. The return of the seventy-five-year-old Pope to Rome was a triumph like Caesar's.

And, like Caesar, John was murdered by a trusted traitor. The priest Gregorius, on an icy evening, offered him a cup of warm poisoned wine. The arsenic was slow in taking effect, as happened with Rasputin a thousand years later at the banquet of Prince Yossopov, and the prelate took a hammer and smashed the Pope's skull. He himself was killed at the Pope's funeral, between the columns of the ancient Lateran portico. For almost two centuries crime was to be habitual at the Lateran.

The most shocking of these crimes was that against the body of Pope Formosus (891–896). As pope, Formosus had committed the political error of favoring the German party and offending the Spoletine party that dominated the Roman provinces. He achieved a natural death, but the vindictiveness of his enemies led Pope Stephen to try his corpse, dead for nine months. "Like a bloody beast he had the corpse of Pope Formosus brought into the meeting." The "putrid cadaver" in its papal robes was formally tried, condemned, mutilated, and thrown into the Tiber. From an anonymous author we learn the sequel to the story: "In the middle of the night in which he had been thrown into the Tiber, in a tremendous roar of thunder and in flashes of lightning, the river moved as if for a gigantic flood and, slowly carrying the corpse for about twenty miles, deposited it whole and compact near the river.

"After three days, a vision appeared to a monk. 'I am,' said the vision,

'Formosus, Pope. Look for me and take care of my body, that has been brought here by the river.' The monk obeyed the order, found the body, and buried it secretly. Not much later, on the order of Pope Theodore, clergy and people brought it back to Rome in great triumph. They carried it into the basilica of the Prince of the Apostles and gave it back to its burial place."

Pope Stephen had inserted the records of this trial that condemned a cadaver into the archives of the Lateran, but they were removed and destroyed by Formosus' party when it returned to power. Destruction of archives documents for political reasons was becoming a familiar procedure.

« 1 »

In the Purple Privilegium, the *Privilegium Ottonis*, the German emperor granted the Church temporal jurisdiction over about three-quarters of Italy. The diploma is in golden letters on a great sheet of blood-red *membrana* or parchment, now hard with the passing of time. Even this document is not an original, but a "synchronous" copy made a thousand years ago. It is kept in a separate drawer of the locked case that holds special treasures of the Secret Archives.

Written in 962, it emerged from a time when the papacy itself, at the mercy of individualistic forces of the feudal world, seemed to be undergoing cadaveric decomposition. For most of the century the choice of popes had been in the hands of the papal bureaucrat Theophylact and his family of viragoes. The gossipy Bishop Liutprand of Cremona writes of these women: "Theodora, shameful *puttana,* seized the monarchy of the city with virile strength. She had two daughters, Marozia and Theodora, even more fitted than she for the exercises of Venus." According to him Theodora (the mother), "*accesa dal calore di Venere,*" had had the Bishop of Ravenna made pope (John X) "because he could possess her only on very infrequent nights of love, due to the distance that separates Ravenna from Rome."

But she must have had a gentler side as well, for in the little Church of Santa Maria in the Via Lata which she had restored in thanks for the recovery of a paralyzed son, one can still see the Madonna that she had painted and read the inscription: "Source of Life, Star of the Sea." Perhaps Theodora's allegiance was less to the Virgin than to the *Magna Mater.* Or had the stone age, the bronze age, unknowingly worshiped Mary?

In the year 931, Theodora's daughter Marozia brought about the election of John XI, who may have been her son, "due to a nefarious adultery." The great round tomb of the Emperor Hadrian, now Castel Sant' Angelo, with the little chapel to Saint Michael on the top, she took for a private residence.

Her grandson Octavian became Pope John XII, and Prince of the Romans, at sixteen. He was an audacious youngster, lacking in wisdom, loving life and its pleasures. His apartments in the Lateran became a gathering place for the teen-agers of the Roman nobility. Chronicles of the time tell of his orgies, "which the devil attended, welcomed with toasts." Whether or not these tales were true, he had enough religious feeling to ask the monks of Subiaco, where that very different boy Benedict had also attained rank at an early age, to sing a hundred Kyrie Eleisons and a hundred Christe Eleisons each day for the salvation of his soul. In any case the machinery of the papacy continued to function, and the Chancellery sent out bulls and encyclicals as usual.

Eventually Rome was alienated by the reported excesses of the pontifex and his *jeunesse dorée* followers and by his preference for the German party in local politics. In this dangerous situation he appealed for help to Otto I. The Charlemagne of Germany, Otto was building a prosperous national state, and like Charlemagne he dreamed of a Christian empire.

His army camped in Nero's field near the Vatican and John crowned him as Emperor of the West. In the phrasing of their pact, the *Privilegium,* we can read the solemn promises that the victorious Emperor made to the Pope, too young, too inexperienced, too overcome by events:

"In the name of the Lord Omnipotent God, Father and Son and Holy Spirit.

"I, Otto, by the grace of God august emperor, give faith and promise with this pact to you, blessed Peter, Prince of the Apostles and doorman of the kingdom of the skies, and through you to your vicar the lord John, Supreme Pontifex and universal pope . . ." He grants the Holy See all that "Lord Pepin, of blessed memory, and Lord Charles, the most excellent emperor, our predecessor" had granted, and more beside, but makes it clear that in doing this he is making a free gift, not restoring ancient rights. In return, no pope was to be consecrated who was unwilling to swear fealty to the emperor.

The pact was less enduring than the parchment, and soon broke down in intrigues and accusations.

But the relationship between emperors and popes had not yet hardened into automatic antagonism, and at about the year 1000 there arose an intellectual and political partnership between a pope and an emperor that might, if they had lived and succeeded in their plans, have opened a strange and wonderful chapter in human history. The emperor was Otto III, the pope was the learned monk Gerbert who, perhaps in memory of an earlier pope who was by legend a magician, took the name of Sylvester II (999–1003). Gerbert was one of the few popes – – the humanist Aeneas Silvius was another — whom history seems to regard as individuals rather than popes, and persistently calls by their own names rather than by their numbered papal appellations.

The *Liber Pontificalis* tells of the "magician pope" Sylvester II in a story that may have been an early version of the Faustus legend: "This Gerbert, when young, was a monk in the monastery of Fleury, but he left the monastery and made an image of the devil so that everything would come out according to his wishes. And that the devil promised to arrange . . . Gerbert was made Bishop of Rheims, then of Ravenna, and finally pope.

"He then asked the devil how long he would live as pope. The answer was, as long as he wanted to, unless he said Mass at Jerusalem. He rejoiced, thinking he was far away from death, as far as he was from the desire to go on pilgrimage to Jerusalem. But during Lent he said Mass at the Lateran in a church called Jerusalem.

"He heard the rattling of the demon and at the same time felt death was approaching. And sighing, he started to cry. Revealing his sin before all, he ordered chopped into pieces that member that had offered homage to the devil, and directed that his lifeless body be put on a horse-drawn cart and buried wherever the animals would have taken him." But the horses returned to the Lateran guided by the mercy of God.

Actually Gerbert's interest was in the scientific mysteries. His visit to Toledo, which had the reputation of being a center of the magical arts, is explainable by the fact that Moslem science was far ahead of the science of the Christian world. He introduced Arabic numerals into Europe; he made a celestial globe that showed the movements of the planets, and a watch that told time by the stars.

As Pope Sylvester II he had great influence over his former pupil, the young Emperor Otto III, who had inherited the throne at three. The combination of a brilliant scholar and a man of action, or a man of power, is sometimes very fruitful and seems to be one of the human relationships in which disparity of age is of little importance. Alexander the Great conquered the world and kept looking for interesting scientific presents to send home to Aristotle — would he have dreamed of a world civilization, a world race, if his only tutors had been retired generals? Gerbert and Otto together planned the *renovatio imperii*, the renovation of the empire, the renovation of the world. The Roman empire was to be restored and to include all Christendom; pope and emperor were to rule it jointly from its capital at Rome.

But Otto was poisoned at twenty-two by the widow of the rebel Crescentius, whose beheaded body he had exposed at Castel Sant'Angelo. Sylvester too was poisoned, perhaps by the same woman. She had, according to the Romans, become Otto's mistress out of hatred, in order to kill him. It was a remake of the story of the Emperor Commodus and the Christian woman Marcia.

« 2 »

The second register in the Secret Archives, that of Gregory VII (1073–1085), Saint Hildebrand, is the oldest original volume of this series. Even here there are wide time gaps and many letters are missing. Its parchment sheets are large, perhaps half again the size of those of the first register, and are evenly perforated to mark the lines. The writing is in different hands but somewhat uniform in style. Many of the initial letters are enlarged and colored red; the name of Gregory is always in red.

Gregory was the pope of the struggle over investiture, study of which in high school has put most people off medieval history for life. He was small, dark, and badly formed. The son of a Tuscan family in modest circumstances, he became a Benedictine monk and was a brilliant success in the Church by the time he was twenty-five. His austere integrity, his regard for regulations, his shrewdness and energy made him a valued executive officer — or, some might say, a hatchet man — for a series of popes. He himself was elected to the papacy in 1073, by acclamation and against his will.

A surprising thing about this register is its inclusion of a few very personal letters, no more in place here than they would be in a modern office's letter file. Some are to Hugo, Abbot of Cluny, who urged mercy on him at Canossa.

His letters to Hugo seem to have something more real, more literal, than the usual I-suffered-awful complaints of medieval churchmen and modern novelists. He describes his feelings at his election: "Suddenly, while the corpse of the Pope was being brought to sepulture in the Church of the Savior at the Lateran, the people went mad and appointed me, so that I must say with the prophet, 'I have found myself in a high sea and the storm has submerged me.' I am in bed, very tired, and cannot write. Pray God for me, so that prayer, that should have kept me from danger, may protect me now that I am in danger."

In another letter he writes of his feelings of inadequacy: "We are weak and without physical or intellectual energy. In this sad time we carry alone the weight of spiritual and temporal preoccupations, and we tremble in fear of not being able to hold up under this weight . . ."

And, again to Hugo, he expresses despair for himself and for society: "Among the secular princes I do not know one who puts the honor of God and justice ahead of money. And those with whom I am living, the Romans, the Lombards, and the Normans — I often tell them they are worse than the Jews and the pagans.

"If I turn to myself, I see myself so crushed under the weight of my mission, and so torn between grief and postponed hope, so shaken by the storm, dying at the same time that I live, that I am expecting Him who tied me with his bonds, to whom I often say, 'Do not be late!' "

Gregory was a reform pope. He carried on vigorous campaigns against the sale of Church offices and the incontinence of priests. The time was long gone when Clement could tell, and Eusebius retell, the tender story of Saint Peter's farewell to his wife as she was being led away to execution ("My dear, remember the Lord.") Under the feudal order, most of the monasteries and bishoprics had become courts wide open to concubines and loose women. A picture of the corruption of the times is given in the *Liber Gomorrhianus* of Peter Damian, which must have been in the papal archives, possibly in its library section, since it was dedicated "To the Very Blessed Pope Leo, by his servant Peter, the last of the monks."

Gregory saw the need of some supranational power to curb the excesses of the nationalistic states, and he believed that power should be the papacy. "We make it our business to provide weapons of humility for emperors, kings, and other princes, so that they may be able to restrain the floods of their pride." The Church was the ultimate authority, and "from her there is no appeal." According to his *Dictatus Papae* temporal power was to be strictly subordinated to spiritual power, spiritual power being that of the pope, "whose feet princes must kiss," and whom he saw not as the servant of Peter but as Peter himself. One phrase in the *Dictatus* foreshadows the nineteenth-century dogma of papal infallibility: "The Roman Church has never erred, nor will it err to all eternity." The copy of this inflexible document that is in Gregory's register looks like a page of poetry; each claim is set forth in a line of its own, and every important sentence is in red.

The *dramatis personae* of Gregory's life included both a woman and an enemy. There was a spiritual tie between Hildebrand and Matilda, Countess of Tuscany, who ruled a third of Italy. A pretty, fragile woman, who was married twice but cared little for her husbands, she gave her life to religion and to charity. Noblemen knelt and trembled when they spoke to her, but she was considerate to the poor and to the clergy, built churches and hospitals, and collected "a great number of books in all disciplines." She was devoted to Gregory, accompanied him to Germany, and was ready to accompany him on a crusade to the Holy Land. "She was always near the pope with such a great spirit of charity that it seemed as if she would never separate from him. Because of this she faced the infamy of calumniators."

Gregory's letters to Matilda show a deep affection, many of them beginning "To Matilda, girl of rare nature," or "To Matilda, beloved daughter in Christ." He urges her to abandon herself in the arms of the Virgin — "What can I tell you of the Mother of God? To whom I will never cease recommending you, up to the day that we see her, as we so ardently desire? She whom sky and earth never cease praising, but cannot praise according to her merit? Keep as a very certain truth that she is the most sublime, the kindest, the wisest of all mothers, and the most clement and sweet toward sinning men and women. Put an end to the bad will of sinning and cry with a humble and penitent heart; you will find her; I promise you certainly."

Another letter to her ends, "I am writing these things to you in my own handwriting, not using any secretary because, if you love me as I love you, I know that you will not prefer any other mortal to me."

The young emperor Henry IV was alarmed at the Pope's influence over Matilda: her domains extended too far toward central Europe. And he saw the Pope's insistence on the right to supervise the appointment of bishops as interference in his nation's internal affairs. There was a personality clash as well — Henry was a notorious womanizer, and he resented the Pope's insistence on morality. Brought up by a weak mother and two corrupt bishops, he early came under the influence of one of his mother's lovers. The contemporary historian Brunone wrote of him: "He ran to pleasure, to the precipice of libidinousness, like a horse to an ass. He forced noble women to his filthy pleasures, then passed them on dishonored to his servants. Having a sister who had become a nun, and chastely lived in a monastery, he had her brought back and, keeping her locked in his arms, obliged a servant to consummate an abominable connubial act in his presence. He had built for himself a fortress at the summit of a high and rough rock. None could climb there but those who knew of his crimes and of his weaknesses."

It was this Berchtesgaden moralist who accused Pope Gregory on the ground of his relationship with the Countess Matilda of Tuscany: "You have filled the Church with almost a fetor of scandal because of your more than familiar cohabitation with a woman who belongs to another.

Complaint has come to us from all directions that every problem, every decree of the Apostolic See is handled by women, and that the whole orbit of the Church is governed by a new senate of women . . . I, Henry, by grace of God, king, with all our bishops, we say to you — come down, come down from the apostolic seat, O damned for eternity. We take back the obedience that we promised to you."

Gregory read the emperor's letters aloud to a council of the bishops, the clergy, and the people of Rome, and swore to his innocence at the altar of the tomb of Saint Peter, before excommunicating the emperor.

Henry's excommunication gave Germany's dissident elements an excuse to rebel, and the emperor had to come to Canossa. The Pope had to forgive him. After all, there was that text in the Scriptures about seventy times seven, and the Abbot of Cluny was urging him to. But he made his forgiveness conditional. At Henry's communion next morning he pointed out that if his penitence was not real he would be "eating judgment to himself."

It was not real, and in the end the two men destroyed each other. Henry died deposed and excommunicate; Gregory, heartbroken at the Sack of Rome by the Normans whom he had called in to protect him, followed their returning army toward Naples and died at Salerno. And Matilda, in a "white marriage" for political reasons, married a boy of nineteen.

« 3 »

The disappearance of the archives in these lethal centuries is the more surprising in view of the fact that they were not concentrated in a single location, but were decentralized to at least three sites. In addition to the old deposits at the Lateran and at Saint Peter's, a third was established at the Palatine, in the Tower of the Papers, the Turris Chartularia.

As early as the ninth century the popes had begun to feel insecure in the Lateran, unprotected as it was and surrounded by the fortresses of potentially unfriendly nobles. The Lateran Palace remained the official papal residence, but John VIII established a Patriarchum on the Palatine Hill, where the palaces of the Caesars, with the weakening of Byzantine power, had come into the possession of the Roman Curia. The new Patriarchum was in the area where the Monastery of Saint Gregory had already built a castle-fortress that included the Arch of Titus and the most beautiful part of the Palaces of the Caesars, the seven-storied Septizonium, that the Romans called the Seat of the Sun.

John's Chancellery and part of the archives probably accompanied him to the new Palatine Patriarchum. Later they came to be located in the Tower of the Papers, also called the Tower of the Seven Lamps, from the seven-branched candlestick that was carved in bas-relief on the nearby Arch of Titus, where the tower's debris lies today.

Important papal documents, especially the registers, were kept in this Tower of the Papers, the *locus tutissimus* ("the very secure place"). It was here that Cardinal Deusdedit, late in the eleventh century, consulted the registers in drawing up his *Collectio Canonum*. Putting documents in towers for safekeeping was an old custom, and storerooms in church belfries were commonly used for this purpose. In the Ghirlandina of the Cathedral of Modena one can still visit one of these thick-walled circular storerooms, that was used for diocesan records from the time of Charlemagne to that of Napoleon.

The defense of this papal section of the Palatine was entrusted to an old baronial family that dominated Roman history for two centuries, and was strong enough to influence the election of popes: the Frangipani, or "breakers of bread," who held the relief concession for Rome and were in charge of the public granaries at the foot of the Palatine. On their coat of arms was a black viper, and two golden lions tearing apart a loaf of bread.

The Frangipani had their own army, with banners in the papal colors, which was supposed to be at the service of the pope, and they possessed several stone fortresses in Rome as well as the Colosseum. They were the official custodians of the Turris Chartularia, and a member of the Frangipani family, with the rank of papal chancellor, usually lived there along with the notaries.

The tower was surrounded by other towers, where the noble families of Italy built their defenses against invaders and each other. Rome had become a skyscraper city. The Orsini built in the Theater of Pompey and by the Bridge of Sant'Angelo, the Savelli in the Theater of Marcellus, and the Colonna seem to have taken their name from the *Colonna Traiana* — the Trajan Column. The materials for the towers came from the buildings of imperial Rome, the "city of marble" that Caesar boasted of having left. Even the tradesmen shared in the plundering of temples and government buildings, and fish stalls and butcher shops had counters of marble that had been chosen for the gods and the emperors. Women carried water from the little local wells in ancient amphorae.

Fighting was endemic among Rome's noble families. They fought each other on the side of the pope, against the pope, on the side of the emperor, against the emperor, following their own interests rather than political ideals, veering from one party to another. The main focuses of this contention were Saint Peter's, the Lateran, the Turris Chartularia, and Castel Sant'Angelo. There was usually an antipope occupying one of these places, and a legitimate pope occupying another; it was not always clear which was which. The Turris Chartularia was the scene of many episodes of papal history. There popes were elected, held as prisoners, or protected until they could escape. It was taken and retaken, destroyed for vengeance and rebuilt.

It was a mistake to bring the archives into an area of warring towers, for at some time during this night of history they disappeared almost without trace. And with them into oblivion went nearly all of the archives kept at the Lateran and at Saint Peter's. "The bust outlasts the throne," but the king's letters vanish.

Some historians have attributed the loss of the archives to a single explanation, such as the treason of one faction of the Frangipani, or the taking over of the tower by the Frangipani's hereditary enemies, the Annibaldi, in about the year 1235. But very likely, as was the case with the Library of Alexandria and the Library of the Caesars, the archives were lost by successive destructions. The disorders in Rome at the end of the life of Gregory VII may have accounted for much of the loss. Henry IV had come to Rome with his antipope and occupied the Lateran; Gregory's nephew had defended himself in the Septizonium on the Palatine, near the Turris Chartularia, until Henry IV destroyed it, smashing its magnificent columns and very possibly looting anything in the vicinity. Gregory called in the Normans and their Saracen allies, who offered Moslem prayers in Saint Peter's. The city was sacked and burned; its citizens were massacred and the wives and children of senators were taken as slaves. The section between the Lateran and the Colosseum was almost destroyed by fire; one of the gates of the Lateran was afterward called the Burned Door. This Norman invasion was of the magnitude of that of the Goths and the Vandals in an earlier century, or the Sack of Rome in a later one. And in 1234 came the Roman revolution, when the people took over the Patrimony of Saint Peter and made it the Patrimony of the City, sacking the Lateran and the palaces of the cardinals. To these major destructions were added the continual feuds among the nobles and among the factions of the Church, in which contesting parties often had the opportunity of destroying each other's records.

Yet the disappearance of the archives was almost too complete to be credible. One wonders whether particularly valuable material may have been hidden in the walls or in secret passages, such as are found from time to time in the Vatican and even in the present Secret Archives. The walling up of valuables was a common Italian practice in times of invasion or internal danger, and in many cases the person who had hidden them died without passing on word of their whereabouts.

If hidden archives were found, what would be left of them? Perhaps nothing recognizable of the papyrus or the parchment. But there is some hope, I think, that the mineral or metallic substances used in making the ink might have remained *in situ*. If so, very careful handling of the debris might make it possible to recover some of the writing. And very likely candidates for hiding in a time of disorder would be the enormously valuable codices made of precious materials, like the psalter of gold leaf written with ink made from melted rubies. I am inclined to think that anything of metal might possibly survive, in spite of Rome's climate. Recently a child at my home at Anzio brought me a Roman safety pin, buried in the earth for perhaps two thousand years and still perfectly workable.

The loss of the Church's central archives for the nine centuries after Constantine has been an irreparable one. Historians have filled in the lacunae as well as they can with material from other sources, but this was a time when only a few copies might be made even of important documents. Often our knowledge of a fact or a situation depends on a single source which may be inaccurate or prejudiced. Perhaps the greatest loss was not in the important things but in the multitude of casual documents that might have made this puzzling era more comprehensible. And since the library and archives were still connected, the disappearance of material must have meant a loss to literature as well as to history. Documents of interest to anthropologists must have disappeared with the reports of missionaries to "the land of the north wind," to bronze-age Ireland, to other countries where the very old cultures of the West survived. There might even have been, in Africa, a missionary priest with leather bags of water tied to his horse's belly, who followed the Roman road past the Tassili Massif where the frescoes of strange space-helmeted humanoids are, in times when the frescoes and the legends were newer. And these lost records, which went back to the time when fragments of the Etruscan culture still survived, might have helped us to decipher this language that has proved more resistant than the linear scripts of Crete.

We have lost, too, the records of certain social experiments that might be of practical usefulness to the Church. The vernacular liturgy was tried out eleven hundred years ago, and the Church had married priests, with varying degrees of official tolerance, for a thousand years.

And there are the little mysteries of the past, to which the very old archives material might have given some clue. What would we not give now for information that would help us to find the contemporary statue of Christ the healer, "an upright figure of a man with a double cloak neatly draped over his shoulders and his hand stretched out," which Dionysius, Bishop of Alexandria, and two other writers reported having seen?

The Viatory Archives

THE time of disaster and the time of rebuilding overlapped, and before the fall of the Turris Chartularia, before the sacking of the Sacred Palace of the Lateran in the Roman revolution of 1234, the new documentation of the present Secret Archives started to accumulate. The regular file of papal registers now available to historians begins with the six registers of Innocent III, pope from 1198 to 1216.

Innocent III, Lothair dei Conti de Segni, in search of simplicity, had the gold and silver vessels removed from his table and replaced with wood and glass. He himself was served only three dishes, his chaplain two. "Action outranks contemplation," this brilliant pope wrote to one of his legates. Elected unanimously at thirty-seven, he died at fifty-five, burned out by the effort to impose his ideals of theocratic absolutism on an unruly Europe.

Innocent III spelled out his policy plainly in an encyclical dated the first year of his pontificate: "Just as God, founder of the universe, has constituted two large luminaries in the firmament of Heaven, a major one to dominate the day and a minor one to dominate the night, so he has established in the firmament of the Universal Church two great dignities, a major one to preside — so to speak — over the days of the souls, and a minor one to preside over the nights of the bodies. They are the pontifical authority and the royal power." Most of the monarchs of the time would have been satisfied with the nights of the bodies, but Innocent claimed authority over those also.

Then, as now, the pope had very few divisions. The wars of the Lord had to be fought with diplomacy and psychological warfare, but Innocent used these effectively and brought the papacy to the height of its power. He excommunicated or interdicted kings and emperors, among them King John of England, who ultimately deeded his realm to the Church; in return John received it back as a papal fief and was promised help in resisting the Magna Carta. This arrangement was euphemistically called a donation, and the Donation of John Lackland is one of the earliest documents in the present Secret Archives. Innocent also brought the peninsula of Italy under papal power, inaugurated the Albigensian crusade, and continued the feud with the emperors.

The Church thought it had gotten rid of Frederick Barbarossa when he went swimming in a pleasant river and drowned on his way to the Crusades: the Germans said he was only sleeping in a cave near Salzburg, and would return when his sword clattered to the rock in the time of Germany's great need. Instead he reappeared in a red-haired grandchild, the little king of Sicily, who was to be Frederick II. The child became a ward of the pope and a pawn of international politics. Innocent wrote to him when he was eleven years old, in terms that could be understood by a small boy: "How much joy entered the Apostolic Scrinium of our heart when from the letter of Your Serenity we learned that the hand of the Lord has liberated you from the disgraceful custody of such people . . . How many times the dispatches of the nuncios have crossed each other as they came and went, taking to various parts of the world the messages that should have assured peace for you. How many times the letters sent for the sake of your well-being and that of your kingdom tired the pens of the notaries and dried the ink-wells of the copyists . . . Hoping in God that you may some day realize in your soul and in your deeds the care and benevolence of the Apostolic Seat, your mother."

Instead, Frederick grew up to hate the papacy and the hierarchy, and to be a thorn in the flesh of several popes. Yet before his outcast's death he wrote a strange chapter in history. Now and then medieval society produced an almost modern man, and one of these was Frederick II. He possessed both genius and power, and in his Sicilian kingdom he ran a private Renaissance. Like Charlemagne, he was in love with learning, and he started with a far richer cultural background. He had the scientific works of every age "from Aristotle to Averroës" translated for him, kept astronomers at his court, knew both Western and Arabic poetry. He had more faith in scientific truth than in God or immortality. And at a time when the Mohammedan world was called the "son of the slave of Egypt" and Christians were urged to follow the Biblical injunction "Send away the slave and her son," he lived in a manner as much Saracen as Christian, maintaining a harem and surrounding himself with Moslem scholars. When he was finally prodded into going, reluctantly, on crusade, the enemy emir sent to meet him found his conversation delightful, and was fascinated by what Frederick told him of Western culture. The crusade turned into a cultural mission. Eventually the two men remembered what they were there for and arranged a truce, omitting the warfare normally regarded as a prerequisite. Both the Muslem and the Christian worlds found such behavior shocking.

Innocent the lawyer and the diplomat was a poet as well, and perhaps the author of the *Veni Sancte Spiritus* and the *Mater Dolorosa*. And he was certainly the author of the obscenely exquisite *De Contemptu Mundi*: "Man is conceived of spoiled blood through the ardor of libidinousness, and the only company of his corpse is the worms of the tomb. Alive he generated lice; dead he will generate worms and flies. When alive he produces dung and vomit, dead he produces putridity and fetor. Alive he fattens only himself; dead he will fatten worms by thousands.

"What is more fetid than a human cadaver, what is more horrible than a dead man? The sight of a man whose embrace we valued in life is now unbearable. O my mother, why did you generate this son of bitterness and grief? O vile indignity of the human condition!

"Observe the herbs and the trees: these produce flowers, leaves, and fruits, and you produce lice. They offer olive oil, wine and balsam; you offer only sputum, dung, and urine. They breathe a sweetness of perfume; you spread the fetor of corruption."

There is nothing peculiar to the Middle Ages in this; it is the cry of Gilgamesh as he watches the worm crawl from the nostril of the comrade-in-arms "whose embrace he valued in life." Gilgamesh's goddess told him: "Let thy garments be pure, thy head be washed; wash thyself with water! Regard the little one who takes hold of thy hand; enjoy the wife in thy bosom." Innocent, like Gilgamesh, wanted only the sacred plant of immortality.

Most of Innocent's arrangements crumbled after his death; the crusades failed, the Church lost control of the Italian peninsula, new heresies arose. England and the empire went their stubborn ways. But like a prince who has been the patron of a great artist, Innocent achieved a lasting merit in the support he gave to the spiritual genius Saint Francis of Assisi.

Francis had grown up in the country of the heretics, but instead of theorizing on the dualism of good and evil, of life and death, of spirit and substance, he developed a philosophy of love without limit for all men, for all creatures sentient and insentient. In the leper's disfigured body there was always a man, with his divine dignity.

Around the jester of God gathered his disciples, the *fraticelli*. They were young men of a type that we know in our own day: I have had many lay *fraticelli* at my fireside. They despise their wealthy fathers, they are willing to engage in hard manual labor (in Latin America or the Congo), they join kibbutzes for a little while, and they long to be slugged by a Southern sheriff. To such men Francis gave direction and comradeship. He later said of them: "Those who came to embrace this life presented all they had to the poor. They were happy to remain with only a tunic, a cord around the waist, and a pair of drawers. They did not want anything more."

Even the handling of money was forbidden to them, unless it was needed to help lepers or to cure the sick, "because for us money must not have any more importance or value than a stone." Each brother was permitted to own the tools of his craft. Actually many of them worked as dishwashers or hostlers, daily work that could be gotten easily and given up when it was time to move on. They begged when they had to; Francis said, "If we are not paid for our work, let us call at God's table, asking for a little food from door to door like other poor men." Like acrobats and troubadours the friars went singing from city to city of the happiness on which the sun would never set.

As Franciscanism spread from Assisi to other cities, Francis decided to ask for papal authorization for his movement, to quell the doubts of bishops and city officials who felt that there was something irregular about these troubadours who sang the love of God on the lute through the squares and countryside.

In the Louvre is a painting by Giotto showing Innocent III and a church. This is not unusual; medieval popes had their portraits done holding church models in the same way that modern statesmen have their pictures taken looking intently at a globe. But in this picture Innocent is asleep, in a bed under a canopy supported by small columns, almost an *aedicula*, luxuriously decorated with encrustations of mosaic. Huddled beside the bed are two old people, watching the sleep of the pope, their bodies draped in the dark folds of their cloaks. His dream, shown in the picture, is of a church that is falling, its columns fracturing and its tower tilted. The church is the Lateran, and propping it up is Saint Francis. The new sect, Innocent thought, might be a defense against heresy, since it took over two of heresy's most attractive features — the cult of poverty that followed the advice of Christ, who told his disciples that they didn't need two coats, and the practice of talking directly to the people in the I-and-thou approach of Martin Buber.

Francis and his twelve companions were introduced at the Lateran by Cardinal Colonna. At his second audience Pope Innocent said to him: "Go with God, and preach as he inspires you. And when the Omnipotent multiplies you in numbers and in grace, come back to me, and I will give you greater missions." He warned him prophetically, however, that as institutions prosper they are likely to lose sight of their first aims.

Later Pope Honorius elevated the Franciscans to the rank of the older orders by approving their *Regula* or Rule. This statement of recognition, now in the Secret Archives, ends with a warning like the ones on Egyptian tombs: "No one of mankind may tear this page, or contradict it with temerarious daring. If anyone attempts this, know my imperative: that he will incur the indignation of the Omnipotent God and of the blessed apostles Peter and Paul."

In Rome for the occasion, Francis stayed with the Frangipani in their fortress-palace on the Palatine. When he left he gave Jacoba Frangipani a baby lamb, as "a symbol of purity and gentleness."

With Saint Francis a new element enters Christian theology. Not his devotion to poverty and the poor (other saints showed the same devotion), but his praise for all of God's creation. The Canticle to the Sun must have been said not with the folded hands and bowed head of medieval man, but with the upraised arms of the early Church. And in his feeling for the animal creation he entered an area of ethics that is still almost *terra incognita* to Western theology. The hermit saints in caves and in desert huts had come to see their animal neighbors as individuals, and the dying Saint Columba, nuzzled by an old cart horse, said, "Let him alone, he loves me." But this was regarded as a peculiarity of the saints, perhaps an aberration brought on by isolation. If here and there an old man saw the shadow of the Madonna in a mother bear holding her cub, he dismissed the thought as blasphemy. But Francis' preaching to the birds, his taming of Brother Wolf, have entered into Christian mythology. His statue, on the birdbaths of American gardens, and the representation of Saint Christopher on traveler's medals, are the only images of saints generally used in the Protestant world. It may not be an accident that two secular saints, Johnny Appleseed and Albert Schweitzer, both had this quality of reverence for all life.

Francis' teachings seem to have had little effect; in the great city that is named for him, little old ladies are being arrested for feeding the pigeons. Yet he has given some shadowy theological sanction, some faint touch of Church approval, to those who believe in civil rights for all the citizens of the planet.

It was Innocent III who began to shift the curial life of the Church, including part of the papal archives, from the Lateran to the Vatican. Shortly before his time the Lateran had been fortified so well that it was now called "The Palace of the High Walls," and the surrounding towers that menaced it had been pulled down, but it was still less defensible than the Vatican. He had already rebuilt the Vatican Palace that Pope Symmachus had constructed about the year 500 and that Charlemagne had enlarged and enriched, and he had provided new quarters for the *camerarii* or chamberlains and for the Chancellery.

To the *camerarii* was entrusted the care of the *Thesaurum nostrum et ecclesiae romanae,* which contained the pope's personal treasure along with that of the Church, gold and silver objects and gems, parchment documents, the registers, precious codices. The Chancellery, charged with preparing, dispatching, and preserving in registers the correspondence and acts of the popes, was headed by a cardinal known as the *Cancellarius* and also as the *Bibliothecarius Sanctae Matris Ecclesiae.* Under him were various officers. Some of these composed the pope's letters and prepared the rough copies of the papal acts. When these letters and acts had been revised and approved in their final form, other officials registered them, that is, copied them into a register, or rather, copied them on parchment sheets that were later to be bound into registers. Different popes used sheets of different size, but all of a given pope's letters were normally copied on the same size of parchment. The parchment sheets were folded to form *quaderni.* In this way two smooth white sheets faced each other, and two rough yellow sheets faced each other, so that the eye did not notice dissonance of color and texture.

The pope's official documents, edicts, and decrees and the seals affixed to them were called bulls. The papal seals are round balls of lead, attached to the document with silken or hempen cords. The "letters with silken cords" of red or yellow were likely to be documents granting a favor or pardon; in some periods the recipient could tell whether a letter from a pope brought him good or bad news as soon as he saw the cords that held the *bulla.* The papacy rarely used golden bulls, except for great occasions such as the appointment of Henry VIII as Defender of the Faith. On the other hand, the kings and emperors who wrote to the pope often used bulls of gold and silver. This favorable balance of trade enabled the papal treasury to build up an excellent collection of precious bulls.

The employees who affixed the seals — the bullators — were expected, for reasons of security, to be illiterate in Latin. They were sometimes called "*fratres barbati*" because they were often drawn from the bearded Cistercian order; many of them came from the Abbey of Fossanova, the first Cistercian monastery in Italy, built not far from the old Temple of Saturn. It is still an agricultural abbey; cheese made of buffalo milk by the ancient hand processes is sold there, and the great high-arched hall that was once the infirmary now serves as a storage place for grain and farm machinery. The Cistercians prided themselves on being an order of working men, and Fossanova was a reliable source of devoted laborers illiterate in Latin.

The Secret Archives' file of papal registers is not complete — often a register is missing, or a gap in dates shows that not all the *quaderni* that should have been bound into a volume have been included. Some of these losses may have been due to the fact that the popes in their frequent travels in Italy and abroad took with them in their baggage trains the archives documents that might be needed, along with a part of their Chancellery. These traveling documents were called the *scrinia viatoria* — the wayfaring archives — and were carried in iron trunks with rounded tops, banded with strips of iron and fastened with enormous padlocks.

Modern popes repair to Castel Gandolfo for the summer months, but medieval popes had many country retreats that served less as places of rest and recreation than as places of refuge. When Rome or other parts of Italy became temporarily untenable, it was wise to have a choice of castles, and they prepared fortified palaces in Assisi, Viterbo, Perugia, Orvieto, Anagni. One has some idea of the splendor of these papal country houses when he sees the Hall of Audiences in the palace at Orvieto, with its series of great arched windows overlooking the plain. Sometimes all Italy was unsafe, and the popes fled to France until the political climate changed. Between the years 1058 and 1304 the popes traveled a great deal in Italy and France; in two and a half centuries they were away from Rome for more than a hundred years. Often they undertook long trips to attend conferences of state.

Travel was so slow that they, like the emperors, found it necessary to follow a policy of govern-as-you-go, and took with them archives documents that might be needed for reference. For a political conference, they took only what would later be called cabinet papers, but for an extended stay the papers taken might constitute a large mass of archives. The transferring of important documents sometimes led to their destruction or dispersion, especially if the popes were involved in armed skirmishes, but this did not affect the bulk of the archives, which remained in their normal location, perhaps no safer than the mule trains of the popes. These were the *archiva stataria, archiva armaria,* or *scrinia palatii* — the stationary, kept-in-closets archives, the "scrinium of the palace."

However, the loss of archives through the travels of the popes was often lessened by the fact that copies rather than the originals were taken. For instance, when Innocent IV, in his conflict with Frederick II, transferred his ecclesiastical court to Lyons for six and a half years, he took with him as supporting evidence the most important grants of privilege and donations to the Holy See. But he did not take the originals;

only copies on long parchment rolls. One of these, known as "the Cluny Roll," is still to be found in the National Library of Paris.

I have searched for a description of one of the papal baggage trains, but have found none for this period. However, the register of the Apostolic Camera gives the details of a trip made by Paul III to Bologna in 1543, which was probably not dissimilar. This document is entitled "The book of mules, and other conveyances, for the trip of Paul III to Bologna and other places. 1543." This Mule Book lists the allotment of mules required to carry the luggage of various functions, such as the Pope's kitchen and his dining room, and of various individuals. The Pope took with him two mule-loads of wax and one mule-load of lead, an indication that considerable office work was to be done, but only three mules were allotted to the chancellery. Perhaps some of its equipment was carried on the wagons, or perhaps the business was to be largely financial, for fifteen or more mules are allotted to the chamberlains. The treasurer had three mules; their loads may have included books and documents. Much of the Mule Book deals with the allotments of individuals. Some had four mules; others a quarter of a mule — half a saddlebag. One has the impression that status at that time could be measured in mules, as modern executives measure it in windows and telephones.

The Road to Exile

THE cold snows of Canossa were supposed to teach the kings of the world that it was dangerous to defy the pope. But the kings drew another conclusion as well — that an institution strong enough to humiliate an emperor was a menace to their sovereignty, their dignity, and their self-interest. Innocent III had played one ruler against another, made free use of excommunication and interdict, and brought the papacy to an unprecedented height of power. But what he had done had been done by a brilliant man, in favorable circumstances, when the luck was with him. He forgot to allow for margin. Boniface VIII followed the example of the great popes, and came to disaster.

At Boniface's election, the Church was still a very powerful institution. All over Europe cathedrals were going up, with their exquisite architecture and their by-guess-and-by-God engineering. But France and England had become strong national powers, Arabian thought was washing the shores of Europe, the universities had arisen to provide a refuge for thinkers in advance of their times, and the ships of Europe had the compasses that would direct them to the New World. The crusades were virtually over; for centuries they had sapped the energies of the papacy as the unfinished tomb of Julius II was to sap the energies of Michelangelo. But now their strong religious appeal was no longer available to cement the Church's public relations. Instead they had brought to Europe new ways of thinking, new ways of enjoying the present life. It was not only the seeds of Saracen fruit trees that the crusaders brought home with them, but Saracen ideas and tastes as well.

Boniface's story begins with a holy man on a mountain. The Church had been two years without a pope, deadlocked between the Colonna and the Orsini factions. Then, as often happens in the case of people with a troubled conscience, the cardinals went to the other extreme and instead of electing a nepotistic pope they elected a saint.

The hermit Pietro di Murrone was eighty years of age when he was elected in 1294. He was of peasant origin, and he had spent most of his life at a mountain hermitage near Sulmona in the Abruzzi. His personality and the reports of his miracles had drawn other hermits to him, and his fame had spread so that he found it necessary to set aside part of the day for counseling people who came to consult him.

In the Secret Archives there is a document that purports to be his autobiography: "This is the Life that the Holy Father wrote, that was found in his cell," supposedly when he had to leave his monks to become a pope. Very probably the author was one of his disciples, who had lived near him and heard him talk about his life. The little book is full of miracles, but they were not considered in the process for his canonization, probably because of the lack of sustaining evidence. All his visions are of an imaginative kind: he tells of a celestial singing that he heard on the first night of his solitude in the mountains; it lasted even after he awakened, long enough for him to say a Paternoster. A mysterious bell always woke him in the morning at the time for prayers, until he made the mistake of accepting the gift of a rooster. He gave the rooster back, but the bell never rang again. Demons came to him in the shape of women — women that he had known when he was in the world.

The Archives also has the astonished letter that the Holy College of Cardinals sent to advise him of his election: "To Lord Brother Pietro di Murrone of the Order of Saint Benedict, elected Highest and Roman Pontifex, by the Divine Providence. Who, like the wind, turns where He will . . ."

Peter pleaded incompetence; he knew that the papacy involved administrative responsibilities and that he was unable to meet them. But his old patron, King Charles of Naples, offered to advise him, and Peter consented to be consecrated as pope if it could be done in a country chapel at Aquila, in the mountains east of Rome. Afterward, instead of going to Rome, he set up a temporary papal court in Naples, where he managed to live fairly comfortably by having a wooden hut put up in a corner of the garden of the palace King Charles had given him.

As Pope Celestine V he was as inefficient as he had said he would be. He was too much under the influence of his old patron King Charles, either because he trusted him or because he thought it better to stick to the devil he knew. Some of the Curia cardinals got away from him and sold blank bulls, to be filled in by the purchaser.

In the same year in which he had been elected, the Pope read his abdication speech in the Church of Santa Lucia of Naples: "I, Celestine

V, moved by humility, desire for a better life, and my conscience, because of bodily weakness, lack of instruction, and human malignity, in order to find the rest and consolation of the life I once had, I freely and of my own will leave the papacy, giving to the Holy College of Cardinals the faculty to elect legally a shepherd for the Universal Church."

Cardinal Caetani, who had influenced him toward abdication, was elected pope and took the name of Boniface VIII. When old Celestine tried to return to his mountain, papal troops were sent to take him into custody. Celestine escaped twice — the troops may have been in sympathy with him — and realizing that papal forces would be waiting for him at his hermitage, took ship for Dalmatia. It was beaten back to Italy and he was brought before Boniface, condemned, and imprisoned in a tiny cell. He must have been a strong old man; he lived ten months after this, and the rumor was that he finally had to be killed by a nephew of Boniface who drove a nail into his temple. In fact, the skull that is supposed to be Celestine's shows a hole. Perhaps his spirit got back to its mountain, for Saint Bernardino told of meeting it there two hundred years later. It was wearing its papal crown; *il gran rifiuto* had changed at last to acceptance.

Boniface's return to Rome after his election was a triumphal procession. From the old cardinal poet Giacomo Stefaneschi's description of the cavalcade and the stag party that followed, we know that the Pope's white destrier had a saddlecloth of purple; "bare its breast and all the forward parts of its body," and the horses of the cardinals and prelates wore white saddlecloths. The horses of subdeacons, chaplains and *scriniarii*, however, were uncovered — archivists apparently lacked status on the saddlecloth scale. The Pope, "the world's highest prince," rode "not as a tired man" under the heavy weight of a crown shaped like a Phrygian cap, woven with peacock feathers and adorned with a "flame of rubies." Trumpets and cornets sounded hosannas, "banners and togas are flitting here and there, and the people waving palms. Youth is like a wind all around." Cardinal Stefaneschi goes on to describe the banquet in the "convivial rooms resplendent in gold," where the Pope dined alone at a raised table from dishes brought by two crowned kings, who "respond to his signals like servant boys." The fathers rose to drink to the Pope from the "gemmed chalices of Bacchus," then "going back to the tables again and again made feast to the Father." Having said this much, the cardinal breaks off abruptly with the comment, "It is better that we keep secret this feast that was held in private."

Under Boniface VIII, the Lateran was again the center of the Church's life. With the building of the tower called the New Palace, it reached the height of its splendor, and its fountains ran day and night. Cardinals, judges and notaries came and went; the palace was staffed by an army of cooks, bakers, wine waiters, hostlers and water carriers. The Secret Archives' *Book of Expenditures of the Holy Palace* shows that enormous sums were spent for fish, meat and wine. The office supplies purchased give us some idea of the activity of Boniface's Chancellery — lead for bulls was bought by the half-ton, and parchment by the hundreds of pounds.

Boniface had four guards of the bedchamber. He may have felt that guards were the more necessary because of the rumors that were going around about the death of Celestine. Three short lauds on the Hermit Pope have come down to us; one of them, addressed to Celestine, says openly that he was murdered: "For holiness you gave up the papacy; people flocked to you and your miracles. For the envy that others had toward you, they killed you . . ."

Italy was becoming dissatisfied with the contemporary version of the Warren Report, and a restrained and formal charge was brought by the Colonna (whose motives are somewhat suspect because a police action had just been brought against them for hijacking 200,000 golden florins from the Anagni-to-Rome coach) and two or three rebellious Franciscan brothers, among them the poet Jacopone da Todi. This discreetly worded *Manifesto di Lunghezza* was affixed to the doors of Roman churches and laid on the altar of Saint Peter's: "We have frequently heard from people of great authority, ecclesiastical men and lay persons, that the abdication of the Lord Pope Celestine V of holy memory was legitimate and canonical. For this reason we ask with great humility that a universal council be called, so that it might declare that the abdication was according to legitimate and canonical principles, and that the election following was carried out according to such principles." Boniface replied by firing the two Colonna cardinals, excommunicating almost all of the family, and razing their feudal base, Palestrina.

More serious trouble arose with the King of France, Philip the Fair, and his minister, Nogaret. A fourth of the land of France was in Church hands, and Nogaret decided to tax it; in response Boniface issued the great bulls *Clericis laicos* and *Unam sanctam*. In the first, he said, "Lay people are always hostile to the clergy and have always tried to exceed their limits." In *Unam sanctam* he went even further: "There is one Catholic and apostolic Church; outside of it there is no salvation nor forgiveness. There was only one ark and Noah was its captain.

"There are two swords, one spiritual and one secular; the secular sword is to be used for the church, the spiritual one by the church. One is in the hands of the priest, the other is in the hands of kings and warriors, but is to be used according to the priest's orders."

This was perhaps too clearly written; it left no room for the ambiguity of interpretation that might have made for peace. Like modern nations faced with the sole alternative of unconditional surrender, the kings fought on, and they had their Italian adherents. In collusion with the French minister Nogaret, a party of the Colonna, under the leadership of Sciarra Colonna (in the *ciociaro* dialect "*sciarrare*" now means "to violate"), captured the Pope in a *coup d'état* at Anagni.

A contemporary account that has the liveliness of good reporting tells of the incident: "On the eve of the nativity of the blessed Virgin Mary, at sunrise there came rapidly and unexpectedly a great body of armed men on the side of the King of France and of the two damned cardinals Colonna. A great cry began around the village, men and women getting up from their beds and opening the doors and asking the reason for the noise. And finally they understood that the army had come to take the Pope and put him to death."

His enemies found him seated on the throne, wearing the mantle of Saint Peter and the crown that Constantine had given to Pope Sylvester. "And when the Pope was under judgment, and was asked if he would agree to renounce the papacy, he kept saying no, that he would rather, if necessary, lose his head. And in the French language he said, '*Ec le col, ec le cape*,' that is, 'Here is my neck, here is my head.'

"This army, as soon as it entered into the palace of the Pope, robbed his room and his treasury of vases, of clothing, of ornaments, of gold and silver, of all the other things they could find, leaving the Pope as poor as Job. And the Pope observing and seeing that everywhere these villains had divided among themselves his robes, and had taken away all the furnishings, said nothing but 'God gave; God has taken away.'"

At that time the papal treasury also included documents. So in this attack the Pope's personal archives which he had with him were subject to rifling or destruction. Apparently one or more registers and other documents disappeared at this time. Fortunately Boniface had taken the precaution of hiding part of his archives in the wilderness caves of Mount Soracte near Rome — the same caves in which Mussolini, during the Second World War, established an emergency headquarters and a storage place for important documents.

Anagni was empty, frightened, sacked. The Pope was in prison, abandoned even by the Colonna guards; eventually he was liberated by his Caetani kinsmen. He had been three days and nights in a dark cellar, on a straw pallet, dressed in his pontifical robes. Brought out into the light, he had himself taken, almost gropingly, to the public square. The reporter tells us what he said there: "'Good men and good women, you know that my enemies came, and took away from me my goods and the goods of the Church. I have had nothing to eat and nothing to drink. If among you there is a good woman who wants to help me, with her offering of bread and wine — and if she does not have bread and wine, a little bit of water — then I will give her God's benediction and mine.'

"Everyone started to shout, 'Long live the Holy Father,' and all the women who were there and all the others ran immediately through the village to the Palace of the Pope, offering him, some wine, some bread, some water; so that at one time all his room was filled with wine and water, and some of them, not finding enough containers, threw the wine and the water on the pavement of the Pope's room in great quantity.

"And all could come before the Pope; the good and the bad; the small and the great; and all of them were able to talk to the Pope as to another poor man."

A heretical saying runs, "Every soul is a city." For a little while Boniface had been Celestine.

A few years later a French pope, Clement V, was to take the papacy to Avignon for a "short stay" that lasted most of the century. The migration of the Archives had already begun, for Boniface's successor Benedict XI had transferred them to Perugia in 1304 to save them from political brigandage in Rome. Even the *archivia armaria* were viatory now, and they had no pope with them to protect them, as viatory archives normally had. In troubled Italy they were "sheep without shepherd, left to chance."

Clement took with him the registers of the last two popes and the jewels for his coronation. The papal library, the bulk of the archives, and the treasury were not forwarded to Avignon immediately — a fact that supports the belief that the move was not intended to be at all permanent. In 1312, when Clement had been at Avignon for three years, he sent for the valuable objects of the treasury. They got only as far as Lucca, where they were deposited at San Frediano. There they were sacked by the Ghibellines in 1314. The library and archives — they were still spoken of as two parts of the same body — were stored at Assisi in the treasure room next to the sacristy of the Church of Saint Francis, but they too were plundered by the Ghibellines in 1319 and 1320. The library was badly damaged; the archives suffered less.

It was not until the year 1339 that what remained was inventoried and sent to Avignon.

Silence had come down on the Lateran, after a thousand years of Christian history. The Loggia of Benediction was empty; the statue of

Marcus Aurelius that was believed to be of Constantine stood alone in the deserted square. And on the bronze Wolf of Rome the cut-off hands of criminals who had committed offenses against the government or stolen religious objects shriveled and dried in the wind.

Interlude at Avignon

T HE rolling plains of Avignon are laced with the silver of olive trees; beyond are the towers of the papal palace, towers in time as well as in space. Seven popes reigned here for nearly seventy years. At first their stay was unintentional; the day of decision, like the day of the Lord, came like a thief in the night. Clement V had been elected by the French faction, and the French cardinals felt safer away from Rome.

Avignon — the Vineyard City — had several advantages: it was on the edge of France but not in France; it belonged to the friendly king of Naples and was surrounded by the Comtat-Venaissin district which was part of the profits of the Albigensian persecutions. A river city, built on the chalk cliffs above the Rhone, and easily defended, it had been a trade center of the Middle Ages. It was also a center for the study of the black arts — necromancy, sorcery, alchemy, astrology — and many bulls in the Secret Archives show that the problem was a persistent one.

Avignon's account books, discovered in the Secret Archives in the last century, tell us a great deal about the little provincial city that became a world capital, about the construction of its palaces, and about the artists who worked there. When the first of the Avignon popes arrived in 1309, the city was a typical small city of Provence, with narrow streets and low buildings made up of little apartments in which master and servants, people and horses, lived together in crowded confusion. One of the largest of these apartment houses is described in the *Collectoriae*, or tax collector's records. The ground-floor entrance opened directly into a very small room with a stable for twelve horses on one side and one for two horses on the other. The kitchen was beyond the smaller stable, though it is not clear whether one got to it by passing through the stable or by going out into the street. On the floor above were three rooms with another kitchen; on the floor above that were three additional rooms. Because of the housing shortage in Avignon this so-called palace rented for three and a half gold florins a month.

Clement V (1305–1314), the first of the Avignon popes, lived modestly with a small court in the Dominican convent, when he was not on progress among the castles of Comtat-Venaissin. Nor did the second Avignon pope, John XXII (1316–1334), seem to regard himself as a permanent resident, although he wanted the Church to have a proper seat in Avignon, and remodeled the ancient episcopal palace. According to the account books, the Pope's rooms had floors of varicolored tile, and the glassless windows were covered with waxed linen canvas, necessitating a great consumption of candles and lantern oil. The palace was heated by wood fires, and the accounts include repeated references to the upkeep and repair of the "stoves of our house," as well as receipts for wood brought to the palace. The cold must have been bitter or the Pope easily chilled, for the accounts often mention his furs, and the items referring to his bed-coverings include quantities of silk and wool blankets and fur coverlets.

John's successor, Benedict XII (1334–1342), had the face of a temple priest of any time from Akkad on. Yet this man who looked so self-indulgent was personally economical to a fault. His extravagance was the palace; he wanted Avignon to have a seat as splendid as the Lateran. He razed to the ground the buildings that John XXII had erected, and in their place put up a palace that was almost a city, with its grandiose square towers, its gardens, and the great hall where the Consistory sat with him in council and in judgment. The papal apartments were in the Tower of the Angels. And the bedroom, in green, is an arboreal pavilion: oak branches and vines intertwine on the wall.

Within forty stairsteps of the Pope's room were the quarters of the *camerarius* or chamberlain, the first dignitary of the court, who had to remain within call. Above was the Pope's personal library, called the High Treasury; below was the square vaulted chamber of the Low Treasury, underground on one side and protected by a great wall on the other. Here in this almost secret area were thirty coffers full of parchments, the archives of the Church. What was left of the archives sent from Rome in 1304 had finally, by 1339, reached Avignon. With them were kept the treasures of gold and silver and the precious gems that the Pope collected. It was probably in rooms near the Low Treasury that a large staff of scribes took care of the confidential correspondence of the Holy See.

Clement VI (1342–1352), who loved the world and its luxuries, again remodeled the palace and created an addition known as the New Palace. On the walls of the papal atelier we can still see the sports of the countryside, the beauty of young men in action. At Clement's death the palace was practically finished. This building, that Froissart called "the most beautiful, the strongest house in the world," had gone up in less than twenty years, because, for the first time, the size of the stone building blocks was rigidly standardized.

With the builders came the painters. One of them was Matteo Giovanetti, whose frescoes remind one of Giotto and, strangely, of the Chinese artists — his prophets look like Chinese sages. Avignon had its poet too, and though the Secret Archives documents published in the last century have given a soberer, more accurate view, it is through Petrarch's bitter, fascinated descriptions that we see the papal court. Dante was not there; the "other people's stairs" that he spent his life going up and down were not in Avignon. But his life overlapped the Avignon period and his strictures on the papacy joined themselves to those of Petrarch. Avignon had its saints also — Catherine of Siena, who kept urging the popes back to Rome, and Bridget of Sweden, who saw Clement VI as Lucifer on the Holy See.

The intellectuals of the world came to Avignon, in search of ancient manuscripts that had survived the Middle Ages in Carolingian refuges, and in search of money from the popes whose munificence they despised. And on the narrow streets that wound between the crowded houses, jostled together like buildings in a flood, the princes and the cardinals rode to prayer or to the tourneys and balls for which Avignon was famous. There were the "women of the Pope's family," wearing the ermine and miniver furs, the fabrics of spun gold and silver, that were forbidden to ordinary women. There were the women of the court — Doucette, Blanchefleur, the Countess of Turenne. And somewhere there was Laura, whom Petrarch met in the Church of Santa Clara.

The poets and the artists came to Avignon, but the plague came also — the plague of the *Decameron*, that depopulated cities and tore the social fabric wide apart. Pope Clement VI had a special mass written for it, the Mass Against Mortality: "O God, remember your promise; call back your punishing angel, so that the land may not be utterly desolate, so that not all may die." These formulas are still repeated during plagues and catastrophes; this is the mass that will be said for us in the days of the fallout.

« *1* »

In one of the oldest indices of the archives of Castel Sant'Angelo I found the notation, "Sacrilegious hands, abusing the trust of the pontifical legates, removed many precious documents. Among the most important was the trial of the Templars," that took place in France in the year

1309. Though this particular record is now in the Manuscript Section of
the Library of Paris, abundant documentation on the subject remains in
the Archives — papal bulls, supplications, scroll on scroll of parchment
with the interrogation of the trials in France, Italy, Spain, England, Scotland, Ireland, Germany, Cyprus. Just one of these records forms a scroll
two hundred and thirty-six feet long, made from eighty pieces of parchment, sewn together, one after the other, with grayish thread. In the lines
of sewing are strange designs that are the seals of the notaries used to
authenticate the documents. The writing is very hard to read; accusations and confessions, truth and lies, seem compounded into a homogeneous dust.

The Templars were one of the élite military groups that appear again
and again in history. The Militia of the Temple had been formed to
guard the holy places of Palestine and to protect the routes of pilgrimage. They took their name from the Temple of Solomon; on that site
their order had been founded. Their rule was said to have been devised
by Saint Bernard, but it was not divulged to the public or, in its entirety,
to any but the highest ranking of its members. Novices were initiated at
night, behind guarded doors. It was even said that the Templars had
secret ports from which they traveled to unknown continents.

As the Crusades declined the Templars became the bankers of the
Mediterranean world, carrying goods to the Levant in their own ships
and handling the transfer of large sums. Their strongholds, at once fortresses and religious centers, spread through Europe and the Middle
East. The Temple quarter of Paris belonged to them with its palaces,
orchards, and gardens; in its tower they kept the treasure of France.

"Their uniform was white, their spurs were gold, and their allure was
pride." The king of France wanted to be one of them, and he was refused. Was it the Templars' blackballing of him, or perhaps his greed for
their wealth, that made him attack their order? Or did he believe the
rumors that they had betrayed the cause of the Crusades and entered
into private agreements with the infidels? We do not know, but at dawn
on Friday, October 13, 1307, all the Templars in France, some two thousand in number, were arrested and charged with idol-worship and obscene practices.

The order was responsible to the Holy See; only the Pope could suppress it. At first Clement V tried, weakly, to defend it, but he remembered what had happened to the last pope who had opposed the French
king, and he feared the threatened posthumous proceedings against
Boniface. The Templars, subjected to tortures more obscene than the
crimes with which they were charged, confessed that they had worshiped an idol with a cat's head, one shaped like a devil, one shaped like

a satyr; that they had spat on the cross; that they had carried on sodomitic practices; that they had betrayed the cause of the Crusades, had plotted against the Pope and the king.

But when the Templars faced the tribunals of inquisition established by the Pope, whom they still trusted, they withdrew their confessions. Clement, pressed by Philip, ended by ordering all Christian princes to arrest the Templars, and forcing the reluctant king of England to torture them.

The Grand Master Jacques de Molay was burned to death at night on the Isle of Jews, in the presence of the entire royal family of France. According to tradition de Molay, covered with flames, pronounced a curse on Clement, on Philip of France, on the minister Nogaret: "I summon you to appear before the tribunal of God before a year is over." Clement died forty days after the Templars were sentenced. Then Nogaret died; his last words were reported to have been "I'm burning up." Philip was stricken in the forest of Pont-Saint-Maxence, chasing a mysterious stag or boar — the stories differ — and died complaining of great thirst.

The verdict of history on the Templars varies between "Not guilty" and "Not proven." The charge of homosexuality was probably true in some marginal sense. But that it was a matter of official group policy seems unlikely.

The charge of idol-worship is now thought to be baseless because of the conflicting testimony elicited. Asked to describe Baphomet, "For one this head was white, for another black, gilded for a third, a fourth had seen its eyes blazing like carbuncles. For some it was the Creator, who makes the trees blossom and ripens the harvest; for others, a friend of God, a powerful intercessor. Others had seen it suddenly turn into a black cat, or a crow, or a demon in the guise of a woman."

To the modern mind there is something familiar in this shifting of mental figures: it is reminiscent of the effects of LSD, which produces different images in different minds, beautiful in some, horrible in others. It may be that what the Templars were really guilty of was experimenting with the Arabs' psychedelic drugs.

The little Princess Joan of Naples, granddaughter of King Robert the Wise, grew up as a cherished child. She was usually dressed in purple velvet embroidered with silver campanulas; her wooden horse had a Moorish saddle and a *couverture* of sandalwood.

In 1343 the Neapolitan statesman Acciaiuoli wrote, "On Wednesday King Robert was buried, and King Andrea married her and knew her carnally." Andrea was Joan's cousin, son of the King of Hungary, a boy

younger than she. There was little love or harmony between the young
sovereigns, and the Archives show that Clement VI did a good deal of
long-distance marriage counseling. Two years after the marriage, Andrea, now eighteen, was assassinated. The Pope, in a formal speech,
summarized the circumstances: "Called by the traitors, he came out from
the bedroom of the Queen. Some of the criminals put their hand on his
mouth, so that he could not cry out and ask for help. Others put a rope
around his neck to strangle him, as the marks show. Others took him by
the genitals and so dragged him. One can say of him what has been said
of Christ, that from the feet up to the head there was not a part of him
left uninjured."

This account of the murder shows two nurses, the king's and the
queen's, each defending her child. The queen's nurse, Philippa, had
closed the door after Andrea so that he could not come back into the
bedroom, and the king's nurse, Hungara, prevented the quiet disposal of
the body when, hearing the commotion, she came with a lighted candle
to look for the boy, and found his body where it had been thrown from
the window, a piece of the attacker's skin in the dead boy's mouth. The
part played by the nurses and the youth of the principals in this historic
murder bring to mind the comment of the American philosopher Eric
Hoffer, that the history of the Middle Ages is absolutely incomprehensible unless one remembers that it was enacted by adolescents and by
adults attuned to adolescent thinking.

The accused Queen Joan, after an inconclusive hearing at the papal
court, returned to Naples and her own eventual murder. Joan remains a
puzzling personage. According to the chronicles of the time, we see her
as a little girl who on Holy Thursday, along with Queen Sancia, washed
the feet of the poor in the churches. Petrarch, describing a great tempest
that struck Naples in the year 1343, says, "the young Queen, feet bare,
with a great number of women around her and following her, kept visiting churches dedicated to the Virgin Mary, Mother of God. In the port
there was no ship that could hold against the tempest." For other historians, she was utterly dissolute, and the lover even of a washerwoman.

It is not for lack of documentary sources that Joan is still an enigma.
Her chief biographer, Émile Leonard, used eleven hundred letters that
he found in the secret and the ordinary registers of Clement VI. Yet most
of the letters in the secret registers touching on the relations between the
queen and the Pope have not been published or fully exploited. Beyond
the masses of papal correspondence, Joan remains unconvicted and un-
cleared — except by the popes, who gave the Golden Rose to her and her
new husband.

"They met in caves of turpitude called paradises." Clement V's bull ran: "We have learned that certain abominable sects of wicked men usually called beghards and of certain unfaithful women called beguines — under the instigation of the sower of weak actions — have risen up with great danger in the Kingdom of Germany, following and teaching sacrilegious and perverse doctrines spotted with the following errors: First, that man in his present life can acquire such a state of perfection as to make him incapable of sin. Second, that it is of no use to fast or pray, after a man has reached a state of perfection, because then sensuality is so truly submitted to reason and to spirit that man can freely offer the body all that the body loves. Third, that those who are in such a state of perfection and spirit of liberty are not obliged to observe any precepts of the Church whatsoever, because, as they state, where the spirit of the Lord is present, there is perfect freedom." (Is there an echo of this idea in a phrase in the Book of Common Prayer — "and whose service is perfect freedom"?)

The arguments quoted in the bull draw to the conclusion, "Seventh, that if women give even a kiss when they are not inclined to do so by nature (*natura inclinat*), they commit a mortal sin. Instead the carnal act — when it is the inclination of their nature, is not a sin, especially if it is exercised at the moment that one is tempted to it."

The bull seems to confuse various movements and sects; this is probably because they actually *were* confused. The fringe religious movements of the Middle Ages — the beghards and beguines, the bizoches, the sect of the Spirit of Liberty — tended to overlap and run into each other in the same way that modern liberal protest groups do. Some of them seem an inheritance from the desert days of Christian heresy, others a rehearsal for the Reformation.

One of these sects, known as the sect of The Spirit of Liberty, turned from the self-abnegating "ascent" of the orthodox saints to a mystical acceptance of the body, holding with Saint Paul that "all things are lawful unto us" once spiritual perfection was reached. It sometimes forgot the last part of the quotation: "but not all things are expedient."

Objective tests were devised to determine whether a follower of the sect had reached the grade of perfection. One such test, given in Umbria, involved putting a young woman, a stranger, into the bed of a male subject whose perfection was to be tested. If the man showed a sexual reaction to this woman, whom he obviously could not love because he did not know her, then it was proved that he was still prey to instinct and to the urges of the body; he was a sinner and not a free spirit. But if no sexual reaction occurred, then he was beyond sin and had attained the liberty of the Holy Spirit. If later the two came to know and love each other, complete union was permitted, since it was a manifestation of the divinity that dwelt in their souls and their bodies.

The caves of turpitude called paradises were emptied by the Inquisition, but the heretics' ideas were to reappear again and again in the subterranean life of the Church.

When the archives from Rome finally arrived in Avignon, thirty years later than the papal court, a new and extensive documentation was already accumulating. Red tape means archives, and during the Avignon period the activities of the Church were becoming more and more complex.

Of the *fondi* that form the framework of the present Secret Archives the records of the Chancellery and the Camera began before Avignon times; those of the Secretariat of State began after them. But some new *fondi* date from this period. One is the series of secret registers. To prevent leakage through Chancellery employees, the pope's confidential correspondence was now handled by a staff of pontifical secretaries working in the so-called Secret Chamber. These letters were then copied into secret registers, distinct from the regular series of registers.

The series of registers of "transcriptions of petitions in their entirety" also begins at Avignon, where the petitions themselves were copied into a *Registrum Supplicationum*, in order to keep a check on graft. The Secret Archives have 7365 volumes of petitions covering the period from 1342 to 1889; forty-six of them are from the Avignon period. These registers not only indicate the existence of papal letters that have not been recovered, but offer much more background information than the bull or brief sent in response, since people who want something are likely to go into a good deal of detail explaining why. The petitions come from every part of the Christian world, from individuals, religious orders, political organizations. They contain references to the construction and restoration of churches, political events, family situations, economic life, and even natural phenomena. Among those who asked for benefits and dispensations were almost all of the intelligentsia of the time, including Petrarch, Boccaccio, Rabelais, Michelangelo and Copernicus.

The papacy's financial affairs were carried on by the Apostolic Camera, an organization hated perhaps slightly more than the Inquisition. The great expenses of the Avignon court, of its charities, and of the wars in Italy, were being carried on a diminished tax base as Germany, England, and France reduced the revenues sent to the pope.

But the Church was still a secular as well as a spiritual power. It had its own states, its vassal states, and large tracts of land in states that were under other sovereigns. Over all the faithful it had the weapon of excommunication, and when other resources were not enough it taxed itself, drawing on its outlying members to feed its central core.

During the Avignon period the devices of the squeeze and the kickback were highly developed. The laity were subject to tithes (an income tax) and Peter's Pence (a head tax); while a newly appointed bishop paid annates (a year's income of his new benefice), and tithes thereafter. A bishop also paid to go on compulsory pilgrimages. And he paid his superior's expenses, if the superior — and his entourage — came to visit him. (If they did not, he paid what it would have cost him if they had.) Finally, he made "caritative" or affectionate gifts, regardless of the state of his affections. When a bishop died, the pope could invoke the right of *spolia* and seize his house and goods, if his neighbors had not done it first.

Like modern diplomats, bishops often found it hard to make their official income meet their official obligations. Some bishops made a very good thing out of their appointments, particularly if they held several benefices; for others it was just another version of the rat race.

Historians have searched the Camera's extensive records as archaeologists scrutinize the numbers on the clay tablets of the Fertile Crescent. At first these historical studies were mainly on the financial structure of the Holy See; more recently they have stressed economic life, production, the movement of goods and money, the customs and life of the times. For example, the series *Introitus et Exitus* (What Comes In and What Goes Out) — the series of cameral ledgers recording the receipts and expenditures of the papal exchequer — lists the expenditures of each department of the papal household, including military expenses, building costs, the names of artists and what they were paid for what services. This series, which runs from 1279 to 1524, contains six hundred and six volumes.

Another series, called *Collectoriae*, has five hundred and four volumes, dated from 1274 to 1447. The *Collectoriae* were tax-collection districts, each under a collector who had the power of excommunication. Beginning in 1217 the collectors had been sent to all Christian countries, from Poland to Ireland. These officials usually sent back short reports explaining the amounts collected. One area had had a flood, an early freeze had killed the crops in another, such-and-such a nobleman had enlarged his domain and could now pay more. Some of these reports are of high literary quality; those from Naples in the time of Queen Joan have the grace and precision of miniature paintings.

The *Collectoriae* records include illuminating inventories of the belongings of deceased cardinals, bishops, and other high-ranking ecclesiastics, which by the *ius spoliae* came to the Holy See. These tell a great deal about living conditions in the various countries of Christendom, particularly those countries that are not much dealt with in secular writings. What was life like in Latvia, in Hungary, in Palestine, in Cyprus? The lists of books give some idea of the prelates' cultural level, and the auction records tell something of comparative values. (For example, juridical codices brought higher prices than religious works.) Now and then there are human glimpses, as when a collector, listing the four books belonging to the Bishop of Malta (who must have given some away to foil the *ius spoliae*) says that he would like to keep a certain breviary at the estimated price "because it is written with very large letters and therefore would be a blessing for my sick eyes."

Then there are the court records, particularly those of the Rota and the Consistory. The Rota, today concerned mainly with requests for annulment of marriage, then dealt chiefly with suits concerning benefices. The oldest volumes of the archives of the Tribunal of the Rota are in the Secret Archives, but not even these can be consulted without the special permission of the Tribunal.

The Consistory, made up of the pope and the cardinals, was a deliberative body, consulted by the pope on matters of great importance, but it could also function as a tribunal. Complaints could be brought to it about the pope himself. The consistorial records are deposited in the Secret Archives, but only their older volumes may be consulted.

The Apostolic Penitentiary deals with moral and spiritual matters — cases of excommunication, suspension from office and priestly duties, interdict, and, sometimes, with marriage dispensations and questions of absolution. The nature of its jurisdiction is shown in its designation as "the tribunal of conscience and extraordinary sins." To this court came such cases as that of Count John of Armagnac who requested absolution for having married his sister Isabella. The archives of the Penitentiary, because of their sensitive subject matter, are barred to consultation and kept in the offices of the Penitentiary. A few very old processes can be found among the papal letters in the series of Avignon registers and in the Miscellanea series.

The young Petrarch, unwillingly a student of law at Montpelier, loved the classics. When his father came to visit him and found "profane books" hidden in his room, he started to throw them into the fire. The boy wept, and his father, relenting, gave him back the *Rhetoric* of Cicero and a Virgil, "for solace, but it should be very rarely." Later, released from the law, Petrarch was able to pursue a lifelong study of the classics, and a lifelong search for the lost books of the ancient world.

There were popes and cardinals who cared as much for books as Petrarch did, and were patrons of literature as well as of art. Cardinal de Cabassole even founded a public library, as Petrarch planned to do in Venice. But the great enthusiasm was the search for manuscripts. France was a good hunting ground, since old manuscripts had been copied in the scriptoria of its abbeys. The interest that the popes and cardinals took in recovering the books and manuscripts of the past helped in rebuilding the papal library, which finally arrived at Avignon in 1339, depleted by pillage. The merchants of Pisa had sent John XXII fifty books recovered from the sack at Lucca, but in general the library had had to be recreated almost *ex novo* from bare shelves. Thus the successive inventories tell us something about the interests of the individual popes.

The right of spoil gave the papal library the proceeds of the book-collecting activities of its cultured prelates, and probably saved many rare codices and manuscripts from public plundering.

In the book inventories of Avignon, Aristotle appears in many copies; in the year 1368 there were already thirty. But there are two strange lacunae — the works of Dante and Petrarch. Even in the long catalogues of private ecclesiastical libraries, that is, of cardinals and bishops, Dante's name is found only twice — and each time the only work listed is the *Divine Comedy*.

Perhaps the hierarchy resented his *Monarchia*, which advocated a world empire like that of ancient Rome, or his assumption of the role of final judge in the *Divine Comedy*, or perhaps it felt that he had come too close to actual witchcraft. Boccaccio tells of a woman who, seeing Dante walking in Verona, pointed him out to her friends: "Look at him — he goes to hell and comes back whenever he likes. And he brings back information."

« 3 »

Slowly and tentatively, the papacy returned to Rome. In 1365 Urban V (1362–1370) ordered the Vatican palace repaired, and vineyards and orchards planted near it, but when he set out for Rome he left behind at Avignon the papal library and treasure. He returned to Avignon in 1370, to die, as Saint Bridget of Sweden had predicted he would do if he left Rome. Seven years later another pope, Gregory XI, left for Rome, though the omens were against it. (Saint Catherine of Siena had assured him that he would die if he remained in Avignon; she omitted telling him that he would also die if he went to Italy.) Apparently Gregory was not certain of the wisdom of the move, for he too left behind him at Avignon the papal treasury (which had been reduced to very little) and the pontifical library and archives.

The great library was hidden in various rooms and chapels. The personal library of the popes, the documents that made up the archives, and the most precious objects of the palace were piled together in the semi-subterranean halls of the Low Treasury beneath the pope's apartments. The doors were closed and covered over so as to look like walls.

In Rome the papacy found, as absentee landlords often do, that things had gone to wrack and ruin in its absence. The repairs ordered by Urban V had restored the missing doors and windows to the Vatican Palace and provided it with a watertight roof, but the ruin to the city could not be so easily repaired. Rome had always been a tourist town, and for nearly seventy years there had been few tourists. The great aqueducts were still cut, and the population was so small that agriculture had invaded the city; the Forum was used as a cow pasture. The classical ideal of *rus in urbe* had been ironically realized.

Son of the Sun and Moon, Pope of the Sea

MATTEO di Giovanni's fresco shows Gregory XI (1370–1378), the last Avignon pope, riding into Rome with an embroidered canopy held over him and the crowds pressing near him; it also shows the body profile of a very sick man. Gregory died shortly afterward, warning future popes against those of either sex who, "under the banner of professed revelation, present their visions to tell the Pope and the Curia how to direct the Church."

There were sixteen cardinals in the conclave that was to elect a new pope; only four were Italian. But the conclave was to be held in Rome, under the pressure of public opinion and under the threat of public action. Cardinal Pedro de Luna made his will before attending it, another cardinal took his confessor along to deal with last-minute sins, still another took the precaution of strapping on a cuirass under his clerical garment. The cardinals could hear the mob's tambourines, its trumpets, its shouts of *"Romano lo volemo"* — "we want him Roman."

The cardinals elected a compromise candidate, the Archbishop of Bari — an Italian but a Neapolitan. When the bells of Saint Peter's rang *ad martellum,* they were unable to bring themselves to tell the Romans whom they had elected; instead, thinking fast, they seized on a senile Roman cardinal and let the crowds assume he had been elected pope. As the rumor of the Archbishop of Bari's election spread, the crowd shouted: "We don't want him!" Asked to resign by city officials, the new Pope Urban VI said, "They don't know me. Even if I saw a thousand swords raised to cut my throat, I still would not resign." This was to be the attitude of most of the popes of the Schism; in fact it is hard to think of any pope except Celestine, who was a saint, who was not afflicted with this early form of Potomac fever.

Urban VI (1378–1389) was devoted to reform, but vindictive and hot-tempered, and given to insulting cardinals. After a few months of this, some of them remembered the circumstances of his election and began to have happy doubts of its legitimacy. In 1378, sure of the support of the king of France, they elected a French cardinal who took the name of Clement VII. He lost the battle for Rome and retired to Avignon, where he established a new Curia and new archives, and put on new balls and tourneys. The great Schism of the West had begun.

Now the Catholic world divided itself into two enemy camps: the Obedience of Clement VII of Avignon, which included France, the kingdom of Naples, Savoy, and the Christian kingdoms of Spain, Scotland and parts of Germany; and the Obedience of the Roman pope, Urban VI, which was made up of the States of the Church, Venice, Milan, Genoa, Flanders, Portugal and England. England was the enemy of France and therefore on the other side. Urban excommunicated the intruder Clement and his followers; Clement excommunicated Urban; nominally all Christianity was excommunicated in one way or another.

Some religious orders were turned into parties of the Schism, and the conflict even became a conflict of saints — Catherine of Siena and Bridget of Sweden for the Roman papacy, and Saint Vincent Ferrer for Avignon's. Catherine's attitude was that of Gilbert and Sullivan's duchess — "He's my husband and I love him. There were some people said it couldn't be done, but I said, He's a duke and I'm *going* to love him." Urban was pope, and Catherine did what she could to civilize him. On the other hand, the great preacher Saint Vincent Ferrer stayed for almost the length of the Schism with the pope of Avignon, asserting that the followers of the Roman pope were either heretics or seduced by demons.

The popes of Rome and Avignon died and successors were elected; the Schism was in its second generation. And now in the confusion of charges and countercharges, of reciprocal excommunications, there began the story of three men: a pope, a saint, and a soldier.

The lifetime of Pedro de Luna, the second of the Avignon popes, who reigned as Benedict XIII (1394–1422?), spans the duration of the Schism. A cardinal before it began, he was the last of the schismatic popes to yield the tiara, and he yielded it only by dying. Of the line of the counts of Luna, and with Arab blood, allied to the royal houses of Aragon and Navarre, he was already aged when elected pope, an elder from Michelangelo's paintings. And like other popes before him, he was suspected of a dual priesthood, of allegiance to a religion older than Rome.

Pope Luna was a man of flawed greatness, imperfect but on the grand scale, feudal in his authoritarianism but surprisingly modern in some of his religious theories. One even wonders whether, if he had been recognized as pope, the Church might not have had a reformation instead of a counter-reformation. The Anonymous Florentine, then in Avignon, wrote of him at his election: "He is a great cleric and a wise man, a good person, not given to simony. I think he will be able to get the church of God and the world into good shape."

It was true that Luna was without venality; but as the English theologian C. S. Lewis has reminded us, the devil knows better than to use common bribes as bait for uncommon souls. Pope Luna had the sin of the angels, and his obstinacy was to trouble Europe until his death at almost a centenarian's age.

Always with him was Vincent Ferrer, who was soon to be sainted. De Luna had known him at Valencia, and when he was crowned Ferrer came to Avignon as the Pope's confessor, chaplain, and apostolic penitentiary. After a miraculous recovery from a severe illness the saint began his mission to the heretics, a mission which he believed to have been assigned him by Christ in the presence of Saint Francis and Saint Dominic, and announced himself as the Angel of the Apocalypse foretold in the Revelations of Saint John the Divine. Pope Luna was not a man to be intimidated by having the Angel of the Apocalypse around the house, and Ferrer continued as his trusted friend.

Luna's friendship once saved Ferrer from a trial for heresy, and perhaps even smoothed the road to sainthood for him. A Latin document that I found in the Secret Archives, apparently written by an enemy of both Luna and Ferrer, tells a charming legend as evidence of horrible heresy. According to the writer, Pope Luna expressly and repeatedly ordered Nicolò Eymerici, Inquisitor of the Kingdom of Aragon, to send him the authentic processes made against the Pope's confessor, Brother Vincent, from which resulted juridical proof of his heresy: "One day at Eastertime, before a great multitude of people, in one of his sermons, he affirmed that Judas the traitor, after having sold Christ, and after Christ was condemned to die on the Cross, was moved by true and sincere penitence and asked to be allowed to go to him, to ask forgiveness for his treachery. But because of the press of the crowd following Christ to the Mount of Calvary, he was not able to reach him. And so in his heart he kept saying, 'As I cannot go to Christ with my feet, I will reach him with my soul, and in this way I will humbly ask his forgiveness.' So he went and hanged himself, and as soon as he died his soul floated to Mount Calvary, and asked and obtained the pardon of Christ. So when Christ ascended into heaven, the soul of Judas also was among the blessed, with the other elect."

On receiving this accusation, Pope Luna "made ashes of the process, so the fame of Vincent suffered no damage whatever, and his horrible heresy was destroyed by fire."

In the conclave that elected Pope Luna, all of the cardinals had taken an oath to resign if this were necessary for the unity of the Church. Soon after his election, a procession came to Avignon to ask Luna to keep his promise — five thousand men led by the lords of France and the king's brother. The Anonymous Florentine describes them with admiring disapproval: "This vainglory surpasses that of Oriental kingdoms; it is like something from another world." The French lords and the delegates of the University of Paris who accompanied them were urging both popes to resign so that the Church could start afresh with a new conclave. But: "The Sovereign Pontifex does not need your advice to govern the Church; the Vicar of Christ has no right to abdicate to please men or to secure his own peace. . . . The sovereign master of the universe has no accounts to render except to God."

Some of his cardinals rebelled; in 1398, the Avignon towers were besieged while actors staged a play about the Trojan War. Part of the palace was put to the torch with the wood that was intended for the kitchens and the ovens; the "strongest house in the world" could no longer be defended. Luna grew a white beard and escaped. Traveling on the Rhone in a small boat, and then by horseback — he was still an excellent horseman — he reached his friend, Louis II of Anjou, who asked for the cut-off beard and wrapped it in white linen as a sacred relic.

Luna, intending to establish his power in Rome, prepared a corsair fleet at Marseilles. The people of Genoa welcomed him with wild enthusiasm, but the Roman expedition failed; disease broke out among his soldiery and the sea drove his ships to Catalonia.

His friend King Martin of Aragon lent him the palace of the kings of Majorca at Perpignan; and there to the drill-field patio and the great audience hall came another procession, this one from the Council of Constance, and led by the Emperor Sigismund himself. With him were princes, ambassadors, clerics, all asking Luna to resign as the other popes had now done. Luna received them in the great hall of the palace, enthroned and wearing a red mantle and an ermine biretta. At the conference later he talked for seven hours: "You say I am a doubtful pope, but before that I was a cardinal, an undisputed cardinal of the Holy Church of God, because I received the investiture before the Schism. I am the only living cardinal from before the Schism. If, for you, all the popes that have been elected are doubtful, then all the cardinals they have appointed are doubtful. And as it is the cardinals who elect the Pope, I am the only authentic cardinal and therefore the only one who can elect an authentic pope." And now even Ferrer turned against him: "You are the true pope, but it is necessary that you resign." His powerful, devoted and generous friends, King Martin the Humane and Louis of Orleans, were dead. The emptiness of abandonment slowly surrounded him.

Luna had an ultimate refuge prepared: his own castle at Peñiscola, near Valencia. He knew that the king of Aragon would not attack him; blood was thicker than theology. As he waited on the beach to take ship, in an armchair that had been brought him, he refused to speak to the kneeling ambassadors who were begging him to remain and reconsider, except for a message to the king of Aragon: "Tell your king for me, 'You have sent me to the desert — I that made a king of you!'"

His last stronghold, his family palace of Peñiscola, was a castle with ogive windows, carved from the red rock, almost a part of the rock, surrounded by sun and sea, and rumored to be an ancient headquarters of the Templars — perhaps even one of the secret ports from which they sailed to unknown continents. "*Hic est arca Dei,*" he said. "Here is the ark of God." And here he lived for eight years, eating from tin dishes when he was alone, from golden ones when there were visitors, sitting on a terrace by the sea, and excommunicating his enemies.

The Council of Constance of 1414–1418, the greatest council since Nicaea, with its mitered bishops like fields of white tulips, had deposed him, and the old man met its Benedictine legates ("Here come the crows of the council!") in the great hall of Peñiscola. He wore the crown that Constantine had given to Pope Sylvester and that the popes of the Babylonian captivity had taken to Avignon. He heard their condemnations and he said, "The Church is not at Constance. The Church is here. Here is the ark of Noah."

In the human sense, what kind of man was Luna, aside from his courage and his obstinacy? A Secret Archives document of 1398, probably by Luna himself, tells of his generous treatment of prisoners in the siege of Avignon. An enemy force, carrying bags to hold the expected loot, had crept in through the sewers — connecting the kitchens with the Rhone had not been such a good idea after all — and had been captured. "He gave them food, in spite of his own followers having so little, ordered his own doctors to tend their wounds, and permitted some of them to leave the palace for necessary medical treatment."

Certainly he was capable of vindictiveness. (King Ferdinand of Aragon, dying in agony, received a bull of excommunication every day.) Yet he was tolerant beyond his times; he tried to bring the learned of Israel's Diaspora into the Church, though he appended some "or else" provisions if they refused to come; he sponsored Ferrer's mission to the heretics.

Always in his enemies' accusations was the charge of priesthood in the

old religion — "Pope of the Moon, Pope of the Sun, Heretic!" This was a
time when the sun-symbol still wakened memories of the *sol invictus* of
the legions, and of an astronomical religion older still; a generation later
San Bernardino of Siena was to be threatened with inquisition for his use
of a Christian mandala bordered with flames like those of the sun's corona. And it was a time when Joan of Arc could be burned as a witch.
(In fact, Margaret Murray says calmly that she *was* a witch.)

Along with the perhaps valid suggestions of his connection with the
old pre-Christian faith there were all the hysterical charges of medieval
demonology. The Council of Pisa brought five accusations against him.
His biographer Pillement summarizes them:

1. He had a strange indulgence toward heretics.
2. He had continuous traffic with spirits.
3. According to one testimony he always had at his service two
   demons kept in a little bag.
4. After he was elected pope he searched everywhere for books on
   magic, and found two in Spain and one with the Saracens.
5. To know the future and what was foretold of him, he was in the
   habit of putting one of these books under his pillow.

Even the Council seems to have had its doubts about the portable
demons, but it convicted him of "notorious and enormous crimes of extreme gravity."

When the Council of Constance excommunicated him it called him a
"dead branch" of the Church. But cut-off branches sometimes take root
again, and he still had many followers. It is in this period that a romantic
hero enters the story of Pope Luna — a rough soldier, a monk, a prophet.
John Carrier was a great friend of the Count d'Armagnac, who was lord
of that forested country. He became a disciple and legate of Pope Luna,
who created him Cardinal of Saint-Étienne. With a small group of faithful, the cardinal carried on an underground resistance against the decisions of the Council of Constance and against Rome. That this movement was strong enough to trouble the Church is shown by a Secret
Archives document among the records of the Council of Siena, held in the
year of Pope Luna's death. "This Holy Assembly, desiring to confirm the
sentence of condemnation on the damned memory of Pedro de Luna,
once, in his obedience, called Benedict XIII, orders to be condemned all
who are his followers, as well as those who receive them, have them as
guests, defend them, or help them with food and especially with medi-
cinal drugs and instruments of war."

At the death of Pedro de Luna, Benedict XIII, his cardinals, at the direction of the King of Aragon, had elected as pope the cardinal Giles Muñoz. Muñoz resigned after a short time. But John Carrier, the Cardinal of Saint-Étienne, who believed simony had been involved in Muñoz' election, went back to a castle near the Forest of Rouergue and alone elected, from among the people of the forest, a pope whose name he would not tell, as head of the new church. "This church was to be open to all, Jewish and Gentile, the humiliated and persecuted. It was to be a church without rites and without hierarchy, that did not need wealth nor luxury to exist, but only devotion. The man of the new church would no longer need penitence or expiation to enter the House of God."

So for the people of these regions there was still the problem of which pope to believe in — the Roman pope, the pope elected by the majority of Luna's cardinals (who was soon to resign), or Carrier's pope. Where could they go for advice in such a situation? The Count d'Armagnac decided to write to Joan of Arc, and he must have been speaking for many a bewildered Christian: "My very dear Lady, there are three contendants for the papacy. One lives in Rome, called Martin V, whom all Christian kings obey; one lives at Peñiscola. The third, no one knows where he lives, except the Cardinal of Saint-Étienne, John Carrier. In the name of Jesus Christ, please let me know which one is the true pope."

Joan wrote back that she was very busy with the war just now, but that when d'Armagnac heard she was in Paris he was to get in touch with her and she would go into the matter: "I am going to let you know which one you must believe, according to the advice of my sovereign lord, the king of all the world." The letter was used against her at her trial.

A pope was named by Carrier and his name was never given. Did this pope, in his turn, name cardinals *in pectore,* and did they elect a later pope? Is there still, perhaps, among the longshoremen of some French port or among the Knights of Malta, a pope of the line of Luna?

In studying the story of Pope Luna, the pope of the moon, Noah of the *arca Dei,* one is left with a feeling of unfulfillment that is not entirely due to the thought of the charismatic old man dying deserted in his fortress palace. Rather one regrets the play that Shakespeare never wrote: the story of a pope perhaps too closely connected with some very old religion; the story of a turncoat saint who deserted him as a matter of duty; the story of a rough soldier (a character so common in Shakespearean plays), to whom the pope turned when he was perhaps a little tired of saints, and who himself carried on the dream of the aged prince of Peñiscola.

The Great Schism of the West, lasting from 1378 to 1417, had its re-percussions on the papal archives, which went into schism along with the Church. When there were two popes, there were two curias, two chan-celleries, and two archives: the archives of the Roman Obedience and the archives of the Avignon Obedience. The popes of the Roman Obedi-ence accumulated records in Rome, while the popes of the Avignon Obe-dience maintained their own archives in Avignon.

When the Council of Pisa elected a third pope in 1409, and the other two popes refused to recognize the Council and its decisions, there were three popes, three curias, three chancelleries, and three archives. The separated archives, like the separated fragments of a starfish, continued to live and grow.

Probably the Roman archives were located in the Vatican, which was sacked in 1404 when a Roman mob under the leadership of the Colonna rose against Innocent VII. While the Pope fled to Viterbo, papal registers and other historically valuable manuscripts were thrown into the streets. Innocent's successor, Gregory XII, in the first year of his pontificate, sold five hundred golden florins' worth of archives documents, including some of the registers. When the Council of Constance forced him to renounce the tiara he took his papal acts and treasure, and those of his predeces-sors, to the Marches, of which he had been appointed rector. There he died, saying, "I have not understood the world, but then the world has not understood me." His archives were eventually found in Recanati, an old city of gloomy palaces and narrow faded streets.

Records accumulated at Avignon while the antipopes remained in resi-dence and their papal chancellery continued to function. But Pope Luna, fleeing from Avignon, took with him part of the archives and part of the papal library.

His library at Peñiscola was enormously valuable, including as it did the personal library of his friend, King Martin the Humane, king of Cata-lonia, Aragon, and Sicily. Martin, a man of great culture, had lost his only son. Although Martin was old, fat, and lacking in energy, Pope Luna arranged a marriage for him with a demoiselle of the court, "honest and beautiful," named Margherita de Luna. The king died after eating a duck that the queen's lady-in-waiting had fed with special foods to in-crease his sexual powers, and the five-hundred-year-old dynasty came to an end. King Martin's personal library, rich in manuscripts and in codices illuminated like jewels, came to his old friend, Pope Luna.

The Peñiscola archives increased through the activity of the papal chancellery — letters to the Pope of Rome, bulls of excommunication, bulls to the University of Paris, bulls or letters to the sovereigns.

After Luna's death his library passed into the possession of the French Cardinal de Foix, who had been one of the last cardinals to abandon him at Perpignan. De Foix took some archivistic material to Rome in 1429, but transferred the codices and manuscripts to a college he had founded in Toulouse. In 1680 they became part of the National Library of Paris.

Some archives had remained in Avignon, and the Holy See regarded this material as a detached part of the Roman papal archives. Its return to Rome was a very slow process. Some documents came back about the middle of the fifteenth century, and were stored in Castel Sant'Angelo. In 1566 a papal commissioner, Mario Lazzarini, one of whose descendants now serves the *Osservatore Romano,* was sent to Avignon to secure the remaining archives, but he encountered such strong local opposition that he had to leave five hundred manuscripts behind. Later in the century Gregory XIII had the Avignon *fondi* inventoried and transferred to Castel Sant'Angelo. Under Paul V Borghese, the cardinal-nephew Scipione Borghese brought back from the Apostolic Palace at Avignon some three hundred manuscript works that belonged to the old library of the popes — documents on theology, philosophy, pastoral care, canon law and history, some of them earlier than the thirteenth century. These were swallowed up by the Borghese family archives and did not reach the Vatican until 1892. The last section of the Avignon archives, according to the historian Battelli, came to Rome in 1784, when the Great Schism of the West had been over for three and a half centuries.

At present the Secret Archives has twenty-six volumes of documents relating to the Schism, called *De Schismate Urbani VI.* This collection contains for the most part reports on the election of Urban VI and on its consequences, gathered chiefly by the ambassadors of the king of Castile. Other important documents on the Schism are to be found scattered in other collections. That the Secret Archives have the documents of the antipopes as well as of the legitimate popes is not surprising, since the two, then the three Obediences were a purely administrative division of the Church, which considered itself always spiritually united even if, from a disciplinary point of view, it was dismembered.

The Archives Under the Angel

CELLINI, designing a large button for the pontifical cope, "represented God the Father sitting in a sort of free, easy attitude." This attitude was characteristic of the Renaissance. The Dark Ages, so like those earlier dark ages that had followed the breakup of the Bronze Age civilization, were ending, and mankind was feeling that elastic unreasonable joy that so often follows disasters.

Rome was still a medieval city. Censuses made for tax purposes in the early sixteenth century show that most Romans made a living from the land, farming, tending vineyards, herding buffalo. Handsome villas stood along the Tiber, but most of Rome's buildings were single-family dwellings of not more than three stories, often with a courtyard — the *atrium* of the old Romans — to provide for light and air. Cardinals, tradesmen, nobles, prostitutes, lived side by side on the same street, as they still do in this city that has been spared the monotony of zoning laws. And in the scanty population of Rome there were many foreigners — people who were here because the capital of the Church was here, and people dislodged by civil or religious strife or by personal misfortunes, who came to Rome as they did to England a little later.

But the city was changing. Money from the new prosperity was flowing into Rome and being spent on art and architecture and the pleasures of the world. As the Communist countries use forced savings to build their heavy industries, so the Church used the forced savings of its tax-collection system to make Rome a visual paradise. The Vatican was a vast workshop, not only for painters, architects, sculptors and builders, but for jewelers, leather workers, and designers of gardens and fountains.

Saint Peter's was fitted with bronze doors by Filarete, crowded with imperial scenes of an equestrian Christianity, the Renaissance counter-part of the new bronze doors by Manzù that show death in its varied forms, the lonely deaths of an alienated age.

The showplaces of the Vatican were being built in these years. The Borgia apartments were decorated with a somber richness relieved by the large fireplaces and by the windowseats where someone (one of the Borgia children, an idle young cardinal, a soldier?) scratched game-boards in the stone. The game must have been played with marbles; shallow depressions are hollowed out where the lines cross. Raphael and his pupils were painting the frescoes that have made "the Raphael Rooms" more his than the popes' ever since. And there were built the small and perfect places, like Nicholas V's private chapel with its carved crucifix — a Christ with his ribs showing — against a rose-red back-ground, and its inlaid figure of the sun and the solar corona on the floor.

Artists had a new self-confidence. Ghirlandaio was so sure of himself that he suggested that the walls of Florence be covered with his murals, thereby making it an open city. Michelangelo, when a cardinal protested a costly change in design, told him "Your job is to provide the money; leave the design to me."

The Secret Archives' volumes of *Diversa Cameralia,* Briefs, and *Introitus et Exitus* have been searched to find evidence of artistic expen-ditures, since these sometimes make it possible to tell how many artists worked on a picture, to authenticate paintings of unknown provenance, or to alert art experts to the existence of unknown works. We not only read of the conditions of employment under which Michelangelo, as Su-preme Architect, painted the *Last Judgment,* but that "to Urbino, boy assistant of Michelangelo, His Holiness gives sixty ducats as a reward for finishing the painting of the Sistine Chapel and for his fatigue in having to sweep the walls and ceilings," and that fifty ducats were paid "to Ra-phael the Florentine for the eyeglasses he has bought for His Holiness."

These Archives records must be used cautiously, since they tell only part of the story. The popes sometimes made direct payments to the artists from bags of gold that they or their attendants carried. At other times payments that went beyond the regular budget were taken care of by the bankers of the Roman Curia. Some receipts written in Raphael's handwriting acknowledging payment for his work have been found among the records of the Chigi bankers in Rome. In later times pay-ments may have been made by the Vatican Curia's Bank of the Holy Spirit, which now has branches throughout Italy. The records of this papal bank have been preserved in the Secret Archives, and examination of them may add considerably to our knowledge of art history.

Old statues were being recovered — that is, those that had escaped being made into lime to spread on the failing fields or to make mortar in earlier centuries. Rome had fallen so long ago that some of its ruins were already covered with soil, in that gradual rising of the ground level that goes on in densely inhabited areas. (I always think of archaeology and the seven cities of Troy when I walk through Anzio's green streets and see the garbage that its inhabitants cheerfully throw in the nearest convenient place.)

By the beginning of the sixteenth century, part of Nero's Domus Aurea had become a vineyard, and there a peasant found the *Laocoön,* already known to scholars from Pliny's description. All of Rome, cardinals and citizens and artists, came to see it, and it was drawn through the city on a cart pulled by flower-wreathed oxen to the Belvedere of the Vatican. The wealthy were collecting ancient art for their courtyards and galleries, and Rome was becoming the city of antique shops that it has been ever since. Enthusiasm for newly created sculpture came later. Isabella d'Este, receiving a gift of a Cupid by Michelangelo, wrote that "for a modern work, it is beyond words."

Much of the life and pageantry of Rome came from the cardinals. In winter they rode through the streets in their splendid cloaks that covered both horse and rider, using the animal's body warmth as an automatic heating device; in summer their hunting parties clattered through before daybreak, provoking a bull from Sixtus IV ordering that "cardinals abstain from clamorous hunting parties, with barking of dogs and sound of horns, which give maximum scandal to secular persons." He also recommended that cardinals should not ride with retinues of more than thirty persons, and that conviviums — get-togethers — be sober and modest.

The reminder was a necessary one, for at that time cardinals were often laymen, given the red hat for political reasons or for their shrewdness and practical ability that provided the tough integument which a spiritual organization needs to protect it from the outside world. To someone who protested that the newly appointed cardinals included "a number whom I would not have as servants in my kitchen or stable," Pius II said: "If this dignity is to be given only to those who really deserve it, we must look in Heaven for those on whom to confer the red hat. We however, as being but men, shall elect men, since it is not Heaven and angels but earth and men that we are to govern."

Often the cardinals were vowed to the service of the Church in childhood by families anxious for financial and political advantage, or simply to provide the child with a vocation and an income. Such children were dressed in ecclesiastical garments for a few hours a day and sent to a sacristy for training. The wonder is not that the cardinals were worldly, but that so many of these worldly cardinals later became excellent popes. Like secret agents, they became involved in their cover.

Foremost among the cardinals were the nephews of the pope. Those psychologists who believe that paternal instinct is confined to such creatures as penguins and timber wolves have not studied the history of the papacy. By the end of the sixteenth century the cardinal-nephew was a recognized part of the mechanism of the Church, serving as head of the Curia and of the pontifical secretariat and therefore in a position to grant or withhold privileges and favors. Papal portraits of the time often show the cardinal-nephews in the background, generally looking rather sinister.

There were practical reasons for the existence of the cardinal-nephews. Even Gregory Leti, who in 1627 published a book on *Papal Nepotism, or the True Relation of the Reasons Which Impel the Popes to Make Their Nephews Powerful,* and who had the distinction of having all of his books on the Index, thought there was something to be said for the system. For one thing, the pope needed to have someone near him that he could trust. The papacy had always been a dangerous job. In the first centuries of the Church, under Roman persecution, the popes came and were killed like priests of the Golden Bough. Later there was danger from invasions, from unfriendly emperors with political parties in Rome, and from men within the Church who wanted the papacy for themselves. When a pope died, rumors of poisoning were almost routine. Leti illustrates the fear in which the popes lived by telling of Sixtus V making a visit to the Convento dei Ss. Apostoli, where he found a monk sitting on the steps happily eating a bowl of beans. The Pope sat down and joined him, using a wooden spoon and asking for a second bowlful, and commented, "These beans will lengthen my life, for I can eat them without fear. Thank you, Lord, for letting a pope eat in peace for once."

Since the cardinal-nephew's high position in the socioeconomic system depended on the continued existence of the pope, the situation was opposite to the relation between a king and his heirs. And aside from contributing to the security of the pope, the cardinal-nephew brought a more youthful viewpoint to the Church. Popes tended to be old men, often splendid old men, but not always in touch with current ideas.

The situation was ideal for art and architecture. The cardinal-nephews wanted to leave monuments behind them, for their own glory and that of their family, but they never knew how long they had before the death of the old pope and the election of a new one ended their privileged status. There was a strong incentive to begin projects early and finish them quickly.

Many of the palaces in which wealthy foreigners now try to rent uncomfortable niches were erected in this period. Raffaelle Riario built the present Palace of the Chancellery perhaps in the same spot where the early Church's archives once stood. It is severe in style, but a humanist saw it with the imagination of a poet as "a city of towers going up to the sky; encrusted with precious marble, spangled with gems, the Golden House of Nero." The slums that surrounded it may have made it seem more splendid than it was.

The cardinals spent great sums on entertainments and theatricals, in which the players were often boys of the Roman aristocracy. At a banquet given by the cardinal-nephew Pietro Riario in the Piazza dei Ss. Apostoli in honor of Eleanor of Aragon, ballets were presented, a battle of centaurs was staged, ferocious wild animals were brought in, and women danced instead of merely being passively decorative as the custom of the time required. A child dressed in golden leaves passed among the audience, sprinkling the guests with scented water. The rumor was that the entertainment ended with a ballet danced by cardinals.

In the time of Leo X (1513–1521) Monsignor Cibo had Ariosto's *Suppositi* presented in his quarters at Castel Sant'Angelo; the scenery, which included a perspective view of the city of Ferrara, was by Raphael. There were lamps in the form of letters of the alphabet, each holding five torches, and the bearers arranged themselves so that the lighted letters spelled "Leo X, Pontifex Maximus." Ambassadors to the Vatican complained that no serious conversations could be held during the run of the performance.

The populace caught the spirit of the papal court, and when the head of Saint Andrew was brought to Italy from Constantinople by a royal fugitive, the streets were hung with tapestries and bright with flowers and torches. The journalist pope, Aeneas Sylvius, wrote: "All the decorations the houses possessed were lavished to adorn the streets for the sacred head. . . . At the crossroads and in all the streets altars sent clouds of smoke. Everywhere incense and branches of fragrant shrubs were burning. Whoever had in his house paintings or fine and lifelike statues displayed them outside in the portico before his door. In many places there were actors in costume; children represented angels. There was no instrument that might not be heard and praises of the Apostle filled the air."

« 1 »

It was the cardinal-nephew system that gave Pope Alexander Borgia (1492–1503) to the Church. Pope Luna had received the first of the ecclesiastical family of Borgias, Alfonso, into Holy Orders in Spain during the Schism. Alfonso later had his schismatic appointment legitimized and eventually became pope, as Saint Vincent Ferrer had predicted, taking the name of Calixtus III. Borgias that were still in Spain were brought to Rome and given papal appointments, and the twenty-five-year-old Rodrigo, the Pope's nephew, became a cardinal. At Calixtus' death, when the Spaniards were being driven from Rome, Rodrigo alone remained by his body to pray for him. Rodrigo was well regarded as a cardinal, though Pius II once found it necessary to rebuke him for attending a party at which "amorous seductions had no limit," and from which the male relatives of women guests had been excluded. But the Pope adds that "we always thought of you as a model of austerity and modesty." The charge that Rodrigo was syphilitic is probably untrue. The suggestion of infection could more plausibly be made in regard to his son Cesare, who often wore a black silk mask to cover a facial eruption.

When Innocent VIII died in 1492, Rodrigo, by now one of the richest of the cardinals and for thirty-five years vice-chancellor, secured enough votes to succeed him. He was sixty-one when he became pope, a man of commanding presence, handsome when the miter covered his tonsured head. With him to the papal court went his four children, illegitimately begotten but deeply loved.

Rodrigo (who took the name Alexander) was a hard-working pope; he reformed the prison system, allowed the people direct access to him, and firmly defended the faith while showing a kindly forbearance toward individual sinners. (For example, he took no punitive action against Savonarola until Savonarola excommunicated *him.*) The tendency of modern historians is partially to rehabilitate his reputation. Many of the documents that have been cited against him date from the pontificate of his enemy Julius II, and the contemporary diary by John Burckard found in the Secret Archives is largely a copy, with added interpolations. Two of his successors, Sixtus V and Urban VIII, listed him along with Saint Peter, Saint Sylvester and themselves as one of the five great popes of history.

No one has ever found the poison called cantarella (too slow in its action for the time of its administration to be fixed) that is part of the Borgia legend. And there is no real evidence of an incestuous relationship between Alexander and his daughter Lucrezia — a charge brought by a son-in-law who was being divorced for impotence.

The Pope's personal reputation has rested chiefly on his relations with three women — Vanozza Catanei, Lucrezia, and Julia Farnese. Historians are not sure who Vanozza was. One rumor said that she was a madam who ran a string of *hosteria,* but from what is directly known of her she was a devoted mother to Alexander's children and as good a wife as her irregular situation permitted her to be. Rodrigo Borgia's relationship with her was not unusual enough to cause any serious comment.

His daughter Lucrezia is described as being "of medium stature and fragile of aspect. Her face is quite long, her nose beautiful and good in profile. Her hair is like gold, her mouth is rather large, her teeth white, her throat well formed — in all her being happy and smiling." Another writer says: "She wore a white and golden dress with sleeves of gold brocade and a headdress of green veiling decorated with pearls. Cardinal Hippolito's eyes were glistening when he looked at her: she really is a seductive and gracious lady."

"Julia la Bella," "the Bride of Christ," as she has been derisively called, was the wife of Orsino Orsini. Her husband's mother was Adriana de Mila, a Spanish relative of the Pope, who acted as an aristocratic governess to the girls of the Borgia clan. At times Lucrezia stayed at the Convent of San Sisto Vecchio out on the Via Appia, a permissive institution where the nuns were allowed to wear low-necked dresses and flower crowns on Church holidays. As a young girl, however, she was entrusted to Adriana de Mila who, according to the Secret Archives, received many payments from the Pope.

Alexander had met Julia Farnese when she was not yet fifteen. We can see her best in a letter from her brother-in-law Lorenzo Pucci: "Today I went to Santa Maria in Portico to see Lady Julia. She had just washed her hair, and was sitting with Lady Lucrezia, daughter of our lord, and Madam Adriana near the fireplace. Lady Julia has put on weight and has become the most beautiful creature: in my presence she loosened her hair and then dressed it — it is the most beautiful I have ever seen and comes down to her feet."

For a time the Santa Maria in Portico household included Adriana, Lucrezia and her court, Julia Farnese, and Julia's baby daughter Laura, all of whom lived on terms of happy intimacy. Then the women left for Pesaro, the feudal domain of Lucrezia's husband Giovanni Sforza. It is in this period of the year 1494 that the letters found in the Secret Archives by the historian Pastor were written. From Adriana: "My only wish, and I can think of nothing else, is to be near Your Holiness and to live under Your Holiness's shadow . . . it seems to me that I am at the end of the world — *in capo del mondo* — here." And Julia writes: "If Your Holiness thinks we are spending our time in happiness here, he is greatly mistaken. I cannot enjoy pleasures far away from Your Holiness — where my treasure is, my heart is also." The letter ends begging the Pope to call them back "to kiss the desired feet." And the Pope writes to

Julia, who has described the beauty of Caterina Gonzaga to him: "Everyone tells me that when you were near her she seemed like a lamp near the sun . . ."

Alexander then ordered Adriana to return to Rome and bring Lucrezia and Julia with her. But Julia, having heard that her brother was dying, had left with Adriana to go to him. The Pope, furious at their failure to return, finally wrote to Julia, on stationery bearing the Greek initials of Jesus Christ, the famous *"Julia ingrata et perfida"* letter in which he reminds her of the many times she has sworn to "be at our command" and not *"accostare Orsino,"* her husband. (*Accostare*, like the term "live with" in English, can mean either "stay with" or "sleep with." Apparently languages sometimes find ambiguity convenient.) He continues, "Now you do the opposite and risk your life to go to Bassanello; and I think you are doing it to get pregnant again by that horse . . . Under pain of excommunication and eternal malediction We command you . . ."

Nothing has been found in the Secret Archives to prove that the Pope was the lover of Julia Farnese. That attraction and jealousy existed seems certain, but the Pope's letter may have been only that of an aged gallant who enjoyed the company of these women and who was accustomed to deferential admiration and obedience. In any case, emotions are not actions. One of the paradoxes of Christianity is that "as a man thinketh in his heart, so is he," yet there is an enormous gulf between the thought and the committed deed.

The Pope's essentially religious nature appears at the time of the sudden death of his son the Duke of Gandia, whose stabbed body was found in the Tiber. In his grief Alexander declared: "With joy we would give seven kingdoms to have him back in life. Because of our too great love for the world, God has punished us for our sins." He promised to abolish nepotism and to initiate reform, first of himself, and then of other officials of the Church.

Many popes had wanted to reform the Church and none had succeeded: it was too large and expensive an enterprise. A pope tired of *vanitas* was in the position of a modern man who has a large mortgaged house and an expensive family. He may read *Walden* or a life of Albert Schweitzer, but he has to keep the money coming in. Pope Borgia's proposed reform of himself and his Church came to nothing, but when the time for reform did arrive, forced on the Church from without, it was accomplished along the lines that he had indicated.

It is unlikely that Alexander Borgia will ever be completely cleared of the more serious charges against him; in popular thought he will always be *"sepultus in inferno."* But if he were cleared, most historians and novelists would lose interest in him, and the word Renaissance would be less rich in its implications.

The surprising thing about the Renaissance passion for classical Rome is that so slight an element of newness and discovery was involved. The ruins had been there all the time, Latin literature had been both studied and neglected, the aqueducts still marched southward to Naples across the *agro romano*. That the intellectual classes of Italy should suddenly awaken to what they had possessed all along is like a man's falling in love with his wife of twenty years. As with many things involving human behavior, one can only say that it happened.

The literati's idealization of ancient Rome centered on the Latin language. Inscriptions in ancient Latin were still visible everywhere, from the formal legends on imperial buildings to that earliest highway sign on a dangerous curve, *"Terribilis est locus iste."*

But the language itself had changed. Medieval Latin, the lingua franca of the Church, had become simpler — less attention was paid to endings, and its speech-rhythm was not the same; the phrases were shorter. When one looks at a passage written in medieval Latin he is often pleasantly surprised to find that he understands it. It served the purpose of communication — in fact it was far better than classical Latin for writing love songs in — but to the humanists it was a debased instrument. Their standard was the Latin of Cicero — Valla even wrote of "the saving grace, the sacrament, of the Latin speech." The prestige of classical Latin was shared by Greek. At the beginning of the Renaissance, most of Italy's scholars had, like Wodehouse's hero, been able to tell Latin from Greek at a glance. But humanist scholars had begun bringing Greek manuscripts back to Italy even before Constantinople fell and the eleventh Constantine died fighting on foot like a common soldier at the gates of his city. Greek literature, science, and philosophy were translated into Latin and made accessible to those who found the actual learning of Greek a counsel of perfection.

Interest in languages extended to Hebrew. The Avignon popes collected not only Latin and Greek but Hebrew manuscripts; Urban V had had a hundred and twenty of them. The papacy had long been tolerant of Jewish physicians, probably for the same reason that American conservative senators vote large sums for research in the degenerative diseases. But now there was an interest in Hebrew literature and philosophy as well, and study of the language itself made possible the scientific criticism of the Bible.

The students of classical language and culture, the humanists, faced the intellectual's usual problem of making a living in some way that would allow them to pursue their studies and plan the reshaping of society. Since the courts of the princes and the popes conducted their correspondence in Latin, it was there that they went in search of easy employment and the opportunity to influence the course of events. The Chancellery was considered the richest pasture of all.

Changes had taken place in the Chancellery at the beginning of the Renaissance; the secretariat had become a college and some of the secretaries had been given specialized duties. The post of *Secretarius Domesticus* or *Secretarius Intimus,* which later developed into that of Secretary of State, involved dealing with the pope's most secret correspondence and was usually given to a cardinal-nephew. But humanists often held the post of apostolic secretary, the official who sent and registered the papal briefs and prepared the notes for the popes' secret letters, often registering them as well. Beside their work on the popes' correspondence, they wrote solemn discourses, speeches, and panegyrics.

Under Innocent VIII the post was a privilege to be sold, and the Pope saw to it that there were an abundance of posts to sell; he had twenty-six papal secretaries and fifty-two *plumbatores* to attach and stamp the papal seals. The posts were expensive, but buying one was a good investment, since the documents handled by the apostolic secretary were loaded with charges. Forging papal bulls was sometimes another source of income. In 1489 Innocent found it necessary to hang two papal secretaries for this offense. Even Paul IV, in his youth, is said to have spent some time as a prisoner in Castel Sant'Angelo for forging a papal brief in the course of his work as an abbreviator for Pope Alexander Borgia.

While leading humanists worked as secretaries, beginners, the less gifted, and the less fortunate served as apostolic scribes or abbreviators, writing briefs and keeping records for the Curia. Platina and Poggio both worked for a time in the College of Abbreviators. Julius II even appointed Raphael as Scriptor of Briefs, "with all the duties, honoraria, and perquisites relative to the office." Fortunately for us, Raphael enjoyed the honoraria and perquisites but neglected the duties.

Pietro Bembo, one of the apostolic secretaries of Leo X, has, on the evidence of a register of briefs that he edited in Venice in 1535 and 1536, been credited with introducing humanistic style into the papal briefs. This register was written in classical style, and since the original was not in the papal archives it was assumed that the Venice edition was more or less a copy of it. Later, however, the original volume of briefs was discovered in the Ambrosiana Library. Comparison of this original volume with Bembo's later version clarified the matter. Bembo, as Leo X's employee, had dutifully compiled the briefs in the usual style of the papal chancellery. Later, on his own, he had done the job the way he thought it ought to be done, revising the Latin in the direction of greater elegance and "making it more harmonious with the spirit of the century."

The humanist who had the greatest effect on the Church was Lorenzo Valla, papal secretary under Nicholas V, who exposed the Donation of Constantine in his *De falso credita et mentita donatione Constantini declamatio.*

The Donation of Constantine is now regarded as a forgery, but it played its part in history as an argument for the secular authority of the Church. The Secret Archives has a very beautiful copy of this document, written in Greek and Latin on rich sheets of parchment in golden letters with illuminated initials, bound in red velvet and closed by two silver clasps.

According to medieval belief, the Emperor Constantine had been cured of leprosy by Pope Sylvester. In gratitude the emperor gave Sylvester temporal as well as spiritual authority over the western part of the empire. "We grant to the Holy Apostles, and in their name also to the blessed Sylvester our father, and to all the pontiffs his successors up to the end of the world, the Lateran Palace of our Empire and the diadem crown of our head." Provision was made for clerical dignity; "And we order that knights precede him in the procession, as for an emperor. And he must have the imperial scepter and the imperial insignia. In addition we bestow on the very reverend clergy of the Holy Roman Church the rights and honors of senators. Their horses will be adorned with splendid draperies, and like senators they may wear red boots." This dignity was to have a sound material basis, and "in order that the pontifical power should not decline, we grant to our father Sylvester and to his successors not only the Lateran Palace but the city of Rome and all the provinces of Italy and the Western regions."

To the modern mind it seems that this document could have been identified as questionable by the internal evidence alone — the touch about the red boots is pure Walter Mitty. Also, a hard-bitten emperor, "most prudent in every way," does not give away half his empire and the diadem crown of his head. Yet it conformed to the facts of Constantine's withdrawal to New Rome in the eastern half of his empire, and to the Church's eventual assumption of imperial obligations and authority in the power vacuum that followed. Another reason for the medieval belief in its authenticity was that it had been found both in the Vatican Secret Archives and in the records of the Eastern Empire.

It may be unduly harsh to speak of the Donation as a forgery. In the Middle Ages, replacing a lost or missing document was not regarded as a serious intellectual offense. And the new documents were sometimes revised in ways that, to their writers' minds, improved them. If you are rebuilding a house that has burnt down, why include all its architectural errors?

Valla used philological comparison to discredit the Donation, examining the text phrase by phrase and using close-thinking scientific methods that he had developed in his study of Roman jurisprudence. His critical sense was also turned on the Apostles' Creed, which the Apostles themselves were supposed to have originated, and on Jerome's translation of the Bible. He even found inconsistencies in the Bible itself. His principles of textual criticism were adopted by Erasmus, who also applied them to the text of the Bible, and they are being used today in the study of the Dead Sea Scrolls. Perhaps this has gone too far; I recently bought a paperback edition of the Psalms, in a new translation approved by the Church, and found that I am now expected to address the Lord as Yahweh.

The humanists even attained the papacy itself, in the persons of such popes as Pius II (1458–1464), who is better known by his own name of Aeneas Sylvius. Aeneas Sylvius was a conscientious and diligent pope who died preparing a crusade against the Turks and expounding the domino theory to an unhearing Europe, but he was a writer at heart. He left a series of memoirs that were not recognized as being of his own authorship until Pastor identified them in the nineteenth century. The manuscript was misleading in three ways: it was written in the third person, much of it was in other handwritings, and it was openly laudatory of the pope. Aeneas Sylvius had the humanists' sin of pride, but he wrote some of the best travel literature of the time. One sees the Roman countryside in these memoirs, for the Pope's progresses seem to have been a series of picnics. "There in a green meadow near a never-failing stream the people of Proceno had made shelters of brushwood in which they received their lord," and he gave audiences "sitting on the riverbank where it was greenest and grassiest."

As a journalist he knew the value of the specific fact, and wrote of Scotland: "It is a cold country where few things will grow. Below the ground is a sulphurous rock; which they dig for fuel. The houses are usually constructed without mortar, and in the country doorways are closed with oxhides. The men are short and brave; the women fair, charming, and easily won. Women think less of a kiss than in Italy of a touch of the hand. Their horses are all small and natural trotters. There is nothing the Scotch like better to hear than abuse of the English. At the winter solstice the day is not more than four hours long."

He was sometimes credulous and sometimes not. He eagerly investigated the tale of a tree that bore fruits which dropped into the water and changed into birds, but "he found that it was all a lie or if true, had been moved on to the Orcades Islands." He uses "it is said" about the village in Kent where children were reported to be born with tails because men from that village had cut off the tail of Thomas à Becket's horse. But when he escaped robbers in northern England after having refused the two young women who had hospitably accompanied him to "a chamber strewn with straw," intending to sleep with him, "Aeneas thought this was the reward of his continence."

The final effect of his autobiography on the reader is not one of lightness. Its character is given in Aeneas' own words ". . . for we ourselves who were both king and priest . . ." These are the memoirs of a monarch as well as of a pope, the work record of a sovereign who had to carry on wars, suppress insurrections, build fortresses, keep a hundred political factors in balance. This was an intellectual who was fully *engagé*.

There were Christian gentlemen among the humanists, but as a group they had the kind of pride that is the sin not of angels but of intellectuals, a pride maintained by ignoring all areas of excellence except their own. Their bitter controversies with each other, their greed for money, their pornographic writings, make one realize why Plato thought it advisable to exclude poets from his Republic. What was the eventual effectiveness of their work? Certainly they failed in bringing classical Latin to enduring life. Cut off from the people, humanistic Latin died when the Counter-Reformation destroyed the special environment that had allowed it to flourish, as a suburban lawn dies when it is not watered. But the flowering weeds of the vernacular had survival qualities.

Some historians have said that the humanists prepared the way for the Reformation. If they did it was indirectly; the policy of the humanists employed by the Church was not so much a boring from within as coexistence. And the philology and textual criticism of the humanists, including Christian humanists such as Erasmus, who hoped in this way to clarify Christian problems, prepared the way not for the Reformation but for our modern uncertainty. The humanists are sometimes credited with introducing appreciation of the joys of this earth; but these joys had been known all along. Most medieval men, like most modern men, lived by the pleasure-pain principle. They turned to the Church when they were dying and religion was the only game in town, but until then they were not unduly restricted by it. The ascetic principles of the Church were never generally accepted; throughout the Christian era there has been a vigorous underground movement of *Amor Mundi* that opposes

Contemptus Mundi in a fluid guerrilla warfare. In fact this lineup is not limited to the Christian countries; in the Communist world *Amor Mundi* is known as revisionism.

The attempt to revive paganism was hopeless from the start. The Roman gods simply were not good enough; they belonged on a lower round of the spiral. Attempts to combine Christianity and paganism were artificial and self-conscious; none of the classicism of the humanists had the vitality and integrity of the ancient mosaic in the Tomb of the Julii under Saint Peter's, where Christ is driving the horses of the sun, the attributes of Apollo. In one thing only had the humanists been fully successful — in bringing back the love of knowledge for its own sake. And in this, through the humanist popes, they founded the present Vatican Library.

Nicholas V (1447–1455) had emerged from poverty and the Florentine Renaissance to become pope — perhaps not as great a triumph to him as his discovery in Switzerland of the works of the great Christian heretic Tertullian. His love of books was not only intellectual but almost physical; he carried them and caressed them as Petrarch's illiterate old servant had done. He had the surviving volumes of the old library of the popes that were still at the Lateran and in the Confession of Saint Peter brought to his quarters at the Vatican. Eager for new books, he acquired a stable of humanists, caring nothing for their morality, their religion, or even their loyalty to himself. He paid them lavishly, hustled them out of Rome whenever plague threatened, and sent them all over Europe looking for ancient manuscripts.

But the library still lacked an adequate physical plant. It was Sixtus IV (1471–1484) who provided it with its own establishment under the Borgia Apartments, on the ground floor of the new palace that he had built between the Courtyard of the Pappagallo — the Parrot — and that of the Belvedere. Until recently the site of this library, with the delicate frescoes of Domenico and David Ghirlandaio faded to shadows, was the storage-place called Floreria Apostolica, full of old picture frames, carpets, and armchairs. The frescoes have now been restored and the area fitted up for meetings of the Synod of Bishops.

The library was large; an inventory compiled in 1484, the year of Sixtus IV's death, lists over thirty-five hundred volumes, about a third of them in Greek. Latin and Greek works were kept in separate rooms as had been done in the very early Church and the libraries of secular Rome. Sixtus' library had four rooms corresponding to its four sections: the common or Latin, the Greek, the secret (including heretic and pornographic books), later called the *parva secreta,* and the pontifical, later called the *magna secreta,* which contained the registers of the popes, many original manuscripts, and more than two thousand deeds and diplomas. And somewhere in the library, probably on the tops of the bookcases and closets, were placed the tools and toys of the new age, astronomical and geographical instruments, "for pleasure to the eyes and for their practical utility."

When the library was completed, set in order, and decorated, the humanist Platina, who had been imprisoned by Paul II for his "splendid invective," was appointed as its first prefect. Melozzo da Forlì's fresco, now in the Vatican Pinacoteca, shows Platina, a handsome white-haired man with a strong intelligent face, kneeling to receive from Pope Sixtus IV the keys that symbolized his appointment as Prefect of the Library.

Platina's learning was as impressive as his appearance; the dazzled English traveler Robert Flemmynge, Dean of Lincoln, wrote in free verse: "Praise to Bartholomew Platina, the glory of his native city Cremona, richly blest by both nature and learning. Blest therefore be both place and guardian: place because its charge is given to a great man." The Pope opened the library to scholars, and Flemmynge wrote: "The most eager of authors will there discover his old friends, and spend there his days and nights among flowing discourses sweeter than honey."

The Church had always been generous in lending its codices, but under Sixtus IV the papal library resembled a modern library, and even the most precious codices went out on loan. To borrow a book one had to sign for it, and we still have some of these early registers of loans. Apparently getting books back has always been a problem, for the series begins: "No matter who you are who write your name here because you have taken books of the Vatican Library on loan, know that you will incur His Holiness' indignation and execration if you do not give them back when they are due. This Platina, Librarian of His Holiness, who is in charge of this important office, states to you, the last day of February of the year 1475." Even the prefect himself signed for the books that he took from the library. "I Platina, have taken for my personal use the *De Republica* of Plato, in parchment. The first day of April, 1475 . . . I have given it back." In one case the borrower apparently forgot to sign, for the note is in Platina's handwriting: "Signor Domenico della Rovere, His Holiness' chamberlain, has taken (on loan), a large breviary, bound in red leather, the last of February." Below it is "As you say, Platina," signed *Domenico della Rovere, Secret Chamberlain.* Then later, "I have given it back. 24 May."

Other names on the registers tell us something of the reading interests of personages of the papal court. One entry reads: "I, the very reverend Signor Giovanni dei Mellini, Bishop of Urbino, have received on loan the

Dialogues of Saint Gregory, in parchment, bound in red, April 13, 1475. It is a small volume." Later Demetrio, the library custodian, writes that he has received the book back on December 13th, and that it is indeed in parchment and red. The Bishop of Arbe borrows more heavily — five volumes of Greek books and two volumes of Diodorus Siculus in paper, the first bound in red leather and the second in black, but he says, "I will give these back as soon as Signor Librarian asks me." Books on poetry, archaeology, and the natural sciences were taken out by Angelo Colocci, the humanist book dealer who founded the poets' Academy of the Orchards in his own villa. Much of his fine personal library now belongs to the Vatican.

Here too are the names of Girolamo Aleander, the friend of Erasmus, who was sent to Germany to oppose the Lutheran heresy, and who was to be, like Platina, librarian of the pontifical library; of the humanist Pietro Bembo, later secretary to Leo X; of John Burckard, master of ceremonies under Alexander VI, whose diary contains derogatory statements, perhaps interpolated, about the Borgia pope; and of a cardinal who was to be pope himself, Alexander Farnese, the brother of Julia la Bella and called the Petticoat Cardinal. The Romans said that he had created the three most beautiful things in the city, the *Chiesa del Gesu,* the Farnese Palace, and his daughter Clelia.

Some books were fastened to the table with iron chains and had to be loosed before they could be borrowed, and certain manuscripts could not be taken out unless some valuable object — money, silver plate, a codex — was left in pawn. But neither Platina's precautions, nor the pope's threatened indignation and execration, nor the exalted rank of the library's patrons prevented extensive pilfering of books and manuscripts.

Over a hundred years later the next Sixtus (1585–1590) erected a new library building, with spacious rooms and palmlike pillars, straight across the long rectangular Court of the Belvedere. This area of fountains and statues and formal gardens was now cut in two, further marring Bramante's plan. Those who regretted the lost integrity of the court were more right than they realized. Only one end of this mutilated section is still a garden — the small patio near the Secret Archives. The greater part is a paved parking lot, once used by the limousines of the cardinals but now crowded with the Fiats of Vatican employees.

When the English diarist John Evelyn visited the Library in 1645, he described it as "the most nobly built, furnished, and beautified in the world; ample, stately, light, and cheerful, looking into a most pleasant garden." Much of this is still true.

The ceilings and walls of Sixtus V's library are so covered with bright paintings that when one walks into it he has a sudden feeling that *all* of

Grand Central Station has been turned over to Eastman Kodak. Then he notices that the pictures center around books — Tarquinius Superbus and the books of the Sybil, Hebrew scholars acting as consultants at the Library of Alexandria, Xerxes' books being packed up for shipping as a war indemnity, Moses giving the Book of the Law to the Levites, and the bad-guys books of the Arians being burned. The contents of the library are, as Evelyn said, "all shut up in presses of wainscot, and not exposed on shelves to the naked eye, nor are the most precious mixed amongst the more ordinary."

Sixtus V's library building had to be large, for the library had grown rapidly, and by now printed books in quantity were joining the hand-written manuscripts of the old archives-library, and parchment had given way to the cheaper, more homogeneous paper. It was an omen for the future that the earliest things to be printed had included not only a psalter and a Gutenberg Bible but an astronomical calendar and forms for granting indulgences.

The archives had space in the Library, but more and safer space was needed. In the latter part of the fifteenth century Sixtus IV had the most valuable documents of the Church, such as the imperial diplomas, taken to Castel Sant'Angelo, the great fortress at the bend of the river near the Vatican, that had once been Hadrian's tomb. It had long been the custom for the popes to keep such documents either in places thought to be safe for religious reasons, such as the Confession of Saint Peter, or in strongly defended places like the Turris Chartularia. Here in Castel Sant' Angelo the two factors of safety were combined, for it was a fortress protected by the sword of Michael the Archangel.

The top of the structure, that had once held a small circular grove surrounding an equestrian statue of Hadrian and his horses, was now built over with crenellated towers, and the high sunny terraces held cannon, piles of stone cannonballs, and the huge horizontal bows of the catapults. War supplies could easily be taken to the terraces, for inside the circular walls of the castle Hadrian had built a great helicoid ramp, halfway between a ramp and a stair — the steps are very wide and slope a little — that rises at so slight an angle that a chariot or a wagon could be driven along it; it is less a ramp than a road.

The archives were placed in the circular room above Castel Sant'Angelo's Hall of Justice, at the top of the castle, just beneath the statue of the angel. At first they were kept in sacks of various colors, and the sacks of archives were stored in great iron trunks along with the papal treasure. Four of these trunks are still in the circular room of Castel Sant' Angelo. Empty now of both documents and treasure, they are of heavy wood covered with metal. The largest, the size of a small trailer, apparently was not intended to be moved, but served as a safe rather than a trunk. The two medium-sized ones (which are larger than any modern trunk) have rings on the outside through which a rope or steel bar could be passed for carrying purposes. They locked with four keys. The circular room has only one small window, and is closed by two doors of heavy wood faced with metal.

At the time of Paul III (1534–1549) walnut cupboards, exquisitely decorated by Sangallo, were built in the same room to hold the archives. Apparently the storage wall was not, after all, an invention of the Americans. Near it is a larger, well-lighted, fireplace-warmed room that was used as a library or study room.

The move to Castel Sant'Angelo was only a change of location; these archives, like those still in the library, were in Platina's custody. At first the Sant'Angelo archives were only a small nucleus made up of the most valuable documents. But as time went on they increased, and at the end of the century the archives of Avignon, finally brought back to Rome, were placed with them. As they became a distinct archives in their own right they came to be called the Archivum Arcis, and had their own prefect and their own inventories.

Castel Sant'Angelo was a place of security not only for the archives but for the popes. Alexander Borgia had built an escape route from the Vatican to the castle, a passage on the top of a bridge that has the look of a tunnel in the sky. Here in the Vatican fortress are exquisite papal apartments — a bathroom heated by warm air circulating through its hollow walls, and rooms with such names as the Room of Cupid and Psyche, the Pauline Hall of the Council, the Room of Apollo. In the salons Europa rides the Jupiter-bull across the ceiling, a satyr pulls the girdle from a nymph, Apollo cuts the male organ from an impotent man and gives it to a woman; but the style of painting is such that these figures have an elegant formality.

It was a January day when I last visited Castel Sant'Angelo; the vines on the terraces were dry and the tubbed trees dormant. Yet I could see what the walks and terraces overlooking the city must be in the summer — hanging gardens of Babylon, a place for lovers.

There is a pleasant little snack bar opening off the terrace, where I stopped for coffee. I heard its manager talking to one of the guards: ". . . the first customer this morning. Except for a foreigner that came in and asked for *due Nazionali*. I gave him two packs and he said no, he meant two *cigarettes*. I told him we didn't sell them that way, then, well,

I *gave* him two. That's what business is like when the tourists are gone."
On the way out I passed a table on the terrace where a bearded young
man sat smoking and writing. In front of him was the second cigarette
and a pile of scribbled pages weighted down with a book — new archives in the making.

X V

Greater than Europe and Africa

IT is strange that the Queen of Sheba should have come down to us as a sex goddess, for what the Biblical writers thought worth mentioning about her was her intellectuality. They tell us that when she came to Jerusalem, to the city where Solomon had made silver to be as stones and the cedars like sycamores in the vale for abundance, it was to prove him with hard questions. Another legend, or the rumor of a legend, repeats this theme of questing intelligence, and forms a tenuous but fascinating tie between the library-archives of the Church and the discovery of America.

One of Columbus' officers, the able but rebellious Martín Alonso Pinzón, captain of the *Pinta*, who had helped fit out the ships and recruit seamen for the enterprise, later felt that his services had been inadequately recognized and rewarded. In 1515, nine years after Columbus' death, an inquest was held as part of the Pinzóns' suit against the Columbus family. In the course of it, Pinzón's son swore that, on a visit he and his father had made to Rome, his father had called on a friend who was a cosmographer at the Vatican Library. This friend had lent him a Hebrew document from the papal library which said that in Solomon's time it was believed that the Queen of Sheba had sailed out of the Mediterranean into the Atlantic and there, "ninety-five degrees to the westward, by an easy passage," she had found a land called Sypanso, which Pinzón took to be Japan, "fertile and abundant and whose extent surpassed Africa and Europe." The Pinzóns claimed that they themselves had intended to make this voyage, and that Columbus, despondent at the king's failure to finance his project, had taken heart after learning of this document. Witnesses were found to confirm the testimony.

The story is not intrinsically impossible, though it seems so because it is so attractive. The popes had been collecting Hebrew codices since Avignon times, and while the account of a voyage a quarter of the way around the world is an odd thing to find in the records of a desert people, there is, when one comes to think of it, a surprising frequency of reference to the sea and its islands in Biblical writings. A reflection of desert man's longing for water, or an unacknowledged heritage from the Phoenicians?

The document, if it existed, has disappeared. It may be in one of the bundles of unclassified documents in the Miscellanea, it may have been destroyed in the Sack of Rome in the next century, or the cosmographer friend may simply have given it to Pinzón, who would have had no trouble getting it retranslated in a Spain from which Jews had not yet been evicted. The fact that Columbus took with him on his first voyage an interpreter who was a converted Jew and skilled in Hebrew, though he knew only a little Arabic, suggests that he may have attached importance to the legend. A fragment of supporting evidence comes from paleobotany: the same variety of cotton was being cultivated both in Peru and in the Indus Valley in 2500 B.C. Since cottonseed is killed by sea water, this may be an indication of intercontinental contact, somewhere back in that megalithic age that seems less and less primitive the more we learn about it.

The great names of the past crowded around the discovery of America, as ancient writings, newly printed, were searched for evidence and opinion. Columbus studied Ptolemy, Aristotle, Pliny. He had a copy of Pope Aeneas Sylvius' *Historia Rerum Ubique Gestarum;* the Pope had modestly planned a universal history and geography, and had completed the section on Asia. He read Esdras, the prophet of the Apocrypha, and was inclined to believe him because Saint Ambrose and Saint Augustine had thought highly of him. Also, Esdras told Columbus what he wanted to hear; his estimate of the earth's relative proportion of land and water made it seem that the Atlantic would be conveniently narrow. Even Prince Henry the Navigator, in his research institute at Sagres, found some of his inspiration and motivation in legend. The route around Africa was to lead not only to the prosperity of Oriental trade but to the kingdom of Prester John and to the gardens at the high point of the world.

Henry was a prince of the blood, lord of the province of the Algarve, and Grand Master of the Order of the Cross of Christ, which had inherited much of the property and personnel of the Templars. Perhaps it had inherited some of their secrets as well; one thinks again of the rumor of the Templars' secret ports and their voyages to unknown continents. But the prince's methods were those of the modern world. He used a systems approach; it was not better charts, or better ships, or better methods of navigation that he needed, but all of them together.

There is little left now of the academy at the Sacred Rock of Sagres except for the great wind-rose compass made of small stones lying on the ground. Like the circles of tent-stones that one sees on prehistoric camp-grounds, it has survived because its parts have no value. Yet this place was the Cape Canaveral of its time, a center for geographers, mathematicians, astronomers, naval architects. Henry's research staff recovered some of what the Phoenicians and the Arabs had known about celestial navigation — and of what the desert saints had known, crossing the sands between one monastery and another in the cool night.

Sagres was under strict security during the time of Prince Henry; the carrying out of its plans would mean financial ruin to many cities. And men of the time were close enough to classical days to remember that Rome had conquered Carthage by making a hundred copies of a wrecked Carthagian ship. For that reason no one knows just what voyages were made during the life of the Navigator and in the generation that passed between his death and the discovery of America by Columbus.

One day of April in the year 1493 the Spanish prelate Giovanni Sánchez — one of the many Spaniards at the Borgia court — told his friend Giuliano Dati, parish priest of Santa Dorotea in Trastevere, that the Vatican had just received an important report from Spain, saying that a Genovese navigator named Christopher Columbus had discovered islands in the western sea, rich and marvelous islands where gold was plentiful.

This report was a copy of the letter that Christopher Columbus, when he returned from his first voyage the previous month, had sent to the sovereigns of Spain, and which they in their turn had transmitted to the Holy See, with a request for juridical recognition of their new possessions.

Giuliano Dati was a highly regarded poet, the author of a pageant of the Passion that had been enacted in the Colosseum. He asked permission to read this report, was fascinated by it, and decided to turn it into a long *ottava rima* poem entitled *La Lettera dell'Isole che ha trovato nuovamente il Re di Spagna*. The poem immediately became a best seller. Written in Italian instead of Latin, it was an answer to the public's excited curiosity about the new lands. Two editions came out in two successive days.

Dati dedicates his poem to "Almighty God, who gives me grace to sing," and reminds Him of the heroes of the past; of Ptolemy and of the kings and consuls of Rome; of Alexander VI Borgia, the Spanish pope, "just in judgment, wholly human"; of Ferdinand, "most Christian king of Christians," who "never tired of mangling traitor Jews"; and of Isabella, whom he describes with a beautiful word that cannot be translated: "*Honesta donna, savia, e peregrina*"— honest, wise and unusual, wandering from the norm, a traveler who does not follow common ways.

With the formalities out of the way, Dati returns to Columbus' appearance before the King of Spain,

> *Saying to him, "My Lord, I want to search*
> *For lands the ancients could not find, and hope*
> *To take them without war,*
> *If you provide the means and I the person.*
> *For fortune often gives, as a free gift*
> *Much for a little price . . .*
> *The King refused him, smiling, but at last*
> *Gave him a ship and two fair caravels.*
>
> *Who travels on the sea is never safe*
> *But fighting always water and the wind.*
> *Reward and tribute often can be lost,*
> *And no help then in saying "I regret."*
> *But as it pleased the Lord, who does not err,*
> *In three and thirty days he reached the land.*

Dati's poem continues:

> *His armed men searched for ambush; there was none.*
> *Three days they traveled through the lands they found,*
> *And saw no house, no human.*

This last stanza is a little out of place, as it was in Columbus' Letter to the Sovereigns, and a little inaccurate. Columbus' men had been met by natives when they landed, and Columbus, rapidly realizing that his Hebrew and Arabic interpreter would be of slight use, kidnapped a few of them and started them on a total-immersion course in Spanish. And here is one of the little mysteries of the first voyage, for the natives, impressed by the Spaniards' appearance and clothing and by their ships, called them "the men from the heavens." Men from the sky had come to them before, they said, to teach them not to make war on each other.

Columbus later remarked with some surprise that they still regarded him as a man from the sky after several weeks of close association in the crowded quarters of shipboard, *"sempre a mangiare, a bere e a dormire accanto a me . . ."* Whatever their men from the sky had been, they had been flesh and blood.

Columbus names the islands, as they are discovered, after his superiors in strict order of rank:

> *The first-found isle I called San Salvador,*
> *The second was Conception, honoring Mary.*
> *The third one Ferdinanda, named for you.*
> *Fourth, Isabella for the honored Queen.*
> *The fifth Giovanna . . .*

for the girl who was to be the Mad Queen Joan.

Columbus had gone in search of gold and trade and dominion, but of none of these does he write with the enthusiasm that he shows in describing the natural beauty of the new land and the goodness of its people. The island country was

> *. . . of various fruits adorned.*
> (E' dotata di fructe molte e varie.)

Perhaps he was influenced by Esdras' account of the third day of creation, but more likely no literary influence was necessary; Columbus writes like a convert to California.

> *Great rivers and maximum mountains,*
> *Trees, fountains, birds, things never seen till now,*
> *My mind, Lord, weeps for joy.*
> *Tall pines that touch the sky,*
> *And nightingales, and cotton.*
> *And in November there are trees that flower*
> *Like May upon the mountain and the plain;*
> *Spices and precious metals in excess,*
> *And little rivers that bring with them gold.*

He sees the future of the new country, its plains where walled cities could be built, its wide cultivatable lands, its ports for commerce.

> *Water and space are here,*
> *In a land no brush could paint.*

And he writes with an almost fatherly pride of the people of the new lands:

> *Although they are nude they are clean.*
> *I cannot tell you of their pleasantness.*
> *They live in peace together, do no wrong.*

There was an advantage in the fact that they were not already Christian, for this meant that they could be taken into slavery. The enslavement of fellow Christians was forbidden.

> *They do not worship planets, sun or moon*
> *But raise their minds up wholly to the sky.*
> *Women and men are pious in behaviour;*
> *Each one already is inclined to believe.*

"Fifty armed men," Columbus remarked in the Letter to the Sovereigns, "could subdue them, and make them do all you wish." But these intimations of imperialism existed along with an ardent love for the new world and its people.

> *Who has not seen these islands and their wealth,*
> *Their trees, their men and women,*
> *Who never leaves the circle of his walls,*
> *Can never give right praise unto the Lord*
> *Not having seen the things that He has made.*

But Columbus was too good a letter writer to paint only a peaceful picture. He has not much to report in the way of monsters — he has heard of a tribe of people without hair, and of a tribe of people with tails; nothing really worth mentioning. But he tells the king about the cannibals who live on the fringes of his paradisal people's territory, and about the island of the Amazons:

> *An isle of women, where they live alone,*
> *Though lovers come and use them;*
> *They have no women's arts; they draw the bow . . .*

The rumor of the Amazons, probably taken from ancient literature, was to appear again and again in the reports of soldiers and missionaries. As late as 1964 a Peruvian civil-military expedition that included a Franciscan friar reported discovering a tribe of giant men and women;

the women, skillful with the bow, were said to resemble the description of the ancient Amazons.

Columbus' account of the Indians, gentle, naked and beautiful, enchanted Europe: the myth of the Golden Age, the Scriptural account of the Garden of Eden, seemed to have come to life. Pope Alexander Borgia himself must have been deeply impressed by the report he had received, for he ordered the king of Spain to dispatch "to the said mainlands and islands learned and honest men, fearful of God, to instruct the inhabitants and citizens of these lands in the Catholic faith and in good customs." In the same bull he granted the king of Spain that part of the world west of the famous Line of Demarcation. "We grant those islands and lands with all dominions, cities and places to you and your heirs and successors the kings of Castile." When Rodrigo Borgia had become Pope he had taken the name of Alexander, the conqueror of the world. This must have seemed presumptuous even in those days, and yet he lived to cut the world in two. If he had been an Italian pope he might have been less inclusive, and have left room for the Papal States to take direct action in the New World. As it was, the papacy had responsibility without authority in American spiritual matters. It issued edicts; Spain followed them or not, as it liked. Even the assignments of priests were made by the Council of the Indies that was set up in 1524.

Columbus' gentle Arawak, taken into slavery, escaped the situation by dying, and Father Bartolomé de Las Casas, hoping to save them from the cruelty of the Spaniards, urged the importation of Negroes. The Portuguese slave trade had already begun with the importation of Negroes from the African colonies, particularly Guinea. Some were kept in Portugal — critics of modern Britain's liberal immigration policy say that "England Portugalizes itself"— and others sold to Spain.

It may have been the treatment of the Arawak by Columbus and his men that led the papacy to rethink the matter of slavery. Columbus' real admiration for the Indians had come into conflict with another and stronger motive: the need to produce for his employer, the king of Spain. When the overworked Indians could not find gold enough, shiploads of them were sent to Spain as slaves: two hundred died on the way.

The early Christians had regarded slavery as one of the things that were Caesar's, of little real importance since there was "neither bond nor free in Christ Jesus." The Church was not entirely consistent in this matter, since no slave could be a priest, but this may have been due to a fear of conflicting lines of authority. At the time of the discovery of America, and for a long time afterward, there were slaves in Rome itself. They were not used for heavy work, nor were they exploited. Rather they were a status symbol, an indication of the wealth of a family. Women slaves often formed the little harem of the lord. The Christian noblemen of the middle and early modern ages thought that less sin was involved in having two or three Negro or Saracen slaves as lovers, since only those who had been baptized could be sinners. In other words, it was a form of chivalric self-abnegation.

It was that unexpected reformer, Paul III (1534–1549), who brought the ethical sense of the Church to bear on the subject of slavery. An old Roman law provided that a slave who could reach the Campidoglio and claim liberty became both free and a Roman citizen; Paul confirmed it by papal authority. He also, at the urging of Las Casas, ordered a study in comparative anthropology. The university science of the day, led by Sepúlveda and his colleagues at Salamanca and Oxford, held that Indians were not fully human, and therefore not possessed of the natural rights ordinarily granted to humans.

Paul III collected information from Jesuit, Franciscan, and Dominican missionaries all over the world. The consensus was that the non-European races were fully human, and the Pope, in his encyclical *Pastorale officium* of May 29, 1537, forbade the enslavement of Indians, regardless of whether or not they were Christians. "These Indians, although they live outside the bosom of the Church, nevertheless have not been, nor are they to be, deprived of their freedom or of ownership of their own possessions, since they are human beings and, consequently, capable of faith and salvation." The following month the Pope declared against all forms of slavery, stating that "people of color" also were "*veri homines*" — true men — and affirming that they had the same rights and the same duties, civil and religious, as Europeans. But it was already too late; slavery was part of the new economy, and American gold was coming to Europe. Tradition says that the first of it, which Columbus had acquired by more or less innocent trading, had been sent to Alexander Borgia along with a copy of the Letter to the Sovereigns, and that he used it to gild the ceiling of Santa Maria Maggiore. In Spain, the effect of the new wealth was toxic; there was no need now to develop a better technology or a modern economic system.

The real gold of the Indies, of the Americas, was green. From the new continents came maize, the potato, the tomato, and legumes to ease the protein starvation of the poor. The new varieties of beans must also have eased the fasting of the clergy — the kind they had before were of the cattle-food type. The American plants could have gone far toward abolishing poverty if population had been stable; as it was they made possible the Industrial Revolution and the new age of urbanization, by enabling a smaller fraction of the population to provide food for the rest.

And in America, "now all is done, save what shall have no end"— the irreversible processes that had been set in motion, the blending of races, of cultures, of religions. A third of the Church's people are presently in Latin America, and a tenth of its priests. Poverty is approaching critical mass — and so far the Food and Agriculture Organization, in its Roman palace, has not been able to give back to the New World what it once gave to us.

The *Avvisi* and the Men Illicitly Curious

ANY member of a military or diplomatic service, business corporation, or other large institution knows how essential it is to listen to gossip and rumor. A person who knows only facts is unable to plan for the future, to prepare alternative courses of action, or to protect himself against the changing whims of authority. In the early modern age, Church personnel, including the nuncios, the merchants and bankers, and the ruling aristocracy felt this need for knowing not only the facts but the gossip and rumor of their times. The need was met by the *avvisi*, or newsletters — "advices" as to what was happening.

Some *avvisi* were legitimate. For example, the banking establishment of the Fuggers required its employees to include, with each business letter, a commentary on events and conditions in the place from which the letter was written. Reports sent by ambassadors, nuncios and their agents were often written as *avvisi*. Even some Jesuit reports of general interest were called *avvisi*, though the news in them might be of the footprints of Saint Thomas on the shore of a Brazilian river, often washed out by the water but always appearing again, or of strange faiths disturbingly like the Jesuits' own.

However, these were not periodicals like the true *avvisi*, the anonymous, illicit, fascinating gossip columns that dealt with everything from troop movements to the follies of the great. When they began, in Italy just before the middle of the sixteenth century, they were hand-written and folded in notebook form. By 1565 printed *avvisi* were appearing, and Venice, a meeting-point between East and West, became a center of this fly-by-night publishing industry. Most of these *avvisi* were written in Italian, a language then known all over Europe.

The authors of the *avvisi* were the *menanti*, forerunners of modern journalists, who gathered material where they could and who had their agents or sources in many a Church and government office. These "persons who usually speak truth" have become the "usually reliable sources" of present-day newspaper articles. It is not clear why the early journalists were called *menanti*. One explanation is that they were leaders of opinion, but this may stem from retroactive vocational pride. Others also derive the name from medieval Latin, but say that *menante* meant intriguer — one who led, but led astray.

Some of the *menanti* were hired by bankers, businessmen and princes to provide them with information; there were even agents, like literary agents, who were instructed to keep on the lookout for *menanti* with good sources. There was always danger that a *menante* without a good lead story might make up something rather than send no *avviso* at all. Even today in Florence, when people buy a newspaper, they sometimes say, "Give me sixty lire's worth of lies." The *menanti* who were in the service of princes were paid two or three gold *scudi* a month. Others, with poorer sources, were paid only one *scudo* a month, and to augment their income sold their *avvisi* on the streets.

These newsletters were extremely popular; everyone condemned them and everyone read them, including the cardinals. Perhaps especially the cardinals, for they could read with professional interest such items as this one regarding Pope Paul IV: "On Monday a consistory was held. His Holiness, in order to arrange the rooms of the Palace to his own liking, has decided to open the hall where the Swiss Guard is stationed, and the one next to it, and to make a door with a window on each side in the Constantine room. The valuable paintings done by the hand of Raphael, showing Constantine and Maxentius, will be lost. In the opened rooms the Pope plans to make hanging gardens. Cardinal Caraffa, speaking for other cardinals as well, tried to deter the Pope from his decision, but he went into a terrible rage shouting that they, his own nephews, wanted to take every comfort away from him, and that they were not nephews but enemies and traitors. He raised his stick to strike them but could not reach them . . ." Senility, the cardinals must have thought; there would be a conclave soon.

But an *avviso* of the following month read: "The Pope went to the Theatine Brothers at San Silvestro the other day, for a change of air and regimen. It seems that he is feeling very well. It is thought that if he continues to live a regular life, he may live seven years more, as was prophesied. It is thought that on Monday he will return to the Palazzo, having deceived the whole world that thought him more dead than alive . . ." But it was the lightening before death, for a later *avviso* says, "The Pope is very ill and has grown worse. He cannot eat, he has lost all his teeth, he has a fever, he has chills, he has a thousand maladies, or so it is said by vulgar, malignant and pernicious people. His relatives are hurriedly clearing the Palazzo of its tapestries, gold and silver. This is the real sign that he is beyond cure." And then — because of religious feeling, belief in prophecy, or discretion — the *menante* reverses himself. "But what folly to believe that the prophecy will not prove true! The Pope has seven more years to live, and you will see that he will do many Christian and exceptional deeds, and will make this Church of his, now so depraved, *pulchra* and *immacolata*."

Pope Paul IV died the following year, in 1559, to the joy of Romans who had suffered under his severity, and an *avviso* reports: "At this hour, that is, at midnight, a courier has arrived with the news of the death of the Pope. This has given great joy to all. Those who had had statues made of him went to break them into pieces as soon as they knew he was dead. Then they set free from prison all those who were there because of the Inquisition, burning documents and court records."

Succeeding popes were also severe, and in an *avviso* of the following year, 1560, we read that "His Holiness (Pius IV, 1559–1565) last Monday, about noon, sent for Cardinal del Monte to come to the Palazzo. It seems that he has been roaming the streets at night like a vagabond and getting into fights with people. Friday night he not only got into a fight with a gang of boys but later on, in the house of the courtesan Marluccia, he had a fight with Signor Giacomo Malatesta, who pretended not to know who he was and beat him with a stick, and also beat the courtesan." Cardinal del Monte was fined three abbeys, "and he is likely to lose his cardinal's hat if he does not come to his senses."

The next pope, Saint Pius V (1566–1572), was severe even against his own relatives, as the *menante* notes in a rather shocked headline. "Yesterday the Pope, after talking with his fiscal officer, had Signor Paolo Ghislieri [his nephew] called into his presence. As soon as he arrived, the Pope, without looking at him, had the fiscal officer read his sentence. Signor Paolo was to be barred from the escort of the Pope and deprived of the governorship of Borgo and of all the pensions he enjoyed. On penalty of decapitation he was to leave the Palazzo within two days, Borgo within three days and the papal states within ten days." When a cardinal tried to intervene for him, the Pope answered that while it was *brutto* to see spots on other people's clothing, it was much worse to see them on one's own. Saint Pius seems to have determined on a general housecleaning, for "the women relatives of the Holy Father must also leave the Vatican and go back to the woods; they sail tonight for Civitavecchia. Every day some prostitute is whipped as she emerges from the brothel. And all live in fear."

An ecclesiastical joke is offered for the *avvisi*-readers' amusement: "The story is told of a noble Carthusian who, thinking the Carthusians too lax in their way of living, went to Rome to ask advice on entering another and stricter order. He had the good fortune to talk to the Pope, who advised him to become a Capuchin. But here too he found the same laxity of life. He went back to the Pope, who was annoyed and gave orders for him to be imprisoned. Consequently, prison is now regarded as the strictest religious order in existence." The clergy were often spoken of irreverently; the *menante* writing of a committee of cardinals, chosen to study the reformation of the Church, comments that "there are more old nags than racehorses among them."

Papal policies were discussed and items relating to the Index must have been of special interest to the writers and publishers of the time. "The Index of prohibited books that has just been printed gives everyone a good deal to talk and think about, especially the booksellers, who see themselves half bankrupted. They are thinking of going to the Very Reverend Alessandrino, head of the Inquisition, to ask that they be at least temporarily exempt from customs duties on the books, or allowed to return them." This plan apparently failed, for a later *avviso* says, "It is rumored that many are burning the prohibited books themselves; others are taking them to the Inquisition. It is believed that the greatest part are burned or will be burned."

There are notes on economic conditions: "Here there is extreme famine; people are starving. The carnival celebration is very poor; dearth is bitter; the grain is ground with barley and millet." Celestial portents are recorded: "We have received news from Milan that in this city have appeared three prodigious suns, chained together in three circles with thousands of extravagant signs." And always human interest stories: A bride named Santilla has been stabbed by a group of knights that included her brother because many rich presents had been found at her home; evidence *tenesse mala vita* (of leading an evil life).

And like modern newspapers, the *avvisi* carried social notes, such as an item on the marriage of the king of France to Elizabeth of Austria. "The Queen arrived at Sedan, in border country, accompanied by two princes of the Empire, by the Bishop of Argentina, and by six hundred horsemen. As soon as he learned of her arrival, the King went incognito to look at her, and came back to Thein le Moustier where he was lodging, very happy and in good spirits at having found her so beautiful." The *menante* goes into great detail about dining arrangements at the royal banquet, where, as at the old papal banquets, princes acted as waiters. The *avviso* even includes a seating plan of the banquet table, probably as proof that the *menante* or his agent had actually been present.

The Roman *avvisi* specialized in Church news and scandal, in gossip and pasquinades, but those of Antwerp tended to be more serious and political in their nature. They included news of Protestant England, closed to Catholic readers as Communist China is closed to Western readers today; England-watchers waited in Antwerp gathering information as China-watchers now wait in the fringe countries of the Orient. They reported the persecution of the Catholics: "They were paraded through the streets as if they were monsters. They were put to death by pressing with a pointed stone on the kidneys and another on the heart. Their bodies were put into a boiler of hot water and then exposed on the walls of the castles; the Puritans came with knives and cut off pieces of the remains. The Catholics went to martyrdom with such a happy expression, as if they were on their way to a wedding or a banquet." But the description of the death of Anne Boleyn was equally compassionate: "She herself took off her headdress and gave it to her demoiselles, saying sweet words to them: 'As you cared for my body in the days of good fortune, now you have accompanied it to its miserable end.' After she was beheaded, one of her demoiselles took the head, another the body, and arranged them on a sheet and placed it on a bier already prepared. The Council of the Crown declared that the daughter of this Queen is the daughter of her brother, and ordered the king to take back the daughter of the first and true queen . . ." and the England-watchers foresaw the day when, under Mary Tudor, England would again be Catholic.

Both the Vatican Library and the Secret Archives have collections of *avvisi*. Many volumes of this very ephemeral form of literature survived mainly because they were interesting and amusing enough to provide entertainment at one of Italy's great ducal houses, the seat of the dukes of Montefeltro, lords of Urbino. The *avvisi* from Rome were topics of conversation for the cavaliers and ladies of the court and for its guests. So instead of discarding the old copies, the duke's librarian had them bound into volumes. The *avvisi* were kept much as bound volumes of *Punch* are kept at English country houses. When the Montefeltro family became extinct and the title reverted to the Holy See in the seventeenth century, the sixty-nine volumes of *avvisi* went to the Vatican. Five more volumes of *avvisi* from Venice came to the Holy See with the library of the Count Palatine of Bavaria; these include some of the Fugger *avvisi*.

That so many *avvisi* should have survived is the more surprising when one remembers that even the possession of them was often illegal. Everyone liked to read them — they were enormously popular — but being part of their subject matter seemed, to those in authority, an invasion of privacy. It was disquieting to have to wonder whether the young man in the outer office was making a bit of money on the side as an agent for a *menante*. And, to the popes, the irreverent tone of the *avvisi* meant *lèse-majesté*. There was also the matter of security — disclosures made in the *avvisi* could bring about international complications.

In 1571, Pius V (1566–1572) forbade the writing of *avvisi*, and an *avviso* sent the following year reports that a "consistory was held on Monday and our lord spoke very bitterly against those who write news, disclose secrets and write of the faults of others, all mixed with many lies. He exhorted the cardinals to forbid them to their households." Two weeks later the Pope promulgated his *Constitutio contra scribentes, exemplantes et dictantes monita vulgo dicta gli Avvisi et Ritorni* — against those who wrote, copied and provided information for the *avvisi*. His successor, Gregory XIII, went further, and a constitution of 1572 ran: "There has recently appeared a new sect of men illicitly curious, who write every kind of information of which they have knowledge, or which they make up out of their own libidinous imaginations, mixing the false, the true and the uncertain with no restraint whatever. As a result, a new profession has already established itself, and most of them, even for a very low payment, take this gossip of the common people, add short comments anonymously and send it here and there, from Rome to different places, and then sell it in Rome as if it had come from somewhere else. And they not only concern themselves with what has happened, but foolishly pretend to foretell what is going to happen in the future. To eliminate these inconveniences we prohibit anyone from daring to write such commentaries or to receive, copy, disseminate, or transmit those written by others." The penalties were to be perpetual infamy, prison and capital punishment by hanging on the Sant'Angelo Bridge.

Even this was ineffective, and still another pope, Sixtus V (1585–1590), wrote against the *menante* in a *bando* very like a speech that Shakespeare was to use in *Othello* twenty years later: "As we try to extirpate homicidal persons, robbers and hired assassins who endanger their neighbor's goods and his life, we must in the same way and with the same rigor extirpate the kind of man who brings offense to fame and to honor, which according to natural and civil law have always been held worth more than life."

Sixtus meant what he said, and the *avvisi* of Rome account the tragic fate of one of their writers named Hannibal Cappello, who was accused of slander, arrested and bound and brought to Rome from Pesaro. "The same Hannibal Cappello this morning was taken to the Bridge of Saint Angelo, where justice is carried out. First a hand was cut off, then his tongue, then he was hanged, because he was a false *menante* for many years, a detractor of the honor of persons of every kind, and because he kept and exhibited obscene figures in various postures and libidinous acts, in dispraise of God and of the saints, and because he wrote *avvisi* to heretic princes."

Not all of the martyrs are heroes, but it may have been the death of little men like Hannibal Cappello, and the perseverance of others who continued in their dangerous profession, that finally brought about a slight relaxation of the ban on the *avvisi*. In the sixteenth and early seventeenth centuries, all *menanti*, even the writers of straightforward news, were regarded as criminal. But a *bando generale* of the Roman government published in 1621 tacitly permits restricted news writing by saying that no one is to have the presumption to write, or to have written, *avvisi* to any person whatsoever without written permission from his lordship the governor or his chief notary, on pain of scourging, a fine of one hundred *scudi*, and prison for five years, according to the gravity of the offense.

But for libel the punishment was to be death. Thus distinctions were drawn between authorized *avvisi*, unauthorized *avvisi* and libelous *avvisi*. Hannibal Cappello, with his libidinous little figures and his letters to heretic princes, was dead, but the new profession was on its way to being securely established. The papal states, beginning their long decline, had good reason to fear it.

Challenge and Response

LEO X, Pontifex Maximus, was very fond of his elephant. The great gentle animal had been sent him by the king of Portugal, as a gift from the newly reached East Indies, and had been given the Carthaginian name of Hanno. Not only the Pope but the young men of Rome were enchanted by this "animal with the intelligence of a man"; for elephants were now unknown in the city where once the juvenile-delinquent Emperor Heliogobalus had raced his elephant-drawn quadriga on Vatican Hill.

Leo X (1513–1521) was a rich man's son, an intellectual and a dilettante, who never committed the sin of living as an ungrateful guest in this earth that God has given us. He enjoyed the papacy as he enjoyed his collection of exotic animals, his codices, the company of artists and poets, his amateur theatricals with scenery by Raphael. He shared John XXIII's dislike of going around in bedroom slippers and wore hunting boots that made toe-kissing difficult, but he was a kindly man, and accepted graciously the little gifts that the country people made him as he rode through the *campagna*. He would have been a great success as a constitutional monarch, but this son of bankers had no sense of money. Julius II had left the Church in good financial condition, but Leo's expenditures were enormous; book collecting is more expensive than the carnal vices.

In addition to the high cost of codices there was the cost of the new Saint Peter's, which was proving expensive even though the marble for it was being looted from the buildings of classical Rome. Leo had inherited the project from Julius II (1503–1513), under whom the need for repairs had become critical. The old basilica had lasted for over a thousand years; not long for a structure of imperial times, but its walls were too high for stability, it was built on a sloping site, and too much wood had been used in its fabric. Even the marble staircase leading to it had been worn away by age and by the feet of many pilgrims; Aeneas Sylvius tells us that he had it replaced at great expense with one that was "easier and handsomer." An anonymous document in the Secret Archives tells us that Julius II had wanted to save the old basilica "for eternal remembrance of its glorious founder Constantine," but he consulted experts, and "taking into account the difficulties of keeping such a great mass stable, grounded in the air, so to speak, over columns many times restored by the supreme pontifexes, he decided with great magnificence to raise from the foundations a new temple, larger than the old." In the center of the new temple was to be a memorial to himself, done by Michelangelo.

Ground was broken for the new Saint Peter's in 1506, and the old basilica, with its patristic elegance, was shattered in a brutal wrecking job. Little care was taken to preserve the columns; perhaps they were worth just as much broken, for they could be cut into the bologna-slices useful for decorating tombs. Many Romans regretted the loss of the old basilica, and Julius was pictured as having to answer for it in Heaven; moderns who read descriptions of it may regret it still.

Since Julius II had other heavy expenses, such as walling Civitavecchia against the Turks, and recovering cities that had been taken away from the papal states, he "asked the people of the world to join in the work of piety, exhorting them to offer alms in order to obtain the remission of sins and other spiritual graces." In other words, he instituted a discreet sale of indulgences.

The sale of indulgences was nothing new. In Egypt of the Second Millennium individuals who feared the Judgment of Souls could buy, from the priests' clerks, scrolls containing a favorable verdict. A blank was left to be filled in with the name of the purchaser. In medieval Europe indulgences had been given to the crusaders, and later to men on the home front whose work and gifts supported the war effort. Boniface VIII had gone back to ancient Hebrew tradition and established the custom of the jubilee year, when large indulgences were given for pilgrimage to Rome, and the jubilee years were such a success that they became rather frequent. Eventually it occurred to someone that the indulgence could be given without the pilgrimage if the financial pain of making a large gift was substituted for the hardships of travel.

One finds material on the Lutheran controversy not only in the regular *fondi* of the Secret Archives but in letters, memoirs, almost all the writing of the time. Even the imperfect indexes give pages and pages of detailed listings.

Heresy had been a problem from the earliest days of the Church, and the Arian controversy, one is convinced as he reads the details of Arius' violent final illness, was ended not only by the burning of Arian books and the persecution of Arian believers but by poison. Many heresies before Luther's are reflected in the Archives, along with records of their extirpation, which was often accomplished by the extirpation of the heretics themselves. But there were factors that made "the Lutheran matter" harder to deal with: the printing press was available for the use of a journalistic genius, the system of copper engraving made possible the reproduction of cartoons, in Germany there was a spirit of ecclesiastical anticolonialism, and in Italy there was a humanist pope with other things on his mind — such as the fact that the thirty-third chapter of Livy was rumored to be in the possession of the king of Denmark.

The precipitating incident was trivial. Archbishop Albert of Mainz had borrowed twenty-four thousand ducats from the banking house of the Fuggers to pay for his dioceses. The Pope, who had extended the sale of indulgences, amiably allowed the archbishop to keep half the profits in his territory; the rest was to be applied to the building of Saint Peter's. Albert delegated the sales campaign to his assistant Tetzel, who promised plenary indulgence guaranteed to restore the purchaser to "the innocence and purity possessed at baptism, so that when you die the gates of punishment shall be shut and the gates of the paradise of delight shall be opened." He neglected to add the Church's normal proviso that indulgence be granted only to persons with "the heart contrite and the mouth confessing." Public response was enthusiastic, and people living outside Albert's territory crossed his borders to buy indulgences. A Holbein cartoon shows payments being collected in a metal-bound trunk similar to the treasure trunks in Castel Sant'Angelo, but with a slit in the top into which coins could be dropped. The trunks had four keys; one of them was held by an agent of the Fuggers.

The commercialization of divine forgiveness had attracted the attention of Erasmus, who wrote against it in his *Praise of Folly*. "What shall I say about those who happily delude themselves with false pardons for their sins? The life of Christians everywhere abounds in such nonsense. The priests allow and even encourage such things. They know that it brings in much profit." But Erasmus, like an employee almost ready for a pension, could be easily managed. Luther was still too young to be prudent.

Brother Martin Luther (1483–1546) was an Augustinian monk of peasant stock. When he first entered the monastery he had often made six-hour confessions, to the vast boredom of his confessor, and had dreamed of living like the desert saints on herbs and roots and cold water. But as time went on his interests turned to theology and disputation. He discovered Saint Augustine and the theory of predestination, which by then the Church had rather forgotten about. (There is much to be said for it logically, but its practical application is disastrous.) He read Valla's exposure of the Donations of Constantine and doubted Church tradition; he read Erasmus' translation of the Bible, was delighted to find that Jerome's "do penance" had been corrected to "be penitent," and arrived at the conclusion that sin, an offence against God, could be paid for only by the atoning Christ. It was not through good works and through the Sacraments but through faith that one could call on the generous justice of God.

When Luther's church-door theses inviting disputation on the subject of indulgences found no takers he had them printed; they met an immediate and enthusiastic response in Germany, particularly among the rebellious young. They also led to immediate reprisals. Albert of Mainz complained to Rome, and in 1518 the Augustinian order received instructions to "inhibit" Luther.

If the controversy between the monk and the Church had dealt only with indulgences it might have had an amicable solution. The Church agreed that Tetzel had gone too far; he was admonished and punished and the necessity of genuine contrition was pointed out. But there were three factors that made rapprochement almost hopeless from the start — the corruption of the Church, the attitude of the German public (the press was performing its usual function of hotting up the controversy, and Luther's writing made splendid copy), and the fact that Luther seemed to be undergoing continuous revelation. At the beginning he had spoken of himself as a devoted son of the Church, anxious only for its amendment in the matter of indulgences. But other dicta followed: the Bible was the sole source of revelation, neither the Pope nor the councils had true authority, the Church must give up temporal power, canon law was to be abolished, priests were to be allowed to marry, there were to be no masses for the dead, papal legates were to be driven from Germany.

Both Luther and the Church showed a capacity for invective that would have done credit to Platina. According to Luther, Rome was a Jerusalem that kills her prophets, the purple Babylon; the Pope was Antichrist sitting in the temple of God, and the clergy were the whole swarm of the Roman Sodom. And the Church called Luther the wild boar invading the vineyard, a scabrous sheep infecting the flock, and a serpent creeping through the field of the Lord.

The emissaries that Rome sent to deal with the situation were not skillful diplomats. The first of them, Cajetan, persisted for some time in the conviction that he was there to receive the confession of a penitent heretic. Later the humanist Aleander, head of the pontifical library, was sent to Germany with the *Exurge Domine* bull and its zoological allusions. There the librarian tried to sway a conference of German knights — not intellectual types — by showing them a medieval manuscript to prove the status of the papacy in the time of Charlemagne. And both Cajetan and Aleander permitted themselves to be drawn into discussing Luther's case before secular conferences.

Aleander soon realized that the Lutheran campaign was making effective use of journalism, and in 1521 wrote: "I say to our priests and rectors in Rome, who seem to have nothing to do but spend months in polishing calumnies against each other, that they must get together to defend our faith in their writings. They could do some good with their knowledge and ability and reduce to silence these newsboys who, only because of their skill as writers and poets, have gained as much prestige with the *vulgus* as if they had succeeded in beating down the true theology. You can't impress them with excommunication; they laugh at it. These gentry must be defeated with their own weapons. The pope could encourage some talented men to make a thorough study of the Bible as the Germans have done, so that they could finally use their pens for the defense of the faith. To confute these racketeers we do not need great doctors of theology; they want nothing to do with them."

But no effective counter-propaganda was ever developed. In fact it would have been difficult to find a writer to match Luther, who used the vocabulary and imagery of his agricultural youth as skillfully as any American politician, and at other times wrote passages of deep poetic beauty.

A change of venue might have helped to bring about a climate of conciliation; the conferences between the Church and the Lutherans were being carried on in a far from neutral area. By the time Aleander arrived the country was largely Lutheran in sympathy and full of the tension that precedes revolutions and race riots. He wrote home that the Germans gnashed their teeth at him on the street and that "I hope the pope will give me a plenary indulgence and take care of my brothers and sisters if anything happens to me." And the new pope Clement VII (1523–34), writing to his legate at the emperor's court, says of the Germans: "The malignity of their souls, hitherto somewhat hidden, has come out into the open. Pretending to hear the Gospel preached, they allow only Lutherans to preach. They allow, or rather induce, priests and friars to take as wives nuns or those women that before were their concubines and prostitutes. In some places they destroy the images of the saints and of Our Lady. In some churches they have abolished the *Ave Maria*, and instead of saying *Salve Regina* they say *Salve Rex*. They do not care for the sacraments of the Church, especially confession. They say that prayers and offerings for the dead are no help. They do not decorate the church. They are enemies of both canon and civil law."

Rome's efforts to seize Luther's person failed because he was protected by the Elector Frederick the Wise of Saxony. Various reasons have been given for Frederick's stand — religious conviction, ambition to be elected emperor, desire to keep the income derived from pilgrims visiting his extensive collection of relics. But a document in the Secret Archives gives another explanation. The Duke of Saxony, it says, had asked a famous astrologer, Giovanni da Monteregio, "to study and see if the House of Saxony would ever regain its ancient grandeur." The astrologer answered that this might occur if Germany experienced religious reformation; and, if the leaders of the new religion could be kept in Saxony, the family would increase in greatness. This story is told as having happened several years before "the devil entered into Luther," and would explain Frederick's fostering of the University of Wittenberg and his protection of the monk Martin Luther.

The controversy dragged on, with endless conferences where too many people talked and talked too long. In 1540 a papal legate, who had been waiting three weeks for a reply to a letter on urgent matters, wrote: "I think Rome has forgotten I am alive." And while the scholars disputed and Rome delayed, the Lutheran Church was establishing itself, a Lutheran tradition was forming, a Lutheran literature was reaching the people as the Church's literature and the humanist literature never had. Much of Germany had been lost, at the conference tables and in the neglected parishes, as much of Europe would soon be lost.

In the Secret Archives there is a letter from Erasmus to Cardinal Campeggio, denying Lutheran tendencies and saying, as our own liberals may say in a coming age, "I wrote many things in an untroubled century . . ."

The fifteen-year-old Prince Arthur of England son of Henry VII, had just been married to the Spanish Princess Catherine of Aragon, daughter of Ferdinand and Isabella. After the ceremony they were taken to a torchlit chamber in the palace of the Bishop of London. There, in the presence of nobles and ecclesiastics, they were put to bed naked, as the Manichaean children had been in the time of Pope Leo the Great. It is uncertain what happened after they were given a last blessing and a cup of warm sweet wine. Fifteen often meant biological childhood in those days, and the boy was soon to die. But years afterward, when the matter had taken on international importance, a courtier related that the prince had said to him, "Last night I was in Spain."

When Arthur died it was decided that the marriage was too good a one, politically and financially, to waste. Eight years later, in 1509, Catherine, dressed as she had been for her first wedding in the white robe and flowing hair of virginity, was married to the proud but rather reluctant young King Henry VIII, Arthur's brother, whom she had first known as a ten-year-old page.

This arrangement aroused misgivings from the first, since marriage to a brother's widow was forbidden under canon law on the basis of a passage in Leviticus: "Thou shalt not uncover the nakedness of thy brother's wife; it is thy brother's nakedness; the union will be sterile." Catherine said that her alliance with Arthur had not been consummated, but her elders seem to have been uncertain of this, for they asked for a dispensation of the sort necessary if a marriage had actually existed. Julius II doubted whether he could give a dispensation from Scripture, but finally did so.

Henry's conscience apparently did not trouble him for a time; only unhappy marriages come up for annulment. But as child after child was born and died, or died and was born, leaving only the sickly and unattractive Princess Mary, he blamed not syphilis but Leviticus. A male heir was badly needed; England had only recently emerged from an exhausting civil war caused by the lack of a clear succession. Henry even thought of making an illegitimate child heir to the throne; perhaps he remembered that it was sin that created Solomon.

Anne Boleyn was the daughter of a merchant politician and the sister of one of Henry's mistresses. She was in her teens when Henry first met her, black-eyed, vivacious, dressed with sophistication. She loved pearls and wore them in her hair, on her dresses, in a double strand around her neck. Later there were rumors that she was a witch; she had an extra little finger that some said was a devil's teat; Cardinal Wolsey called her "the night-crow." But she played the lute and sang well, and some of the songs were her own.

Henry sent her poems he had written; in one of them he reminded her that no bird can resist the eagle, no metal the heat of the flame, the hardest stones must yield to iron, and the wisest lose their minds in the company of princes. But Anne kept hers for a while; probably she had seen enough of her sister's life to feel that there was no future in such a status.

"Me and my heart," the king writes to Anne Boleyn, "put ourselves in your hands." A series of seventeen letters from the king to Anne somehow reached the Pope and his Consistory and, later, the papal archives.

They now belong to the Vatican Library. It is not certain how they came to Rome; probably they were stolen from the house of Anne's father at Hever or from her own apartments. They could be expected to work against Henry's plea for annulment of marriage, since they showed that it was not actuated by religious conscience.

These letters, the first of which probably dates from the year 1527, are written on fine parchment, which was later pasted onto stiffer material for durability They are in both French and English, chiefly French. The handwriting of the earlier letters is large and clear, but in the later ones the characters run into each other, the ink is blotted, and the width of the pen strokes is variable.

Here we see a man very much in love, but still able to turn a pretty scientific conceit, like those of John Donne, on the subject of Anne's absence — ". . . reminding us of a point in astronomy, which is that the longer the days are the farther off is the sun and yet the hotter; so is it with our love." He is uncertain that his feeling for her is returned and is determined not to pine for a woman who doesn't want him: "Absence from you is very grievous to me, but if I understood that in truth you yourself wished it I could do no other than complain of my ill fortune while abating little by little my great folly."

He is uncertain of her feelings toward him: "In debating with myself the contents of your letters I have been put to a great agony; not knowing how to understand them, whether to my disadvantage as shown in some places, or to my advantage as in others." Nevertheless, in the same letter, he makes her a firm proposition: "If it pleases you to do the duty of a true, loyal, mistress and friend, and to give yourself body and heart to me . . . I promise to take you as my sole mistress, casting off all others than yourself out of my mind and affection, and to serve you only."

Anne apparently accepts, for in his next letter he thanks her "for a present so beautiful that nothing could be more so (considering it as a whole). I thank you very cordially, not only for the handsome diamond and the ship in which the lonely damsel is tossed about, but chiefly for the fine interpretation and too humble submission which your kindness has made of it." The arrangement apparently is not a physical one, for he speaks of "my unchangeable intention, which is *aut illic, aut nullibi.*" He ends by assuring her that "henceforward my heart shall be dedicated to you alone, with a strong desire that my body could be also thus dedicated, which God can do if he pleases; to whom I pray every day to that end." And he signs himself "H seeks AB no other R" — no other queen.

Anne does not allow him to forget his promise, and in the next letter (or a postscript), he writes: "The reasonable request of your last letter . . . causeth me to send you now these news: the legate we most desired arrived at Paris on Sunday or Monday last past so that I trust by the next Monday to hear of his arrival at Calais, and then soon after to enjoy that which I have so longed for to God's pleasure and our both comfort; no more to you at this present time mine own darling for lack of time, but that I would you were in my arms or I in yours, for I think it long since I kissed you; written after the killing of an hart at eleven of the clock, minding with God's grace tomorrow mightily timely to kill another." His next letter says that he has scant leisure, but has arranged lodgings for her "by my lord cardinal's means." He manages to combine love with his passion for hunting in a passage less graceful than that based on the earth's orbit: "Seeing my darling is absent I can not do less than to send her some flesh representing my name; which is hart flesh for Henry; prognosticating that hereafter God willing you must enjoy some of mine, which he pleased, I would were now."

Anne falls ill of a sweating sickness, a peculiar epidemic unknown in later centuries. Henry sends her one of his physicians and an expression of concern that is the more convincing for its arithmetical qualification: "I would willingly bear the half of your illness to have you cured." Other letters of love and concern follow, with assurances that everything that can be done concerning "our matter" is being done, and as speedily as possible. The tone of the letters has changed now; they are not letters to a fiancée but to a mistress, familiarly known: ". . . wishing myself (especially of an evening) in my sweetheart's arms, whose pretty duckies I trust shortly to kiss." In the last letter Anne has apparently made some protest concerning her situation, and failed, for the king writes "to inform you of what joy it is to me to understand of your conformableness to reason, and of the suppression of your inutile and vain thoughts and fantasies with the bridle of reason . . . for thereby shall come both to you and me the greatest quietness that may be in this world."

The legates came and went, but no dispensation came from Rome. The papacy was playing for time. It had just been through the Sack of Rome; the city was plundered and at the mercy of the Emperor Charles V, Catherine's nephew. Henry had the compliant Cardinal Wolsey send to Rome to ask that legates come to decide on the validity of the king's marriage to Catherine, and a year later the legatine court was held in England. Evidence was taken on the question of the consummation of Catherine's marriage to Arthur; courtiers repeated the boy's remarks, the sheets that had been sent to Catherine's mother in Spain were retrieved and inspected. And the court adjourned without a decision. Henry referred the matter to the universities, which appointed study groups, al-

Chapel erected on the Appian Way to commemorate the meeting between Saint Paul and the Christians of Rome (Paolo di Paolo)

The Tiberine Island (Paolo di Paolo)

Basilica of San Clemente. Lower floor, Mithraic area (Paolo di Paolo)

Basilica of San Clemente, lower floor. "The Secret Water of Rome"
(Paolo di Paolo)

The skull of Saint Lawrence the Librarian, preserved in the Matilda chapel, Vatican City (Paolo di Paolo)

Church of San Gregorio Magno. Chapel of Santa Barbara. The stone table is the one at which the saint daily served twelve of the poor. Legend says that once the poor were joined by an angel (Paolo di Paolo)

Arch of Titus.
ABOVE: *Detail of the Seven-branched*
Candlestick of Jerusalem (Paolo di Paolo)

Pepin makes the historic Donation to Stephen
(Copyright by Leonard von Matt)

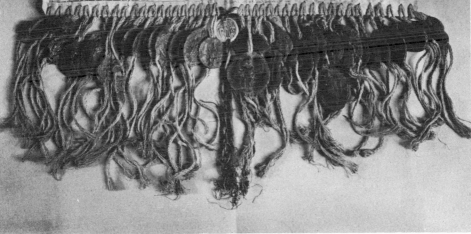

*The decree of the first Council of Lyons, 1245, which ended with the
excommunication and deposition of the Emperor Frederick II
(Copyright by Leonard von Matt)*

The Lateran in the year 1500 (Vatican Library)

*Executions of men condemned for having stolen relics and religious objects
(Vatican Library)*

The Archangel St. Michael on the top of Castel Sant'Angelo (Paolo di Paolo)

Circular room of Castel Sant'Angelo, where the treasure and the most precious archives of the Church were kept (Paolo di Paolo)

The "Borgo" Passage between the Vatican and Castel Sant'Angelo
(Paolo di Paolo)

*Castel Sant'Angelo, cells used as prisons. Among the names scratched
on the walls are those of Benvenuto Cellini and Cagliostro
(Paolo di Paolo)*

*One of the rooms of the Secret Archives, built during the reign of Paul V
(Courtesy of the Secret Archives)*

The safe in which the golden seals and the most precious documents are kept (Courtesy of the Secret Archives)

An example of the Secret Archives' famous collection of golden seals (Copyright by Leonard von Matt)

Ground floor corridor, Vatican Secret Archives (Courtesy of the Secret Archives)

*Reading room, Vatican Secret Archives
(Copyright by Leonard von Matt)*

Shelves of the Archives (Copyright by Leonard von Matt)

Historical "carrousel" in honor of Christina of Sweden (Oscar Savio)

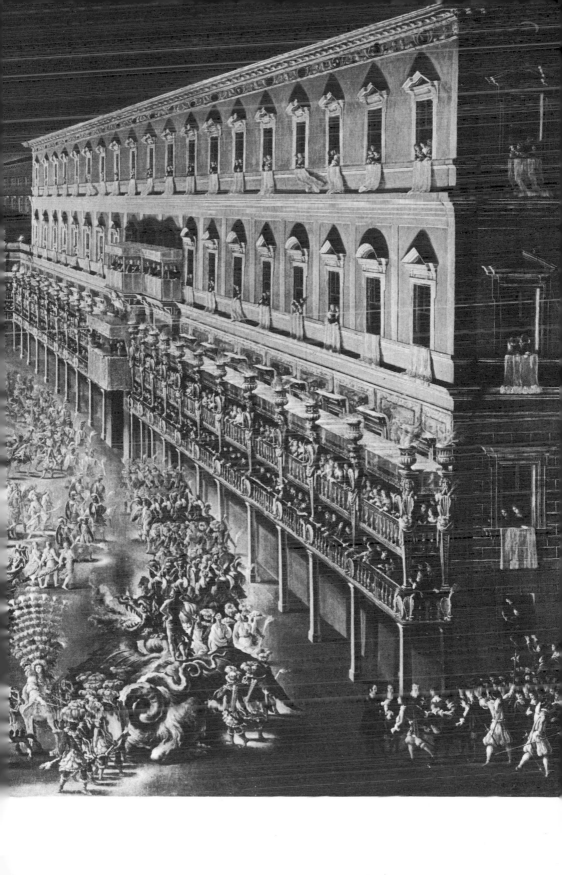

The ban on the new profession of journalism (Vatican Library)

The original of one of the stolen letters of Henry VIII to Anne Boleyn (Vatican Library)

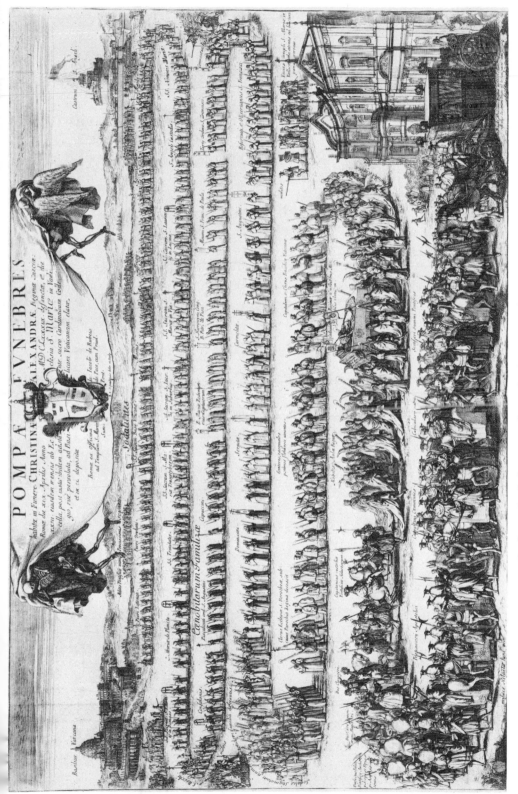

The funeral of Christina of Sweden (Vatican Library)

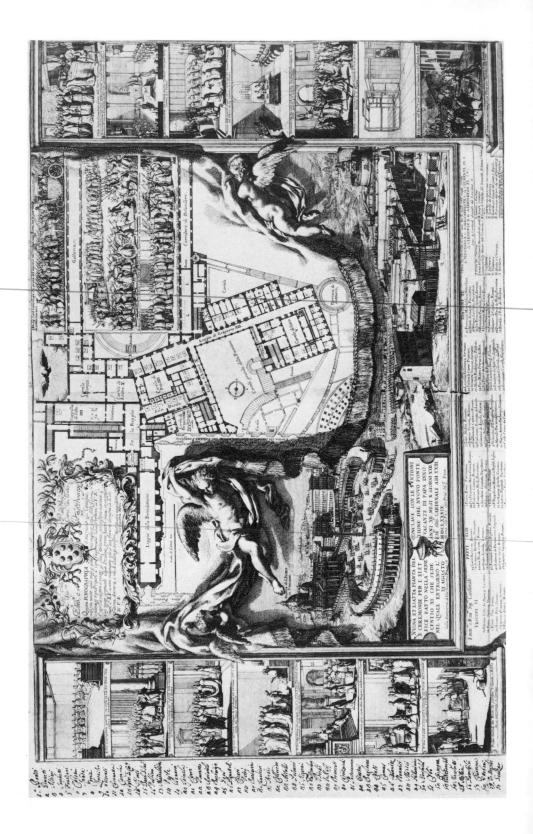

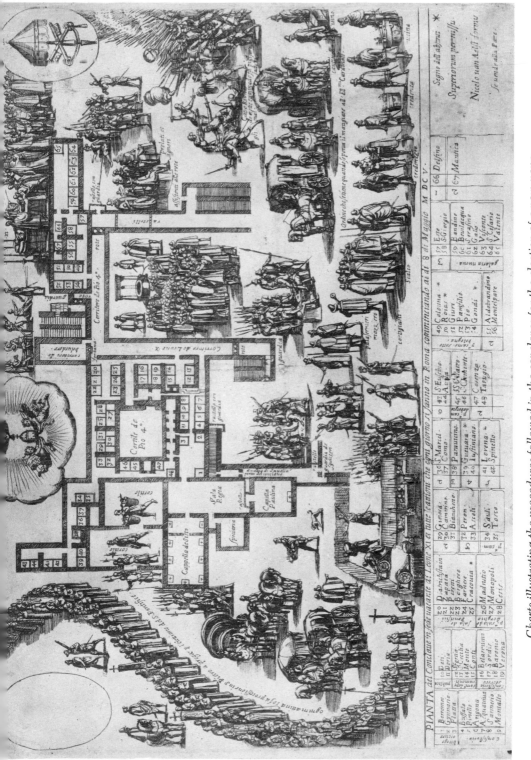

Charts illustrating the procedures followed in the conclaves for the election of a new pope
(Vatican Library)

*Frescoes from the Tower of the Winds and the Meridian Room
(Photographic Archives of the Vatican Museum)*

Fresco from the Tower of the Winds. Archives documents are visible just below the fresco
(Photographic Archives of the Vatican Museum)

Palazzo della Sapienza, where the State Archives of Rome, taken over by the Italian government in 1870, are located (Paolo di Paolo)

Palazzo della Sapienza. One of the halls of the State Archives of Rome
(Paolo di Paolo)

ready a useful device for avoiding action. But by 1533 the king could wait no longer for papal permission; Anne was already pregnant with the child that he hoped would be the next King of England. He married her, secretly, in January; and a month later had Parliament pass an act forbidding appeals to Rome and declaring that even cases involving spiritual matters were to be tried in England. An obedient court headed by an archbishop declared the marriage to Catherine null and the marriage to Anne valid. The Pope's opposing judgment for Catherine was not made until the following year.

Henry's Reformation Parliament rejected papal authority but not the doctrine of the Church; the Church was now in schism. But the transfer of spiritual authority from the pope to the king made later attack on doctrine easy. The monasteries were closed, and the last Abbot of Glastonbury, before they hanged him, had just time to send the wooden cup that may have been the Holy Grail into hiding in Wales.

The pontificate of Clement VII (1523–1534) was disastrous, marred as it was by the Lutheran controversy, the loss of England, the Sack of Rome by imperial troops. Charles V had hired an army of mercenaries, the *Landsknechte;* they were joined by the Duke of Bourbon's army that had been occupying Milan, and swept south. Clement bought them off with a bribe, the bribe was not large enough.

There had been warnings of catastrophe. A mule had given birth in the Chancellery; wafers of the Eucharist put in the Pope's chapel on Holy Thursday had been found on the floor. As usual, Rome was unprepared for invasion. Clement thought its walls would protect it, and his ministers advised against his leaving for the better-defended city of Florence, or sending valuables into safekeeping.

A report in the Secret Archives contains a bitter accusation against the papal government for failing to "maintain civil and worthy customs under the shadow of military discipline, without which no peace, no real greatness, is possible." Its writer is less critical of Clement, a man lacking in courage, badly advised, and suffering for the mistakes of his predecessors, than of the Curia, "the graceful, delicate prelates, delicate courtiers," who even in normal times could not bear "the tough discomfort of the body, the great griefs of the soul, or even the tickle of flies." And he blames the Roman populace, "those Romans, lost in effeminate and libidinous laziness, dedicated to amassing gold and silver for themselves by fraud and cruelty, under cover of Christian piety." The Italian people were "frightened little sheep penned in the slaughter house" as "four thousand, six thousand, twelve thousand *ultramontani,* not professional soldiers, without good officers, conquer this province of ours."

The city's walls were breached under cover of fog, and the report tells of "the flight of our lord to Castel Sant'Angelo" over the aereal escape route that Alexander Borgia had thoughtfully prepared, of the hurried getting together of provisions, of "priests, cardinals, merchants, noblemen, courtiers, women, soldiers, all mixed together at the portal of the Castle begging to enter." One of the latecomers was Cardinal Hermellino, minister of finance, a leader of the economy party that had been unwilling to spend money to defend Rome. He is described by a contemporary as so money-thirsty that he regretted not being able to put a habitation tax on flies or a transportation tax on ants. The cardinal was hoisted to an upper terrace of the Castle in a large basket like the small ones that some of my Roman neighbors let down from their upper floors to the grocery below.

When the doors were closed on May 6, 1527, about three thousand people were inside — and the figure is chilling to anyone who has visited Castel Sant'Angelo, for its rooms and ramps and terraces would hold far more than that. Someone had done what modern designers of atomic shelters fear that no one will be able to bring himself to do — close the doors as soon as the number who can be fed and cared for are inside. In this flight of the papal court to Castel Sant'Angelo even the elementary ethics of a baboon tribe, where the old males stay behind and die to cover the retreat of the pack, had been abandoned. But our modern leaders too have their Castel Sant'Angelos.

Eight days of atrocity followed. The behavior of the invading forces was far worse than that of the barbarians who had invaded the city in imperial times. For the Germans, an element of religious warfare had entered in — what mercy need be shown to Antichrist? Victims were torn to pieces in the streets, and "many threw themselves from the windows to escape torture and death. Chalices, ivories, gold and silver vases were taken from the altars with bloody hands. Virgins and modest matrons were violated. Many noblewomen and young girls and nuns were ransomed, but there was a flood of libidinousness." The writer comments disapprovingly that there were not enough suicides: "One would think that some noble and pure virgins, in order not to be contaminated, would have spontaneously killed themselves with iron or thrown themselves into the Tiber or onto the pavement. However, I have not heard of any such virtue and honesty. And that is not surprising, considering how corrupt and full of vice the city was." Another writer, however, says that many women drowned themselves in the Tiber after being raped.

Citizens were tortured to make them tell the whereabouts of hidden valuables; blood and mutilated members mixed with the mud of the streets. "Many were strung up for hours by the arms. Many were stretched and bound in a strange way by the sexual organs, buried in the cellars, branded with hot irons. Some of them were made to eat their own ears and nose and testicles that had been roasted."

But the reporter seems more amused than shocked at what was done to the prelates and high authorities of the Church, many of whom had remained in their palaces, thinking themselves safe because they were members of the imperial party. "One time they brought in Cardinal Araceli in a coffin, singing his obsequies as if he were dead. They killed a priest because he refused to give the sacrament to a dressed up donkey. Other priests were forced to perform very humble services, in torn tunics and without stockings, currying the horses, turning the spit, or washing dishes, as maybe most of them used to do before acquiring with questionable vices a dignity that they never deserved."

Another story of the Sack is told by a Benedictine nun, Ursula Formicini. For greater security, her sisterhood was moved from San Cosimato in Trastevere to the Monastery of Saint Lawrence in Panisperna on the Esquiline, part of which had been vacated for them. "They had been ordered to walk two by two, in procession, an old one and a young one. Altogether there were thirty-five couples. The frightened little virgins came out with their veils down to their mouths, and they told me that while they were walking they did not see any light, both because they were afraid, and because the veils did not allow them to see."

Sending women on a walk across the city at such a time seems a dubious plan, even though they were accompanied by monks and relatives, and Sister Ursula apparently realized it. "And here we found a miracle, that having to cross the city for such a long way, they did not find even one of the enemy."

The brothers of the monastery had hired some of the invading soldiers and paid them well to protect the place, "but these people being wicked, they did not keep their promise, and being loaded with wine, began to shout and noisily demand that the monastery be opened. The brothers advised that this be done, so that they would not climb over the walls or set fire to them, as they were threatening to do, or break the doors down. They promised not to hurt anyone, and said that they only wanted to look for things that they thought were hidden in the convent." The credulous brothers let them in, and "anyone can imagine the terror, agony, and fright of these pure doves. They all gathered together in the church behind the choir and the old nuns made a front. [For protection, or to make the group seem less attractive?]

"The Lutherans came in, but because of a divine miracle they did not see any of the brides of Christ, who were kneeling on the floor and praying to the celestial bridegroom to deliver them from such great danger.

Then a very presumptuous soldier entered that choir where our nuns were" — and here Sister Ursuline forgets the Christian ethic of submission and shows admiration for a Sister Innocentia di Campagniano, who operated according to the barbarian ethic. "Seeing this soldier come in where our girls were, going here and there like a blind man, not knowing what he was doing or where he was going, the sister pushed him strongly so that she threw him quite far away from the choir. Such a strong push was certainly not a woman's but from God, who gave her strength and valor. The soldier ran away, not like a man-at-arms but like a thief who has been surprised in a robbery, saying, 'But who is this woman?' "

The soldiers afterward confessed that they had entered the monastery with bad intentions, but had been unable to see any nuns. "And they threw themselves on the beds of the servants of Christ like pigs, though no nun was there, while the nuns, like little lambs afraid of the wolves, were in church praying to the celestial bridegroom."

Rome's libraries, with no old Amazon to protect them, were less fortunate than the little nuns. There are serious gaps in the Capitoline archives and in private and monastery archives as a result of the Sack. Some of the Church's precious documents, and its collection of golden seals, were safe in Castel Sant'Angelo, and the Vatican Library was fortunate in being made the headquarters of Philibert, Prince of Orange. Europeans have learned to be very hospitable to enemy headquarters, since the places they occupy are saved from general destruction and usually undergo only discreet looting. Even so the Vatican Library suffered serious losses. Saint Peter's and the Vatican were plundered; manuscripts and papal documents were scattered in the streets and used as litter for horse's stalls; the registers of the Apostolic Chamber were torn to pieces to make wadding for cannonballs, and all the Acts of the Secret Chancellery fell into the hands of soldiers. Pastor quotes the Protestant hero Sebastian Schertlin of Burtenbach as saying that all written material, such as registers and letters, was under particular attack. He says — and many veterans could echo him — "We have behaved very strangely . . ."

Some of the lost treasures were finally recovered. Five years after the Sack, according to a letter of 1532 from one Bonaventura Samuellis to the pope, it was learned that in Naples "a few people, Christian as well as Jewish, have securely hidden some cloth made of gold and very beautiful silk, of a great value, received after the sack of Rome." (After the last war, stolen objects showed this same tendency to drift toward Naples.) "It seems that they are the tapestries of the chapel of the Holy Palace made under Pope Leo of happy memory"— the great tapestries of the life of Christ, woven in Brussels according to designs by Raphael's

school. Samuellis asks for money so that he can negotiate for their recovery; we do not know what answer he received, but the tapestries now
hang the length of the Vatican's Tapestry Gallery. I always like to visit
them after seeing the *Last Judgment,* for here a very different Christ sits
with two friends in a suburban garden, a bird and a bottle on the table
in front of them and a wine cooler in the grass at their feet.

Every new pope had declared his intention to carry out reform, just as
new heads of state declare their intention to balance the budget, and
with as little effect.

The excesses of the Renaissance made the need for reform more apparent than ever, and in 1517, before the Lutheran controversy or the
Sack of Rome, Gianfrancesco Pico della Mirandola, nephew of the philosopher, delivered a stinging address on the corrupted customs of the
clergy before the Pope and his assembly. According to a report of the
speech: "Pico does not ask very much; only that ecclesiastics not offer salt
that has completely lost its savor. He does not ask them to be learned;
only to know the duties of their office. He does not ask them to martyrize
themselves like Jerome and Benedict, but to give up Sybaritic luxuries
and stop adorning their servant girls with precious stones; he does not
ask them to clothe the naked as Saint Martin did, but to refrain from
clothing their beasts in purple, and that the churches should not be like
stables while their own apartments shine with gold and the luxury of
carpets." And Pico added a comment that some of his hearers must have
remembered ten years later: "If Leo X leaves these crimes unpunished
any longer, then one must be afraid that God himself, with fire and
sword, will amputate the diseased members."

With much of Europe lost, the Church finally came to reform.

It seemed improbable that Paul III Farnese (1534–1549) would be a
reform pope. He owed his cardinalate to Alexander Borgia's affection for
his sister Julia, and one of his own first acts as pope was to give cardinals'
hats to his two adolescent nephews, provoking the pasquinade: "To the
very new reverends; praise the children of the Lord." But Paul also gave
other cardinalates to men who were learned and of strong moral character. He then appointed a commission to report on the state of the Church
and to make recommendations for emending it. "Courage before the
Vicar of Christ in his triple crown is even rarer than courage before the
thrones of kings," but this commission reported that the prime source of
the Church's trouble was the assumption of an excess of power by the
popes. It went on to speak of moonlighting bishops with their multiple
benefices, of absentee parish priests, of "spoiled convents," and ended:

"You have taken the name of Paul: we hope you will emulate his charity. Make alive in our hearts and in our works that name already forgotten by the pagans and by us priests, the name of God."

The difficulty of convening the reform council, the Council of Trent, is shown by the many bulls of convocation and suspension that preceded the definitive bull of opening in 1544, the bull called *Laetare Jerusalem*. These words are the opening of the Introit for the Fourth Sunday in Lent: "Rejoice, O Jerusalem, all you who love her, you who were in sadness, rejoice and drink at the springs of her consolation" — a moment of joy in a long season of grief.

The Council opened several months later; the bishops in their miters of white linen, and the cardinals in their miters of white damask and their red copes embroidered in gold, which had arrived from Venice the night before, joined in singing *Veni Creator Spiritus*. The Council lasted until 1563, with varying periods of suspension, and the Secret Archives contains one hundred and fifty-five volumes of official reports, in addition to private journals. From the diaries of Angelo Massarelli, who was secretary throughout the Council, and from the protocols, one gets some idea of the enormous quantity of work, of diplomatic dealings, of theological and canonical discussions, of dispatches between Rome and Trent.

As time went on the Council, like the recent Vatican Council, developed its own subculture. In the second session, begun in 1546, a decree was issued on suitable conduct for all those attending. They were to refrain from satisfying their fleshly desires, to confess and take the Eucharist often, to attend church every Sunday for as many services as possible, and to pray for the peace of Christian princes and the unity of the Church. "And as it is necessary that the bishops be blameless, sober, chaste, at their table let there be sobriety and moderation in food. And because long idle conversations often arise at the table, at the tables of the same bishops let there be added the reading of the Holy Scriptures." (At the last Vatican Council the coffee bars that Pope John ordered installed just for the purpose of encouraging conversation were a great success.)

Perhaps the recommendation about sobriety of food was intended for Cardinal Madruzzo, Prince of Trent, who on the previous Easter had given the legates a three-hour dinner with seventy-four courses. Madruzzo apparently regarded himself as host to the Council, and sent the legates lavish gifts of food: "Today an enormous sturgeon, then splendid melons, pheasant, and so on, not to mention wines more than a hundred years old." This cardinal had not quite entered into the reform spirit, and "one time Madruzzo, on the occasion of a marriage in the bishop's residence, induced the bishops who were present to take part in the quadrille of the newly married pair, according to local custom, giving rise in the presence of the legates to serious scandal."

One side of the work of the Council of Trent — reformation of the government and organization of the Church — could be compared to the work of the American constitutional convention. The main tasks of any government are to keep order, to cut down on graft and crime, and to get some work out of people. The Roman Catholic Church is now regarded as one of the world's most efficiently run organizations.

The other side of the Council's work dealt with doctrine, and here its decisions were extensive and definitive. They were strongly influenced by the Jesuits, who were informed and able and followed a party line. The Jesuits had done their homework, and for this reason they could often dominate debate. The commission Paul III had appointed had warned of the assumption of too much power by the popes; the Council of Trent confirmed their power and made obedience to the pope as much an article of faith for every churchman as it was for the Jesuits.

Many of the decisions seemed to be aftereffects of the Lutheran controversy. Man was to be saved by both faith and works; the bread and wine of the Eucharist were Christ himself; the celibacy of the priesthood was affirmed. The Bible and tradition had equal status as means of revelation. Erasmus' Bible was declared invalid — Erasmus had suffered the usual fate of moderates and was damned by both parties — and Jerome's old Vulgate was declared authentic, though it was soon revised.

The principle of indulgences and "spiritual graces" was affirmed, but the conditions under which they were granted were to be controlled. (The control has not always been rigid. A few years ago, when the Friday menu was still a matter of faith and morals, I had dinner with a Spanish friend of mine whose devotion to the Church makes Loyola's seem rather lax in comparison. While I nibbled my frozen fish she was happily tucking away a steak. We were old enough friends so that I could ask for an explanation; she told me that she knew a little church in Spain that sold meat-on-Friday dispensations for *very* little; it had been granted the privilege so that it could raise money for the crusades. She would have told me about a delightful little dressmaker in exactly the same way.)

Finally, there was a non-dogmatic declaration on the Immaculate Conception of Mary that met a profound response among the faithful and led to the cult of the Immaculate. This and papal infallibility were to become dogma three centuries later.

The Council of Trent got more done than the Second Vatican Council; in fact it may have gotten too much done. It spelled out the tenets of Catholic theology so clearly and unmistakably that the ambiguity that might have made for agreement was destroyed. It was harder now for the heretics to come home. And in the coming Age of Enlightenment, and in ours, the exact statements of doctrine have created a difficulty for men who were committed to the new science, the new thought, but who in their hearts wanted to give allegiance to the Church as well.

There was very little change in Church doctrine in the time between the Council of Trent and the recent council; only extension and intensification. Paleontology seems to show that a creature that becomes highly specialized in one direction is headed for extinction if the environment changes, that nature cannot reverse evolution. But more than nature is involved here, and with God's help we may be able to find our way back to the plasticity of our desert days and a new patristic age.

The Rebels

IN authoritarian organizations it is easy to become a rebel without realizing it, by violating some unenforced rule that others have been violating with impunity. Of four men who suffered for their beliefs — Pico della Mirandola, Savonarola, Giordano Bruno, and Galileo — probably only Savonarola was fully aware of the risk that he was running. Certainly Giovanni Pico della Mirandola, Count of Concordia, a favored child of the Church, had no intention to rebel.

One way to understand Hamlet is to remember that he was a graduate student, and the same is true of Pico. He was a tall and beautiful young man, gifted and perhaps overly learned, idealistic, intellectually proud, and, I think, going through a period of over-ideational excitement that would now be dealt with by the Student Health Service rather than the Inquisition.

Great things were hoped of Giovanni Pico, by his family, by the Church, by his friend Lorenzo the Magnificent. At fourteen he began the study of canon law at the University of Bologna. Later he absorbed the humanism of the court of Ercole d'Este, went deeply into Aristotelianism and Averroism at the University of Padua, and at the University of Paris acquired a completely inaccurate idea of how much it was safe to say in the late Quattrocento.

Pico took all knowledge for his province; he explored Jewish and Arabic mysticism, he showed too much interest in magic and astrology, and he fell under the spell of the third century theologian Origen of Alexandria, whose grace and imagination made many a scholar forgive him for being a heretic. Origen himself had no idea that he was a heretic; he lived an austerely Christian life and at sixty-five withstood torture in the Decian persecutions. He was reputed to have written six thousand books in his long life (his posthumous enemy Jerome said that it was only eight hundred).

Pico, having woven Origen's ideas and many others together with his own, decided to share his wisdom with the world in a work entitled *Novem Centuriae Conclusionum Secundum Opinionem Propriam* (Nine Hundred Conclusions According to His Own Opinions.) And these theses he would defend publicly in Rome, the heartland of orthodoxy.

His *Conclusions* were already known in the Holy City, where they were arousing great interest, perhaps because they touched on forbidden subjects. But Pico was never allowed to defend them in public as he had planned to do. Instead he found that he had been the subject of a communication from Innocent VIII, gentle and almost apologetic in its tone, but shocking to a young man who had had so little disapproval from his superiors: "We have had news that our beloved son Giovanni Pico, Count of Concordia, has set forth many and various conclusions on various subjects. Of these, some, from what we can understand from the words themselves, seem to deviate from the straight way of the orthodox faith; some of them instead are dubious and of ambiguous significance because they depend on new and not commonly used words, and are so involved and obscure as to require explanation." Conclusions that departed from the Catholic faith and had the color of heresy were to be pointed out and "those that could be understood in a wrong way must be put in such a way as not to be repellent to faith." Those "in which an unexpected novelty of words has been introduced" were to be rewritten "in a clear open way." Innocent VIII sounds plaintively like a twentieth-century pope faced with the intricacies of Teilhard de Chardin.

Pico had the Pope's assurance that no harm would come to him, and his friends urged him to let well enough alone. But Pico, in the folly of his youth, spent twenty nights writing an *Apologia* made up of thirteen *Disputationes*, in which he restated his belief in magic, in freedom of thought, in Origen. Innocent VIII recognized the challenge for what it was, and ordered the tribunal of the Inquisition to punish Giovanni Pico della Mirandola according to the canon law regarding heretics. A Secret Archives document announces the fate of the Nine Hundred Conclusions: "Taking the advice of our venerable brothers, the cardinals of the Holy Roman Church, we condemned and reproved the book of the nine hundred conclusions mentioned above, in spite of their containing some Catholic and true propositions, because of the admixture of condemned statements . . ." (and also, no doubt, because plowing through all nine hundred of them was more than could be expected of any man). "Under pain of excommunication we order those who possess it to give it to the flames within two days."

Pico himself was arrested on the way to Paris, but was set free through the intervention of Lorenzo and the Gonzagas. He returned to Florence and continued his work, now in a deeply Catholic vein. His *On the Dignity of Man*, an assertion of freedom of the will, is powerfully written but full of self-references and boasts about his achievements at an early age. He urged Lorenzo to bring Savonarola to Florence, and in repentance and humiliation became his disciple as he had once been Origen's. He died at thirty-one, perhaps of poison, perhaps because he was weakened by a deep conviction of guilt.

The orator's art is as evanescent as that of the actor, and we can only guess now at the power and charm that made it possible for the Fundamentalist preacher Savonarola to take over a city as intelligent and sophisticated as Florence. There was little in Girolamo Savonarola's early life to foreshadow it. He was the son of an upper-middle-class Ferrara family, an odious youth who wrote condescendingly to his parents, "I am still flesh and blood like you." At twenty-two he became a Dominican monk, and was regarded as a very poor preacher until, suddenly, he became a very good one. Probably he had learned to slow down and to talk without notes; more probably still, he had experienced and enjoyed that sudden rapport with the audience that is like a declaration of love.

He was in his late thirties, a thin dark little man with the Incan profile that one sees so often in Italy, when Lorenzo the Magnificent brought him back to Florence. An Archives manuscript by "Certain Parties" — probably by one of his followers — says: "To see him out of the pulpit he looked as if he were truly a little lamb, full of humility and charity. No one ever saw him angry. But when he was in the pulpit he seemed to be much taller than his usual stature, showing a soul virile and invincible, completely free of all worldly considerations, and not afraid of any living man. He was like the ancient prophets, apostles, and martyrs."

Not long after his arrival in Florence Savonarola became prior of the Monastery of San Marco, a place where the Middle Ages must have lingered, for the Archives has a signed account of a miracle within its walls that sounds as if it had come from Gregory's Golden Legends: "And I, Simone di Mariano Filippepi, I have heard from a man of good fame . . . that the night after the holy Christmas, to a young brother in the convent who had never sung Mass, there had appeared very clearly in his cell on the small altar in front of which he was praying, Our Lord in the form of a small child." It was time to go to matins, and there was a conflict in the brother's mind as to whether he ought to leave the Holy Child, "and deprive himself of such a great sweetness," or to take it along. He finally hid the child under his cloak and "all shaking for great happiness, and for fear, he went into the choir without saying anything to anyone. But when his time came to sing and he approached the music rack, the child disappeared from his arms."

We have glimpses of Savonarola's life in the monastery; of the impromptu processions that assembled at night and wound through the grounds, to end with a sermon in the church; of the orchard seminars: "In summer time, in the evening after supper, Father Girolamo used to go with his brothers into the orchard, and with Bible in hand he had them sit all around him, and talked to them and posed them questions." The other side of his character appeared in the pulpit where he preached his thunderous and moving sermons against the corruption of the government and the Church and against the sins of princes and prelates, described in fascinating detail.

Lorenzo the Magnificent died, and his ungifted son eliminated himself by trafficking with the enemy from beyond the mountains. Savonarola came to power, and Florence became a Puritan theocracy: a fact to remember when we think that Italy will never go Communist because it is incapable of accepting a rigid code of conduct.

For a time Savonarola was enormously popular; seventy or eighty "gentlemen of good sentiments" accompanied him on his way to church, and the street between San Marco's and Santa Maria del Fiore "was filled with men and women who came only to see him, as if they never had seen him or heard him." Crowds of eight thousand attended his sermons; three thousand children sang in the choir. "One had the feeling of being in heaven." He passed laws regulating the details of personal conduct, and Florentines gave up their colorful medieval garb for sober clothing. He even — and here the chronicler seems astonished — "reformed the women and the young people, and that was certainly a very holy work of great importance."

This reformation of the young was accomplished by the organization of youth groups that in some ways resembled the youth organizations of twentieth-century totalitarian countries. In fact they had much in common with Mao's Red Guards. Some of the young, given authority over their misbehaving elders, made the most of it. They "spread terror among all the rascals of the common people and cleansed the city, both inside and outside, talking to and persecuting gamblers and similar persons," and, on occasion, tearing the clothes from women whom they regarded as improperly dressed. These young zealots, again like the Red Guards, gathered up "vanities" — things of which they disapproved — and threw them into bonfires in the Piazza della Signoria. If the fires had destroyed only such objects as wigs and playing cards they would have done little harm, but paintings of nudes and precious manuscripts were burned with the same wild joy.

Meanwhile Savonarola had been carrying on a running feud with Pope Alexander VI Borgia, who he compared unfavorably with the fathers of the early Church. For a time the Pope was patient under Savonarola's attacks; he knew as well as anyone that the Church needed to be reformed. Later, "with great art," he asked Savonarola to stop preaching for two or three months, "because in addition to his sermons being painful to the pope himself, they were very irritating to the Moro of Milan and to Pier Francesco de' Medici." But Savonarola resumed preaching against "that shameless prostitute," the Church.

Alexander finally banned his books, and ordered that no one, on pain of excommunication, might wear or possess the little crosses of red wood that he had given his followers; they were to be turned in to the Vicariate. However, none came in. A search was made, through the city and the countryside, and thousands of the crosses were found and brought to the Vicar, who gave them to his cook for kindling and to provide a quick light fire for cooking the *cocina*. "But certainly," one chronicler states, "I did not give up mine."

Opposition to Savonarola grew as the economy of Florence declined and as his recriminations came to include new groups of fallible humans. "He reprimanded with great acerbity the sins and vices of laymen as well as of the religious of his time." Local opposition was added to that of Rome, and Savonarola, on Palm Sunday of 1498, knelt before the crucifix and said: "My Lord, I thank you, because you will soon make me like yourself." But when the opportunity for martyrdom came, in a proposed trial by fire between himself and his Franciscan enemies, he let his young disciple Domenico da Pescia volunteer in his place. Domenico is one of the most attractive figures in the Savonarola story, a strong young man, utterly, unquestioningly devoted to the Church and to his teacher.

On the morning of the day of the trial, Savonarola's party went in procession with the Host to the square where the contest was to take place. "Not only the square, the streets and the balconies were overcrowded with people, but even on the roofs a grain of rice could not fall, they were so full." The Franciscans were already waiting, and with them, in spite of the Signory's order, were armed men, "all as paladins in favor of the brothers of Saint Francis."

The day became a series of postponements; one has the impression that everyone concerned except Domenico was playing chicken. He was to be first to enter the fire, but the Franciscans "to delay things and use up time in order for night to come, started to claim that they wanted the brother to be undressed, alleging that some enchantment might have been within his clothing." In one way and another the day was wasted until evening came. Savonarola, carrying the Host, Domenico with the crucifix, and their party started home; as they went the crowd threw rocks at them. And on the door of the Church of San Marco, and at other places in the city, cartoons were posted showing Savonarola in intimate conversation with a novice.

Later his enemies attacked him in church, and seized him with the two brothers Dominic and Sylvester, though Dominic laid about him with a heavy candlestick. The Signory wrote to Rome for judges; Rome sent them happily: Romolino, the Governor of Rome, and the Father General of the Dominicans, both unfavorable to Savonarola. They were welcomed in Florence as cardinals, and a chronicler says that "the first gift made to Romolino was a beautiful girl dressed as a boy," given him by one of Savonarola's enemies. He kept her with him throughout the trial, then took her to Rome; when she escaped and came back to Florence she "complained to many of the wickedness of Romolino, and of his many ribaldries."

The chronicler, who says he had his information from an eyewitness, tells of the questioning of Savonarola. Romolino asked how he had learned the things he preached about catastrophes to come, and the reforms needed by the Church; Savonarola raised his eyes to a nearby crucifix and said, "I have it from God." He was tortured for days, then ". . . as they were unable to get from him what they wanted, they attached him to a rope and beat him. As he was very frail and delicate physically, exhausted by great pain, he said, 'Take me down and I will talk.' And they took him down, and Romolino took him aside and for a long time they talked together, face to face, with no one present. Never was heard, never was known, of what they said." But at some time Savonarola denied being a prophet and confessed to vainglory. He was thrown into prison, chained and bound, and only his enemies were allowed to see him. Here the chronicler says he had his information from Savonarola's guard, assigned to him because of his violent dislike for the prisoner. "But according to God's will, while living in the same room with Savonarola, the man became converted, then was always in favor of him and by a miracle was healed of the French sickness which was greatly rotting him." It was through the guard that the small book on the rules of good living that Savonarola wrote in prison, "by his own hand, but with great fatigue, because of the tortures," was preserved.

The Secret Archives contain another account, utterly ambiguous, from this period. A letter had been written by "a very bad religious" to Giovanni Manetti and Franceschino degli Albizzi, enemies of Savonarola, asserting that he was a hermaphrodite and used one sex or the other according to his desires of the moment. They asked the Signory's permission to visit the prison, and there Giovanni, "who was a cultivated man, said a few words in Latin to him. Savonarola answered, 'I cannot persuade myself to believe that the Signory, or you, come to me with such an enormous accusation; and treat a poor servant of God in such a way.' They said that they had to do it, and that Savonarola had to obey and submit himself. In answer he requested that Manetti at least be satisfied to do this alone, and as decently as possible." Manetti agreed, sending out Albizzi and the guard, "then, taking a lighted candle, he examined him and touched those parts as much as it pleased him, with the right hand. But then, not much time passed before he became seriously sick. Questioned by his wife and relatives, he did not want to confess, but always shouting 'This hand! This hand!' agitating it very miserably, he ended his life."

Savonarola and his two companions were allowed confession and communion before they died. His monk's clothing was taken away from him, but he asked to be allowed to hold it: "Holy dress! When I wanted you, God gave you to me, and I have preserved you immaculate . . ." Three scaffolds were raised in the Square of the Signory; the men were hanged one after the other, "and immediately the fire was lit. And dust and ashes were made of them." People who tried to gather relics were pushed back by the guards, and the ashes were thrown into the Arno from the Ponte Vecchio. Downstream a miller took a heart from the water and "with a few experiments it was proved that it was the heart of Savonarola."

Because of Savonarola, Pico della Mirandola became a Puritan, Botticelli turned to religious art, Michelangelo went in fear of the Last Judgment all his days, and Macchiavelli, thinking over his success and his failure, concluded that people will believe anything and that the only power, ultimately, is the power of force. Luther regarded him as a forerunner of the Reformation, but Raphael, a dozen years after his death, included him among the saints and doctors of the Church in his painting of *The Dispute on the Sacrament.* And for present-day Catholics he is part of the Church's past, and close to us for that reason, as in old age even the enemies of our youth seem closer to us than the uncaring strangers of today.

Giordano Bruno, born in 1548, was a Dominican monk who had fled his monastery and drifted north through Europe, arriving at last in England, "that net in the sea set to catch the wild and restless of all nations." At Oxford he knew Sir Philip Sidney and the avant-garde of Elizabethan England; he was so much one of them that he wrote of the queen as "that singular and incomparable Diana of our times, who from these frigid regions so close to the Arctic parallel sheds light and glory over the whole terrestrial globe."

It was in England of the age of discovery that he wrote the work on which his martyrdom, in modern eyes, depends — *On the Infinity of the Universe and of the Worlds*. The universe, he said, stretches endlessly, since only an infinite universe could be worthy of an infinite God. "Why should we, how can we, think that divine power is inactive? Why should we assume that divine goodness would will to be scarce, to remain sterile, rather than to become reproductive, a father, prolific, adorned, and beautiful? Why should you think that God is limited?" And this God of the unlimited worlds was immanent in His universe, present in every atom, every grain of sand, anywhere in the worlds. Like Teilhard after him, he believed that all matter was moving toward consciousness.

Even more dangerous was Bruno's belief that the infinite worlds are peopled, like our own. "For the infinite excellence manifests itself incomparably better in innumerable individuals, than in those which are numerable and finite. Therefore it is necessary that of an inaccessible divine countenance there be an infinite image . . ."

Bruno's stay in England ended when Oxford dismissed him from his post because of his Copernican views. He returned to the Continent, adhered to the Lutheran Church for a time until he was excommunicated, and finally, homesick for Italy, turned southward.

Everywhere he went he wrote, and everywhere he went he talked. His ideas were a mixture of rebellion and insight, and sometimes seemed intentionally shocking. (His *El Candelaio* was banned in San Francisco in 1965, nearly four hundred years after it was written.) He satirized the Church, and the social order; he questioned transubstantiation and the virgin birth. Bruno was a loud-mouth, fatally indiscreet in a Europe where freedom of speech was only a gray light on the horizon. But his return to Italy was not as rash as it seems, for it was to Venice that he went. Venice had a reputation for resisting the Inquisition; Galileo's friends felt that he was safe as long as he stayed there. But Bruno in his wanderings had become a stateless man.

He came to Venice as tutor of the patrician Giovanni Mocenigo, who wanted to improve his memory by taking a course in mnemonics. Mocenigo's memory showed little improvement. It was probably a case of what the Jesuits call invincible ignorance, but he came to believe that Bruno was intentionally withholding material from him. In this mood of ill feeling he reported some of Bruno's remarks to his confessor and was ordered to act as an *agent provocateur* in leading Bruno on to still rasher statements. Bruno finally suspected that he was in danger, but was arrested before he could escape, and was tried and condemned by the Venetian Inquisition. Like Galileo after him, he recanted. He was sick from the treatment he had received in the dungeons; the tribunal often had to order him to stand up instead of sitting on the floor.

His recantation was useless; a few months later the Venetian Inquisition turned him over to the Roman Inquisition, which kept him for seven years in Castel Sant'Angelo's "underground cellars in which neither the light of the sun or the shining of the moon could be seen." Here he withdrew his recantation. Perhaps he was now convinced that he would be punished in any case, as witches were burned in spite of their repentance.

The original records of Bruno's Roman trial, which went on for seven years, have been lost; extensive searches in the Secret Archives and in the archives of the Congregation of the Holy Office have failed to bring them to light. Apparently they disappeared sometime between 1815 and 1817, the years in which the Secret Archives were being returned to Rome after the defeat of Napoleon. Probably they were among the vast quantities of documentation sold to a Parisian cardboard manufacturer. However, a fifty-nine-page summary of the trial was discovered, in the Eighties of the past century, in one of the cabinets of the Miscellanea of the Secretary of State. This document, a transcription *"quod frater Iordanus male sentiat de fide catholica,"* was part of a volume not registered in the inventories. The discoverer, an assistant custodian of the Archives, must have been disappointed to hear that Pope Leo XIII failed to share in his joy, and even gave emphatic orders that the trial records were to be shown to no one. By now the Church realized that burning geniuses was bad for public relations; disclosure of the document would have been a gift to anticlericalism. Normally the volume containing the trial would have been classified, given a number, and restored to one of the fifteen cabinets of the Miscellanea of the Secretary of State. Instead the cardinal in charge of the Archives took possession of it, along with the copies that had been made, and placed, or rather deliberately misplaced, it among the personal archives of Leo's predecessor, Pius IX. There it remained until 1940, when Angelo Mercati found it after a fifteen years' search.

This unsigned document is a summary of the proceedings of the trial, drawn up for the use of the assessor and of Cardinal Bellarmine. The compiler sometimes reproduces the testimonies verbatim and sometimes summarizes them, but is always careful to indicate in the margins the corresponding page of the original document, which he must have had at hand. From this we can tell that the lost process of Giordano Bruno, from which this summary was made, had at least 295 pages. The summary deals with twelve main points: the Trinity, divinity and incarnation, transubstantiation and the Holy Sacrament, hell, the existence of many worlds, the adoration of the Magi, (whom Bruno saw as riding on giraffes), the eternity of the world, Cain and Abel, Moses, the prophets, the virginity of Mary, and the immanence of God. Even without Bruno's cosmological views, the Church had enough to hang him.

The summary contains elements from both the Venetian and the Roman trials: the accusations of the informer Mocenigo, damning excerpts from Bruno's writings, the depositions of two booksellers, Ciotti and Brittano, who in general seemed friendly toward Bruno, and the testimonies of five of Bruno's fellow-prisoners. In Italy, having been in jail with someone is a recognized human relationship for which we have a special name; we call such persons *compagni di carcere* — our companions of incarceration. Bruno's companions of incarceration were Brother Celestine, a self-styled Capuchin who was burned in 1599 for doubting the saving power of Christ, Brother Giulio da Salò, a Carmelite, Francesco Vaia, a carpenter, Matteo de Silvestris of Orio, of whom nothing is known, and Francesco Graziano, a translator of ancient manuscripts and a transcriber of prohibited books. Graziano was regarded as a cultivated person and a good writer, but slightly insane and not to be taken seriously.

Mocenigo's testimony conveys something of the fear Bruno felt when he first realized he was in the hands of an enemy. "I asked him if he was not afraid I might accuse him of so many wicked words against Christ and the Catholic Church. He answered that he was not afraid of the Inquisition, because he did not offend anybody in living in his own way, and that he did not remember having said anything bad to me. And that even if he had he had said it only to me. He told me that if I would let him go he would teach me everything he knew. Your Holiness must forgive me for not having brought this accusation before; I did not realize his depravity until I had him in my house for a month or so." He reported that Bruno felt that the Catholic faith had strayed from the teachings of the Apostles, who converted the people by preaching and example instead of by force. Monks were all donkeys and should be deprived of income. Ciotti the bookseller agreed that Bruno was "a man without a religion," and Brother Celestine said he had uttered many heresies. Bruno denied having said that the Catholic faith was blasphemous, but admitted having said that "the Apostles did more with their good preaching, exemplary life, and miracles than is now accomplished by force."

The informer further testified, "I have heard him say that the Catholics' greatest blasphemy is saying that bread is transformed into flesh, and that he is opposed to the Mass." Bruno replied that he had never doubted any of the sacraments, and had refrained from attending mass only because, as a defrocked priest, he was excommunicated. The informer reported him as saying that "in order to live well it is enough not to do to others what we would not like to have done to us"; Bruno answered that he had always considered that good works were necessary to salvation. Mocenigo and other witnesses accused him of having said that Christ "did a wicked thing in seducing the people," and apparently died very much against his will, and that both he and the Apostles had performed false miracles by the use of magic. Graziano was quite certain he remembered Bruno's saying that Moses had surpassed the magicians of the pharaohs, and had gone alone to Sinai to prepare with smoldering wood the "fumigations" that would give the effect of dark clouds, and that the Mosaic law could not have been of divine origin because it was a tyrannical and bloody law. Bruno admitted having said that Moses was a great expert in the learning of the pharoahs' magicians. "I believe that before he spoke with God he might have operated as an expert in magic, which is not in itself illicit, being grounded in the forces of nature . . . As to mathematic and superstitious magic, I believe it to have been alien to Moses and to all honored minds."

Mocenigo asserted that Bruno himself had claimed to know the art of divination, and that, "When I had almost come to the point of denouncing him, he asked me to give back a booklet of conjuration that I had found among his papers. And when he was put in prison we found a small book full of strange characters that I entrusted to the Inquisition." Bruno explained that he had studied astrology only to see whether it contained any grains of truth.

Brother Celestine and Graziano agreed that Bruno had defended Cain's killing of Abel on the ground that Abel was an executioner of animals, and killed the most beautiful of his lambs. Bruno defended himself, saying, "God liked Abel's sacrifices better than those of Cain. But at first, laughing, I said that Cain was a Pythagorean, because he loathed the killing of animals. I remember having said, in a sort of jolly mood, just talking, that of these two brothers, one was a wicked person because he killed animals, but the other, who had it in his soul to kill his brother, was worse."

Brother Celestine accused him of joking about the relics of the saints, and laughing at the Genoese for revering the tail of Christ's donkey. Graziano supported this: "He said you could take the arm off someone who had been hanged and pretend it was the arm of Saint Hermaiora."

A more serious charge was the informer's statement that Giordano "in speaking of people's great ignorance in regard to the Trinity, spoke also of the virginity of Mary, and said it was impossible for a virgin to give birth to a child. And in saying that he laughed and made jokes." Bruno denied this: "I believe that it is not physically impossible for a virgin to conceive, but I maintain that the Blessed Virgin did not conceive Christ physically, but through a miracle of the Holy Spirit." And then, the summary remarks, he went on to explain by what method a virgin could conceive physically. This is one of the places where one regrets the loss of the original documents.

His prison companions were unanimous in saying that he did not read the breviary, and Graziano reported him as saying that it was so badly written that it made him nervous, like a lute out of tune. Bruno insisted that he had nothing against breviaries in general, but that some of them contained stories not accepted by the Church. One Dominican breviary that he had examined in the jail at Venice said that Saint Dominic had given the devil a whipping. How could one beat the body of a spirit? Besides, it was Graziano, not he, who had said that the breviary in the Roman prison was like a lute out of tune. And one reason he did not read the breviary more was that the works of Solomon impelled him toward *luxuria.*

Brother Celestine accused him of having said that the cross worshiped in the churches was not the kind of cross on which Christ died, "and that this shape of cross that is now kept over the altars was a symbol worn on the breast of the goddess Isis, and that the ancients had always venerated it, and that the Christians had stolen it from the ancients." "I said that the cross did not have four arms as it is usually portrayed," Bruno admitted. Instead, he asserted, criminals at the time of Christ were put on a forked cross. (A few weeks ago I saw a Y-shaped crucifix of the kind that Bruno described, on sale in a religious-art store within a block of Saint Peter's.)

The accusers agreed, and Bruno admitted, that he did not believe in eternal punishment. It was also charged that "he said that he liked women very much, and that he had not yet had as many as Solomon did, and that the Church committed a great sin in making a sin of sex, which suits human nature very well and which he himself regarded very highly." Bruno admitted having said that of the many sins, the sins of the flesh were minor ones.

His hedging and compromising disappeared when the inquiry dealt with his ideas on cosmology. To the informer's charge that he said, "there are endless worlds and God makes endless numbers of them," and to Graziano's "he asserted that there were many other worlds and that the world was a star, and that to the other worlds ours seemed to be a star," he answered that his beliefs on this matter were clear from his books, that the universe is infinite and in the universe there are numberless worlds. "Whosoever holds that God produces limited effects thinks of God as something finite and of finite virtue."

From all this Bellarmine distilled eight propositions that Bruno was to accept or deny. He recanted, then withdrew his recantation and stood firm to the last. He refused every comfort offered by the Brothers of Saint John the Decapitated, who were responsible for the care of condemned criminals, and the register of their confraternity says that although "they talked with him affectionately and with much discussion of doctrine in order to show him his mistakes, he remained in his accursed obstinacy, his mind always playing with a thousand errors and vanities. And he so insisted in his obstinacy that he was taken to the Campo de' Fiori and there, undressed and nude and bound to a stake, was burned alive." Alive, and with a wooden wedge driven into his mouth to stop his blasphemies. As he died he turned his head away from the cross that was held out to him.

Bruno was without honor in his own country until the last century, when a statue of him was erected on the Campo de' Fiori. It is very much like the one of Leonardo at the Da Vinci airport, but Bruno's is darker, heavier, sadder. We seldom look at it, because we are shocked at ourselves for what we did to him, shocked at him for refusing the crucifix. Perhaps some future pope, as an act of grace, will remove his excommunication. Meanwhile the Russians have given him a better memorial than ours: a large crater, on the order of the Tycho Brahe Crater, on the far side of the moon has been named for him. "Above the graves of the Inquisitors,/The quiet stars still bear their Arab names."

One of the Archives' great treasures is a bound volume of handwritten original records of the trial of Galileo. It is often exhibited on state occasions, though I am not quite sure in what spirit, since the Galileo episode was not our finest hour. Perhaps it is shown in a gesture of historical objectivity, perhaps as an example of the mistakes that men can make. But I think that the main feeling is one of muted pride.

Only one volume is left of the original three. The others, like the acts of Bruno's trial, probably ended in the maceration-vats of Parisian papermakers. It is not certain how this one survived. One version of the story says that France returned it at the middle of the century, on condition that it be published. But Angelo Mercati, Prefect of the Archives, discovered in the Secret Archives letters "of the rubric of the nuncio of Vienna" saying that documents relating to Galileo's trial had been returned to the nuncio by the widow of the Duke of Blacas, who had accompanied the French king Charles X into exile. In any case, publication of the materials was very slow. A few excerpts, carefully chosen, came out in 1850, but there was no real reprinting until 1877.

Galileo's sin was not heresy but *hubris*. He was a man of multiple gifts. Milton saw him primarily as an artisan, "the Tuscan artist" who viewed the moon through optic glass "at evening from the top of Fiesole," a maker after the order of Leonardo. He saw himself as a philosopher; the figure of the research scientist was not yet clear enough to be a major self-concept. In addition he was a brilliant writer. And like Shakespeare's golden lad he knew his estimate; Galileo anticipated one of the more annoying habits of modern intellectuals by referring to his mind in the third person.

He was one of the fortunates who find their calling early; at nineteen he had already discovered the law of the pendulum. He became professor of mathematics at the University of Pisa and then at the University of Padua; he experimented with magnetism; and he became a devout Copernican in the conflict that was dividing the learned world. It was a time of great interest in astronomy; contemporary portraits show astronomical instruments lying casually on tables and bookcases as intellectual status symbols. The idea of a turning earth that swung around the sun was perilous and exciting, and some thought that it "saved the appearances" (conformed to the facts) better than the Ptolemaic theory. But Solomon himself explicitly said that "the sun goeth down, and hasteth to the place where he ariseth."

In Galileo's time discussion of the Copernican theory was permitted as long as it was regarded as a hypothesis; in fact the new Gregorian calendar had been worked out on the basis of the Copernican theory. If Galileo had been a little more cautious and the Church a little more flexible, the hypothesis might have passed over into principle without painful conflict. The issue was forced too soon. In another generation or two the evidence would have been overwhelming, and the Church would have decided with Saint Augustine that an institution holding opinions that everyone else knows to be false is likely to get itself laughed at.

Even after the Council of Trent there had been a tacit agreement that thinkers were not to be disturbed if they refrained from rocking the boat, and one could argue that if the Inquisition had been as voracious as is generally thought, Bruno and Galileo would not have spoken as openly as they did; that their folly must have rested on an assumption drawn from the observation of many undisturbed acquaintances.

The Copernican controversy might have remained an academic one if it had not been for the coming of the telescope and the consequent introduction of masses of new evidence. Galileo billed himself as the instrument's inventor in the subtitle of *The Starry Messenger:* ". . . with the Aid of a Spyglass recently invented by him," but whether he actually invented it is a matter of semantics. He had heard that such an optical instrument had been made in Holland, and with no more information than that he built a far better one, "after first being illuminated by divine grace." Eventually he had a telescope that enlarged by nearly a thousand times and brought objects over thirty times closer. The mountains of the moon, and its maria, were visible now; it clearly was not the perfect spherical body that the old theory required. Jupiter had its satellites, like the Earth, and Galileo named them, for his patrons, the Medicean Stars: "Four Planets swiftly revolving about Jupiter at differing distances and periods, and known to no one before the Author recently perceived them." The dispute about the Milky Way was ended "by making its nature manifest to the very senses as well as to the intellect," and it was a pleasant and elegant thing, Galileo said, to demonstrate the nature of the nebulae.

The Starry Messenger created a sensation in the intellectual world; its author was a celebrity. In gratitude for the Medicean Stars, Cosimo II made Galileo chief mathematician and philosopher to the Grand Duke of Tuscany, and Galileo, against the advice of his friends, left the employment and the safety of Venice. He was now within reach of the Inquisition.

Everything seemed to be going well; even the Jesuits were favorable to him. Old Father Clavius, head of the Roman College and the astronomer of the new calendar, was finally induced to look through the telescope, and by the time of his death in 1612 was almost a Copernican. Galileo's visit to Rome in 1611 was a triumph; Paul V Borghese granted him a friendly interview and the Roman College put on a Galileo Day. But before he left the city Cardinal Bellarmine had secretly ordered an investigation of his possible connection with a suspect heretic. Galileo continued publishing, and the *Letters on Sunspots* in 1613 spoke of "the great Copernican system, to the universal revelation of which doctrine propitious breezes are now seen to be directed toward us, leaving little fear of clouds or crosswinds."

But the clouds were gathering and the crosswinds beginning to blow; little ones at first, as one cleric and then another challenged the astronomer. And Galileo responded, as abstract geniuses often do, with maladaptive behavior. Instead of lying low as his friends urged, he tried to put things more strongly, more clearly, confident that once people understood they would agree with him.

His *Letter to the Grand Duchess Christina,* not printed at that time

but privately circulated, dealt with the apparent conflict between science
and Scripture, and was subtitled "Concerning the Use of Biblical Quotations in Matters of Science." The letter was long and learned; the Grand
Duchess must have had a hard time getting through it. And Paul V Borghese, a man trained in canon law and "impatient of novelties and
subtleties," had no inclination to examine scientific evidence.

In February of 1616 the Qualifiers of the Holy Office and its assembled
theologians declared heliocentrism to be "foolish and absurd, philosophi-
cally and formally heretical," and the Pope ordered Cardinal Bellarmine
"to summon before him the said Galileo and admonish him to abandon
the said opinion." The word *admonish* was a euphemism; he was to be
imprisoned if he did not agree. Galileo acquiesced. He was free to return
to Florence now, but not to "hold or defend" the Copernican theory. He
remained discreetly silent for some time, but in 1623 he published *The
Assayer*, ostensibly an attack on an unhappy colleague but actually a
work on the philosophy of science. It was in this year that his friend
Maffeo Barberini came to the papal throne as Urban VIII. Barberini was
something of an intellectual; he is credited with having kept Paul V from
making the decision against Copernicus an *ex cathedra* statement, an
action that would have settled the infallibility controversy. Galileo again
visited Rome, and renewed his acquaintance with the Pope in several
friendly audiences. The climate of official opinion seemed to have
changed, and soon afterward he began the work that was to bring him to
trial and recantation — the *Dialogue Concerning the Two Chief World
Systems*. He had been forbidden to hold or defend the Copernican theory, but that, he felt, need not prevent a character in a literary work from
holding and defending it. An added factor of safety was that it dealt not
with cosmology directly but with the tides, which Galileo thought were
caused by the motions of the earth.

In its way the *Dialogue* is a deeply religious work. Whether or not a
man has a reputation for religious feeling depends partly on whether he
happens to be drawn to that particular aspect of the Trinity that is in
vogue at the time; many of our generation who regard themselves as
agnostics are devout worshipers of God the Holy Ghost. We are more
able than men of the seventeenth century to see the piety in Galileo's
cry: "Is the Work less noble than the Word?" and less shocked when
Galileo, in veiled but vivid language, suggests that mankind is only a
single grape in the vast vineyards of the Lord.

His casuistry in putting his cosmological arguments in dialogue form
instead of stating them directly was unsuccessful. In the American frontier phrase, Galileo outsmarted himself. He forgot that he was dealing
with men who had as much social intelligence as himself. And worst of

all, he had insulted the Pope; Prince Hal was now the king. Urban, in one of their amiable conferences, had given him an idea that he thought might be useful: the argument that we cannot say in just what way a given cosmological effect is achieved, since God in his omniscience and omnipotence might have done it in a hundred ways. Galileo used the argument, but he put it into the mouth of his dullest character, the Aristotelian Simplicio.

In 1632, when Galileo was called to Rome by order of the Pope to face the Inquisition, his friends urged him to flee to the safety of Venetian territory. Galileo refused; he was old and sick and a Catholic. But he might have accepted the suggestion if he had known of a document in the files of the Holy Office stating that Cardinal Bellarmine had, in 1616, forbidden him even to discuss the Copernican theory. It was once thought that this document had been added to the archives at the time of Galileo's trial, in 1632 or 1633, perhaps through alteration of an earlier document. But investigations made in 1927, when the Vatican permitted it to be examined by X-ray and ultraviolet analysis, indicate that it is genuine. The fact that other documents near it are in the same handwriting also leads to this conclusion. Galileo's biographer de Santillana is inclined to agree that it is of 1616 provenance, but thinks it was intentionally seeded in the files at that time by someone who knew the situation, and knew Galileo, well enough to plan on his writing or talking himself into trouble sooner or later.

The Pope wanted Galileo convicted; therefore the doubtful injunction was regarded as valid by the prosecution. But to strengthen the case it was also charged that he had both held and taught Copernican views. There was no defense but what the old man himself could provide: "I remember that the command was 'not to hold or defend.' It may be that 'and not to teach' was also there. I do not remember it, neither the clause 'in any way whatsoever,' but it may be that it was; for I thought no more about it . . ." Galileo was to function as a great genius up to the time of his death nine years later, but age brings its fears of fading powers, even before they have faded.

Again, he went too far in defending himself, and made statements that any intelligent reader knew were not true: "I have neither maintained nor defended in that book (the *Dialogue*) the opinion that the Earth moves and that the Sun is stationary, but have rather demonstrated the opposite of the Copernican opinion and shown that the arguments of Copernicus are weak and not conclusive." One is forced to agree with the Counselors of the Inquisition who reexamined the book and found that "The accused does teach, he does defend, he does hold."

A compromise solution was reached when Galileo expressed, to a commissary who was himself a Copernican, his willingness to confess his errors. When he returned to court he reported that he had reread the *Dialogue* and, "I freely confess that in several places it seemed to me set forth in such a form that a reader ignorant of my real purpose might have had reason to suppose that the arguments brought on the false side, and which it was my intention to confute, were so expressed as to compel conviction by their cogency."

In the document in which "I, Galileo, have abjured as above with my own hand," he admits the validity of the 1616 injunction against "teaching in any way whatsoever the said false doctrine." And most degrading of all, he promised: "Should I know anyone guilty or suspected of heresy, I will denounce him." The sentence pronounced on him consisted of two widely disparate penalties — imprisonment at the pleasure of the Pope and the weekly repetition for three years of the seven penitential psalms. Three of the judges did not sign; one of them was Francesco Barberini, the cardinal-nephew.

"An old unhappy tale of things done long ago, and ill done." And yet, in a sense, the Inquisitors were right. Unable to judge the scientist intellectually, they judged him *ad hominem*, as servants judge a house guest. And the servants are often surprisingly right. Galileo *was* lying, he *was* a jumper to conclusions, and he *was* wrong — not about heliocentrism but about many other things: the cause of the tides, the shape of the earth's orbit, the three-bodied Saturn and the horned Venus. The real victim of the Galileo trial was not Galileo but his illegitimate daughter Virginia, Sister Maria Celeste, who died shortly afterward of illness brought on by anxiety and, perhaps, by the conflict of conscience she must have undergone in helping her father's friends hide his papers from the Inquisition. Galileo in prison, forgetting his age while he slept, as old people often do, wakened thinking he heard his young child crying.

Italian science walked very softly for a while. Botany was popular as a safe subject; no one foresaw that Gregor Mendel's peapatch would be far more dangerous than Galileo's telescope. Descriptive astronomy was still possible, and the globe of the moon that I have on my coffee table shows name after name of Italian origin. But in the enchanting lunar nomenclature — Mare Crisium, Mare Imbrium, Oceanus Procellarum — there is one kind of name that is lacking. Places all over the earth were being named for the Trinity and the saints, but I find no religious names on the moon. There is no Sea of the Conception; only the Mare Foecunditatis. The long, needless dichotomy between science and religion had begun. They had turned away from the Church as Bruno, in the flames, turned away from the crucifix.

The Copernican theory gained ground even in religious circles, and within twenty years of Galileo's death the Jesuit astronomers were hastily calculating a back azimuth. After all, they pointed out, heliocentrism had never been condemned *ex cathedra*. Galileo's trial had been effective in acquainting people outside scientific circles with the new astronomy. And I think that the popularity of the carrousel, that one sees in old pictures, may have had something to do with getting his theory accepted, for the moments of silent, slow circular motion at the end of a ride produce a convincing illusion of a circling environment, like the illusion of the revolving sun.

For intellectuals, at least, the world was enormously enlarged. When Milton's Lucifer was thrown out of heaven it was not a tumble from some celestial Tarpeian rock, but a fall for nine days, earth time:

> *Nine times the space that measures day and night*
> *To mortal men, he with his horrid crew*
> *Lay vanquished, rolling in the fiery gulf . . .*

Some historians suggest that the Galileo controversy was ultimately of benefit to the Church, since its recent defeat in the field of astronomy may have made it reluctant to risk another defeat when the argument over evolution arose. While the Protestant churches were angrily resisting the new Darwinian philosophy, the Catholic Church wisely decided that its concern in regard to man's beginning was not with the evolution of his body but with the creation of his soul. In general it avoided direct confrontation with science until its twentieth-century challenge to the laws of geometrical progression.

This caution may be a matter of policy rather than of intellectual conviction, and it is not hard to foresee the stand that the Church will take in the coming age of biology. When new and identical individuals can be grown from a single cell, when "old age becomes the handsome child at last," the faithful will be told that it is their duty to die in the traditional manner. We will exhort and decree and excommunicate, and the conflict will end with our christening the test-tube babies — the formula recommended for the baptism of multiple monsters ought to do very nicely — and doing our best to bring them up as Christians. Perhaps it will help us then to remember that acceptance of the Copernican system, of the idea of a turning and traveling earth, of an enormous universe, had little effect on the Faith.

It is only occasionally that we have to think of the implications of Galileo's ideas. A year or so ago I visited Palomar Observatory on its southern California mountaintop. Seen from a distance it is a beautiful thing, a combination of the male and female sex symbols, and I wondered again why the utilitarian artifacts of our time are the best of its abstract art. Even inside it, where the delicately balanced mechanism gathered the light-rays, it was a work of man — something to give one confidence and pride. But below the observatory, a little way down the mountain, was a small museum given by the mother of a boy who in his short lifetime had loved astronomy. Its directors, perhaps working with limited funds, had provided only pictures — enormous illuminated photographs of superb quality, hung on all four sides of the room, with explanatory legends beneath them. I saw the pictures and I read the distances and the numbers — a hundred billion stars in the galaxy, a hundred billion galaxies in the universe — and I felt utterly lost. How could God care for everyone in the shining dust-clouds of worlds? I thought how the mother of the dead child must have felt, picturing a small soul adrift in all of this. I wanted to leave and find a church — a small church with a good roof on it — or, failing that, the hamburger house down the road, where there was coffee and companionship.

A junior high school class, shepherded by their teacher, had been going through the museum. Now most of them had left, but two boys had lagged behind. Instead of only glancing at the inscriptions, as the others had done, these two were reading them. The brightest of the lot, I decided, and very good friends, from the way they accepted body contact as they leaned toward the pictures. One of them put his finger on a spot of light in one of the photographs. "That one's Alpha Centauri," he said. "We'll get to that one first." His tone was confident, proprietary.

The teacher came back to round up her young star-captains, and I realized with relief that the mother who had donated the museum must have understood her son. The stars no longer seemed distant and intimidating; instead they were like the lights of town, like the lights of Rome as they look from the Abruzzi. And I could see that a time may come when man will be proud that he is of no mean city.

Beatrice Cenci

THE Middle Ages were fascinated by the idea of incest. One reason for this may have been the Church's definition of the term, which was so inclusive that priests in small villages and landlocked valleys had to ignore the regulations if their parishes were to have any legal marriages at all. This noncognizance was more difficult in the case of the aristocracy. One could even venture a theory that much of the political chaos of the medieval period was due to the canon laws that prohibited cousin marriage: in a day of the divine right of kings, the requirement of extreme exogamy prevented the building up of stable hereditary strains.

Consanguinity was not required for incest; relationships by marriage or through a baptismal sponsor also ruled out sexual union. Some persons of the time found the Church's inclusive ban very convenient, for it made possible a medieval version of divorce Italian style. A husband and wife who had nothing else in common could discover with suitable horror that they had a common great-grandfather. But for the average Christian the wide range of relationships that came under the laws against incest must have added to the individual burden of guilt, for almost everyone would, at some time in his life, have felt at least a momentary sexual attraction toward some persons within the prohibited degrees of relationship. Normal and innocent persons must have thought themselves possessed of unnatural tendencies.

Whatever the reason, the Cenci scandal that broke in 1599 aroused extreme public interest and quickly became part of the folklore of the Italian people. Shelley, over two hundred years later, found it a topic of lively interest and discussion. Because of the prominence of the persons involved, and because the case was tried in the Sacred Rota, the Cenci murder left traces in the Archives. One of these is a worn parchment, often very difficult to read, entitled "Report on the Death of Giacomo and of Beatrice Cenci, and of Lucrezia Petronia Cenci, their stepmother, for patricide, in Rome on Saturday, September 11, 1599, under the Pontificate of Clement VIII." This manuscript, discovered in the Secret Archives by Angelo Mai, is in the Italian of the period and apparently dates from the time of the trial. Its author is unknown. However, his sympathies were obviously with Beatrice, even to the extent of shading her age by a few years: "The Lady Beatrice was sixteen years of age, small and rounded, with a beautiful face, small eyes, a profiled nose, round cheeks and wavy blonde hair."

The papacy was at least partially aware of conditions in the Cenci family. The atheistic Count Francesco Cenci, a little under fifty at the time of his death, had three times paid heavy fines for sodomy, and Roman wits said that the Aldobrandini Pope, engaged in founding the family fortune, resented his murder because it cut off a reliable source of income. However, the papacy had ordered him to provide proper support for his two older sons, and to furnish a rich dowry for the marriage of his elder daughter to a nobleman of Gubbio. Beatrice is said to have written a letter to the Pope complaining of her father's treatment of her and asking the Church's assistance in ending the situation. This letter was not answered, and may not have been delivered; it has not been found in the Archives and we can only guess what it contained.

The anonymous writer of the report says that the Count "was living in such a disorderly fashion that he took the boys that were always around the house, along with women of pleasure, into his wife's bed. Not satisfied with that, he attempted with threats and force to violate his daughter Beatrice, who had grown up and become beautiful. He was not ashamed to go to see her in bed nude, or to go around the house nude, or to take her into bed with his wife so that she could see by candlelight what he and his wife were doing. He used to tell the poor girl a very new heresy, that when the father used the daughter, saints were born."

The Count's wife, Lucrezia, was the stepmother of the children; she was sympathetic but could do little to protect them. Equally ineffective was Monsignor Guerra, a priest who frequented the house and listened to the confidences and complaints of Beatrice and Lucrezia. The chronicler describes him as "handsome in face, large and well-built of body, touched by love of Beatrice."

As long as the Cenci family was in Rome the Count was subject to the force of public opinion. The city was still small, and an aristocracy is always a village. It may have been for this reason that he sometimes took his wife and daughter to an old Colonna castle between Rome and Naples. La Rocca Petrella was an abandoned mountain stronghold, rocky and remote as the cave above Zoar where Lot lay with his daughters.

Here, on one occasion, the Count's sadistic tendencies took the form of locking his wife and daughter into their rooms for months, under the most squalid conditions. And at some time during their stay at La Rocca Petrella it is said that he attacked his daughter. We do not know that the attack was successful, or even that it actually occurred. But something happened that confirmed the Cenci family — Beatrice, her stepmother and her brothers who were visiting — in their conviction that the Count must be killed.

It was planned as a perfect crime, but ineptly planned, for the conspirators included Beatrice's mentally deficient young brother Bernardo, and the act was to be accomplished by hired assassins. One of these was Olimpio Calvetti, the caretaker of the castle, with whom Beatrice is said to have been having an affair: the other was a certain Marzio, who was also, according to the chronicler, "touched by love of Beatrice," a condition that seems to have been fairly general.

The assassination was originally planned for Trinity Sunday, but Lucrezia protested against having it done on such a holy day. (Later, at her trial, she claimed to have withdrawn from the plot at this point, and to have tried to dissuade the others from carrying it out.) But on September 9, 1598, the Count was given opium in his evening beverage. After it had taken effect, the two hired killers, Olimpio and Marzio, crept into his room, but came out again saying that they could not bring themselves to kill an old man in his sleep. (Was it from this that Shakespeare drew his inspiration for Lady Macbeth's: "Had he not resembled my father as he slept, I had done't"?)

Beatrice is said to have gone into a rage. "If you don't do it, I will, but that will be the end of both of you." They then went back into the Count's room and drove an iron spike through one of his eyes into his throat. The women wrapped his body in a sheet and threw it from a balcony at the back of the castle which was used as a passage to the outdoor toilet, so that his death would seem to be the result of a fall. In the morning when the body was discovered in the old, half-wild orchard under the balcony, they broke into cries of shock and grief.

The Cenci family returned to Rome, but the Count's death was regarded as suspicious and was investigated by an agent of the Kingdom of Naples. No evidence could be found against the Cenci brothers, but Beatrice had given the sheet to a washerwoman, telling her that she herself had stained it during the night. Interrogated, the washerwoman said that the spots did not resemble menstrual blood.

Chance took a hand when Monsignor Guerra decided that it would be safer to do away with the assassins. Olimpio was successfully killed at Terni, but before Marzio could be eliminated he was arrested in Naples for another crime. Thinking that he had been arrested for the Cenci murder, he confessed his part in it.

The Cenci family was imprisoned at Castel Sant'Angelo. Later, one of the men who had killed Olimpio was also arrested for another offense, and repeated what he had heard from him about the killing of the Count. Lucrezia and Giacomo, Beatrice's brother, were put to the torture and confessed. Beatrice at first denied the charges and "it was only at the moment when her beautiful hair was to be cut that all her strength left her. 'I will tell what I want to tell, and what I know.' " The position of the Cenci had been weakened by the fact that Monsignor Guerra had escaped, disguised as a coalman. He had bought two donkeys for props, filled his cheeks with bread and onion to change the contours of his face, and blackened his blond hair with coal-dust.

Beatrice's trial was colored by the animosity of Pope Clement VIII (1592–1605), who took the position that he didn't know what young people were coming to. "Shall we live so long as to see children murder their own father?" At one time he changed Beatrice's lawyers, suspecting that they too were touched with love for Beatrice, but in one way he was just, for the lawyer he finally gave her was Prospero Farinacius, one of the great legalists of Rome. Though Beatrice herself, at her trial, did not accuse her father of attacking her, he based his defense on her right to defend her chastity. The case was lost, but his appeal to the Pope for mitigation of the death sentence is a legal classic. "May God be with me, Holy Father, though Beatrice Cenci impiously procured the death of her father, Francesco Cenci, yet if it be true, as is believed, that Francesco by imprisoning Beatrice in the dungeons of the castle of Petrella, and there barbarously treating her, endeavouring to overcome her chastity, it is not contrary to law to hold that she is deserving to be judged with some degree of clemency. In Plutarch we read of Cyane, who stabbed her father Cyamnus with a sword because he had debauched her, and of Medullina who, having been violated by her father Aruntius while he was intoxicated, put him to death. Whatever Beatrice may have done she must have been held to have done because of imminent or future danger or fear, and she is on that ground deserving of legal excuse, as having committed homicide in defense of her honor."

All of this was an appeal to classic precedents, but in Prospero Farinacius' pleading there were also two very modern ideas — that of diminished responsibility due to age, intellect and emotional conditions, and an almost open distrust of confessions gained by torture or the fear of torture. He is at his best in his defense of the young Bernardo, condemned in perpetuity to the galleys. "Again I submit to the consideration of Your Holiness the fatuity and the imbecility of intelligence of this youth, which render it not astonishing that giving way, in all probability, to the influence of his brother Giacomo, he should have been persuaded to give his consent. Therefore, by reason of this imbecility and fatuity of mind, added moreover to his tender age, he should, in my opinion, be excused from the ordinary punishment."

The boy had not been tortured because of his age — "*propter minoram aetatem*" — but Farinacius held that even a fear of torture could distort a testimony. "Holy Father, I cannot omit to say, that though Bernardo's confession may be generally true, yet it is not to be argued that, as it came forth without the use of torture, it is to be considered as a spontaneous confession. The fear of torture very probably induced this boy to confess as he did."

Public opinion was strongly on Beatrice's side; crowds shouted for "the Roman virgin" and prominent citizens sent in petitions for clemency. But the sentence of execution stood. "The Pope is stern; not to be moved or bent, a marble form, a rite, a law, a custom, not a man." Situational ethics might not have a name for another three hundred years, but Clement had recognized the concept and rejected it.

On September 11, 1599, a year and two days after the murder, Beatrice, her brother Giacomo and her stepmother Lucrezia were put to death. Giacomo, after having had his flesh torn away with red-hot pincers, was struck with a mace, drawn and quartered. The two women were beheaded. Beatrice, after the first shock of the sentence ("Oh God, how can it be possible that I am to die so soon?") had become calm and resigned. The chronicler describes her at her execution: "The lady arrived at the place on foot, after having traversed the Via Crucis. Her dress was as the nuns wear, of wine color with large sleeves and a great girdle and a silver veil. The sleeves of the garment under it were very large, and showed her arms. With one hand she held the crucifix, with the other a handkerchief to dry her eyes and to wipe the sweat from her face. At the moment of execution she left her white slippers, trimmed with ribbons and lace, at the foot of the stairs and very quickly offered her neck to the knife-blade, adjusting herself to keep the executioner from touching her."

And Clement, in the country for the weekend, raised his arms and gave her plenary absolution as he had promised to do. A year later he pardoned young Bernardo, though the enormously rich Cenci estate remained confiscated.

"And finally the body of Beatrice was brought to an isolated place, washed and dressed in a white dress trimmed with flowers." A funeral procession with five hundred torches accompanied her to her burial in the place she had requested — near Raphael's *Transfiguration* at Saint Peter's of Montorio.

In the Church of Saint Gregory there is a picture by Guido Reni of the martyrdom of Saint Andrew. The girl in the foreground may be Beatrice Cenci. She wears the lilac-colored dress that Beatrice often wore, and her right hand, in a maternal gesture, is caressing the turned head of a blond child, as if she wanted to keep him from seeing the flaying of the saint. Beatrice's young brother Bernardo, before being sent to the galleys, was made to watch his sister's beheading, as a means of preventing further delinquency.

Scandalosa, Impia, Contra Verbum Dei

THERE have always been rebels to challenge the Church. Their de
fiance is sometimes open, like Luther's; more often covert — the
passive defiance that assents and disobeys. And sometimes it is more subtle still, and consists only of obedience; anyone who has ever seen a rebellious convent, or factory, or military unit, knows what Shakespeare
meant when he wrote, "Those he commands move only in command;
Nothing in love."

From century to century the Church has had to combat heresy, sorcery,
corruption in the monasteries and the convents. The emphasis changes
but the problems themselves seem endlessly viable. One thinks of witchcraft as being something far in the past, or at least confined to primitive
and disadvantaged areas. Yet present-day Rome is said to have many secret societies, cutting across social classes with that democracy characteristic of underground organizations, and engaging in magic that ranges
from the relatively innocent to such practices as calling up the Doppel-
gänger of a living person and extracting secrets from it. I do not know
whether current rumors of the Black Mass are true or not, but there is
one house in Rome where I no longer go.

Belief in witchcraft and diabolism has existed throughout the Christian
era. The desert saints were troubled by visitations, some of which sound
very much like amateur attempts at psychotherapy, and devils enlivened
the dullness of monastic life. Among the many causes of the medieval
belief in diabolism — helplessness in the face of illness or other disasters,
survival in degraded form of the old religions, carry-over from Christian
supernaturalism, absorption of the Zoroastrian doctrine of polarized
good and evil — one of the most important may have been that demon-
ism, and its dangers, provided material for excellent tales of mystery and

suspense. Devil stories were as fascinating to people of the Middle Ages as murder stories are to us.

Occasionally there were inquiries in regard to clergy who were suspected of practicing the magic arts, and there were even dark suspicions of a pope, Sylvester II (999–1003), who had studied at the sorcerer's city of Toledo. In Spain, they said, he had not only learned to make celestial globes of purple leather, but to build fires in which the spirits of the dead took on a wavering but recognizable outline. Petrarch's reputation was such that Pope Innocent VI was afraid to listen to readings of his work, suspecting incantation, and a deposition in the Secret Archives says that Dante was a skilled sorcerer whose powers were to have been used, if necessary, in the Visconti's attempt to kill Pope John XXII by witchcraft.

In the countryside paganism survived longer than in the cities, and country priests sometimes officiated at the rites of both religions. Perhaps something of the old idea of the priestess had also survived, in the wise women who understood herbs and spells and cared for the health of both the human and the animal population. Some of the spells were pagan, but some made use of the new religion, as in the Irish charm for the closing of wounds:

> *No more blood, no more pain,*
> *Till the Virgin Mary bears a child again.*

These women were sometimes very capable; Paracelsus is quoted as saying that he learned more from them than from the universities. But the very existence of a pharmacopeia of powerful drugs constituted a temptation. The same garden that grew digitalis for heart patients could also grow the devil's oatmeal that was used to procure abortion, as well as the deadly nightshade that could kill a wealthy relative who had lived too long, or a rival, or an enemy.

One gets the impression that the witchcraft of the countryside was somewhat less vicious, less blasphemous, than that of the cities; more of a turning toward the gods of nature and less a parody of Christianity. Yet it was in the Alpine valley of Camonica that, according to the Venetian records, investigators uncovered rites that were a strange mixture of beauty and repulsiveness.

The ancients had a pleasant way of naming roads for the imports that they carried: the Silk Road, the Incense Road, the Amber Road. The prehistoric Amber Road ran southward from the Baltic across the Alps to the great civilization that wanted the resinous melted gold, then regarded as a precious stone.

The Amber Road is still in use; it is now a popular smuggling route. A little way off it is the Val Camonica, under a mountain where the gods once lived. On the valley's glaciated rocks are thousands of stick-figure carvings done by the Camunu tribes, a Stone Age people islanded in the Bronze Age. With the stick-figures are the drawings, carved and then painted in red and yellow, of the Battle-Axe People, the Celts — sun symbols, oxcarts, mounted warriors. The valley is thought to have been a cult center, a place of pilgrimage for thousands of years. Dante mentions it, perhaps this bit of "in" information is another of the half-confessions of Canto XX, for in the late Middle Ages it was the scene of a witchcraft trial that took sixty-four lives.

One of the reports in the Venetian archives describes it as it was at that time: "The Camonica Valley, where each year our butchers go to buy geldings, is a barren place inhabited by people without any rule of civilized life, of a rustic way of living." The writer's account of witchcraft's methods of recruitment bears out Michelet's theory that poverty was a precipitating factor, for each warlock, knowing that his status depended on the size of his following, was on the watch for people in desperate circumstances. Then "with good and artificious words showing sympathy and desire to comfort, he offers him a paradise of delights if he will do what he is told to do." When the victim took the bait "as the fish to the hook, or the flies to the honey, or the mouse to the pumpkin," he was taken to a lonely place, introduced to the devil, and made to have carnal intercourse "if it is a man, with a woman, if it is a woman, with a man, of beauty much greater than Paris or Helen." At these rites the devil was "enthroned, very richly dressed, having two horns on his forehead that represent truth." Then there were banquets and orgies at which some artificial device apparently was used: "When they take joy together, they say that they have the feeling of having intercourse with a frigid thing, and according to the voluptuous preference of the person, she who wants the penis great has it, and she who wants it of medium size has it . . . nevertheless, they say it is always a frigid thing that they feel."

This coldness of the instrument brings to mind the viability of frozen sperm. The idea of artificial insemination was nothing new in the world: Zoroaster was said to have had three sons born a thousand years apart, of semen preserved in a sacred milk. Thomas Aquinas had thought it possible that demons could transfer semen from a man to a distant woman. It was in the fourteenth century that artificial insemination came into use in horse-breeding — and the Val Camonica was horse-breeding country.

Another interrogation tells a similar story of the initiation of witches: "By some old women, sometimes by their own mothers, they were induced to deny their faith, and make a cross on the earth, riding over it with their feet, as if on horseback, and spitting on it. Immediately a beautiful horse appeared, on which they all of them mounted, and in a short time they found themselves on a very beautiful plain located over a mountain [a plateau, or a country of the mind?]. There they say they have seen a great multitude of men and women, who went around two by two, dancing, singing, or playing musical instruments. Everyone showed great joy for the new woman that had arrived, praising her and stroking her. And she, thinking she was the most beautiful and honored lady in the world, was very happy. There was a chair all in gold, on which was seated a great master and lord, and all around many barons and many masters, all dressed in gold and silk; nearby there were beautiful young men. The guide presented the new disciple to the lord.

" 'Daughter, may you be welcome,' he said, making a great deal of her, and touched her with his hand," and she says that "his hand was not as our hands." (The old writings have an irritating way of being silent just when one would like them to be specific. How was the devil's hand different from ours — in touch, in temperature, in structure?)

« *1* »

The great witch-hunt, that set bonfires to burning all over Europe, that made the slaughter in the Val Camonica seem trivial, was touched off by Innocent VIII's bull of 1484; one of a long series of bulls against witchcraft:

"It has recently come to our ears, giving us a great deal of pain, that many people of one and the other sex have sinned with diabolical incubi, and succubi and, enervated by enchantment, have committed crimes and delinquencies. They have made perish, suffocate, and die the deliveries of many women, the fetuses of animals, the fruits of the earth, the grapes of the vineyard, the orchards, the pastures, and men and women and mares. They have done injustice and tortured things, the men, the women, the mares, the sheep, and other animals, with terrific internal and external pains. They have kept men from impregnating and women from conceiving, so that men cannot give the due of marriage to their wives, nor wives to their husbands."

The Pope's concern here was not only for the souls of Christians, but for the organic world, for "men and women and mares." In its first intention, the fight against witchcraft was to protect the natural world, to defend life against death, fertility against sterility. But in its execution it became a means of judicial murder, for in the same bull the Pope named as legates to Germany, with power to inquire into the rumors of witchcraft, two cold-blooded fanatics named Jakob Sprenger and Henry Kramer. Later, Sprenger published a classic work on witchcraft, the *Malleus Malofioarum;* the fact that the Pope's bull assigning him to Germany was printed with it lent it official status. It influenced the Church's thinking for centuries, and is still consulted by students of the black arts.

The method followed by the inquisitors was to go to a place where witchcraft was said to be practiced, preach a rousing sermon in the local church, and then ask the members of the congregation to report any suspicions that they had. There was no penalty for false accusations unless they were proved to be malicious. Charlemagne's rule that false charges of witchcraft and cannibalism were to be penalized with about one-third the punishment of the crime itself had been forgotten, and it must have been easy for personal spite to disguise itself as spiritual concern.

The presumed witch was then seized, while guards searched her home for unguents and other incriminating evidence. She was often taken to prison in a basket or tied to a ladder, to keep her from touching earth and so being helped by the devil. When she was allowed to have a lawyer, his defense was limited by special rules not applicable in ordinary cases. He was instructed not to take advantage of small legal points, not to bring counter-accusations, not to defend heresy. Accusation nearly always led to conviction, for while confessions were not to be extracted under torture, this was interpreted to mean *present* torture; torture ten minutes ago, or ten minutes in the future, didn't count. If the accused confessed, he was given the sacraments before being put to death.

The rationale for the death penalty was a passage in Exodus: "Thou shalt not suffer a witch to live . . . He that sacrificeth unto any god, save unto the Lord only, he shall be utterly destroyed," but there were other grounds as well. Sorcery and witchcraft came to be defined as a form of heresy, for which death was the normal punishment. Or, if the witch had been convicted of preventing coitus between husband and wife, this was classed as homicide, also punishable by death.

The persecution seemed to spread the disorder rather than control it, and the witchcraft fever infected some of the convents, where it found ready victims among young women, already suffering from various forms of deficiency disease. We read of young religious running through the fields, climbing trees, swinging from branches, and imitating the cries of animals. They confessed to congress with the devil and with their confessors; some of the priests went insane or made confessions of their own.

« 2 »

There were also individual instances of aberration, as in the case of Sister Cristina del Rovales, a nun of the Third Order of Saint Dominic in

Naples, a summary of whose trial is found in the Archives' Miscellanea. This is probably one of the cases that has convinced the Church that the only dependable saint is a dead one.

Sister Cristina was famous for her sanctity and revered even by her confessors. In the city her name was invoked, and small images of her were sold. She suffered the pains of crucifixion almost continually; her hands and feet and side were scarred with marks that gave promise of becoming stigmata, and a crown of thorns grew from her flesh. The Holy Office thought she was too good to be true. Would a woman so young, who had had no practice in heroic virtue, really be given the reward of the stigmata? Besides, there was circumstantial evidence. The wound on her side was on the left side, not on the right as Christ's had been. Also, "the thorns that emerged were small like ordinary thorns, not like the ones of the crown of our Lord, that one can see venerated in many sanctuaries of Christianity."

Alerted by these discrepancies, the Inquisition changed her confessor and locked her up in a Carmelite convent. When she attempted to escape, she was put under the supervision of "a nun of holy life, who day and night should not leave her." They must have made her sleep in a lighted room, as the Texans did Jack Ruby, for one night the nun of holy life "saw the blankets of the bed of Sister Cristina rise two palms high over her body. Going near her, she asked 'What is that that I see?' And immediately the blankets came down. And Sister Cristina, awakening at this moment, asked what were the noises of bells, and it was just then that the bells sounded the matin."

In time "the guilt of her conscience and the continuous insistences of her confessors" led her to admit everything to the Holy Office. The little five-year-old boy who had appeared to her was not the Christ-child, as she had said, but a handsome blond young man in his twenties, "to whom she consented with her mind, and had great pleasure. Often, to her great delight, he put his hand in the natural vase, pressing it with art." Cristina's property was confiscated, and she was forced to undergo public degradation before spending the rest of her life "enclosed in the prisons of the Holy Office."

In time — a very long time, as it must have seemed to the people living then — the witchcraft fever burned itself out. By 1538 Spain was putting a brake on the popular demand for more witches to burn, and in 1634 the Holy Office ordered the preaching of sermons cautioning against abuse of the concept of witchcraft. The Inquisition had never been as severe in Italy as in Germany, and in 1657 the Church barred arrest on suspicion and the indiscriminate use of torture.

The persecutions might have ended earlier if a singularly inept group of conspirators had not tried to murder Pope Urban VIII by the wax-image method. According to Giacinto Gigli, whose diary was originally in the Secret Archives but is now in the Vatican Library, one of them was a nephew of the *papabile* Cardinal d'Ascanio, and the plan was that, when d'Ascanio was elected pope, his nephew would procure papal favors for the entire group. They held a dry-run rehearsal of the crime, killing a woman of the court by burning a wax image of her, but when they tried to burn the Pope's image it refused to melt. On thinking it over they decided that, naturally, special treatment would be required for the image of a pope, and that human blood, the blood of one of the conspirators, would be the best thing. But when they drew lots, the role of sacrifice fell on the cardinal's nephew, who very reasonably pointed out that he could not procure favors from the future pope if he were dead. They drew lots again, and this time the chosen victim went to the Inquisition and told everything. The conspirators were burned in the Campo de' Fiori.

In the collective madness of the persecutions many thousands of people had been killed — a single judge in Wittenberg is said to have sentenced twenty thousand. The mortality in Germany was so heavy that it may have had its effect on the nature of the population, if we assume that those who were killed were a little different from the others, more individualistic, more imaginative, or possessed of what Kramer and Sprenger called "venereous charm." And their accusers survived. Perhaps the gas ovens of the concentration camps were lit from the fires that burned the witches.

« 3 »

Besides the sin of witchcraft, the Church had to deal with the endemic problem of corruption in the monasteries and convents, not all of which conformed to the spirit of the Council of Trent. A report on the reformation of the convents of Naples in the time of Paul IV (1555–1559) points out that difficulties were partly due to the fact that in some convents abbesses were chosen by election. After a hard-fought campaign the disgruntled minority sometimes took off and founded a new convent elsewhere. This new convent, short of endowment, took in any nuns it could get for the sake of the bit of money that they could contribute.

This brought in "people of low and ill-born social conditions." And many of the nuns were in convents only because their families could not provide dowries for all the daughters. Parental concern then moved the families to take the girls out and give them a holiday now and then, in the parks or at the theater. If no parents were available, a nun could "have a little pain in the head, or show a sad and weary spirit, or some other indisposition, true or pretended, of the body." Compliant physicians often certified these illnesses, and the girls "with all these excuses and fictions, and with the laxity of their superiors, in the spring and in the autumn were used to go to the hot springs of Pozzuoli, where according to their own will they could stay fifteen or twenty days." Furthermore, some abbess with political gifts had inaugurated the custom of giving the girls one day a week off. "And as the supervising vicar could not keep spies in all places, nor have a list of these days, unfortunately when a nun was found out of the convent, she would say that she had permission from the abbess, and that this was just the day that she was allowed to be out of the convent."

These offenses continued "up to the moment that the blessed God, wanting the good of our souls, inspired the mind of the very excellent Duke of Alcala, viceroy of this kingdom, to entrust a cardinal with the task of having all the monasteries checked in order to know how things really were and remedy them." Many of the facts found by the investigators could not be made known because they would have "offended the honor of such nuns and, in consequence, of all their relatives, that are very noble and well-known in these cities." The report ends with the discouraged comment that to put an end to the minor abuses it had taken the authority of a pope and the work of three very famous cardinals and a canonized saint.

Many of these offenses seem to fall short of mortal sin, and one is inclined to hope that the girls had a good time at the hot springs of Pozzuoli. But in some convents there were grave abuses, and in one of them the worship of the life-force passed over into madness, and an entire convent was given over to a sex cult. A report of the abjuration made in the Convent of Santa Croce in Florence, November 16, 1641, details the confessions of Canon Pandolfi Ricasoli de, Baroni della Trappola, confessor of the convent, and of Lady Faustina Mainardi, the abbess, and three others. The statements of the principals show that this was no new philosophy but a heresy that was old at the time of the Avignon popes, at the time of Leo the Great: the belief that all things are permitted to the perfect. The recorder says of Ricasoli: "He has taught and he has practiced that all carnal acts between men and women are not only allowed, but meritorious, if one keeps his mind united with God. He called such exercise an exercise of purity. He called the sexual organs of men and women holy and sacred parts, and therefore he respected them and he said they ought to be respected, and that the hair around them was like the veils around holy and precious images. He said that such an exercise of purity was not for everyone, but only for the very few whom God called to such perfection. Such acts, he said, had been practiced even by Christ our Lord, with the Magdalene, the very holy Virgin with Saint John, and the *Beati* who are in heaven."

Perfection was to be attained through sexual acts done as exercises of purity. "He taught such exercises of purity to many religious people and to most of the girls in Faustina's care. Practicing with them, he used to make them say the Pater and then added that they should thank God for the gift they had received, and should practice it with other women. Christmas Eve he slept with two girls in order to greet the day with greater devotion."

One of the worst offenses of this scoundrel was that he used the time of love to give lessons in theology. He taught Faustina to say, at the time of union, "I renounce you, Satan, and all your iniquities. And I unite myself with you, Jesus Christ." He explained the stories of David and Ruth, "saying that such acts never did offend the Lord, but were of great perfection and had greater value than the fasting of Saint Paul, Saint Anthony, and other anchoritic saints. With such acts one did not lose virginity, but acquire it and make it perfect." This philosophy may have been widespread at the time, for in England John Donne had written: "Tonight put on perfection and a woman's name . . ." But his "Epithalamium at Lincoln's Inn" was for a lawful marriage.

Under Ricasoli's tutelage the convent engaged in mass perversion and in a primitive phallus-worship. The sexual organs were applied for healing purposes, and Faustina put Ricasoli's semen in a handkerchief among the relics of the altar. In view of all this the two principals in the case were dealt with very lightly. Both were declared heretics, but Faustina was not excommunicated because she abjured. Ricasoli was excommunicated for a time but later absolved in view of his abjuration and public repentance. His wealth was confiscated, but the Pope gave some of it back to him, keeping the rest to build prisons.

« 4 »

It is a relief to turn from the obscenities of the Ricasoli trial to the remoteness of astrology, but astrology also was a sin in the eyes of the Church, and in another trial it brought a better man to a worse punishment.

Those of us who have never let our eyes slide toward our own birthdate in a newspaper horoscope column are presumably free of any belief in astrology. There were few such unbelievers in the courts of the Cinquecento and the Seicento. Interest in the "lore of the Chaldeans" had declined in the centuries following the fall of the Roman empire, perhaps under the influence of Saint Augustine. The saint had a friend whose skeptical father had carefully observed the life courses of two children born at the same time and had found little similarity between them; Augustine then reflected that an astrologer would have had to cast the same horoscope for Esau and for Jacob. But the flooding of Arab learning into Europe brought astrology with it.

The motivation of the astrologers was scientific; their pseudo-science was an attempt at quantification and an admission that man was an integral part of nature. The Church disapproved of astrology because it assigned too much influence to the natural world, though it would seem that Thomas Aquinas' theory that the stars were guided by angels might have taken care of this difficulty. Astrology's effort to achieve exactness of prediction was the first cold touch of the mechanistic hypothesis. Though many of the cardinals maintained private astrologers, the papacy was prepared to take a dark view of a churchman who was an astrologer himself.

Two *chirografi,* or directives, of Pope Urban VIII (1623–1644) in the Secret Archives order the bringing to trial of Orazio Morandi of the Monastery of Santa Prassede in Rome, formerly Abbot of Vallombrosa, accused of practicing the astrological arts. The charges were to be prepared not by the Holy Office but by the governor of Rome, and the names of cardinals and their relatives were not to be mentioned. Instead, white spaces were to be left where their names would have occurred.

Orazio Morandi was one of the leading astrologists of Rome, as well as being a political scientist and a journalist. He kept copyists in important Roman offices, and wrote *avvisi* and articles in depth on political matters. In 1630 his astrological studies convinced him that Pope Urban VIII would die within the year. Other astronomers, including Abbot Cherardi of Padua, agreed with him, although Father Raffaello Visconti, later on Galileo's board of review, held that if the Pope stayed in Rome he could live until 1633 or 1634. The cardinals prepared to gather for the conclave, and the Pope was furious; the assumption of his early death had caused all sorts of political complications. And he may have felt as Franklin Roosevelt did when he attended a church service in a Washington cathedral and the minister suggested that he might like to be buried there — Roosevelt was angry all the way home, from time to time muttering "The old buzzard. . . ."

The judge assigned to the trial went to the Monastery of Santa Prassede, put seals on Morandi's library, and took the astrologer-abbot to the prisons of Torre di Nona. Later, when the judge returned to the library to look for incriminating documents, he found the seals still in place but no compromising material. During the night Morandi's monks had gotten into the library by removing the floorboards, and had taken away all the books and manuscripts that could have been used by the prosecution.

Some of them were burned, others hidden. Later, however, the abbot's servant told the story to the lawyer Teodoro Ameiden, whom he trusted because of his twenty years' service to the monastery. Ameiden repeated it and it came to the ears of the authorities. He and the servant were arrested. The servant would not talk again, even under torture, but the lawyer confessed.

There was still no evidence to convict the abbot. But in stealing the astrological materials Morandi's monks had reached a height of courage — or a depth of iniquity, according to the way one looks at it — that they were unable to maintain. When the judge issued a decree promising lenience if they would tell where the books and manuscripts were hidden, cartload after cartload of incriminating material took its way to the tribunal. The abbot admitted everything and gave the names of some of his colleagues; a week or so later he died in prison, apparently of poison. Astrology was a worse offense than astronomy; Morandi's friend and one-time guest Galileo was still living in freedom.

The Tower of the Winds

LATE on a winter afternoon of 1564 Michelangelo died in his workshop-house near the Baths of Caracalla. The latter part of his life had been darkened with religious fears and regrets. He had complained of old age early, and was troubled by many illnesses. Among his original letters in the Vatican Library is a long list of eye remedies ("for sickness of the eyes that derives from heated blood, gather dew with very white linen.") By the time of his death even his art failed to comfort him, "I cannot paint or sculpt in such a way as to bring peace to my soul."

An official inventory lists the belongings in his possession: the great bureau that held his personal linen and that of the house, his bed with a straw mattress, the little chestnut horse, with saddle and bridle, in the stable, the hoarded golden coins from a lifetime of labor for the popes. And with them were the vast playthings of genius; collage plans for Saint Peter's, and unfinished statues — not beings like the *David* now, but figures more bone than flesh. There was a chiaroscuro of a skeleton with a coffin on its shoulder; on the coffin was written "I say to you, who to the world have given/ Body and soul and spirit together/ In this dark coffin you must take your place." At the beginning of the Renaissance Masaccio had done a similar painting; the Renaissance began and ended with a skeleton.

Even before Michelangelo's death, Paul IV (1555–1559) had had Daniele da Volterra paint clothing on the athletic nudes of the Sistine Chapel — the "trousers of Volterra" that Rome could still joke about. It is difficult to tell how much the outlook of the average man, or even of the average cleric, was changed by the Council of Trent. When the power structure makes its views clear, most people have sense enough to go along with them. The sudden outburst of liberal expression after the Second Vatican Council suggests that a great deal of opinion is suppressed even in our milder age.

From the historical viewpoint the early baroque period was a tragic time, a period of religious wars in which the behavior of Christian toward Christian was such as to give one hope for the Congo. The Church was busy with maneuverings to save Germany for Catholicism; to replace that "servant of vice, Elizabeth" with a Catholic sovereign — by assassination, if necessary; to hold what it had and to get back what it had lost. The Inquisition built an invisible Berlin Wall around Catholic Europe, and behind that wall the Church became more intensely what it already was, emphasizing the very points on which it differed with the heretic sects. The Protestants denied the intercession of the saints; Rome set up a marble ballet of saints and angels. The Protestants denied transubstantiation; Saint Catherine drank the blood of Christ on the altars, and in Bernini's *Allegory of the Spilled Blood* the Madonna offered blood from her Son's pierced side to the thirsty souls in Purgatory. And at the Church of the Capuchins on Via Veneto the monks arranged the bones and skulls of four thousand of their dead brothers into decorative designs, where arches of bones are stacked in skillful stonework, small skeleton-cherubs hover in the ceiling, and the graceful curves of ribs are woven into a frieze.

Yet Rome was beginning to have the look of a modern capital. Sixtus V had ordered the construction of ruler-line roads, and ancient palaces, churches, and monuments had been cleared away to make room for them. At the nerve centers of these splendid road-nets were the obelisks, Christianized now with crosses or statues on the top, but still belonging to the wider world of the empire. And everywhere new buildings were going up, as new families took their place in the Roman aristocracy.

It seems paradoxical that the age of the Counter-Reformation, the age of the Inquisition, should have produced baroque architecture, with its curved lines, its vitality, its playfulness. If the term "organic architecture" had not been preempted by something very different in our century, we might say baroque was organic; one is not surprised to hear that in some of the missions of the New World, built in baroque style, the tiles for the roofs were moulded on a virgin's thigh. It is said that baroque built modern Rome, but this is not entirely true, for the Rome that baroque built was something gayer and greener. The new palaces and churches were put up in the shady suburbs, so that the white curves of the buildings were seen against a background of foliage.

The new Saint Peter's was finally finished in 1626 — rather quickly by cathedral standards. At first its interior was left a plain white. Then the decoration began, and Bernini's *Gloria* went up at the tomb of the Apostle, a sunburst of bronze and stucco like dawn and its clouds, with the dove of the Holy Ghost circled by a radiance of colored alabaster. Soon Saint Peter's began to fill with baroque curves and with human figures, adult and infant, apparently equipped with invisible antigravity devices.

The decorators had a clear field, since the wreckers of the old Saint Peter's had destroyed even the tombs of the popes who were buried there. But a little had been saved, and by an architectural accident there was room for it under the new building. The floor of the new basilica was three meters higher than that of the old, and in this nine or ten feet of space the architects built the upper level of the Sacred Vatican Grottos. Here are inscriptions, mosaics, sarcophagi, some dating back to the fourth century. Lower still, in the crypt of the old Basilica of Constantine, are treasures that one wishes were shown in Saint Peter's itself — the tranquilly beautiful sarcophagus of Junius Bassus, and a statue of Saint Peter that is more human, less hieratic, than the one we have; a statue of an intelligent old man sitting and talking things over with his friends.

In 1663 the Bernini colonnades were completed, two curves of roofed columns that enclose Saint Peter's square, with its fountains and obelisk, and are said to represent the sheltering arms of the Church, though they were intended for the protection of horses and carriages. Their pillars are set so close together that one wonders whether Bernini may not have been unconsciously influenced by the aqueducts, which were built to resist the weight and thrust of water. But they have turned out to be highly functional in an unexpected way, for each of the two hundred and eighty-eight columns is set on a square plinth large enough to provide four sittable corners. The colonnades are cool even on the hottest days, water blows toward them from the fountains, and one can buy cherries from the vendors and eat them while he watches the long hot lines of sight-seers filing into Saint Peter's and the shadow of the obelisk moving across the square. It is easy to laugh at the pilgrim-tourists sitting there, so obviously fed up with culture, but the colonnades go back to something in the earliest days of our religion, to "the shadow of a great rock in a weary land."

One by one the landmarks of today's Rome appeared. The Quirinal Palace was built, on the green slopes of the highest of the Seven Hills. (In Rome all large buildings are palaces, and the United Nations' new, very modern and functional building is called the Palace of the Food and Agriculture Organization.) The Quirinal's altitude saved it from mosquitoes, and the popes spent their summers here to avoid malaria until it was taken over by the kingdom of Italy in 1870. Bernini's Palace of Propaganda Fide, the administrative center of Catholic missions, was erected near Piazza di Spagna in 1627, and a hundred years later the Piazza took on its modern aspect when the Spanish steps, named, like the square, for the nearby Spanish Embassy, went up to Trinità dei Monti.

The rough old days were not entirely over — in the seventeenth century the wall of the Janiculum Hill was enlarged to protect the Vatican from pirate attacks — but the invention of gunpowder had affected domestic architecture in the city as well as in the countryside, and when the new family palace of the Barberini went up on the Street of the Four Fountains it was not an enclosed feudal mass, but half villa and half palace, in the form of a horseshoe, lying open to its gardens.

Fountains were built, bringing the stone city to life — the Fountain of the Rivers in the Piazza Navona, with its deities representing the Nile, the Ganges, the Danube, and the Rio della Plata (the Amazon and the Mississippi failed to qualify), the Four Fountains with their fat old satyr sitting among the reeds, and at the very end of the baroque period, the Trevi Fountain of *Arrivederci Roma.*

Rome was a theater, and a lively social drama was playing on its stages. The ambassadors of the newly powerful nation-states gave a cosmopolitan aspect to the city. The Romans had something new to talk about, and bets were placed on who would sit where at the next feast, who would stand next to whom at the horse races. The ambassadors were rivals socially as well as politically and tried to outdo each other in entertainments, thus filling the ecological gap in the social structure caused by the quieting down of the cardinals.

The non-official *avvisi* of Rome, the gossip columns of the time, give a vivid picture of the seventeenth-century city's social and diplomatic life. On the Sunday of Carnival, one *avviso* tells us, the Spanish Ambassador issued a general invitation to the ladies and gentlemen of Rome; besides the feast there was a bull-chase, with stage horses made up of two men, and a ballet with lit torches in the hands of the dancers. Then "the success of the feast given by the Ambassador of the King of Spain stimulated the very Christian ambassador of the King of France to see that his own feast was not inferior." The floorshow began with the entrance of twelve lackeys dressed as bears, with lit torches in their hands, and continued with a parade of *macchine* — the theatrical "machines" that were moving bits of scenery often draped with female figures. One represented sleep, and was drawn by four children dressed as bats; others were "a tortoise, a mountain peak, and a sea rock which moved to the music." The *avviso*-writer assures us that "everything went very well because only the finest nobility were permitted to attend." One noticeable feature about the entertainments of the time is that their guest lists read very much like those of Roman parties of the current season. Not only the surnames but the Christian names accompanying them are familiar — Don Francesco Borghese, the Prince of Sulmona, Don Ferdinando Ursino.

Rome was beginning to attract travelers who came for sightseeing rather than for religious reasons. Among them were Montaigne and Milton, who took over the baroque style for his *Paradise Lost*. And to this city that loves royalty there came two exiled queens, Christina of Sweden and Maria Casimira of Poland, and the dynasty of the Stuarts.

The Church itself added to the theatrical quality of the city's life, with news of the doings of the cardinal-nephews, rumors of the plans and attitudes of the popes, processions, spectacular canonizations, dramatic exposures of relics, occasional scandals. And there were the executions, open to the public so that they could see justice done and guide their conduct accordingly. The crowd could watch a young murderess beheaded, a philosopher burned, or, under a particularly punitive pope, ordinary citizens killed for carrying concealed weapons. Catharsis was achieved not only through art but through actuality.

New musical forms were being developed — the opera, the oratorio, the orchestra — and there were musical centers to make use of them. The Sistine Chapel for the pope and his cardinals continued the tradition of Gregory the Great's Schola Cantorum, and Saint Philip Neri's evangelistic Oratory, with its principle of *"State allegri!"* brought the oratorio to the people. The baroque oratorio was much less restrained than ours, and was a theatrical as well as a musical performance. Production was sometimes on a lavish scale; when Taddeo Barberini put on "Saint Alexis the Roman" in his private theater on the Street of the Four Fountains, the singers were from the Philippine Oratory, the scenery was by Bernini, as that for the Renaissance cardinals had been by Raphael, and the libretto was written by Cardinal Rospigliosi, the future Pope Clement IX. This drama of a rich and noble young Roman who on his wedding night flees to Edessa to live as a holy man and later returns to Rome incognito to work among his family's slaves ends with a spectacular of chained slaves around a *Roma* throned in glory. The singers were the most famous *castrati* of Rome.

Some of the Philippine Oratory's prefects were Rome's leading music teachers, and from their schools came the best of the *castrati* or *evirati* singers. The use of children's voices was discontinued as these stronger voices, in the late sixteenth and early seventeenth centuries, came to be used in the Philippine Oratory, in the Sistine Chapel, and in the other Roman chapels. There was a constant tendency for music written for such voices to become theatrical in character; many bulls in the Secret Archives protest this drift toward musical secularism. The use of *castrati* was not, however, regarded as immoral; perhaps it had not occurred to anyone that high financial rewards for *castrati* singers encouraged the mutilation of children.

Italy was the center of this artistic-surgical activity; the other parts of Europe got their castrates from here. The musical value of the operation derives from the fact that it affects the development of parts of the body unevenly; the vocal cords grow only a little but the chest and diaphragm much more normally. The result is a voice with the height and sweetness of a child's and the power of a man's — the kind of voice angels were imagined as possessing. It was possible to regulate the type of voice produced by varying the age at which the child was castrated — twelve if you wanted a contralto, much earlier for a soprano. The operation required the consent of the father and, sometimes, that of the child. The State Archives of Rome, a part of the Vatican Secret Archives until they were taken over by the new kingdom of Italy in the last century, is said to contain one of these certificates of permission for castration, in which a musician of the Oratory of Saint Philip Neri gives a written authorization to a barber in the region of the Chiesa Nuova to castrate his son so that he could join the staff of the Oratory. One imagines this little boy on one of the healthful country picnics that the Oratory arranged for its young people's group.

One of the great *castrati*, Farinelli, "with a voice like the cry of a great lonely bird," even became a power in eighteenth-century politics. Philip V of Spain was melancholy to the point of madness, and his wife, anticipating the theories of musical therapy, arranged for him to hear Farinelli sing. Farinelli became David to King Philip's Saul and exercised great political influence. But public opinion was changing; and the liberal Pope Benedict XIV condemned the practice of castration in the middle of the eighteenth century.

Somewhere along the line the Church had forgotten Constantine's law against the mutilation of the body. But the thought of these ravaged children brings another thought to mind. What are we doing now that will seem, to the people of the future, as bad as the Inquisition, as bad as making human beings into musical instruments?

At the time of the Renaissance Europe was still using, with slight changes, the Julian calendar that Sosigenes of Alexandria had worked out for Caesar. As centuries passed it became apparent that there had been a very slight error in calculating the length of the year, so that the vernal equinox kept occurring earlier and earlier in the calendar year.

The Council of Trent recommended the revision of the calendar, and to carry out the task Gregory XIII (1572–1585) built an observatory in the Vatican, in the middle of the Belvedere galleries, called the Tower of the Winds. It is part of the Secret Archives now, and books fill its ancillary rooms, lapping against the frescoes. One can reach it only through the Archives; visiting it is impossible for the tourist and difficult, for the scholar.

The Tower is built above the Gallery of Geographical Charts, a long corridor of vividly colored stylized paintings of the various regions of Italy, showing their topography and their forests, with bright blue oceans, attractive sea-monsters, and dolphin-driving saints. The Tower seems more a temple than an observatory — an old temple, with the pictures flaked and fading, for this is a place where no tourists come, where there are no guidebooks to be sold at twice the price of admission. Yet one can imagine what it must have been when the young Queen Christina, newly come to Rome, lived here for a day or two among literature and science and legend. Pictures cover the walls; personifications of the seasons, Biblical pictures where the wind is blowing or the rain is falling. The bark of Peter is struck by the north wind, representing "the northern heresiarchs," until the waves almost cover it; Saint Paul is shipwrecked on Malta; Christ calms the tempest on the Sea of Galilee; a sleeping pharaoh looking very much like a pope dreams of the blasted corn. Elias prays for rain on Mount Carmel; Ezekiel sees whatever it was that he saw by the River Chobar — "a whirlwind and a fire enfolding it, and in the midst thereof the likeness of four living creatures"; a house is builded on the sand by a foolish man, and it looks very much like the big houses among the vineyards at Anzio. Moses calls up "a burning wind blowing all the night" and the Red Sea is divided; Daniel sees the "four great beasts, different one from another," come up out of the sea. And, most significant of all to a modern, there is the neurotic indecision of the man in Ecclesiastes who did nothing at all because the rain did not come, the man with the unplanted seed-corn and the unyoked ox. "He that observeth the wind shall not sow; and he that considereth the clouds shall never reap."

On the ceiling of the Tower's Meridian Room is an anemoscope, an indoor pointer moved by an outdoor windvane so that it moves when the wind changes direction; Thomas Jefferson was to install one like it at Monticello two centuries later. This "instrument for showing the winds to our most holy and blessed father, our lord Gregory XIII" was surrounded by concentric circles and by rays reaching to them. The circles, the rays, and a large inlaid circle of white marble on the floor beneath are in-

scribed with the names of the winds in three different nomenclatures —
beautiful names, Septentrio, Scirocco, Subsolanus.

But the primary purpose of the Tower was astronomical; it was of the
family of Stonehenge and all the other temples where the light of the
sun, on a certain day of the year, fell on a certain place. In the painting
of the storm on the Sea of Galilee there is an opening in the mouth of the
figure representing the South Wind; through this opening the light came,
of course in different directions at different times of the year. Through
the large white marble circle in the paved floor there is a wide white
marble line along the middle of which a thin black line is drawn, the
meridian from which this principal room takes its name. It varies from
the true meridian by a little more than one degree; perhaps Father Ignatius Danti, the famous astronomer and mathematician, spread himself
too far, for he had the responsibility of designing and executing the geographical charts in the gallery below, supervising the paintings on the
theme of the winds and seasons, designing the anemoscope, and placing
the meridian and the astrological signs.

The report on the new calendar, probably written by the Jesuit Clavius, was a folio of six hundred pages. The calendar which was worked
out on the basis of the data gathered in the Tower of the Winds was a
remarkably accurate one, with an error of only twenty-six seconds a day,
or one day in 3,323 years, and in 1582 Gregory XIII ordered this new
Gregorian calendar into effect throughout the Catholic countries. The
Protestant nations decided they would rather be wrong than Romanist
and resisted the change for nearly two centuries.

In the nineteenth century the Tower of the Winds was again used as
an astronomical observatory, but in 1906 the instruments were transferred to Leo XIII's villa in the Vatican Gardens, and in 1933, when the
lights of Megalopolis had begun to put out the stars, to Castel Gandolfo
in the hills south of Rome.

Top Secret

ABOUT the middle of the sixteenth century a Sienese family of jurists, magistrates, and ambassadors decided to go where the action was and moved to Rome. There Camillo Borghese, an expert in canon law, was made a cardinal. He became pope in 1605 as Paul V Borghese, and in 1612 founded the Vatican Secret Archives as an institution in its own right, distinct from the Library.

Paul V was a conscientious though rather rigid pope, who fought vigorously for the Church, and took so much interest in the Thirty Years War that his monument in Santa Maria Maggiore shows, along with some unusually attractive angels, battle-zone scenes with the lace-garbed Pope examining military maps. Perhaps it might better have shown the Trajan aqueduct that he restored to bring the *aqua Paula* — the Pauline waters — to Rome. They still flow through the gateway that he built for them, using pillars from the old Saint Peter's Basilica. Rome has its connoisseurs of water as well as of wine, and the Pauline water is said to be one of the finest of Rome.

The Borghese family had come late to the capital, and to establish it as one of Rome's princely families, Paul rebuilt a palace in the Ripetta area, The Romans called it the Borghese *cembalo* — the harpsichord — because its terrace and its hanging gardens looked like a keyboard from a distance; there, through his two nephews, Marcantonio and Scipione, Paul established a family. (To found a princely house a pope needed two nephews, one for cardinal-nephew and one for breeding stock.)

The cardinal-nephew Scipione was twenty-seven when his uncle gave him the red hat two months after his own accession. He was the son of Paul's sister, a tie that seems to have been particularly strong for the popes, who would have understood King Arthur's grief at going "far

down to that great battle in the west, where I must fight against my
sister's son." Scipione was an open-handed, open-hearted young man, the
delight of his uncle and, if one can believe the epithet *delicium urbis*, of
the city. He loved the arts and architecture, was a friend and patron of
Bernini, and used some of the Pope's rich gifts for building projects. One
of these was the Villa Pinciana, on the hills above Rome, with its lakes
and forests and ancient statues. He opened part of it to the poor; all of it
now belongs to the people of Rome, who take refuge in its coolness when
the summer heat lies on the city.

It may have been the Pope's professional background in law that led
him to found the Vatican Secret Archives. As a lawyer he would have
had to search for evidence and precedence among the Church's accumulated documents. Attempts had already been made to unify the archives
in a single well-guarded depository. Julius II in 1507 ordered the return
to the Apostolic Camera, within eight days, of all the public and private
acts pertaining to it. This demand was only partially successful, and later
in the century Pius V (1566–1572), who planned to build an archives in
the Vatican Palace, ordered Vatican officers to search everywhere for the
books and papers that belonged to the Church. They were to take any
such material from the Vatican Library, from Castel Sant'Angelo, from
the Italian states, "and from all the world if possible." The heads of monasteries were to admit the Vatican officials to their libraries and archives
"to copy what they wanted to copy and take what they wanted to take."
The palaces of aristocratic Roman families were to be searched for books
and documents, by force if necessary. Much material was recovered, but
the reaction to these drastic measures was such that the program was
discontinued after the Pope's death.

Paul V Borghese finally succeeded in setting up a separate and unified
archives, and once again the Church's records, scattered so often by the
varying fortunes of the papacy, had a secure establishment. The site he
provided for the Secret Archives was next to the Vatican Library, and its
entrance was from the Library, through a door (now kept locked) with a
bust of Paul V above it. The rooms set aside for the Archives were frescoed with paintings of historical personages — Constantine, Pepin, John
Lackland, the Countess Matilda, Frederick II — engaged in humbly
offering great donations to the Church. Wall cupboards of fine workmanship, carved with the Borghese arms, were provided for the documents.

More important, he began to gather in the dismembered fragments of
the papal archives from their scattered storage places, such as the papal
wardrobe rooms and that corner of the Vatican Palace called the Vig-
nola. From Castel Sant'Angelo he brought the most important evidence
of the rights of the Holy See, the acts of donation and the *privilegia*,

together with the oldest part of the series of papal registers and the letters of his immediate predecessors.

The Archives and the Library, now separated, soon began to develop individual characters and traditions, and as they grew each demanded more and more space. Archives documents invaded the Tower of the Winds, which is now surrounded and infiltrated by them.

Setting up the new Archives was only a partial answer to the problem of security. These were state documents, and among the researchers who asked to use them were men in the pay of foreign nations, willing to use every means, including bribery, to get the material they wanted. In 1614 Paul V issued an order that was almost an exact copy of Philip II's order regarding the Spanish archives. This document, discovered in 1887 and then lost again, read: "For the conservation of the Archives that we have set up near the Vatican Library, and to prevent the inconveniences that arise from individuals' searching among the books and taking what they want, we order you, custodian of our archives, under pain of our displeasure and other pains according to our judgment, to allow no one whatever, on any excuse, to consult these books in searching for bulls or other documents. This also holds for the notaries of the Apostolic Camera, but upon the request of such notaries you may look for the deeds and bulls needed for private negotiations. You will do this only upon our personal authorization or that of our ministers."

In 1616 Cardinal Scipione Borghese, as head of both the Library and the Archives, issued a more complete set of regulations. "We, Scipione, Cardinal Borghese, Librarian of the Holy Church, to you officers and ministers of the Vatican Library and of the Vatican Archives, order the following: The custodian, each day that is not a holy day, will keep the Library open for at least three hours, starting one hour after noon." All officials and employees are to be present and "doing what is pertinent" (that is, at work) at this time.

The duties of other employees are laid out in a rudimentary form of the modern job-description: "The *scriptores* must make copies of books ill-treated by time; they must make indices and titles for the books, without taking codices, indices, or other library documents to their own homes. The prefects of the Archives are to file the documents according to a rational system, make the indices, and for no reason allow anyone to read such documents without specific permission." The fact that Scipione forbade scriptors to take materials home, but failed to mention the matter in relation to the prefects, was to lead a year later to the prosecution of a prefect.

Bookbinders were to work in a separate room so as not to disturb the other employees; janitors were to sweep the floor and dust the books daily, "open the windows when the weather is fine and close them at the prescribed hour." Students were not to bring inkwells or pens into the Library, the custodian was to assign them a seat in the scriptors' room and furnish them with whatever they needed. The regulations end by reverting to the problem of security: "When someone asks to copy a treatise or an entire book, the first custodian must bring it to our knowledge, and we will judge what is best to do. *The Cardinal Borghese, Librarian.*"

The records of the trial of Michael Lonigo, Prefect of the Archives, were found by the historian Casanova in the Italian Archives of State, which were a part of the Secret Archives until the "forced dismemberment" of the nineteenth century.

The sad little story of Michael Lonigo (1572–1639) not only tells the tragedy of a dedicated man, but gives a picture of life in the newly founded Secret Archives. Lonigo, a priest in holy orders but no longer engaged in the cure of souls, had held a minor office at the Vatican as master of ceremonies, but he gravitated to the Secret Archives as his natural home; Lonigo loved documents as a botanist loves plants. There he did odd jobs of research and ghost writing, and eventually came to the notice and employment of Cardinal Cesi. A biographer writing later in the century says that it was Lonigo who suggested to Cardinal Cesi, who suggested to the Pope the unification of the archives in a single location. When Pope Paul decided to move the oldest archives from Castel Sant'Angelo to the Vatican, Cardinal Cesi was appointed as one of the committee to select the material to be transferred. Lonigo was his assistant in the task.

In 1607 Lonigo was made a notary, which gave him the right to make authentic copies of Archives documents for a fee, and he gradually attained a high reputation as an archivist through his little research papers and his ability to find needed documents. He became known as "the oracle of foreigners" for his assistance to them — a fact that was brought up against him at his trial, when he was accused of "having received many people, French, Spanish, Italian, and Roman" in the Archives.

In his work for Cesi he compiled a Summary of Investitures which was presented to the Pope, and it may have been this that led to his appointment in 1610 as *Praefectus Archivii Sanctissimi.* The position must have had much less prestige then than now, for Lonigo had only one key to the Archives, which had to be entered through three locked doors. The route to the Archives led through the room of the scriptors and then through the Library; to reach the Archives the prefect often had to wait for someone to open the outer doors. And when he worked overtime, as he often did, the only way he could get out was by making noise enough so that someone could hear him.

Lonigo seems to have been one of those people who rather enjoy disorder because it is so much fun putting things in order again, and the newly transferred archives must have presented him with abundant opportunity. He catalogued the contents of the wall closets and pasted on the front of each a statement of what it contained, and worked on a general index of the Archives.

He roomed and boarded at Palazzo Rusticucci, where his *padrona,* or landlady, was Giovanni Maria Crescentini. It was there, "about the middle of the night" that the police of the Borgo's criminal court broke in and found one hundred and twelve books and documents belonging to the Secret Archives. Inquiries were made in the neighborhood about what gifts Lonigo had received lately; it was reported that he had received six pairs of socks, a cloak, two chickens, and some bottles of wine. Furthermore, the judge's inquirers heard gossip about him and the *padrona.*

The judge consulted the Pope, then charged Lonigo with violating the *sanctitas archivorum* by taking Archives documents to his house and letting other people see them, probably for profit. Numerous testimonies were taken, and the *padrona* was put to torture.

Lonigo was not popular with the students or the notaries. Librarians and borrowers are natural enemies, for the librarian, with many examples of human iniquity in mind, thinks first of safeguarding library property, while the borrower, if his intentions are innocent, regards the librarian as paranoid. At the trial, one notary said that Lonigo had accused him of not returning some materials, and had told the Pope about it; later the materials were found in a trunk. Others complained that they were not allowed access to needed documents, that Lonigo had his own scribes copy them, and took the fees that would normally have gone to the notaries; that he was "avid of emoluments." Probably the most accurate testimony was that of the man who commented that Lonigo was so unpopular that the least little slip could ruin him.

It was also brought out that he had once accepted a gift of a hundred scudi from the king of Portugal, in thanks for having found and copied a needed document. The document was one that the king was entitled to have; nevertheless Pope Paul V said that Lonigo should not have taken the money. The only time the prefect's calm manner changed during the trial was when the judge asked him if he knew of the Pope's letter of 1614 and of the Archives rules established by Cardinal Borghese. "I wrote that letter myself. I suggested it, I composed it, and I didn't intend to impose rules on myself!" Lonigo said. He freely admitted having Archives documents in his rooms, and explained that he was making a general index to the Archives, and was writing summaries of the documents for this. In view of the situation regarding keys it is not surprising that he took material home to work on when he wanted to work overtime; probably what the Romans found difficult to believe was that anyone could *want* to work overtime.

Lonigo was found guilty and sentenced to ten years in the triremes. This could have been a death sentence for a man of forty-five; the Pope commuted it to ten years in the prisons of Castel Sant'Angelo. Lonigo served five of them before the Pope died, but was pardoned by the new pope, Gregory XV. In 1886 his general index of the Vatican Secret Archives was found and formally presented to Pope Leo XIII. The summaries and indexes he prepared are still in use.

Just after the Council of Trent Cardinal Commendone spoke sharply of papal nepotism: "The principal things that lead popes astray are a taste for secular life and wanting to govern like secular princes — to accumulate treasure and search for unsuitable glory. Through nepotism the greatest part of honors and benefices are made hereditary and kept in the family. Such warnings make a doctor anticipate plague, and pilots a future tempest."

Nepotism continued after the Reformation, but it changed its form. A distinction was made between the grand, or political, nepotism and petty or bourgeois nepotism; a distinction roughly equivalent to that between grand and petty larceny. The Borgia, the Medici, and the Farnese popes had given entire states to their nephews, and this had involved the papacy in wars to protect the nephews' territory. Political nepotism of this kind fell into disrepute after Pius IV (1559–1565) sentenced the Caraffa cardinal-nephew to death by strangling for embezzlement of the Church's funds and other offenses. The next pope, Pius V, in 1567 issued a bull "Let us admonish ourselves" in which he forbade the giving away of papal territories. The popes then kept to the letter of the law by rewarding their nephews in other ways; instead of states they gave them money, lands, and lucrative assignments, in what has been called bourgeois or petty nepotism.

In 1692 Innocent XII decreed that the popes no longer had the right to give money or estates to members of their families beyond the assistance normally given to the poor, and that only one cardinal-nephew at a time might be appointed, at a fixed salary. But it was not until the twentieth century that nepotism was eradicated. The nephews of Pius XII became princes by the action of the king of Italy, and John XXIII was proud of the fact that his family remained poor.

Paradoxically, these seventeenth- and eighteenth-century popes who enriched their families were usually virtuous in their private lives. Since they had not taken vows of poverty, the surplus income of the Church was regarded as their own. Modern corporations pay their presidents and vice-presidents extravagantly high salaries on the same principle.

Commendone, writing in 1564, painted a gloomy picture of the life of a cardinal. The popes were often old, so the government changed frequently; life in the Curia was "a sea of changeable things. Changes of times, of masters, and with the changes in masters, changes of customs." Rome was "a marketplace, with a perpetual flowing." Serving in the papal court was like making a voyage by sea; "few there are who enjoy a lasting spell of fortune, without some bad accident." The master might die, or one might lose his favor; "anyone who is not loved at court or does not have convenient qualities can easily come to ruin." But with the founding of the Congregations, the work of the cardinals took on a new importance. In the Middle Ages the problems of the Holy See had been handled by the Consistory, made up of the College of Cardinals and the pope. But the increasing number, complexity, and variety of these problems now made some degree of specialization necessary. A system of Congregations, very like the committee system in the American Congress, was finally set up.

The first Congregation to be established, in 1542, was the Sacred Congregation of the Holy Office — the Inquisition, patterned after the Spanish Inquisition. Paul III said it was made necessary by the devil: "As through the actions of the enemy of mankind, the souls of the faithful day by day and increasingly are contaminated by heresies, we have called some of our beloved sons to take care of the matter." Each individual case was studied by prelates and by doctors in theology and canon law; afterward it came to the pope and his group of cardinals.

A second Congregation was founded in 1564 to make sure that the decrees of the Council of Trent were carried into effect. It was given very strong coercive powers; whoever disobeyed it was to be excommunicated, deprived of all benefices, and might also be handed over to the secular arm.

In 1571 the Congregation of the Index was formed to update, continue, and publish the "Tridentine Index" that the Council of Trent had issued seven years earlier. This was based on Paul IV's *Index auctorum et librorum prohibitorum,* which had banned not only authors and books but publishers. From 1516 the Imprimatur — a statement that the book had passed prepublication censorship — was required.

Actually the policy of prohibiting certain books went far back in Church history; the Council of Nicaea had burned *Thalia* by Arius. The type of books prohibited and burned in public executions varied with the times. In the early Middle Ages they were heretic or apocryphal books and unauthenticated acts of the martyrs. In the late Middle Ages they were likely to be books on magic and necromancy; though this period also saw the burning of the Joachimite texts of Giovanni da Parma, not entirely a successful operation, since their philosophy later influenced Columbus. The Index, therefore, was not a new policy, but the updating and implementing of an old one to meet the new danger of Protestantism.

It was Sixtus V (1585–1590) who founded most of the Congregations, as part of his reform of the College of Cardinals. The number of cardinals was set at seventy, the "seventy of the elders of Israel" who with Moses had come up unto the Lord. Apparently Sixtus had noted that Exodus contains a very sound chapter on the subject of personnel management and the span of control. But instead of setting his elders over certain numbers of people, Sixtus set them over certain classes of problems. "We appoint fifteen Congregations and to each of them we assign special matters."

Later, in 1622, the Church's department of missions — *Sacra Congregatio de Propaganda Fide* — was established. To *Propaganda Fide*, in its palace near Piazza di Spagna, came questions from missionaries all over the earth. From China: could a Chinese Christian official make obeisance before an idol, as his position required him to do, if he hid a cross among the flowers and made his true obeisance to that? What should be done about artists who portrayed Christ in a Chinese-style beard and shoes? From Persia: when a missionary was called to pray for the dying child of a non-Christian family, was it licit to baptize it and so send it to Paradise without the parents' knowledge? And from America: could Negroes just taken from Africa be baptized without preliminary instruction? Hundreds of years earlier, missionaries in the new lands of the Church, trying to adapt the faith to alien cultures, had sent similar queries back to Rome. How should a Christian dress? Was it all right to use pagan enchantments in a real emergency, such as going into battle? Was it Christian for a king to eat alone? Could one take communion after having had sexual intercourse? We can only guess what questions will come back to *Propaganda Fide* in the future, from its missions on the moons of Jupiter or on the planet that circles Cygni 61.

The setting up of the Congregations meant a diminution of the workload of the papal Chancellery. This very old office of the Church, where

Saint Jerome had served Pope Damasus, continued to function, as did the Dataria and the Apostolic Chamber, but the series of Vatican papal registers had nearly come to an end.

Some historians regard the setting up of separate Congregational archives as a loss to the Secret Archives of new materials relating to certain fields, but officially the archives of the Congregations remain part of the Secret Archives, even though they are geographically detached. This is supported by the fact that some of the Congregations send material beyond a certain cut-off date to the Secret Archives. Often material on a given subject is split between the main Archives and that of the Congregation, sometimes according to no discernible rule. For example, when I was looking for the records of the process of sanctification of Mother Cabrini, I found six volumes in the main Archives and the remainder in the archives of the Congregation of Rites.

The diversion from the Archives proper of materials belonging to the Congregations was compensated by a greatly increased inflow of diplomatic materials. From about the time of Leo X (1513–1521) the most confidential political correspondence had been in the hands of a *secretarius intimus* or *domesticus*. From this office developed that of the Secretary of State, usually a cardinal-nephew, and, next to the pope himself, the leading officer of the papal government.

By the time of the Seicento there were three domestic secretaries, one in charge of diplomatic correspondence, one in charge of briefs in general, and one in charge of briefs to princes. After the Apostolic Secretariat was abolished in 1686 the names of these offices were changed; they became the Secretariat of State, the Secretariat of Briefs, and the Secretariat of Briefs to Princes. Each of them has left an important series of records in the Secret Archives.

The Secretariat of State gave rise to one of the most interesting archivistic series, that of the nunciatures, which include letters from the Secretary of State to the nuncios, letters and reports from the nuncios to the Secretary of State, and the archives of the nunciatures, themselves, returned to Rome when the nunciatures closed. These last, like melting glaciers, brought with them an enormous amount of miscellaneous material.

The Church had seldom been a strong military power; perhaps it was weakened by the old conflict of conscience as to whether fighting was licit to a Christian. Yet it regarded temporal power as a right and a necessity; therefore it turned to diplomacy, the manipulation of the power of others. The nunciatures enabled the pope to keep track of what was happening in Europe and to intervene more effectively in political-religious affairs.

Legates had been used from the first century of the Church; Saint Peter had his Sylvanus. A little later the popes sent "apostolic vicars" to provinces far from Rome; Pope Damasus appointed the Bishop of Thessalonica as apostolic vicar for Illyria across the Adriatic Sea, and Pope Zosimus in 417 named an apostolic vicar for Gaul. But the apostolic vicars were usually local bishops, and their loyalty was often to their own country rather than to the pope. Modern departments of state have to switch their diplomats around frequently to prevent them from going native and developing too much sympathy with their adopted country; the problem was worse when diplomats were native to begin with. The pope needed representatives who were not part of the local hierarchies, who were dependent on the Holy See. The official collectors of Church taxes met these specifications, and in the fifteenth century we find collectors in Spain, Portugal, and Naples charged with the additional duty of acting as nuncios. The nuncios later sent from Rome were at first called envoys; one of the most famous was Baldasar Castiglione, author of *The Courtier,* a book which is still recommended to young diplomats by their seniors, and which may be responsible for some of our striped-pants traditions.

The files of correspondence between the Holy See and its nuncios began to be systematically maintained about the middle of the Cinquecento. They are listed according to regions, with about 2,000 volumes or folders for Vienna, 818 for Germany, 715 for France, 643 for Naples, and so on. Material is very scanty for the earlier period of the nunciatures; the probability is that these records were lost during the Sack of Rome.

Letters to and from the nuncios are among the best historical sources. To see what this material is like we can follow the career of a nuncio appointed to a new post and see what documents it produced. On receiving his appointment the nuncio was told what his date of arrival must be; there was to be no dallying along the way. From the time of Alexander VII (1665–1667) he also had strict instructions regarding his journey. Before leaving he was given a letter of accreditation to the authorities of the place to which he was assigned; these letters are now filed in the Archives' *fondo Brevia ad Principes.* From the Secretary of Cipher, whose post was established in 1555, he received two codes: the *cifra commune,* to use in writing to other nuncios or diplomats, and the *cifra propria,* to use in writing to the Secretary of State. He was given a mass of instructions from the Secretary of State; from the time of Clement VII (1523–1534) they were in Italian instead of Latin to make sure that he understood them, and they provided a background briefing on the country he was going to, its problems and political situation, the personal characteristics, ideas, and preferences of the princes and statesmen he was to deal with, and a statement of his mission. For example, Alberto Bolognetti, the papal nuncio in Venice from 1578 to 1581, was instructed to support the Inquisition, see that tithes were paid, defend freedom of navigation in the Adriatic, send *avvisi* from the Levant, Germany, and Flanders along to Rome, and support revolutionary movements in Cyprus "to see what might come out of it." It was not unusual for nuncios to act as secret agents, or *agents provocateurs;* they took part in most of the international plots of interest to the Holy See.

Before leaving, the new nuncio had an audience with the pope and the Secretary of State, and called on a former holder of his post and on the ambassador of the country to which he was assigned. Their suggestions were often written down in the form of memoranda. In fact, he was given a much better preparation than some of our modern diplomats receive.

Once he arrived at his post a lively correspondence with the papal Secretary of State began. The Secretary wrote to him weekly or oftener; he was likely to write very frequently at first, to help the new man get settled into his duties. Even afterward nuncios sometimes received four or five letters a day from Rome, because the Secretary of State dealt with only one subject in each letter. Thus the letter could be exhibited if necessary without giving away information on other problems. The Archives' file of registers containing copies of these letters of the Secretary of State to the nuncios are generally in the *Nunziature* series, but sometimes in private family collections like the Borghese archives.

In return the nuncio was expected to write to the papal Secretary of State frequently, at least once a week. One nuncio who omitted writing because he had nothing to write about was told by Clement VIII to copy his last letter and send it, so as not to get out of the habit of writing. Besides the letters there were the regular dispatches called *avvisi*. These were collections of information on current affairs in the place where the nuncio was stationed, gathered from all sorts of sources — spies, paid reporters, refugees. When an important matter was to be discussed the nuncio sent not a letter but a formal report called a *relazione,* and on being recalled from his post he wrote a full final report. This was of course sent to Rome, but a copy was left at the nunciature for the instruction of his successor. Theoretically copies of all the departing nuncio's correspondence were left at the nunciature for the same purpose, but very often, especially in the case of nobles, they were annexed for the family files. Most of these have not yet been published.

Bolognetti's lengthy final report is divided into sections dealing with such matters as papal interests in Venice, dangers to the liberty of the Church, suggested countermeasures. He has a triumph to report — he has successfully protested against Venice's plans to send a representative to England, which he says has turned again to its vomit after the death of Queen Mary. But he also has to include an account of what went wrong with his mission, for he is being recalled to Rome for insisting on carrying out the required apostolic visits to convents and monasteries. These were actually inspection trips and were unpopular with the institutions called on, as inspection trips normally are. But in Venice there was more resentment than usual, and the Senate told him to stay out. Venice wanted its convents to be left alone, to be dissolute, if they liked, in privacy, for the convents were a part of an intricate system of social and economic balances. It was the custom to send excess daughters of the aristocratic families there to save the high cost of lavish dowries. Having sent the girls to the convents, they wanted them to be as happy as possible; they seem to have thought of convent life as a prolonged boarding school. The result was that the girls wore low-necked dresses and had *cavalieri serventi*, or, Bolognetti darkly thought, even worse. The nuncio Castiglione had taken a less serious view of such things, repeating a story about a bishop who, preparing to throw the book at a confessor who had gotten five nuns pregnant, was urged by the man's friends to show mercy. "And when they repeated their pleas, the bishop said: 'What answer shall I give to God on the Judgment Day when He says to me, *Give an account of thy stewardship*'? Then Messer Marcantonio at once answered: 'My lord, say what the Evangelist says: *Lord, thou deliveredst unto me five talents: behold I have gained beside them five talents more.*' Whereupon the bishop could not refrain from laughing, and greatly mitigated his anger and the punishment that was in store for the offender." But Bolognetti insisted on making his visits, even though the Senate protested that enforcing strict rules would mean that the girls would flatly refuse to enter the convents, and parents would be left with daughters on their hands. Also exposing conditions in the convents "would bring dishonour on noble families."

Bolognetti must have been glad to go on to less personal subjects, such as the information he had gathered from merchants about the Coptic Christians in Venice's sphere of influence, who branded the cross on their children's foreheads, "badly interpreting the words of John the Baptist, who said that someone greater than himself would baptize with fire and the spirit." Those in Egypt were called Irini, those "further down and farther away" were the Abasini. There in Ethiopia the emperor must come from one of three families founded by the three Magi, Caspar,

Balthasar and Melchior. The Abasini "follow the rites of secret things from a fabled book called *The Secrets of Saint Peter.*" Another people, the Georgians, whose archbishop lives on Mount Sinai, take their name from their protector Saint George, "but the general opinion is that they were converted by the holiness and miracles of a poor woman brought as a prisoner to their country in the year 325, Saint Sylvester being Pope and Constantine son of Helena Emperor."

Bolognetti goes on to tell of the Christians "spread partly in the realm of the Soffi and partly in that of the Turks," and has a hard time describing a religiously pluralistic society of the kind now familiar to us in the West. "There are different sects that recognize different patriarchates, each one of them having its own bishops and archbishops. And these, the bishops and archbishops, have their own subjects with regard to spiritual government. They are different in regard to rites and religion but not in regard to locality. In the many places in which there are bishops of different sects, each of them has the government of the Christians who belong to his own sect and does not interfere with the others. Those who follow one bishop talk with the followers of another bishop, they do business together, they eat and drink together; that is, they share their temporal life together." In sixteenth-century Europe such an arrangement took a good deal of explaining.

Bolognetti's final report, so conscientious, so carefully written, failed to save his career. He was not reassigned as a nuncio, but went back to making his living as a notary. He had committed diplomacy's unpardonable offense of interfering with the social structure of the host country. Lonigo was destroyed because he disregarded the letter of the law; Bolognetti because he obeyed it.

The Queen of the Vandals

IN 455 the Vandals sacked Rome, as they had already sacked other cities of the empire, burning the precious books, the irreplaceable manuscripts, the scientific articles that had, in duplicate copies, survived the fire at Alexandria. Over a thousand years later their queen came to Rome, not as a conqueror but as a convert, in love with the Church as she had all her life been in love with learning. Christina Alexandra, Queen of the Swedes, the Goths, and the Vandals, had abdicated a throne that required adherence to the Lutheran faith, after being converted to Catholicism by two rather surprised missionaries who had expected no such results.

The daughter of Gustavus Adolphus had become queen in 1632, when she was six years old, and had assumed control of the government at eighteen. She had been given the training of a crown prince. The rest of her education she had gotten for herself, from hours of study in the early morning and from minutes of study snatched from the duties of royalty. She was a conscientious sovereign, concerned with the trade and productiveness of her country, but with her gift for government there were two other tendencies — her love of learning and her stormy and wandering emotional life. The first she satisfied by bringing scholars to her court, by her studies and by her writing. She learned languages and read history; she worshiped the arts with the humble reverence that one sometimes sees in men and women of action. In her wooden capital on a frozen coast she collected art treasures from the Italian Renaissance, ancient manuscripts from the early centuries of Christendom — though she had an advantage that many collectors would envy: conquering armies to bring home the libraries and art objects that she wanted.

Her personal life was such that Europe speculated on the number, sex, and degree of relationship of her lovers. There seems no doubt that Christina was a biological variant. The only question is to the extent of her variation, and whether there were one or two divergent tendencies at work.

Princess Lucien Murat gives this account of Christina's birth: "The infant presented itself, its little bottom in the air, black as a marmot and so covered with hair that it would frighten you. It cried, my faith, it cried with a voice so strong that the wise women of Stockholm, doubtless trusting their ears, ran happily to tell Gustavus Adolphus that the queen had given birth to a boy. Premature eagerness, a hurried glance, boy or girl? The matter was contestable, the sex capricious. No doubt these ladies, a little short-sighted, should have put on their eyeglasses: 'Look, ladies, light the candles.' "

But the "little marmot" grew into a child that was strong, intelligent, and loved for her own qualities as well as for her rank.

Among the Secret Archives' documents is an unsigned description of the life and personality of Christina Alexandra of Sweden as a reigning queen. It begins, "The Queen of Sweden has a small body, a spacious forehead, and large, clear, friendly eyes. Her nose is aquiline and thin. She is nothing of a woman. Her voice, her way of talking, her walk, her gestures, are fully virile. She rides like a hussar. Unless one sees her from nearby he thinks that she is a man. When she rides she wears a hat and coat as the Spanish do, and it is only from the long dress that one knows she is a woman. She puts her horse to the gallop without her feet in the stirrups; no one could follow her." There is a note of disapproval in the report-writer's description of her clothing: "Her riding costume is so ordinary that it could not cost even five gold *scudi*. She wears ordinary clothes even at court. She never wears jewelry; only one ring. Her shirt is often stained with ink from all the writing she does, and sometimes it is ragged. If one suggests that she ought to take better care of herself, she says that that is for people who have nothing to do."

This was a working queen: "Each morning she dedicates herself to public matters, and each day she attends the council, even when for sixteen days she had a very high temperature. Alone, she receives the ambassadors of the crowns, alone she answers them. Generals who have terrified Germany by force of arms tremble before her. She has grown up such a woman that she has remained free in a free kingdom. She loves all nations, and in everyone she loves goodness and nothing else; she says that there are only two kinds of men in the world: honest men and wicked men." And like Elizabeth in the century before her, "She does not allow marriage to be mentioned. No one has been able to persuade her to marry. She says that she was born free and she wants to die free. She sometimes turns very quickly from smiles and laughter to royal dignity and majesty. She has a retinue of noble ladies in waiting, but more for form than for personal service. She talks very little with them and prefers to talk with men."

In our time, even a royalist like myself feels rather relieved when a young prince or princess turns out to be educable, but the seventeenth century was nearer to the origins of kingship. "She knows ten or eleven languages, even the Saracen of the Hebrews and the Arabs. She has read all the ancient poets and the modern French and Italian writers; she has studied the ancient philosophers. As for the ancient holy fathers, she has read Augustine and Tertullian for the most part, but she does not like them very much. She greatly enjoys Lactantius, Clement of Alexandria, Ambrose and especially Jerome and Cyprian. Her memory is more than human. She has called to Sweden very learned men, artists and scientists from Italy, from Germany, from France." Comenius had been called in to reform Swedish education. Pascal had presented her with a computer and the mechanist Descartes, had failed to persuade her that living and non-living things were alike, or to kill in her that reverence for life that is the latest and least recognized of the virtues. And Grotius, father of international law, was a scholar-in-residence. The slogan-makers of the time called her capital the Athens of the North.

The unknown correspondent, apparently not a man to listen to gossip, concludes by saying, "Only one thing is lacking to this very queen, and that is the true faith. But to discuss it is forbidden by the laws of the kingdom. For her to embrace the Catholic faith would mean to lose her status as queen, and to lose the kingdom."

The very fact that it was forbidden may have made Catholicism attractive to Christina. Or it may have been, at first, a matter of intellectual curiosity. The Secret Archives has a copy of a letter signed with the name of the Jesuit Father Malines, who assisted the queen in her conversion, although Vatican experts have some doubt of its validity. In any case, it sets forth the official explanation: "The very serene Queen Christina of Sweden had for some years found certain dissonances in the Lutheran sect in which she had been reared, and she determined to make every study to ascertain the true faith. She wanted to evaluate the substance and foundations of every religion and sect, and not satisfied with that, she desired and created an opportunity to discuss the matter with men who were in that part of the world, to make the acquaintance of the most celebrated, and to invite them with great rewards to her court under the pretext of acquiring their knowledge, in order to investigate their beliefs. She began to discover the truth of the Catholic faith, and wanted to have members of the religious who could fully instruct her."

At her request, the Vicar of the Jesuits secretly sent two Jesuit missionaries to Sweden, one of whom reported: "As soon as we arrived in Stockholm we were admitted to the Queen's presence. In public we were gentlemen travelers; in secret we were religious. We were amazed to find in a princess of twenty-five years a soul so disillusioned with the vanity of human greatness. Not long afterward, she clearly stated that she definitely planned to embrace the Catholic faith, and to renounce for it the kingdom in which she was not only respected but worshiped, and had an authority stronger and more absolute than her own father had had." Arrangements for the abdication — and the queen's final decision — took some time, but "on December 24 of the year 1654, at midnight, she made her profession of faith."

Historians are uncertain why the queen sought conversion at such a cost, though many explanations are offered. Certain elements in Sweden had rebelled against her policies and her extravagance: she may have abdicated in the same to-hell-with-it spirit that leads workmen to resign their jobs and that caused the Emperor Diocletian to go off and raise cabbages. Or it has been suggested that she rejected Lutheranism because it preached predestination; that only the free will of the Church could satisfy so imperious a queen. She was strongly attracted toward Roman cultural life; for her, exile would, in a sense, be homecoming. Or she may have felt it necessary, as most of us do not, to keep a vow made in illness. Certainly her health had been poor, and the warmth of Italy offered a promise of recovery. And there was probably a deeper, instinctive drive toward the south, to the lands she had seen in Technicolor in the great paintings she collected. There is an atavistic pull in the direction of Africa — man became man in the warm countries; there were no icy Edens. But I think that her conversion was real, and that it was brought about by her reading of the patristic philosophers. Neither the Jesuit missionaries, so dazzled by the throne, nor our standard "Thy Spouse, the Lamb" type of religious literature could have reached such a woman. But the patristic writers were men of her own quality — men like Clement of Alexandria, Ambrose, Jerome, Cyprian.

Christina's act of abdication was signed; its three hundred crimson seals affixed. The queen made her abdication speech in the white dress of a convert, but she left Sweden disguised as a man, *incognita* as Count Dohna. And then, like many wanderers, she turned toward Italy.

Pope Alexander VII thought it best to have her make a public conver-

sion before coming to Italy, or at least before she entered the papal
states. To arrange this, and perhaps to keep the queen in line — he may
have heard those stories about the seduction of barmaids — he dis-
patched Monsignor Lucas Holstenius to join her traveling party. The
Pope had chosen his emissary carefully; Holstenius was, like Christina, a
convert from the Lutheran faith, and he was chief librarian of the Vatican and a deeply learned man.

An undated "Report on the Journey and on the Reception Made by
His Holiness Alexander VII in the Ecclesiastical States and in Rome to
Her Majesty Christina Alexandra, Queen of Sweden," is in the Archives'
Miscellanea. "Our Lord appointed four nuncios to meet her at the borders of the papal territory. He ordered that one of the most noble carriages, two very sumptuous beds, and two canopies and stools to match
in golden linen, and a precious credenza all of gold and silver with the
necessary services be there so that the queen might know not only his
affection but also his pontifical magnificence. On Sunday, November 21,
she entered into the papal states escorted by three companies of horsemen. All her journey was a triumph." Salvos of cannon welcomed her in
Ferrara. In Forli the square had been made into a forest with poles of
wood adorned with leaves and flowers. In Assisi she attended the Church
of Saint Francis; in Spoleto poems were sung in her honor; ". . . at Terni
she was a guest in the Bishop's palace. Perfumes eddied through the
rooms, breathing of *Arabia felix*. In the evening, to provide her with
spiritual entertainment, there was an oratorio in the Roman style," and at
Bracciano, the lake north of Rome, which has told centuries of travelers
that they were nearing the Holy City, "very virtuous musicians, with
their sweet voices, proved that Rome was heaven on earth, not guarded
by an angel with a burning sword, but in the care of God's vicar."

A cavalcade from the Pope came to meet her at Bracciano, as another
cavalcade had come there to meet Charlemagne. "First came two pages
dressed in red, then the trumpeters followed by an army with shields . . .
Then a great number of noblemen, Italian and German, the cardinals,
and the Roman nobility . . . Then came the cardinals' carriages, each
drawn by six horses, too few for the weight of the treasures with which
they were decorated." This was regarded as an informal affair, and the
cavalcade, after the meeting with the queen, took her *incognita* to a
roadside meeting with the Pope.

For her formal entrance into Rome from the Olgiata suburb, the Pope
sent her a carriage chair and a litter, "all of light blue velvet with splendid silver decorations and interiors quilted with silver." The *ghinea's*
stirrups were of heavy silver, and the carriage itself outdid our prewar

limousines by having not only vases but statues. The queen, in gold-embroidered riding breeches and a plumed hat, was surrounded by cardinals as she went to the *Te Deum* at Saint Peter's.

The Chigi pope Alexander VII (1655–1667) was as new to the papacy as Christina was to Catholicism, but he had had a distinguished career in Church diplomacy. One of his cardinals described him a few years later: "The Pope demands an exquisite refinement in all things, especially things that have to do with food and clothing. He likes vestments with all the ornaments that can make him more handsome. When he goes to the country, he wears decorations with little diamond buttons. . . . At the reception of the Queen of Sweden he omitted nothing to make it illustrious and equal to the triumphs of the Romans. And he himself with his magnificent face made all things vibrate."

But the pyrotechnics display in the evening, with the queen's coat of arms and that of the Pope blazing together as if for a royal marriage, may have meant less to her than her visit to the Vatican Library, and her stay in the guest apartment in the Tower of the Winds, with its stormy paintings and its astronomical devices.

Christina came to a Rome that was a hundred years into the Counter-Reformation. The Thirty Years War was recently over; Galileo was a dozen years dead, and the Church was finding relief from unhappy solutions by turning to music and to building. Michelangelo's plan of functional porticos, designed to keep horses and carriages out of the rain, was being elaborated into the triple-aisle magnificence of the Bernini colonnades. Alexander VII was carrying on an urban renewal program; squares were being opened up and new streets cut through houses and palaces. To an immigrant from the north, Rome of the mid-seventeenth century must have seemed a busy, growing center of civilization.

Christina had difficulty in adapting to her new life, and Alexander and his successors needed all of their training in diplomacy. Not even the spiritual battle plans of the Jesuits contained adequate instructions on how to deal with transvestite queens. By the terms of her abdication she was to retain the rank of queen and revenues were provided for her support, but they were not easy to collect and at times had to be supplemented by the Pope. As always, she spent too much, particularly on books, art objects, and gifts. The real difficulty, of course, was that she had no work to do. By genetic makeup and by training, she was one of Plato's Guardians of the City, and now she had no city left to guard.

At one time she intrigued for the throne of Naples, and it was in the course of this, while she was a guest of Louis XIV at Fontainebleau, that the Monaldeschi scandal occurred. Monaldeschi and Santinelli were part of her entourage, and Monaldeschi at least was her lover. According to her early biographer, Princess Murat, the queen received an anonymous note charging Monaldeschi with betraying her, and searched his belongings. There she found copies of letters to his mistress in Italy in which he ridiculed the queen and told of the disgust he felt at her "infirmity" and her "*fantasque*" body. Christina had him killed; she called it execution.

The Secret Archives has some of her letters to Santinelli, the aide who killed Monaldeschi and was also, apparently, the queen's lover. One of them suggests that she was telling Santinelli what account to give of the affair. "Marquis, I am sending you a report on the death of Monaldeschi, who betrayed me and tried to make me believe that you were the betrayer. Then finally, dying, he confessed his crime and our innocence, showing that he had invented all his violent accusations in order to ruin us. Do not try to justify my actions to anyone. I do not have to give an account to anyone but God, who would have punished me if I had forgiven the traitor. I know in my conscience that I have acted according to divine and human justice." But she knew that she did have to "give an account" and the letter ends, "Be happy, and be sure that I will defend our action against all. Christina Alexandra, Fountainebleau, 17 November, 1657."

Another letter, written to Santinelli a year or so afterward, is the letter of a jealous woman striking back at a man who has slighted her. "To Marchese Santinelli: I have been very much surprised to receive your letter, sent from some place I can't pronounce, with a name so barbarous that I doubt if it is on any map but your own." She tells him to come back immediately, "near my person," but while he is in Vienna, "I do not want you spending my money foolishly. And you had better know that if you remain in Vienna any longer you do it at your own expense, because you will have neither money from me nor the title of ambassador. I am speaking very plainly to you. Think what you are doing, and do not do foolish things if you want my protection. Have honor, faith, brain, and I will do more for you than you deserve, more than you can hope, because I want everything good for you. But please do not be your own enemy."

The nature of the queen's "infirmity" is not certain. Was it a structural variation, or the masculine hair distribution of her variant hormones? Or had the hairiness of the baby princess been something more than the *lanugo* that usually disappears before birth? The legends of Charlemagne tell, in an incidental, casual mention, of a tribal company of soldiers who had hair growing on their backs. The scattering of genetic material, as population mobility broke up the tribes, might have caused such a condition to be occasionally existent, though extremely unusual, if it depended on the possession of two rare recessive genes.

Like that of Queen Elizabeth I of England, Christina's physical makeup is a fascinating medical mystery. There is no doubt that she was physically and emotionally attracted to both men and women, that she was one of the bisexuals for whom the fullness of life demands communion in both kinds. But the mistake in her sex at birth, the hints of something greatly variant, and the fact that in her youth she spoke seriously of hoping to become a man, suggest a more serious duality.

Whatever the condition, one has the impression of an increasing feminization as time went on. This may have been due to her love for Cardinal Azzolini, one of the few men who had ever given her shelter.

Ibsen speaks of the life-lie on which our shaky integrity depends. But for some persons there is a life-truth also, a conviction, so early appearing that it seems to be innate, that is with them from infancy to the grave. Christina's life-truth was the love of learning; it had been with her in the cold palaces at Stockholm and in the guest apartment at the Tower of the Winds, and it cared nothing for the sex of the hormones that gave it vitality.

Christina's theology sometimes veered toward the philosophers, but she remained a Catholic. In a sense the queen and the Church were stuck with each other. If she had renounced Catholicism it would have made her abdication a foolish mistake; if the Church had excommunicated her for her sins it would have been an admission that it had misjudged her in accepting her as a convert, or had set its judgment aside in its pleasure at capturing a queen. Yet Christina possessed what seems to be genuine religious feeling, and the Church has always had a particular fondness for its fascinating sinners.

Nevertheless, some of the queen's unused energy went into rebellion, not against the Church, but against its representatives. The popes had an uneasy time with Christina; the child who had lost her father too early had found a new father to torment and tease. Some traces of the queen's intransigence remain in the Archives. One is a reference to a note of the pope's confessor, in which he states that the pope has forgiven Christina "for what happened," but that he intends to punish the criminals. A strain was put on the relationship when Sweden failed to send the revenue promised to the queen and the deficit had to be made up by the pope. Like modern undeveloped nations, she resented taking what she had to take. One year the pope withheld this allowance to her, and she wrote to Cardinal Azzolini, "I assure you that you have given me the most beautiful news. The twelve thousand *scudi* that the pope gave me were the only blot on my life. I have always received them from the hand of God as the greatest humiliation with which he could abase my pride. Now I know I possess His grace, because He has done me the favor of taking away the *scudi*. I want you to thank Cardinal Cybo and the Pope on my behalf for the great favor he is doing me in abolishing this obligation."

A major source of friction was the extraterritoriality of the area (*quartiere*) in which the queen lived. Various undesirable elements were taking advantage of its exemption from Roman law, and eventually the Pope, in order to get the area quieted down, asked the queen to renounce her extraterritorial rights, as the ambassadors were being asked to do. The queen answered, "Most blessed Father: To obey the wish of Your Holiness, and to abate the scandal of the area, I will give up for good what is yours. There is nothing I ask from Your Holiness, and nothing I want. I hope you will accept not only my offer but my example, which may prove useful. Your most devoted and obedient daughter, Christina Alexandra." Written on this document is an unsigned comment, "So little respect for the Pope."

The matter caused much discussion and an "Invective" was circulated around the Vatican condemning the queen's attitude. Then some anonymous defender produced an Apologia for her, writing the "Invective" in one column and his Apologia in another.

Suddenly this attempt at objective analysis is too much for the writer of the Apologia, and he breaks out into, "Oh, you writer of the Invective! Not animal, not man, but beast all the way through! To think that the high and religious soul of Her Majesty, who with inborn and never-sufficiently-to-be-praised magnanimity has abdicated a vast domain made up of three powerful kingdoms and many wide provinces, would have tried to claim possessions of a few hand's-breadths of ground!"

The Invective is the only evidence of Roman ill feeling toward Christina that I have found. Other documents and letters suggest that the city gave itself happily and even affectionately to Christina-watching.

If we ourselves, in our time, were to write an Invective and an Apologia for this contradictory queen, two things that would have to go into the right-hand column are the facts that she worked for the cause of peace in a time when the Church had almost forgotten it, and that, in Rome of the Inquisition, she spoke for the rights of heretics. The early Christians had been pacifists, and so had Augustine until the Vandals got too close; after that he decided that fighting, while wrong for priests, was permissible for other ranks. Later the popes, accepting this distinction, had wholeheartedly embraced war as an instrument of ecclesiastical policy. Yet this woman, whose great regret was that she had never been in combat, harried her ambassadors into ending the Thirty Years War by the Treaty of Westphalia, which the papal nuncio refused to sign and which the Pope denounced. And with subtle tact she urges mercy toward his enemies on the king of Poland when she writes to congratulate him on the liberation of Vienna: "I no longer possess any kingdom, and have the independence and quiet that I value more than all the kingdoms in the world. I thought I could never envy anyone, but Your Majesty has proved to me that I am capable of it. I envy you the beautiful title of Liberator of Christianity, and the pleasure of giving life and liberty to the many unhappy persons among your friends and enemies."

Christina "loved all peoples," including heretics. At the time of the Revocation of the Edict of Nantes, which had given protection to the French Huguenots, she wrote to Abbot Talbor on the extirpation of heresy in France: "I am not convinced of the success of this great design." (And here a modern phrase comes to mind — "the final solution.") "I cannot rejoice over this policy as I could over things that would be favorable to our religion. Are you truly convinced of the sincerity of these new converts? I would not want to have on my conscience all the sacrileges that those forced into Catholicism . . . will commit. Men of war prefer to kill, to rape, to loot, rather than to persuade. I weep for those who were born to error, but it seems to me that they deserve pity rather than hate. France today is a sick person whose arms and legs are being amputated to heal her of an illness that with some patience and kindness could have been entirely cured. Jesus Christ did not use such methods to convert the world." In many ways she was a woman of the twentieth century, trapped in the seventeenth.

There are numerous letters, signed and unsigned, dealing with the last period of her life and with her death in 1689. There are clinical accounts of her illness and of the treatments attempted, even the most humiliating ones, and speculations on her will. There are records of plans to get noble children accepted as pages, to share in the queen's generosity toward her household.

Christina accepted her illness with stoicism and good humor: "I have eight devils — four doctors and four bloodletters." The daily reports give a dramatic account of her illness: "Our queen is better. Her eyes are very lively, as they normally are. She has joked. The queen is out of danger. The Viceroy of Naples wants to send three doctors rushing to her. The Pope wants to have a doctor come from Bologna. The ambassadors of France, the ambassadors of England, come to offer their services. The couriers run back and forth . . . the queen is at Nettuno. The cardinals come very often to see her . . . A new attack of breathlessness. Our queen has lost her speech. Our queen has been believed dead . . . The queen has been given an enema and after she went to the toilet she felt better and she has been able to eat with pleasure. All Rome has been concerned. On Tuesday we wept for our queen, but now we believe she is out of danger. The queen has entrusted her will to the notary Belli."

On the back of one of these letters is written an account in quick and careless writing. The queen was resting after a bad day, when her attendants heard a noise in the apartment above. Fearing that it would awaken her, they sent guards to the apartment. Finding it closed, they forced the door. "Advancing into the apartment, the guards found Monsignor Vaini in bed with Signora Angela Giorgini, consummating holy marriage. The guards were about to throw him out of the window, but Monsignor Vaini, afraid of being killed, offered 3,000 *scudi* for his life and for their silence in regard to the matter. Another thousand *scudi* were offered by the Giorgini woman, who also offered the many jewels she was wearing." But Cardinal Azzolini, called to give his advice on the matter, ordered that the Monsignor be freed.

A "Report on the Illness, Death and Funeral of Her Royal Majesty Christina Alexandra, Queen of Sweden," is in the Archives Miscellanea. "In the morning of April 19, as if she had had a long rest, lying on her right side, without moving, without contortion, better to say, with an unusual calm, she went to enjoy heaven." She had asked to be buried in a simple funeral at the Church of the Rotunda, but the Pope, "to honor this princess who had brought so much honor to the Holy Church," ordered that she be buried with great pomp in the Vatican Basilica of Saint Peter. Only half a dozen noblewomen, and only one other queen, were buried there. Christina was to be in the company of men, which she had always preferred. "Her body, embalmed according to custom, was exposed in her palace from Tuesday morning until Friday night, under a canopy, dressed in white embroidered with gold, continuously attended by barefoot Carmelite friars." And from Rome and the villages near it, the common people came bringing narcissus and other spring flowers gathered in the nearby hills.

Her funeral was as elaborate as her entrance into Rome. "First came the *literati*, then the orphans, then the various religious orders, then the queen's court; pages dressed in mourning carried the coffin. Over her white dress was the royal mantle of purple, embroidered with golden crowns, and with a wide border of ermine. On her head was the royal crown, and in her hand the scepter."

The Archives contains several copies of "The Testament of the Queen of Sweden, Dead in Rome April 19, 1689," along with many drafts and notes. It begins: "*Christina Alexandra, Suecor. Gothor. Vandalorumque Regina.*" She thanks God for having called her to the true faith, and humbly asks mercy for "our endless sins." Twenty thousand masses are to be said for her soul, and charities given to the poor but most of her estate was to go to "our very universal heir, Cardinal Decio Azzolini," with the Pope as executor. The Pope is to have the statue *The Savior* by her friend Bernini, and various kings and cardinals are to have legacies. There are legacies for the members of her household, and she particularly mentions that her little slave Christina Alessandra, apparently recently acquired, is to have the same legacy as her other little slaves. Her body is to be dressed in white and buried in the Church of the Rotunda in Rome, or another church "according to our heir's wish"; her tomb is to be inscribed "D.O.M. Vixit Christina."

Cardinal Azzolini survived her by only two months. Most of the library and the rich collection of manuscripts she had left to him came eventually to the Vatican.

She was buried with the mantle, the crown and the scepter. But the variant was like everyone else at last, and the Queen of the Vandals had made atonement for the sins of her people.

Where Afric's Sunny Fountains

IN present-day Africa there is a class of persons called been-tos. A been-to is a native African who has visited one of the centers of western civilization — London, New York, Paris — and has returned to Africa, never to be quite the same again. In Constantine's time the queen of Ethiopia was a been-to. Her parents had sent her to Alexandria as a girl, to learn Greek and the manners of civilization, in that time when Alexandria was a city of splendid culture; then she had returned to the barren tablelands of Ethiopia to marry the king and bear his sons. One day two young boys, brilliantly educated, ardently Christian, survivors of an ambushed trading expedition, were brought to her court as captives. The queen who had been to Alexandria at last had someone to talk to. She made them tutors to her sons, and the land became Christian.

There had been other Christian contacts; Christian traders came from time to time, and according to legend Saint Matthew, in those years of confidence that followed the Resurrection, had taught in Ethiopia and been martyred there.

Stories from Christian legend, and yet something real, something decisive, must have happened, for Ethiopia to have become and remained Christian. With Islam attacking from both sides and pagan Africa lapping at its foothills, the islanded culture kept its identity and its faith. An unsigned document in the Secret Archives suggests that there may have been institutions making for stability. Many of these were the work of still another been-to, King John the Holy (1667–1682?), who had traveled to Jerusalem and had come back with ideas.

To avoid wars of succession, "he ordered that the brothers of the living emperor, along with other close relatives, were to be put on Mount

Amara, and there be governed with all the grandeur in the world, with the exception of the firstborn son, who was to serve the emperor. There, there are palaces and fountains and gardens, very delicious indeed, and splendid rooms." Mount Amara, long a center of learning, was not only a prison for princes, a place for the safekeeping of unneeded royalty, but a library repository. "There are preserved also all the holy books and all the Scriptures which have been recovered from Jerusalem, from Antioch, from Constantinople, from Alexandria, in various languages. Cardinal Sirleto, having heard of this, tried to get a list of the documents, but death put an end to such thoughts."

The country's many kings were to wear robes of aqua blue, "and on their necks a chain of golden stars, and under it a Saint Matthew, who is Protector of Ethiopia." No man could be made a noble until each of seven generations of his family had done some very notable thing on behalf of either the Christian religion or the empire.

In our day, when Africa is slowly struggling toward literacy, it seems strange to read that Ethiopia had compulsory universal education. "He ordered, in addition, that in each city a great palace, like a monastery, be built, where all the sons of the nobles, the citizens, and the common people, would definitely have to go at the age of eight years, and there learn reading and writing and all things necessary to know for Christian life, up to the age of sixteen. They then joined the armies according to their rank."

Each city was to have a women's convent, where the nuns were dressed like the knights of Saint Anthony, and "in such monasteries there is a house where are put the *zitelle,* young girls who are twelve years of age, and they remain there by force of law, like the boys in the other monasteries, and learn Christian life and all the things that women should know." John gave civil-service status to the prostitutes, who were not to stay within the city, nor be dressed in any color except yellow. These women were only for single men. "A married man is not allowed to go to such a place, since by doing so he would commit a sin. In case he is found there, according to the law he is fed to the lions."

In addition to a guaranteed annual income, the prostitutes had time off, and the chronicler says, "There is also a chapel, with images of the saints, so that they can hear the Mass and sermons, and pray to our Lord."

In the religious fervor of the period that followed the Council of Trent a new age of missions began. The Secret Archives contains many reports, diaries, and letters written by the missionaries. Most of these are segregated in the archives of *Propaganda Fide,* but occasionally one finds summaries of long reports, intended as staff papers for the use of the pope.

Some of the early missionary writings are hard to distinguish from travel literature, and for this reason are valuable source material for such subjects as economic history. For example, the developing nations think they had a golden age of plenty before the white man came. Sometimes the missionaries and travelers write such things as "The land is bitter and sterile of nourishment; the wheat is scarce and so is the wine," but at other times they give a picture of prosperity. A traveler to Persia in 1572 says, "There is a great abundance of grain and of meat. The old as well as the young eat four times a day and very well," which may tell us something about the conditions of the old in Renaissance Italy. He goes on to speak of the city of Taurus, which took one a whole day to walk across, with its endless gardens full of "fruits beyond description for goodness and beauty," a city divided into forty-five areas, each with its own bazaar. And in the Philippines, a seventeenth-century Jesuit missionary writes, "The whole country has a great abundance of many foodstuffs. Rice is raised not only in the valleys but in the mountains, as grain or hay are raised in Spain. Beans and lentils grow as very high herbs and trees. The country is full of palm trees and coconut-gathering goes on all year long for the liquid that they contain. A great quantity of silk comes in from China, and everyone wears silk, even the sailors."

Later in the century Jesuit missionaries were sent to Russia on a diplomatic mission to ask the help of Ivan the Terrible against the Turks. The Pope chose as apostolic nuncio Antonio Possevino, a Jesuit of the same age as the czar — an interesting and perhaps very valid principle for choosing diplomats. A 1581 letter from Father Possevino to the Cardinal of Como gives an account of his entrance into Muscovy; four hundred horsemen dressed in brocade came to meet him in the name of their prince. The czar sent Possevino a Chinese horse, but counter-gifts to the czar were a problem, for Possevino had learned by now that the picture of a Madonna with four doctors of the Church which he had brought was unsuitable; "they would not have accepted it under any circumstances. Our Lord, though still a child, is painted nude and Saint John the Baptist is mainly nude." An *Agnus Dei* was hurriedly substituted.

Diplomatic relations were difficult; audiences with the czar were very short and each time he was mentioned all of his titles had to be recited. Possevino was enraged to see that after each meeting with him the czar washed his hands in a golden basin as if to cleanse himself. Nevertheless Possevino went on a second mission to Moscow, and from these two expeditions he drew the material for his manuscript *Muscovy*, published by the Jesuits in 1592.

Missionaries of the early modern period, like those of earlier ages, tended to follow what economists call the trickle-down theory. If the ruler and his family could be converted, then the whole country would become Christian. There was no objection to forced conversion. In the fifteen-thirties Paul III could write to the Congolese King Alfonso, "My very dear, with the greatest joy it has come to our knowledge that Your Majesty encourages with continuous exhortation and catechizing these people, not only yours, but those nearby, to the Catholic faith, and to propagation of our holy religion, without respite, with exhortation and admonition to the other unbelieving kings, and also with constriction if necessary." This is very like a letter sent to an English ruler a thousand years earlier. Perhaps form letters *are* used that long; on a recent trip to America I had to fill out a blank that asked whether I had brought any horses, mules, or emigrant's wagons with me.

From time to time during the Middle Ages priests and friars had made their way into the Asian land-mass, and had written of the grasslands where thirty-foot-wide mobile homes were drawn by teams of twenty-two oxen driven eleven abreast; travelers had described Chinese cities, their extent, their luxury, their marble bridges. Asia was entering into the mind of Europe; even Milton's *Paradise Lost* speaks of

> . . . *the barren plains*
> *Of Sericana, where Chineses drive*
> *With sails and wind their cany wagons light.*

And knowledge of the West was penetrating into Asia. By the seventeenth century China was ready to appreciate Western science; through it the Jesuits hoped to teach Western philosophy. The emperors were delighted with clocks and sundials; through teaching them time one might also teach them eternity. For the Jesuit Matteo Ricci and his followers, a particular opportunity existed in the condition of the Chinese calendar. China had had a scientific calendar at one time, but it had become increasingly erroneous, and someone had lost the instructions; revisions had to be on an empirical basis. In 1594 Matteo Ricci received a formal request to revise it. Knowing that this was beyond him, he wrote to his superiors in Rome asking them to send a real astronomer, but the years went by and none arrived. When news of Galileo's discovery of the telescope reached Peking, the Jesuits wrote to him for help; he did not answer. Kepler, however, answered all the questions that the missionaries had put to him and sent them copies of his works. When the Chinese government cannily asked the three local schools of astronomy —

Chinese, Mohammedan, and European — to predict the exact time of
an expected eclipse, only the Jesuits gave it correctly.

In 1634 China adopted the new Western calendar. Western art was
less appreciated — the Chinese wanted to know whether the originals of
portraits really had one side of the face darker than the other.

The cultural exchange went in both directions, the Jesuits began to see
more and more to admire in Confucianism. The Chinese, they said, were
not worshiping their ancestors, but *reverencing* them — something directed in the Ten Commandments. In fact, they found that they could
make a very attractive catechism out of quotations from the Chinese
philosophers. The tradition of Jesuit liberalism survived for centuries in
Peking, and some of the Vatican's alarm at the ideas of Teilhard de
Chardin may have been due to their geographical origin.

Meanwhile the Jesuit Roberto de' Nobili was proselytizing the Indian
upper classes by following Indian customs. He wore a long robe of yellow cotton, tied with the Brahmin cord to which he added strands: to
him, three of them, in gold, represented the Holy Trinity, and two, in
silver, the body and soul of *"adorabile umanità."* He presented himself
as a Roman rajah, a *sannyasi* who had renounced the world. Visitors
were told that they could not see him because he was meditating on Divine Law. Those whom he converted to Christianity were allowed to
continue to follow native customs: to retain their caste, to celebrate the
winter equinox with its sun-god implications, to wear forehead-marks of
the ashes of sandalwood, which de' Nobili himself blessed for them. This
assortment of adaptations came to be known as the Malabar Rites. And
the Jesuits' rivals, the Dominicans and Franciscans, watching the success
of their methods and believing them to be an adulteration of Christianity, made formal protest in Rome. Letters took years to come and go,
and it was a very long time before the matter was resolved — if, indeed,
it has ever been. At times the pope tried to speed matters by sending
conditional directives — if the rites were such-and-such, they were permissible; on the other hand, if they were as so-and-so described them,
they were illicit. In the end, however, the Malabar Rites were forbidden.

When the controversy over the Malabar Rites broke out, the Jesuits
were teaching Euclid, liberally laced with theology, to the Chinese emperor, but the dissension within the Church, and the papal rejection of so
much that the Chinese valued, "irritated and wounded him deeply."
Centuries later, in 1940, the Secretary of *Propaganda Fide*, Monsignor
Celso Constantini, commented: "The emperor was on the verge of conversion. If he had been converted, all China would almost certainly have
followed the example of the Son of Heaven. The sad conflict of the Rites

was probably the main cause of alienating the emperor from the Christian religion."

The modern churchman, accustomed to making every possible concession to native opinion, finds it strange that the Church was willing to lose China and India for points of custom. We think of the tom-toms in the Vatican, of the Church literature in pidgin English ("Jesus him the foreman belong you-me."). And yet, what would have been the practical consequences of early Christianization of China and India? Greater cultural interchange, better acquaintance with Oriental life and thought, more rapid Westernization and industrialization of the Orient, progress toward the old dream of Alexander? Or earlier wars?

In Paraguay the Jesuits went to the other extreme, and tried communism with such success that their settlements — the *reductiones* — entered into European thought. It is unlikely that the Peace Corps will ever adopt the system used by the Jesuits for bringing modern civilization to the undeveloped peoples. It was tremendously effective but it involved methods now forbidden in the democratic nations — authoritarianism, religion, communism, and complete manipulation of the environment.

From about 1610 to 1750 the Jesuits maintained a paradise in Paraguay, and when it fell, it fell not because of inner weakness — though weaknesses existed — but to outside invasion. Their achievement is more notable in that the Guaraní Indians involved were not among the most advanced American peoples. They were agriculturists, cannibal only in war, weavers and cultivators of rubber, but without the social infrastructure of the Incan empire, with which they sometimes traded. They had no developed region, and when the missionaries tried to explain hell to them, they said tranquilly, "That's fine; it won't be cold there."

The Jesuits probably got much of the inspiration for their communistic settlements from European monasteries; religious groups have always been a refuge from the competitive economy. Other possible sources were More's *Utopia*, located somewhere "beyond the line equinoctial," Augustine's *City of God*, and Plato's *Republic*.

Each of the *reductiones* or communes had at least two thousand, and more often five or ten thousand, people; when they became too crowded a new town was built, on a principle later used in the "New Towns" of Britain. The plans of the towns were uniform. There was a great central square with palms and orange trees; around it were the most important public buildings — the church, the priests' residence, the workshops, the guesthouse, the community hall with its arches and columns — the same number of arches, the same number of columns, in each *reduction*. Streets were straight so that one could look across the city; the sidewalks were covered to protect against the sun. Orchards were rich with oranges, lemons, peaches, almonds. Travelers of the time greatly admired those planned cities, and compared them with Buenos Aires and La Plata, built with reed and mud roofs "*à la manière des hirondelles.*"

The Guaraní were transformed into livestock raisers, masons, carpenters. They worked not more than eight hours a day, and they worked to music and singing. The community provided everything needed. Their industrial progress was incredible. By the end of the experiment they were running printing presses and making watches and musical instruments. All the children were educated; adults said their multiplication tables to the Lord after mass.

They progressed more rapidly than the Jesuits realized, and toward the end of the experiment they were demanding the right to enter the priesthood. But when the *reductiones* were turned over to Portugal, in a royal barter deal, the people of the *reductiones* fought bitterly for five years to protect their communities. The settlements were ended forever by a conclave far away in Rome, when the cardinals chose a candidate pledged to the suppression of the Jesuit order. But the Guaraní settlements had existed, and succeeded; they must take their place with the state-owned galleys of Venice as one of history's contrary facts.

The methods the Jesuits used in these little republics are available to the Communist countries. Could they be modified and adapted to the democratic system? If so, the black ghettos of America, the crowded cities of India, might become the orchard-shaded towns of the Guaraní Republics.

Missionaries and travelers left Rome for far countries, but travelers from the far countries were also coming to Rome. In the Room of Sixtus V in the Vatican Library there is a fresco showing Sixtus taking possession of the Lateran in 1585. In the procession are four young Japanese in European clothing — long robes of black velvet. These were the Japanese Christian princes who had come on a pilgrimage to Rome. The Secret Archives gives us glimpses of their visit — the two and a half years of travel from Japan, King Philip II of Spain asking one of them to take off a shoe so that he could see how it was made, their gifts to the Pope (the horn of a unicorn, an ebony writing-table, and "two goblets of rhinoceros bone to drink from, efficient against poisoning").

In 1585 they left Rome to return to Japan by way of Venice and Genoa, and in Venice "a very solemn procession was made for their edification, in which, in addition to many holy relics and great quantities of silver, gold, and jewels arranged in different ways, several *tableaux vi-*

vants of sacred history of the Old and New Testaments and of the martyrdom of saints were shown." The last may have been an omen, for a dozen years later Japan crucified thousands of its Christians.

An unsigned report of 1659, in the Secret Archives, relates "some customs and habits of the Muscovite ambassadors, who at present are in Leghorn on the way to their embassy in Venice." The report-writer's attitude is that of a biologist observing a new species. "There are two ambassadors. The first is a prince and the second his secretary of state, but they treat each other as equals. They have with them four noblemen and their *papasso* or priest, who always has on his neck a tabernacle with small lighted candles in which is the Madonna or Saint Nicholas, their protector. They pray to Saint Nicholas for everything they need, and if they do not obtain the mercy they ask for, they beat the saint furiously." However, the writer thought the ambassadors very handsome. The visitors wore sable-lined garments with the front of them embroidered with pearls. "They think it is as cold here as in their own country." Or, perhaps, they had no lighter garments. The writer continues with disapproving comments on the Russians' interpersonal relations. "They beat their servants personally and so brutally that four or five of them have almost died. When they found their priest drunk they punished him severely and tied him up one day and one night to the bedpost. They have very little money, or letters of exchange, but they have a fortune in sable furs, and in addition a great quantity of caviar, and some other salted fish that smells terrible. They are very stingy in spending money, as they are not accustomed to using it. . . . Although in Leghorn they have been lodged in a very large house or palace, they use only two rooms where all of them stay, and they sleep on the floor" (there were thirty-two in the party). It was impossible to get the prince to sleep in the bed; he was afraid of falling out.

Their drinking habits were puzzling to the writer: "The government of Leghorn, on behalf of the Grand Duke, gave them great quantities of excellent wine, which they rate very highly, but then they put all the wines they have into a barrel, white and dark together, without distinction of the kind of wine."

When the governor took them around in his carriage, they got out not by opening the doors, or waiting for them to be opened, but by jumping over them — a natural gesture for a horseman. Their table manners failed to meet Italian standards, though they were obviously trying to learn. "At a formal dinner the Muscovites, having noticed the governor eating soup with a spoon, took the soup with their hands and put it into the spoon, and took meat in their hands and impaled it on the fork. The ambassador, having put a piece of meat into his mouth without the fork, spat it out, put it on the fork, and ate it again."

The ambassador had a weakness for beautiful women, and made them generous gifts of sables and caviar. "One day, having seen an extremely beautiful woman in a carriage, he kept asking who she was. And learning that she was the wife of a doctor, at home that night the ambassador began to shout that he had a terrific pain in his stomach, and asked that he be taken to the home of the doctor who was her husband."

Their next stop was Florence, and they were taking with them "a ridiculous sort of luggage, empty boxes, empty wine jars, and even empty bottles, saying that it is a sign of grandeur to travel with much luggage." They had fifteen boatloads of it to take to Florence. The report-writer's advice to Florence was to give them plenty of parties.

True or exaggerated, these anecdotes are remarkably like the stories that one hears at the United Nations about the representatives of the new republics.

The Church and the world intersect in modern Rome, for the missionary efforts of the nineteenth and twentieth centuries established the faith in many an African and Oriental community. We no longer object to the ways of the native cultures; in fact we seem prepared to accept almost any native practice short of female circumcision. The emphasis on indigenous priesthoods, and even on indigenous hierarchies, has brought young men from all over the world to the seminaries and religious establishments of Rome. Handsome, eager young men in their proud soutanes, carrying their cheap plastic briefcases. They visit the shrines of Christian history to gaze at Saint Peter's table, Saint Gregory's chair, and Saint Benedict's boardinghouse; they try to figure out the Forum with little maps. But they have a modern place of pilgrimage, too: the *Standa*, Rome's equivalent of Woolworth's. One sees them there, intent, utterly accepting, looking at the coiled green serpents of plastic garden hoses, at the hen-shaped clay chicken-cookers, at the colored glass that all of us could recognize as beautiful if it were in a properly authenticated mosaic instead of in cheap jewelry. Their love for these wonders is so apparent that even the cross little clerks of the *Standa* are almost pleasant to them. In a year or two they will return to Asia, to Africa; sometimes to a lifetime of hard work, sometimes to martyrdom, now and then to politics; the newest of the Church's long line of been-tos.

The Conclaves

THE anthropologist Ruth Benedict tells us that the Zuñi of the American desert, when it becomes necessary for them to choose religious officials, put the eligible candidates into the underground *kiva* or ceremonial chamber and fasten the hatchway. I do not know what device takes the place of the Vatican's smoke signals in announcing that the election has been accomplished. But when one comes to motivation the analogy breaks down — the Zuñi find it necessary to incarcerate their *papabili* because, in their culture, the dislike for exercising authority is so great that no one wants to hold office.

The Church's conclaves are a relatively new institution. Some of the early popes recommended their own successors, in a system rather like the adoption of adult heirs by the emperors. Later the Bishop of Rome was chosen by the local clergy, then by the local bishops. Lay participation, now regarded as one of the daring possibilities opened up by the Second Vatican Council, existed as a tumultuous reality in the people's right to approve or disapprove the choice that was made. Papal elections were often the occasion of open fighting; even the scholarly Pope Damasus came to power after a conflict that involved dozens of deaths. Pope and antipope were familiar figures almost to the time of the Renaissance. Interference by the nobles complicated matters, and Charlemagne's son Louis the Pious acquired an imperial veto over whatever choice was made — a right not abrogated until 1904, after it had swayed a papal election.

A canon of 1059 decreed that if Rome was too dangerous, as it often was, cardinals might gather elsewhere to choose a new pope. Also, the approval of the Roman populace was no longer required. Later it was decided that a new pope must have a two-thirds majority — two-thirds plus one, in case the leading candidate was so lacking in humility as to vote for himself. To eliminate long periods of *sede vacante*, the canonists borrowed an idea from the laity of northern Italy, who had sometimes had trouble in electing the magistrates of their communes. If the cardinals failed to come to an agreement, they were to be locked up (*clausura*) by the civil authorities. Then, if they still failed to elect a pope, their food was to be gradually reduced. (The same idea is used in modern corporations, which sometimes prolong conferences far beyond the lunch hour as a means of encouraging consensus.) *Clausura* was used successfully in the Perugia conclave of 1216, though in 1241 most of the cardinals escaped by electing a dying man. In the Viterbo conclave of 1270 and 1271 the citizenry found it necessary not only to reduce the cardinals' rations to bread and water but to cut a hole in the roof so that they would be exposed to bad weather. The pope elected by this two years and nine months' conference, Gregory X, decreed that in future conclaves the cardinals were to meet in the papal palace in the city in which the pope had died, and there be kept on diminishing food supplies, sent in through a guarded window, until a new pope was elected. A cardinal could have only one servant if he was well, two if he was ill — a ruling that tended to increase the morbidity rate. The secret ballot was not introduced until the 16th century, and Aeneas Sylvius, writing of his own debated conclave, complains that some cardinals, fearing that Aeneas would be elected, "left the conclave, pretending physical needs, but really with the purpose of escaping the fate of that day."

The Secret Archives has volume after volume of conclave records, many of them with pictures showing the decor of the conclave rooms and diagrams showing the numbered cells occupied by the cardinals. Records of all the scrutinies, or votes, are available, but the most revealing of the conclave records are the diaries kept by the participants, usually by the pontifical masters of ceremony. Some of these are in the Secret Archives; others have been transferred to the Manuscript Section of the Vatican Library. A particularly interesting one is the diary of Bondone de' Branchis di Fermo, master of ceremonies at the conclave that followed the death of the inquisitor pope, Paul IV, in 1559.

This conclave was a struggle between the French and Spanish parties of the Church, and particularly responsive to political influence. One of the leading candidates was Cardinal Morone, Bishop of Modena, whom Paul IV had thrown into prison for heresy. Another was Cardinal Ippolito d'Este, elegant, worldly, politically corrupt, connected with the French nobility. D'Este had been reprimanded by Paul IV for trying to buy the 1555 conclave; he was prepared to buy this one. Another candidate was Cardinal Giovanni Angelo de' Medici, regarded as unsound because he felt that communion wine for the laity and, if necessary, wives for some of the clergy, would be a small price to pay for bringing the Lutherans back into the Church. The diary of Bondone de' Branchis di Fermo recounts the struggle of these men for power, and incidentally gives us a picture of this unruly conclave.

September 5. The Sacred College meets, its cardinals robed in purple, and gives audience to the representatives of the secular princes, in silk and velvet set off by lace and the metallic glitter of swords. The master of ceremonies reads the oath of allegiance to the Holy See, and the conclave is in session.

September 6. There seem to be more people present than the number of cardinals would indicate; some of them have brought more servants and secretaries than the rules allow. All the conclavists are gathered in the Pauline Chapel and the master of ceremonies calls the roll. There are at least twice as many people present as there should be.

September 26. There is a rumor that the French cardinals plan to elect Ippolito d'Este by acclamation, as a surprise move. The Spanish party reacts violently to this, and Alexander Farnese of the French party and Christopher Madruzzo, Archbishop of Trent, seem to be on the verge of hand-to-hand fighting. There is an "agitated situation" for a day and a night.

October 1. It is discovered that the Cardinal Ascanio Sforza di Santa Fiora, a great lord homesick for the pleasures of his court, has somehow gotten his dwarf into the conclave.

October 2. When the door is opened to let the litter of a sick cardinal pass out, two noblemen dodge in on the excuse that they have to see two of the cardinals. After the scrutiny (vote) is taken, a committee of four cardinals is formed to establish order in the conclave. One is Cardinal d'Este; another is one of the hated Caraffa cardinal-nephews. The committee orders the conclavists to cease scandalizing the people by looking out the windows of the loggia to watch the courtesans walking back and forth in Saint Peter's Square. The committee also discusses the fact that a physician and some servants have escaped by means of the revolving door through which food is sent in.

October 5. There is another ban on unauthorized personnel. Agents of the princes have gotten in to support the French party or the Spanish party, and bankers are there to pay for votes with the cash bribes called dung of the demon. At night the conclave is so noisy that the older cardinals have difficulty in sleeping. Security has gone to pieces; information is leaking out through doors, windows, holes cut in the wall, into the *avvisi*. The Romans are making bets on the new pope, bets properly drawn up and notarized, and so large that the losers are sometimes ruined men.

October 13. Philip II's Ambassador Vargas comes to the door of the conclave and complains that the conclave is lasting too long.

October 20. The vault of the antechamber of the Consistory, in which some of the cardinals' cells are located, has begun to creak and there is fear that it will fall (not an impossibility in those times when the dreams of architects sometimes outran the skill of engineers and the strength of materials). The cardinals, alarmed, have the door to the great hall of the popes opened, and install themselves in the luxury of the Borgia Apartments. The other cardinals are envious, and break down the doors of their own rooms to get some fresh air, badly needed by now in this palace without plumbing. A general meeting is held and the cardinals ordered back to their cells.

November 18. The cell of Nicolò Caetani, Cardinal of Sermoneta, in the Sistine Chapel near Michelangelo's *Christ of the Universal Judgment*, catches fire, but the chapel escapes destruction.

November 22. A group of municipal officers and noblemen are received in audience, and complain that Rome is suffering from lack of a pope. "Misery is increasing and everyone follows his own idea of justice." Resentment is rising against the conclavists, who "confuse everything with their conflicting reports" and are coming and going from *clausura* too freely.

November 28. Several noblemen who have disguised themselves as conclavists are evicted. The conclavists are assembled in the Pauline Chapel while their cells are shaken down. About a hundred unauthorized persons are found and sent away. The deacons reduce the cardinals' food to one main dish.

December 15. The Administrator of the Apostolic Chamber, the equivalent of a modern finance minister, points out that the treasury of the Holy See is empty, and that there is no money for food or for paying the troops.

December 18. News spreads that Cardinal Pacheco has been elected, and his house is sacked, according to custom, before the mistake is known. The window of the conclave pharmacy has to be closed, because a representative of the king of Spain, "coming over the roof like a cat," is lobbying for the Spanish party.

December 25. Late at night Cardinal Giovanni Angelo de' Medici, one of the best cardinals of the conclave, is elected, in spite of his leftist views on wine and wives for the Lutherans, in the hope that he may be able to reconcile the French and Spanish parties.

As Pius IV (1559–1565), the new pope reconvened the Council of

Trent and saw it through to its conclusion, softened the rigors of the Inquisition, and continued Michelangelo as architect of Saint Peter's. It is true that he had the unpopular Caraffa cardinal-nephews executed, and made his own nephew cardinal at twenty-one and archbishop at twenty-two, but this was in accordance with the ethics of the times — and his own nephew was Saint Charles Borromeo.

Modern conclaves are quiet and reverent (as a Catholic, I prefer this to the alternative explanation that security has improved). But even at their worst the conclaves provided a democratic element in monarchy, like the thudding of spears on the ground by which Germanic warriors elected their chieftains. In an age of the divine right of kings, they upheld at least the idea of leadership through merit. And like the American presidential nominating conventions that they so much resembled, they sometimes chose surprisingly good men.

The Saints

"FIRST of the actresses of Antioch was she, and riding on an ass. Bare of head and shoulder and limb . . ." The fifth-century Saint Pelagia the Harlot, experts tell us rather unnecessarily, is not to be confused with the other Saint Pelagia of Antioch, who died defending her virginity. Pelagia the Harlot was one of the saints of the *Vitae Patrum*, but we know her through the beautiful prose of Helen Waddell, in a translation of a translation from the Greek of James the Deacon. Her story was one of those written to be read aloud in refectories; I do not see how it can have contributed to the tranquillity of the brothers.

A convocation of bishops was sitting in front of the Basilica of the Blessed Julian; all but one of them turned their faces away as Pelagia and her retinue rode by. Only Nonnus, Bishop of Edessa, saw her with delight, and recognized the beauty that would sit in the presence of God, "in judgment of ourselves and our episcopate." She sent him a note by two of her servants, reminding him of Christ and the woman of Samaria, "for I have heard the talk of the Christians —" and was baptized. Then, "on the eighth day," because they dared not be near each other, Pelagia fled, in the bishop's tunic and cloak, to a cell on the Mount of Olives. And there as the Holy Pelagius she died of prayer and fasting.

The story of Pelagia is an eyewitness account: James the Deacon was servant and secretary of Bishop Nonnus. Perhaps this is why he can make us, fifteen centuries later, see her as she was when she rode past the Basilica — "and of the beauty and the loveliness of her there could be no wearying for a world of men."

We know some of the early saints through historical or semihistorical accounts such as this, some through the court records that preceded their martyrdom, and some, like Augustine and Clement, through their own writings. The first to be venerated were the martyrs — people who had been killed for their faith, like the Apostles, or had suffered for it, like the popes who were condemned to hard labor in the island mines. The Tomb of Saint Peter seems to have been an object of reverence from the beginning, and when Saint Martin of Tours visited it in the fourth century he prostrated himself before a jeweled shrine in an apparently well-established ceremonial procedure. Similar reverence was shown to the tombs of the martyrs buried in the catacombs, and then to the tombs of the confessors — priests and bishops noted for their ardor and charity — as word spread of the miraculous favors they had granted.

Sometimes little sanctuaries, like Peter's *aedicula*, were built above the tomb, sometimes the body was transferred to another place where worship would be more convenient or safer. This was hard to do in the imperial period, for Roman law regarded the resting-places of the dead as inviolable. "Let the oak lie where it falls" — I have seen the graves of Nazi soldiers placed diagonally across suburban lawns in accordance with the same principle. For a while the Church concurred in this view and taught that whoever violated the tomb of a martyr, even unintentionally, would die. Pope Gregory the Great recounted a story of some laborers who, working around the tomb of Lawrence the Librarian whose body was buried in the raw earth, moved the great piece of silver plate that covered him, and died within a few days.

To counter the opposition of the authorities, the early Christians developed techniques of civil disobedience. If the offense was committed by enough people, and by important enough people, arresting them would be regarded as impractical. Exhumations were attended by the bishop of the diocese and the bishops of neighboring dioceses, regional magistrates, and other *ottimati* or best people. On some occasions, when this open exhumation was thought to be unsafe, the tomb was opened secretly and a miracle declared. Gregory of Tours, in his book *De gloria confessorum,* tells how the pavement broke open above the tombs of three holy priests and the bodies rose up one after the other "as if they were asking for honor and glory." The digging up of bodies was called *elevatio* and moving them *translatio;* together they constituted an informal canonization.

A new literary genre appeared in the lives of the saints and martyrs: the flowery, though partly true, stories of Lawrence the Librarian, Saint Polycarp, "Saint Martin with his colonel's cloak," Paulinus of Nola selling himself into slavery to ransom a widow's son. And there were women among them: Saint Catherine, who confounded the philosophers in a debate before the emperor; the little servant-girl Blandina who was tortured at Lyons; Monica, the mother of Augustine; and old Helena, the barmaid empress whose son was Constantine.

And there are other saints that exist for the sake of a beautiful and perhaps imaginary anecdote, like Saint Dorothea, who tried to convert the captain of the guard as he led her to the arena. "Dorothea, Dorothea, I will believe when thou sendest down the fruits and flowers of Paradise." And that night in the officers' mess the table was showered with yellow roses and yellow apples. These stories, polished and often augmented by oral tradition, were written down in the monasteries of the Middle Ages. According to the Jesuit *Bollandisti* of the nineteenth century, most of the hagiographic legends, when subjected to textual criticism, are unacceptable or acceptable only to a limited extent. Some of the *Bollandisti* books were condemned by the Holy Office, but were defended by Pio Franchi da' Cavalieri, scriptor of the Vatican Library, who had reached the same conclusions independently. The Church itself is now applying the test of scholarship to the saints, and some of them have been demoted to legend; the little Church of Saint Philomena that I used to attend in the mountains beyond San Diego will have been renamed by now.

As Christianity spread to the countryside the people began to make their own saints to take the place of the little gods and goddesses of the Roman pantheon, the small, useful, approachable deities who understood a workingman's life, who could be invited into the kitchen. One could hardly ask Saint Augustine to help with a sick sheep, or with bread that came out stringy.

The minor gods and goddesses had operated on a system of division of labor, and this system was taken over by the saints. There are saints for places, for the various occupations, for specific diseases; others guard one or another of life's crisis points. In my youth I made — and broke — many a pre-examination vow to the saint of students, Rita da Cascia.

The cult of the relics began with the cult of the martyrs, as the faithful soaked small cloths — *brandea* — in their blood, or put them in contact with the coffin. The cult of relics *ex ossibus* spread rapidly when elevation and translation began to be practiced, and bones became easily available. Every altar of the growing Church was supposed to have a relic under it, and kings and princes collected them, housing them in reliquaries that became objects of art. The demand for relics exceeded supply, and some saints, particularly venerated in several places, have a head in each place. Gregory the Great refused a Byzantine empress's request for a piece of Saint Paul, but later there was no hesitation about dismembering a body on the share-the-wealth principle; churchmen cut up the saints as farmers cut up seed potatoes, confident that the vital principle was in each fragment.

Besides the relics of the saints there were other relics with slips of ancient parchment attached to them saying that they were the bones of archangels. These brought a very high price and were thought to be particularly effective. (And yet I remember reading a casual phrase: "Twelve young men, four of them angels . . ." Will some dilettante scientist sometime find a way to count the chromosomes in these impossible relics?)

The number of saints increased rapidly; there were over twenty-five thousand of them by the tenth century. Most of them were only local; getting a saint nationally recognized required the approval of a sovereign, international recognition that of a pope. The cults of really popular saints spread nearly as fast as the cults of motion-picture stars do today — the earliest representation we have of Saint Thomas à Becket is in a Sicilian cathedral.

Gradually canonization came to depend more and more on the Holy See, and when Sixtus V overhauled the Church organization toward the end of the sixteenth century he delegated canonization to the Congregation of Rites. Later Pope Urban VIII forbade all new and spontaneous cults; if cults did arise they were to be regarded as an impediment to canonization. Stories of the lives and miracles of possible saints were not to be published without ecclesiastical approval. In our own century Pius XI tightened the requirements still further by establishing a historical section for critical review of documentation. The Church is now so cautious in regard to possible saints that the Capuchin priest Padre Pio, said to have had both the stigmata and the gift of bilocation, was forbidden to write or to preach.

The canonic process usually begins in the diocese where the Servant of God (a term that avoids the use of the word candidate) lived and worked. The requirement that it begin at the Servant's birthplace has been abrogated; the saints, like the rest of us, move around too much.

First, inquiry is made into his virtues, which must have been practiced with heroic intensity. This is said to be a serious impediment to the canonization of John XXIII — no one doubts his great virtue, but was it heroic? Was enough struggle involved? (This seems rather like faulting a musician for having absolute pitch.) The evidence regarding the virtue of the Servant of God is filed under three classifications, faith, hope, and charity. If heroic virtue is found, the Servant is given the title of Venerable. Later, if the process so decided and if the Venerable has been responsible for two miracles proved by circumstantial evidence, he is given the title of *Beatus*, or Blessed. Finally, if further miracles occur, the *Beatus* can be declared a saint and his cult extended to all of Catholic Christianity.

The canonic process requires long investigations, careful search for documentation, evidence, and witnesses, taking of oaths, printing of documents. The saints usually come from the regular clergy — that is, from the religious orders. Only very rarely are they drawn from the secular clergy — those who serve the Catholic laity — or from the laity itself. This is not because heroic faith, hope, and charity are lacking among the secular clergy and the laity, but because the process of canonization is extremely expensive. Not only are there lengthy investigations, but when the time comes to proclaim the saint, his biography is usually printed, large pictures of him are painted, often by good artists, a valuable silver reliquary is presented to the pope, and Saint Peter's Basilica and dome are illuminated. To make a parish priest a saint would be a very heavy financial burden for his diocese. In rare cases the costs are paid by the saint's family, but they mean a financial strain even for a princely house. After the beatification of Saint Aloysius Gonzaga young boys gathered around his mother to congratulate her. "Be good boys," she told them, "but don't be saints."

Because of the costs of canonization, or for lack of evidence, processes are often left unfinished. The files are kept, however, and the matter remains open for further action. In the Secret Archives and the archives of the Congregation of Rites there are hundreds of these unfinished processes. From time to time the Congregation publishes a list of them.

I was able to see a few of these, including one for the canonization of Mary, Queen of Scots, and other members of Britain's Catholic Resistance. The first volume of Mary's process is of ivory parchment lined with silk of a soft blue. There are many seals of blood-red wax. On the first page is a cross of pink ribbon, with a seal at the end of each arm. Much of the evidence offered is from the Secret Archives, and was discovered by a Scottish archivist searching for documents relating to British history of the Elizabethan period. In it one sees the queen in captivity, demanding that Elizabeth send her a confessor, asking the Archbishop of Glasgow whether her little flock of servants and companions may pray in their own language when making their private devotions, assuring Sixtus V that she is willing to give up not only life but dignity for the Faith — "I leave it to the prudence of your Holiness to decide in what way I may serve you." And finally the incredulous announcement, "I have been condemned to die — I, a free queen."

With the story of Mary Stuart are stories of other children of the

Church, in another hemisphere and centuries later. An old man is standing in front of a Christian home when soldiers enter the village and ask if he is a priest. He is in ordinary clothing, but he answers, "I am a true priest of the true Church," and is slain. Again, a witness tells of seeing a procession of mandarins leading a martyr, "dressed in white and with a smiling serene face," to a ring where he was trampled and tossed by a maddened elephant. These volumes leave one with a feeling that there may be many more saints than have ever been formally canonized.

The records of the processes for the beatification and canonization of Servants of God formally belong to the archives of the Congregation of Rites, a detached part of the Vatican Secret Archives. Actually they are in various places: the archives of the Congregation; the National Library of Paris, which kept some of them, including those of Ignatius Loyola and Rita da Cascia, when it returned Napoleon's loot; and the Secret Archives of the Vatican. Often the volumes of a process are divided between the Secret Archives and the archives of the Congregation of Rites. The number of processes in the Secret Archives is estimated at about four thousand two hundred and fifty. They are only partially indexed, and the indexes are in Latin and are themselves highly classified. The Servants of God are listed alphabetically, and also according to the religious order to which they belonged. Beyond that, no analytical index exists, and to construct one it would be necessary to examine all of the four thousand two hundred and fifty processes. Very often different processes are bound together, and documents that do not belong with a process are sometimes included in it.

This is one of the most inaccessible of all the archives of the Church. The records of saints' lives, of saints' actions in their most intimate detail, are sometimes of a nature to require the secrecy of the confessional. Also, the witnesses, who were often very prominent people, had to give a great deal of information about themselves — their lives and actions, their true opinions on various matters, and their family situations. The processes are all secret. Only after a hundred years have elapsed can some details of them be disclosed.

I was fortunate in being able to examine one process, that of Saint Frances Xavier Cabrini, the first American saint. It consists of fourteen volumes. Eight of them, handwritten, are authentic copies of the ordinary and apostolic diocesan processes carried on in Lodi, Italy, where she was born, and in Chicago, where much of her work was done. These volumes are in the Secret Archives of the Vatican. The remaining six volumes, which are printed, deal with the final process carried on in Rome by the Congregation of Rites, and are kept in its archives. The volumes of the Cabrini process are in white parchment, worked to resemble wood. On the cover of the first volume, surrounded by golden sunlike rays, is a great blood-red heart enclosed in flames and a crown of thorns, the symbol of her order. This volume contains a magnificent map the size of a tabletop, showing Western Europe and the coast of Africa, the Atlantic Ocean, and North and South America from Alaska to Tierra del Fuego. Elegant lines in red traverse the ocean — the routes traveled by the saint. Small golden stars on the coasts and the continents mark the stops in her voyage, the cities where she founded her hospitals, orphanages, schools, and convents — one for each year of her life.

Mother Cabrini's personal history does not present exciting or tragic events, nor, as far as we know, does her spiritual life present those conflicts which have sometimes devoured the saints up to the end of their lives. This may be an illusion; her portrait shows a handsome face that might have belonged to one of the young men at Oxford who took part in the Anglo-Catholic movement. One is reminded of Oscar Wilde's description of Cardinal Newman — "and in his face the ruin of great beauty."

But she was meant for sainthood from the first; she never belonged to the world, except as the world manages to penetrate the Church. When she was born, to a peasant family, a wave of white doves lit in the farmyard, stayed a moment and then flew away; they had never been there before. She grew up in the isolated farmhouse in the Lombard plain, in the summer flooded with sun and loud with the singing of crickets, covered with fog in the fall and the snow in winter. She was a pretty child, with enormous blue-green eyes and blonde hair that for the health of her soul was not allowed to curl. She was called Cecchina (a diminutive of Francesca; the pet name is still used among the peasants of the Lombard countryside, though modern children reject it as soon as they have acquired a little age and sophistication). Too delicate to attend school regularly, she was taught by her schoolteacher sister and later attended a Catholic girls school. Somehow she must have acquired an extraordinary education, for in later life, when she inspected the schools of her order, it was her custom to walk into any classroom unexpectedly, ask what was being taught, and take over the teaching herself.

In the smoky kitchen of the farmhouse the little girl read the pamphlets published by the Society for the Propagation of the Faith, and determined to be a missionary. Perhaps a desire for travel had something to do with it; sometimes it is not only the souls that call "from many an ancient river, and many a palmy plain," but the rivers and the plains themselves, that draw people to the mission field. At eleven she made a vow of virginity; she was a farm child and may possibly have known what the word meant. She was rejected for reasons of health when she tried to enter a convent, but through her work in a nearby orphanage she was able to found a small religious group known as the Missionary Sisters of the Sacred Heart. And somehow this delicate child, brought up in the sheltered environment that even poor families sometimes manage to create for a child that is different and greatly loved, found in herself great reserves of energy and efficiency. Her order was a success; the institutions she founded prospered. When she was thirty-seven she went to Rome to establish a house there as a way-station toward the mission field, and a surprised cardinal found himself giving his consent.

Her personality and administrative gifts attracted attention — even the attention, admiring and amused, of Pope Leo XIII (1878–1903). Leo was old when he came to the papacy, but he was tall, brilliant, and a nobleman, and his friendship was to be one of the continuing influences in Saint Frances' life. When he told her that she must go, not to the Orient and martyrdom as she had hoped, but to America to work among the emigrants, she reluctantly consented.

In the economic troubles that followed *Risorgimento,* Italy had turned to emigration as a solution for some of its problems. Emigrants not only did not use up the new nation's jobs and food; they sent money home and thus improved the balance of payments. But emigration is a remedy for underemployment and overpopulation only in the way that throwing a few passengers overboard is a remedy for conditions in a crowded lifeboat. Italians do not travel well; even today there is a strong reverse stream of immigration from the excellent opportunities offered by Australia. In nineteenth-century America, the emigrant found exploitation of labor (sometimes by Americans and sometimes by other Italians), only the roughest and most dangerous kind of work to do, housing conditions so filthy and unlivable as to make a modern ghetto seem luxurious in comparison, and a great loneliness. "Thames and all the rivers of the kings ran into Mississippi and were drowned," but the waters of the Tiber were slow to mingle. The slight difference between the Mediterranean peoples and those of northern Europe was increased by the fact that many of the early immigrants came from Sicily, and the image of Italians in the American mind was Sicilian. Even today an Italian visitor who is tall and blond finds himself continually explaining the Lombard invasion.

Another barrier to their assimilation, beside language, was their religion. The Church in America, still a mission church, was too weak to give them much assistance, and even discriminated against them: services for Italians were sometimes held in the church basement. At the same time it discouraged friendship with Protestants; consorting with heretics was officially forbidden. And intermarriage with the older stock, that quickest of all methods of assimilation, was of course out of the question. The result was the growth of Little Italys, crowded and poor, in the great American cities.

Saint Frances and her nuns started schools, hospitals, orphanages, doing much of the building and most of the menial work themselves. She had, by nature, an aesthetic dislike of caring for the sick, until she dreamed that she saw the Virgin changing a filthy bed and saying, "I will do what you are not willing to do." One institution after another was established; Saint Frances, with her dreams and her visions to guide her, was a plunger. In America today advertisements for houses often state, not the price, but the down payment. Saint Frances would have found this perfectly sensible. Her task was to get the down payment, to get things started; they would operate by themselves after that. And so her installations multiplied; the gold stars on the tabletop mark the great cities of the United States, of Latin America, of Europe. And in London her order may have entered English literature with T. S. Eliot's

> *The nightingales are singing near*
> *The Convent of the Sacred Heart . . .*

Pope Leo was her friend as long as he lived, and she usually saw him when her travels took her to Rome. On one occasion the Pope, blessing her with his right hand, put his left arm around her and drew her to him. Saint Frances, apparently well versed in the official interpretation of the Song of Solomon, said, "Holiness, the arms of the Church are embracing the Missionary Sisters of the Sacred Heart."

She loved the poor and the orphans and the great Pope, but one cannot help feeling that she would have been a dangerous woman to cross. An archbishop entangled in politics once let her down badly, and while she didn't exactly curse him, she *predicted* that he would never be made cardinal. The archbishop, pondering his lack of promotion, may have felt as one of my American visitors did when, against advice, she refused to give even a small coin to a Trastevere gypsy, and within a week lost both the filling from a tooth and the setting from a ring. On another occasion a group of younger nuns in one of the Sacred Heart convents, touched with progressivism, demanded democratic reform. After they had been slapped down by the appropriate Congregation, Saint Frances spoke of them forgivingly and used a pejorative still thirty years in the future: she said they were sick. In her letter of maternal charity to the offenders there is a distinct suggestion of shape up or ship out. She was shrewd in real estate deals; men who tried to cheat her ended by regretting it. And on one occasion she bought a large tract of land from the Jesuits, who had been unable to find water on it; the next morning she took some workmen to a certain spot, told them to dig, and brought in a fine spring. Pope Leo may have been underestimating it when he described her as "a woman of marvelous intuition."

She died at the winter solstice of 1917; it is said that her body never passed through *rigor mortis*. The procedure for canonization was begun almost immediately, and her sainthood proclaimed at Saint Peter's in 1946. This was rapid recognition; some processes take centuries.

The miracles presented on her behalf were, like most modern miracles, depressingly medical. The time has passed for Saint Benedict and the mended bowl, for Gregory the Great's bees that built a waxen chapel around a stolen fragment of the Host. Still, it is medical miracles that we need now; we already have the loaves and fishes. And plastic dishes don't break, and the bees are dying of insecticide.

I was particularly interested in seeing what part the so-called devil's advocate would play in this canonization. I couldn't see that he had much to work on, though one might be able to do something with the C. S. Lewis approach.

The devil's advocate, officially known as General Promoter of the Faith, is opposed by the Postulator of the process, who represents Michael the Archangel and must combat criticisms and doubts. The Promoter and the Postulator do not meet face-to-face as in an ordinary tribunal. Instead the devil's advocate writes down his accusations and the Postulator answers them. I was surprised to find that there were two volumes of the written dialogue of the two adversaries. Let us summarize them in the form of question and response, accusation and answer.

Devil's Advocate: It is known that the Servant of God, Cabrini, was a member of the Third Order of Saint Francis. How does it happen that no testimony shows that she followed the rules of the order?

Defender: Because no testimony has been asked for on this point. However, a sister, in the course of her interrogation, declared that Cabrini was devoted to Saint Francis and very happy to belong to the Third Order. And up to the end of her life she wore the scapular and the girdle (*cordone*).

Devil's Advocate: There is a saying that *Raro sanctificantur qui multum peregrinant*. That is, those who travel too much do not become saints. How then can we say that Cabrini, who traveled continuously, especially in the Americas, was a saint?

Defender: Cabrini traveled all over the world to spread the knowledge of Jesus. Does not the Church worship saints who have traveled as much or even more than she, like Saint Francis of Assisi?

Devil's Advocate: Cabrini used to travel in the first or second class, never in the third class where the emigrants she claimed to pity were.

Defender: But she traveled in the company of other sisters, some of them young, and she could not allow them to mix with the crowds of people, sometimes rough-mannered.

Devil's Advocate: And what can you tell me of the many sisters that were thrown out from Cabrini's institutions?

Defender: I can answer that immediately. In thirty-seven years of activity, there were twenty-one expulsions or resignations at the time of the taking of vows, because the persons leaving lacked religious spirit. Only two sisters left after taking their vows, and they had the permission of the Congregation.

Devil's Advocate: Cabrini used doctors and lawyers of the Protestant religion in the houses under her direction. This is not advised by the Church.

Defender: It is not prohibited when done for civil or social reasons, and such were Cabrini's motives. And how much good came of it! I can mention the case of a Protestant lawyer who asked for a medallion of the Immaculate Conception and always carried it with him.

Devil's Advocate: But did she not compel them to go to mass and to walk in processions?

Defender: She invited them but did not force them. And they were people who, if they had not come to our religious ceremonies, would not have gone to their own. And they too needed to pray.

I was a little disappointed with the work of the devil's advocate; I know at least three people who could have done it better. Perhaps he was hampered by knowing that he was fighting a losing battle, for the testimony in her favor was very strong.

Depositions given in the early part of the process by the sisters who knew her best provide fragments of information that help a little in understanding her. They say that she had no patience with sexual conflicts, and was able to tell by looking at a nun's face whether such a problem existed. They were convinced that she had divinatory gifts, and cited not only the water-witch episode but her clear and exact description, twenty-seven years before her death, of the place where she would be buried. The sisters say that she greatly worshiped the relics of the saints, and that she always carried with her a reliquary that she used to call her Crusade. She worshiped the Pope, whom she used to call, in innocently Freudian terms, "the organ of the Holy Spirit . . . the column of fire that guides me through all danger."

It was said that she had the power of winning over everyone with whom she came in contact. Not quite everyone, for Gabriel d'Annunzio, whom she met on shipboard, refused conversion for fear it would damage his genius. (Saint Frances pointed out that it had not damaged Saint Augustine's.) Men who had known her thought it was a pity she was a woman; she could have been a great diplomat, a great general. Her ambition was not for herself but for the poor and the Church, but she often said, "The whole world is too small for my desires."

I found nothing in her story to lessen my devotion to Saint Pelagia, and yet I find myself hoping that somewhere in a wiser world the arms of the Church are again embracing the Missionary Sisters of the Sacred Heart.

In reading the lives of the saints one wonders why the earlier ones, chosen by the informal will of the people, often have so much more spiritual charm than the later ones selected by scrupulously exact and thorough procedures. One longs for San Isidro, taking a prayer break in a nearby chapel while his oxen plowed the field for him, or for Saint Ambrose lassoed by the Lord. It may be because the early saints were not only individuals but legends. Beautiful phrases, actions of grace, that belonged to many unknown people were attributed to them. The genius of the race transformed them into something more than human, into better bread than can be made of wheat. Then, too, we know too much about our modern saints. We are shocked at Saint Bernardino's pleasure at the burning of a witch, at Cardinal Bellarmine's and Thomas More's burning of heretics. Or perhaps it is our method of personnel selection. The rigid screening given to the Servants of God, like that given to American government employees, may tend to rule out people who have flaws in their greatness, while passing others who are smaller but have no criticizable features. Or perhaps, for some qualities, the principle of objective measurement is intrinsically unsuitable. One can find the tallest of a group of guardsmen by objective methods, but to find the handsomest it is best just to look at them.

Who are the saints? I believe they are something more than improved versions of ourselves, notable for their religion and their goodness — that the saints (the real ones, not those that got in on a technicality) are literally of a different breed, with powers beyond our own, like us in most ways but with trace elements that we do not possess. The instances of clairvoyance and precognition are numerous and rather convincing.

Professor Rhine of Duke University has commented that the greatest mass of material on parapsychology is in the records of the Church, almost unexplored by science. Perhaps the saints are the latest surge of evolution, something a little above the surface of Teilhard's noösphere.

Or perhaps they are what is left of something very old. Once on the American desert I gave a larger bill than I could afford to an aged Polish workman, making his way on foot back to Saint Louis in search of Social Security evidence, and in thanking me he said, "You must have angels' blood." I had never been called angelic before; in fact my husband sometimes commented that he thanked God the Inquisition was over. But when the pleasure of the compliment wore off I began to think about the phrase itself. It had the sound of a folk saying, as if, in the unwritten tradition of the people, there had once been a time when some families had a strain of some very alien inheritance, as some families now have a strain of Saracen blood, or of American Indian blood. And not always unwritten tradition. . . . When the sons of God came in unto the daughters of men like sailors on a Polynesian isle, what genes did they leave behind them? Perhaps they left us something that, in the shifting permutations of heredity, occasionally gives rise to people as different, as alike, as Pelagia and Saint Frances Cabrini.

I Am Charlemagne

THE Italy that Napoleon found was an Italy which had lived for two centuries and a half under the decrees of the Council of Trent, an Italy in which people thought before they spoke, in which scientists chose safe channels — such as biology — for their work. Isolated as we were from northern Europe, we still had many visitors — young Englishmen on the Grand Tour, viewing classical remains and carrying home with them chunks of marble and the memory of chambermaids; writers and thinkers like Andersen and Goethe in search of a *Citronen-Land;* archaeologists excited about the ruins of Pompeii. The Reformation was so long ago that some of them could even regard the Church aesthetically, and admire its stylized beauty instead of arguing its theology.

The papal court was less a part of Roman social life than it had been, though the cardinals and the ambassadors still entertained generously. Rome had two aristocracies, the old medieval aristocracy founded mainly on the nation's military past — the legendary families of the Conti, Cenci, Frangipani, Orsini, Colonna — and the new aristocracy made up of the great papal families — the Borghese, the Barberini, the Chigi, the Odescalchi, the Albani. The rich gifts of the popes had made them enormously wealthy. Italy was a country of the very rich and the very poor: the crime rate was extremely high.

Rome must have been more beautiful then than now, for the splendid baroque buildings were new, and greenness was not yet being crowded out of the city. Attempts were even being made to keep it clean; a sign carved in stone near my house in Trastevere warns that, "by order of the very illustrious Monsignor who is president of the street, it is prohibited to throw garbage in this alley, or to create a dump here, on pain of ten *scudi* and corporal punishment as judged." The plaque is dated 1763;

there was a large pile of garbage under it when I came past this morning.

But Rome was still a country town. The Forum was a cattle-field grazed by herds of oxen, there were stables next to the Via Crucis of the Colosseum, and barnyard mud around the Arch of Constantine. The Montgolfier fire-balloons that the Romans loved had to be banned from the city because their pans of burning coals set fire to the haystacks when they came down.

The streets at night were dark except for the flicker of the small oil lamps before the images of the Madonna. The shops were little, like those of Pompeii. Goods and services were advertised by pictorial signs; large red or black hands for a glover, a brass bowl for a barber. One of the barbers in the Via Papale had another sign as well: "Singers castrated here for the papal chapel choirs."

Cafés had begun to appear; the first was the Café Veneziano, with its cloth windows and its Etruscan lamps burning in the dark interior; a meeting place for ladies and their abbots. A little later there was the Café del Greco on the Via Condotti, now the most elegantly Bohemian snack bar in Rome, its marble tables and leather benches graced forever by the English and German poets who frequented it.

The Secret Archives too were moving gradually into the modern age. The cardinal-archivist Garampi was compiling his tortuous, mysterious card catalogue, with its cards glued together into a hundred and twenty-four folio volumes and its puzzling signs and abbreviations. When he died in 1792, leaving his library of sixteen thousand volumes to the Vatican Library and Archives, he was succeeded by another great archivist, Angelo Mai, who introduced the systematic use of one of the most interesting of archivistic games. As a young seminary student, Mai had hunted out parchments that showed evidence of erasure and rewriting. The reusers had, of course, written not on the erased lines, but on the undamaged parchment between them. Over the erased lines he passed a small brush dipped in *noce di gallo* coloring — and the old writing came to life. Later, as a monsignor and cardinal of the Church, he made discoveries that contributed greatly to scholars' knowledge of the early world. One of his palimpsests yielded a mixture of Roman letters, Greek letters, and what looked like Nordic runes — the alphabet that fourth-century Germans had worked out to write their own language, as the illiterate halfbreed Sequoia, centuries later, devised a version of "the silent speech" for the Cherokees. The manuscript was the *Skeinrein*, the Explanation — Bishop Ulfilas' Gospel for the Ostrogoths, Danubian barbarians who had not yet migrated to the west. Bishop Ulfilas had prudently deleted the more warlike sections of the Old Testament as being a bad influence on his people; the measure was not completely effective. And yet, because of this improvised alphabet, our first invaders were Christian; the great churches and the people packed into them were saved. Other discoveries of Angelo Mai were juridical texts, Cicero's *Republic,* and fragments of his speeches. The *noce di gallo* coloring is now supplemented by infra-red radiation, but the principle is unchanged, and an erased manuscript is still more exciting than a perfect one.

Rome was a pleasant place, if one had money enough, or the guaranteed annual income of the Church to protect him. But there was a *fin de siècle* uneasiness, a sense of coming change. Other countries had progressed and Italy had not; tension was building up along the earth-fault; sooner or later slippage would occur.

France was a matter of concern to the Church long before the Revolution, for liberal thought had turned against Catholicism. By 1791 diplomatic relations between the Holy See and Revolutionary France were seriously deteriorating. The French minister to Rome was called back to Paris; the papal nuncio to Rome. An effigy of the Pope, Pius VI, was burned in front of France's royal palace.

Abbot Louis Joseph de Salamon, who remained in Paris as internuncio, was a man of ingenuity and courage, something of a Scarlet Pimpernel type. His weekly reports to the Pope were almost magazines; each letter was accompanied by clippings, editorials, cartoons, and little jokes. The Pope said that he did not read them but devoured them. Salamon engaged in active espionage; he attended meetings of the Assembly disguised as a Jacobin and military reunions as one of the regiment. At night, disguised as a peasant, he walked under the arcades of the royal palace. There is an adventurer's enjoyment in his description of the way he got the Pope's bull of excommunication into Paris in 1792. He had it wrapped as an ordinary package and addressed to a member of the National Assembly, the Deputy from Ardennes. He then disguised himself as a messenger and called at the post office to pick it up. "The postmaster came, hat in hand, to ask what I wanted. All the people around me were shoved out of the way, all the packages that had arrived in that shipment were turned over to find mine. I signed the register and I went away very fast indeed with the package under my arm."

But in the letters of this brave, good and intelligent man we can see why the Church and the new France could not understand each other. "The decree in favor of the people of color has been passed. Here is the end of our colonies and of our civilization." He is shocked at the democratic tendencies of the French royal family. "Honestly, this monarch is incomprehensible. Even those who have lived near him since he came to the throne do not understand him. On the night of the same day that he came to the National Assembly, he went down to the ground floor of the palace and showed himself at the window, talking to the people. The queen did the same thing, showing the little royal prince in her arms. There are people who are sure they heard the king shout, 'Long live the nation!' What can one say? What can one think? . . . The king would not attend the *Te Deum,* which for that reason did not take place. He has said, 'I have accepted the Constitution. It at least gives me freedom to think and to follow the cult that I like . . .' Everything has changed; one no longer knows who God is, who the king is, who the priests are." Later, "I think that the *Grande Dame* is not intriguing any longer. People of her household have assured me that when she is alone she cries; the king also is quite a different man in the privacy of his room, which offers us some reason for hope."

The letters break off abruptly in the summer of 1792, when five men with the tricolor worn diagonally across their breasts presented themselves at Salamon's door. He and his boxes of documents were taken into custody, and he died, with hundreds of other priests, in the September massacre.

Clergy and aristocrats were fleeing France; so many of them came to Italy that a special Congregation was set up to deal with them, the *De Charitate Sedis Apostolicae Erga Gallos* — "The Charity of the Apostolic See Toward the Gauls." The Archives' *"Fondo* on Refugees from the French Revolution" grew to fifty-three volumes.

The Germans, after the Second World War, took comfort in the idea that it was German generals and admirals who defeated them, counting the names on their fingers —"Eisenhower . . . Spaatz . . . Nimitz . . ." In the same way the Italians took a possessive pride in the new military genius Napoleon, born in Corsica a year after Genoa had sold that troublesome depressed area to France. His mother had the gift of second sight, and he may have had a strain of the blood of the Comnenus emperors. His Italian heritage did not keep him from repeatedly invading Italy. Even the midwinter mountains were no barrier to him — "Where two men can go an army can go" — and the guns could be encased in hollow logs and dragged across the ice. His first invasion was half-welcomed — there was much liberal thought in the north of Italy — but the excesses of his armies and his greed for profits soon disillusioned us. His method was to conquer and then impose an indemnity as large as the victim could pay. Genoa fell, and Venice; the last of the doges dropped dead. In Rome the French agent Bassville was wounded and left to die without medical attention in a papal guardroom; for a multiplicity of such reasons Napoleon led a punitive expedition that ended in the Treaty of Tolentino. In addition to heavy territorial losses and financial indemnities, a hundred works of art and five hundred valuable manuscripts were to be surrendered. Since not enough gold was available, the invaders took silver objects, often masterpieces. To pack them more efficiently the soldiers had orders to stamp on them so that they would take less room, but even so the plunder filled a hundred wagons as it started north to Paris.

"The Roman Republic" mined the monasteries as well. An Archives document addresses the Brothers of San Callisto: "Citizens, by order of the consulate you are invited to hand over to the nation as a forced loan the sum of four thousand *scudi*. Not only money is accepted, but precious metals." Saint Paul outside the walls was stripped of its linens, San Callisto of "beds, blankets, sheets, shirts, kettles, dishes, glasses, chamber pots, pierced chairs, etc." for those wounded in action. "This is how you can give the liveliest proof of your patriotism. Give us more beds; your people can sleep two to a bed. Everything will be returned."

Napoleon found an excuse for further action when one of his generals was disembowelled by the people of Trastevere, and his retribution took the form of kidnapping the Pope.

It is unjust that Pius VI (1775–1799) should have been the martyr of the Napoleonic era, for he himself was a man of the new age, concerned for the poor and for the welfare of the secular city. Pius was eighty-one when Napoleon's representative Haller came to arrest him. An eyewitness tells of the encounter:

" 'I have come for your valuables,' Haller said.

" 'But I have given you everything I had for the peace of Tolentino.'

" 'You have two fine rings. Give them to me.'

" 'I can give you one of them; it is my own. The other belongs to my successor.'

"When the Ring of the Fisherman had been stripped from the Pope's hand, Haller looked around the room and saw a little box.

" 'Your jewels!'

"But it was only candy."

The Pope, old and sick, pleaded for the right to die in Rome. Instead he was dragged to a coach and taken north on a long and difficult journey to imprisonment at Valence. There he died, watched by soldiers, in the last year of the century. His death, and that of the Duc d'Enghien, were incidents that Napoleon's long apologia on St. Helena could not explain.

To liberal onlookers it seemed the withering away of the Church. The eighteenth-century precursors of Marx and Lenin had said that an institution so backward and primitive would succumb quickly. They forgot that in times of crisis it is often the backward and primitive things that are most useful. Even in the most lavish of our houses we keep candles for the times when the lights go out, and if the bombs fall a countryman's knife, its blade nicked and its handle wrapped in masking-tape, will be of more use than the electric carving knives that the Americans are unaccountably selling.

It had seemed impossible to get a conclave together, but cardinals met in an old tenth-century Benedictine monastery on the island of San Giorgio Maggiore in fallen Venice, and elected a new pope. In homage to his predecessor he took the name of Pius VII.

The Archives' "*Fondo* of the Napoleonic Era" contains numerous interchanges between Napoleon and Pope Pius VII (1800–1823). Napoleon wanted spiritual power and the Pope wanted secular power; they could not leave each other alone. Napoleon's position was that he was, to all intents and purposes, Charlemagne (or, when it seemed more useful, Constantine). And what Charlemagne had given, he could revoke. The Pope tried to make peace, putting aside the memories of the massacred priests, of the tearing down of the great church at Cluny, and signed the Concordat of 1801, preserving at least some status for the Church in France. The Archives has the original Concordat and a record of the four *pour-parlers* leading up to it; they remind one of the Church's present attempts to keep up communication with the countries of eastern Europe.

Rome has always absorbed her conquerors; perhaps it was this consideration that made her welcome Pauline Bonaparte as Princess Camillo Borghese. Pauline, widowed, had returned from the Indies and had been put under the strict chaperonage of one of her brothers "lest her mourning take an undesirable direction." Camillo was dark and handsome and one of the great princes of Italy; he was also, according to both history and the tradition of his family, quite remarkably stupid. Perhaps any man would have seemed dull to her beside Napoleon, who some gossips thought was her lover. He himself, on St. Helena, said, "What keeps me from marrying my sister? Morality. But if it were on a desert island . . ." Whatever the reason, the marriage of Pauline and Camillo was never a happy one. The Duchess d'Abrantès, in her memoirs, tells of Pauline stating that to be with her husband was to be alone . . . "That idiot!" Nevertheless she valued the marriage, since it meant being "a real princess." The Duchess shows her to us as queening it over her sisters-in-law, with all the Borghese diamonds sewed to her green velvet dress. She had no taste, the Duchess says, and she looked beautiful.

When she arrived in Rome, Cardinal Consalvi described her to Cardinal Caprara in terms that make one wonder about the perceptiveness of diplomats: "I come to give Your Eminence news of the bright Princess Borghese, sister of the First Consul. I went to pay my respects to her a few minutes after her arrival. I found her tired with the trip, but in good health, very gracious indeed, and very gentle in manner. It seems she unites the favors of nature with those of the soul." She was met by members of the Borghese family and, Consalvi says, "so great was the cordiality and confidence with which they dealt with each other that it seemed as if they had known each other for years. I will not mention the love between the two spouses, which could not be greater." The Pope was equally impressed with her. "His Holiness gave her the special distinction of receiving her in his own rooms and not in the garden as is usually done for ladies. (Your Excellency knows that this is an important distinction.) Last night, at six o'clock French time, she was introduced by the Cardinal and by the Princess Mother. Without exaggeration I can say that the Pope has been very well satisfied. She showed me a splendid coronet with a superb cameo that our lord has given her. The Casa Borghese certainly could not have better luck in all possible ways . . ."

It could hardly have had worse luck. Pauline was extravagant, promiscuous, and sterile — unless one counts as her descendant the cool white statue by Canova.

The Bonaparte-Borghese marriage did not even save the Borghese treasures, for in 1807 the Secretary of State wrote, "Three days ago, all of a sudden, three French commissioners appeared. They went to the Villa Borghese and very carefully looked over all the ancient statues and bas-reliefs . . ." Napoleon had forced his brother-in-law to sell them, and at a very low price. The Pope could do nothing. The Borghese statues, like the Vatican's art treasures, took the road to Paris — the Gladiator, Silenus, the Hermaphrodite, and Hadrian's young Antinoüs.

In attempting to appease Napoleon, Pius VII had even officiated at his coronation, traveling northward across the Alps to the time and place of Napoleon's convenience. Napoleon had had a replica made of Charlemagne's scepter, but did not copy him to the extent of being crowned in Rome.

Cardinal Consalvi, the papal Secretary of State, who accompanied the Pope on the Paris journey, describes in his memoirs the indignities that he says he prefers not to mention: "The Pope was called to Paris as *Aumonier*. I do not want to speak of what he had to suffer in Paris. Nor to tell in detail of the encounter between Napoleon and the Pope at Fontainebleau when Napoleon appeared disguised as a huntsman with fifty hounds . . . nor of his having kept the Pope waiting an hour and a

half at the altar, dressed in sacred garb, on the morning of the ceremony . . ."

And the Duchess d'Abrantès, pitying the old man as he waited so long,
listening to the magnificent liturgy of coronation ("Thou who hast
spread the sacred oil on Saul and David alike . . .") remembered another pope's journey across the Alps a thousand years before, and Pope
Zachary's assurance to Pepin: "The man who has the power is the man
who should be king."

News of the festivities following Napoleon's coronation came to Rome
by a balloon that traveled in one day from Paris to Lake Bracciano. The
people regarded this as a miracle, but there was a difference of opinion
as to whether it was accomplished by God or the devil. More slowly, the
Pope returned to Rome, having received none of the concessions that he
had hoped to gain in return for his *Vivat in aeternum Augustus.*

New causes of friction followed. Eventually in 1809 Napoleon annexed
the Papal States and arrested the Pope. The Quirinal was silently surrounded, but when General Radet came into the Pope's presence he
found him robed and seated under a canopy. Pius wrote a letter to his
people just before he was taken away. "When you are old you have to
hold out your hands and let people take you where you do not want to
go . . ." On the way north groups of people, alerted by flying rumor,
gathered in front of the carriage, but Radet later recounted that he had a
method of dealing with them; he asked them to kneel for the Pope's
benediction, "then all of a sudden I ordered the postilions to dash forward. By this means the people were still on their knees whilst we were
already far away at a gallop. This plan succeeded everywhere."

The Pope was kept in prison and, as far as possible, brainwashed;
denied writing materials, surrounded by soldiers who might or might not
be soldiers, by cardinals who might or might not be cardinals. But the
people were still Catholic. Napoleon made the best of it and wrote himself into the catechism.

It was in 1810 that Napoleon took over the Secret Archives, as part of
his plan for a world library. Europe's learning as well as its art was to be
gathered in Paris. Only branch offices, under an imperial archivist, were
to remain in other countries; people who wanted documents from the
central archives could send for copies of them. The prices to be charged
were high; the project was to be a source of public revenue. The building
used for the new archives was the Palace of the Dukes of Guise and
Soubise, known as the Hôtel Soubise. It was of the finest Louis Quatorze
architecture, but not well suited for an archives building.

Officials of the French National Archives scattered to the various conquered countries to select archives for removal; some to Simanca in Spain, some to Piedmont, some to Holland. Because of the value and importance of the Vatican Secret Archives the chief archivist himself, Daunou, came to Rome.

We have two main sources of information, which usually agree in regard to facts, about the seizure of the Vatican Archives. One of them is French, *Les Archives du Vatican* by a writer who was able to consult in the National Archives of Paris all the papers concerning the transfer of the Rome Archives and their subsequent handling. The other is the memoirs of Marino Marini, nephew and secret chamberlain of the old Prefect of the Archives, Gaetano Marini. With his uncle and Father Altieri, Marini was sent along with the Archives to Paris. Officially, he was to assist in their arrangement; unofficially, he was to keep an eye on them and do what he could to prevent loss and damage. Marini was candidly resentful; the French found him difficult.

Marini writes of the preparation of the Archives for shipment: "First to be packed were the volumes of bulls. Father Altieri and I were in charge of supervising this operation, and our eyes melted in tears. Many documents were specially requested at this time: the bull of excommunication against Napoleon, the trial of the Templars, the process of Galileo. (Daunou was particularly interested in getting "the papers, the diplomas, the original or copied correspondence, the registers containing deliberations on matters of importance, in a word, all the acts that have to do with public rights, legislation, general administration, and political history.") Marini hated to part with these, probably realizing the use that would be made of them, but "how could we refuse them such documents, the archives being in their power?" The packers were alert and it was hard to remove documents without their being aware of it, but Marini and his friends did succeed in holding out a small amount of material, which they put in "a hidden place of the Vatican Library." But this incident is an example of the continuing fallacy of selecting certain documents for preservation, for among these treasures of the Vatican that the archivists risked their lives to save were the acts of the Council of Trent.

The Archives were being shipped in wagons drawn by multiple teams of mules and oxen — many wagons, for over three thousand cases of material were being shipped. It was not only the Secret Archives (including the Castel Sant'Angelo documents that had been brought to the Vatican in 1798) that were being sent, but nearly all the archives of Rome, taken from its churches and monasteries. En route they were joined by an almost equal number of cases containing the Imperial Archives of Vienna. The mass of materials flooded the Hôtel Soubise;

trunks and chests full of registers and documents were everywhere, in the salons, the halls, even the colonnades of the Court of Honor.

The Italian archivists were ordered to arrange the materials in the same way in which they had been arranged at the Vatican. Relations between the Italian and the French archivists were somewhat strained, and Marini writes: "The Imperial Archivist was very much annoyed at my lack of collaboration. I told him that I was not in the service of the Imperial Government, but of the Holy See, and that I was expected to share in the fate of the Archives."

The search soon began for political material that would be ideologically useful to Napoleon. "The Minister of Cults wrote to my uncle to make diligent search to see whether there had ever been a French bishop appointed without the approval of the Holy See. The government's intention was to deprive the pope of this sacred right, if it could be proved that before the Pragmatic Sanction there had been even one bishop appointed without the approval of the Holy See." No such instance was found, even though the research was done under the supervision of imperial employees.

Daunou, the French archivist, was strongly anticlerical, and in an 1811 directive ordered that particular attention be paid to any documents that would show the ambition of the Roman court. The commission was to "search in every part of the papal archives for all documents showing the abuses committed by the popes against the sovereign authority and the peace of the people." In 1810 Daunou had published a work entitled *Essai historique sur la puissance temporelle des papes*. He now printed a new edition, using unpublished Vatican documents. On the whole, however, little was found. In fact very little scholarship, factional or otherwise, resulted from the Archives' stay in Paris. The historian Laborde says that "in the years in which the Archives of France contained the secrets of two of the most mysterious courts of Europe, Rome and Madrid, not a scholar, or an historian, or a man of letters, asked permission to do research in the Archives. No room had been prepared for study purposes . . ."

Marini tells of Napoleon's visit to the Archives: "Napoleon in November of the year 1811 came to the Archives and asked Altieri and me if we could point out some papers worth publishing. We answered, 'Sire, everything you see here is precious; letters of popes regarding the government of the Church, donations made to her by emperors and princes.' Altieri spoke with such energy on behalf of His Holiness that Napoleon looked as if he had been hit. 'So you are priests! Fine, if you follow the teachings of Christ. But if you follow those of Gregory VII you are priests of the devil. What have I not done for the Church? What do I want more than to give peace to her?' "

Napoleon pointed out that he could have followed Henry VIII's example, "but I want the Catholic religion. I don't want to keep the Pope in prison, but neither do I want him to divide himself between the holy faith and temporal matters. His kingdom is not of this world; my authority comes from God. The Pope has always opposed my wishes. He hates me . . . I am as much Italian as you are. Don't tell me that he loves me; what kind of love? I wanted only good for Italy. I wanted her to be united into one state, and she will be . . ."

But Napoleon's power failed with his sudden aging. "Biology is destiny." With his defeat came the liberation of the Archives, and Marini wrote: "The Lord God finally blessed us with a day of happiness. March 31, 1814, the Allies entered Paris, and April 19 a decree was issued for the restitution of the Archives, of all the parchments, books and papers brought from Rome after the French Revolution, of the sacred objects and the triple crowns. M. Daunou, the Imperial Archivist, when the moment came to turn the responsibility over to us, became extremely pale, for he knew the great value of each document."

Sixteen packing cases were immediately filled with the treasures of the pontifical chapel, the miters that the queen of Etruria had given the pope when he passed through Florence, the Triple Crown that was the gift of Napoleon.

But the returning of the Archives was a more difficult problem; a problem of three thousand packing boxes instead of sixteen. Consalvi and Talleyrand took it under advisement. And while they were conferring, and Marini was looking for the Trial of Galileo and for the bull *Unigenitus,* Napoleon came back from Elba for the Hundred Days. Marini had to flee; probably his behavior during the period of the emperor's imprisonment on Elba had been insufferable. "Finally, the Allies returned to Paris, and all the potentates of Europe were there, united." Marini was sent back with orders to recover not only the Vatican Archives, but the codices and other treasures that had been ceded by the Treaty of Tolentino. Poor Marini found all kinds of difficulty in regard to permits, money, and customs. "I was simply all turned around . . ."

One of his most trying experiences was being asked to give two of the Pope's codices, one of Virgil and one of Terence, to what was now the Royal Library. "I left the Virgil but I took the Terence away with me. The reason I left the Virgil is because we have another copy two or three centuries older at the Vatican Library." Later, backed by a letter from the Pope, he managed to retrieve the Virgil, in spite of French claims that it had originally belonged to the Abbey of Saint Denis. He did have to part with thirty-nine codices requested by the Palatine Library, since the Pope wanted to express his gratitude for German aid to the Holy See, "but in the meantime I succeeded in getting back the fifth-century Sistine Bible, the fragments of Dio Cassius, the Samaritan Pentateuch, and many others," including the fifteenth-century incunabula.

The journey south was a dangerous one for the Vatican treasures and Archives. The first wagons, loaded with priceless objects, were left standing all night, unguarded, in the streets of Turin. The Laocoön statue was damaged when the wagon carrying it overturned in the Moncenisio Pass. The main convoy of Archives was accompanied by troops, but their behavior aroused so much ill feeling in the territory through which they passed that the Archives were endangered. Marini hastened south, and arrived just in time to keep the Archives from being soaked in the crossing of the Taro River; the wagoners and troops had given no thought to the possibility of water damage. One wagon had already crossed, and the cases it carried, Marini says, "were in such bad condition that the papers were just something to cry over." He saved the other seven hundred cases by having them removed from the wagons and taken across the river by boat.

But the greatest danger to the Archives was in Paris. The usual pilfering went on, as was to be expected in a time of tumult, and Marini comments, "How many documents were stolen, how many acts of animosity by the French military took place, ingratitude on the part of the clergy, selling of documents, removal of documents in order to spread wrong doctrines . . ." but the greatest damage may have been done by our own representative, Count Giulio Ginnasi, who was in charge of getting the remainder of the documents back to Rome. Ginnasi was faced with a dilemma; the money for transferring the great mass of material simply was not available. Daunou advised cutting down on expenses by removing from the Archives those sections that were, he said, of little interest. The papal commissioners at first refused, and Louis XVIII finally granted a small sum for transportation. Nevertheless a great quantity of papers that were judged unimportant were sold by weight in Paris in 1816, for wrapping-paper and the making of cardboard. It is not clear how this happened, nor to whom the responsibility belongs. Perhaps Daunou or others planned to buy the material from the paper-makers; if so, fragments of it may sometime reappear. (At Trinity College in Dublin there is an important collection of documents which, according to the orders of Ginnasi, should have ended in the rotting vat.) But if there was such a plan, it was only partially successful, for the horrified Marini, returning to Paris, found in the butcher shops seven hundred volumes of the registers of the bulls of the Apostolic Datary.

So the Archives returned — some of them — like the young men of Italy whom Napoleon had drafted to fight for France. One thinks of that most heartbreaking of military parades, in which the soldiers march in ragged ranks, with spaces left for the dead. Some of the men we lost might have been great men in their century, and some of the documents we lost might have helped to answer the great questions, or the questions that we do not know enough to ask.

Fondi Gained and Lost

AT the end of the Second World War the village square at Anzio was a mass of rubble from the fallen buildings around it. Its trees were shattered; nothing was left but the place itself, its position on the earth's grid of latitude and longitude. When it was rebuilt no experts or town planners were called in. We wanted the square exactly as it was, down to the last park bench, the last tree, the last sidewalk table. Now the new trees have grown, and again the church and the Bank of the Holy Spirit, side by side, watch over the square as it was in 1939.

After the Napoleonic Wars the Council of Vienna felt the same longing for things as they had been, and, like the village council of Anzio, it reconstituted its world. The papacy regained most of its territory. The persecution of the Church had led to a Catholic revival, and people who had seen, in the French Revolution, what a godless nation could do, regarded the Church much as the democracies, after the last world war, regarded the Christian Democratic parties of Germany and Italy. Pius VII (1800–1823) had returned to Rome, unembittered by the gall and vinegar of his imprisonment; he welcomed Madame Laetitia, Napoleon's mother, to her retirement in his city; did what he could to alleviate the conditions of Napoleon's imprisonment; and ordered Pauline Borghese's disillusioned husband to return to her.

Whatever Napoleon was, he was one of the movers and shakers. Some of the effects of his rule came indirectly and much later; the deciphering of the Rosetta stone, the finding of some old engineering studies by a young vice-consul named De Lesseps. Others were more immediate. Italy, under Napoleonic rule, had enjoyed the benefits of an efficient and progressive government. New parks and roads and schools had shown what such a government could provide. Another influence was the draft.

Thousands of young men had been conscripted to fight in the Napoleonic wars, and for those who survived it was a maturing experience. Nothing short of the draft can get Italian boys away from their mothers; with luck an Italian can be spoiled by one woman or another all his life. The lost little faces of the young recruits that one sees in the Roman Terminal suggest that their army experience may be painful, but the effect of military service in building self-reliance and the capacity for independent action is noticeable in those who have completed it. In the early nineteenth century, such men were ready to enter the fight for Italian unification.

Italy had had the experience of unity under Napoleon; a peninsular government was no longer only a memory left from imperial times. A strong underground movement for Italian independence began to grow among the secret societies. Cagliostro "the Immortal" and some English noblemen had established Masonry in Italy; one of its organizational offshoots was the Carbonari. Nationalism was opposed by the Church, which became strongly reactionary under the rule of the Zealot popes. Perhaps one influence removing the popes from contact with the people was the disappearance of the cardinal-nephews, the last of whom, old Cardinal Albani, had fallen on evil days and had to sell his art collection and precious library before the Revolution. The passing of the cardinal-nephews removed a lingering trace of corruption from the Church, but it also removed a channel of information and criticism that the papacy needed. The cardinal-nephews, in a privileged position but also young and worldly, had been able to keep the popes aware of current opinion, and to move them toward acting in accordance with the *Zeitgeist*.

In this period of cold war when nationalists were being sentenced to monthly confessions and compulsory retreats, the Archives were again under strict security. Even before the returning documents were unpacked from their wagons a problem of blackmail had arisen, for during the chaotic period in Paris when Archives were being sold as waste paper, a group of bankers had acquired thirty-seven volumes of trials by the Holy Office. They offered these for sale to the Church, threatening otherwise to turn them over to the liberal *Minerve Française*, successor to the *Mercure de France*, for publication. The papacy bought them in 1819 and they vanished from view, along with the list that told which trials were involved.

The rearrangement of the Archives must have been a time of sadness for the archivists, a time of counting losses. But even during this period of decimation new Archives had been accumulating in Rome, and these were arranged in a *"Fondo* of the Napoleonic Era" — roughly, the last five years of the eighteenth and the first fifteen years of the nineteenth centuries. The Napoleonic *fondo* was divided into two main sections, according to whether the records related to France or to Italy.

A major change took place in Archives structure in this period. From the sixteenth through the eighteenth centuries, the main sections of the Archives concerned the correspondence of the Secretary of State with cardinals, with bishops and prelates, with princes and titled persons, with private individuals, with soldiers, and with nuncios and nunciatures. This organization was now abandoned, and in its place came an arrangement with two general divisions, "Internal" and "Foreign," each divided into subdivisions and these into subsections. This may have reflected a drawing-in of the papacy upon itself — an "Us" and "Them" way of thinking — or it may have been a mechanical simplification.

In spite of the Restoration, in spite of the concordats, the secular power of the papacy had lessened, and new dangers were feared. For that reason the nineteenth century saw a flood of new *fondi* entering the Archives. The Church adopted a policy of concentrating in the Vatican not only the Curia archives but all archives in any way connected with papal history. The Castel Sant'Angelo Archives had been incorporated in the Vatican Secret Archives in 1798, closing the Miscellanea collection of manuscript volumes that had been begun in the seventeenth century. But a second collection, the Instrumenta Miscellanea, continued to receive ancient documents that could not be assigned to any particular *fondo.* This second collection (which now has over eight thousand documents and three thousand parchments, some of them going back to the ninth century) is still open.

In 1835 the *fondo* of the archives of the Chancellery of the Venetian Nunciature returned, with over three thousand volumes and files and nearly seventeen thousand parchment and paper documents. Along with them came other archives that had been committed to the care of the Venetian Nunciature, including those of suppressed Congregations such as Saint George among the Algae (*S. Giorgio in Alga*), and the Archives known as the Tuscan *fondo,* which for some reason were in Venice. These include a mass of small archives of churches and suppressed monasteries, with very old miscellaneous documents.

The *fondo* of the Chancellery of the Venetian Nunciature is almost unexplored, but scattered fragments that have come to light — such as copies of the bulls of the sixth century Pope Pelagius II (579–590), the predecessor of Gregory the Great — suggest the possibility of future important discoveries. Among the records of a suppressed Congregation of

Verona are valuable documents on the history of agriculture, and Saint
George among the Algae has yielded the original contract for Tintoret-
to's *Presentation of the Virgin.*

The papacy's documents of secular government, stored in the Quirinal,
remained where they were, which made it possible for historians to
swarm through them during the brief and finally unsuccessful revolution
of 1848.

The sponsors of the new kingdom of Italy were eager to have Rome as
its seat of government. For a moment I wonder why, as I look out over a
city strangled by traffic and strikes, and speculate on just when the particular aqueduct that serves my apartment will be repaired; it seems
rather like suing for the custody of a juvenile delinquent. But Rome had
been the capital of the old empire; nothing less would do for the new.
When Napoleon III withdrew, Victor Emanuel's army had no difficulty
in overcoming Pius IX's troops; the battle was a token battle with few
casualties, staged to indicate that the decision was imposed by force. The
secular power of the papacy was ended.

For the second time Pius IX (1846–1878) fled from the Quirinal; it
would be a royal palace now instead of a papal palace. Behind him he
left the massed documents of the papal state, along with the other deposits housed in such palaces as Madama and Montecitorio, to be taken over
by the new government of Italy. The documents lost to the Church were
largely administrative, financial, and judicial; those dealing with spiritual
affairs were at the Vatican. The Vatican Archives and those in extra-
mural areas such as the Lateran, that still belonged to the papacy, remained the property of the Church.

The archives taken over by the state are now housed in the Sapienza
Palace, once a papal university, which takes its name from the inscription
over its façade: *Initium Sapientiae Timor Domini.* There is little difficulty in getting permission to use them, though consultation is normally
limited to materials originating before a certain date — thirty to fifty
years ago, depending on the nature of the subject matter. Nevertheless,
research work is even more difficult here than in the Vatican Archives,
for the indices are very inadequate and the attendants, although expert
and polite, are overworked and unable to give much assistance.

Collaboration between the Vatican Secret Archives and the State Archives is limited. However, the taking over of archives by the Italian
State was less of a tragedy than the Napoleonic adventure, for no material was destroyed; there was simply a change of ownership.

With *Risorgimento,* Pius IX became the Prisoner of the Vatican. This
was not a genuine imprisonment, as many seem to think, but a look-what-

you-did-to-me ploy. Actually the Pope was free to come and go as he liked. In the same spirit the papacy refused the compensatory income offered by the government, because it had been arranged unilaterally. For many years Catholics were forbidden by *"Non expedit"* either to vote or to hold office. This had the predictable result of making the government more anticlerical than it would otherwise have been, since there was no Catholic vote to act as a counterweight.

But in this century when the papacy moved into its splendid isolation, Rome itself was becoming part of the modern world. American tourists began to appear, New Englanders just emerged from Puritanism and experiencing a pleasurable culture shock at our wicked city and our seductive religion. The great English poets came, to drink and talk at El Greco's before going on to their deaths in storm and revolution, and to write about Rome in verses of appreciative disapproval:

> . . . *ages, empires, and religions here*
> *Lie buried in the ravage they have wrought . . .*
> *Go thou to Rome, at once the Paradise,*
> *The grave, the city, and the wilderness . . .*

And later there were the Brownings, flaunting an intellectual love affair, with their velvet child riding his pony through the Roman parks. Browning tried to do research for his historical poems at the Vatican, but wrote resentfully that you had to be a converted cardinal — Manning or Newman — to get any help around there.

New inventions were changing the conditions of life, and in 1874 when ex-Prefect of the Archives Augustin Theiner, dismissed from his post by Pius IX for overuse of Archives documents in his writings against the Jesuits, lay dying, his servant and his landlady telegraphed to obtain absolution for him; with it, by telegraph, came the special benediction of the Pope. And slowly the industrial revolution crept down from England, bringing the problems of the new age to add to the still unsolved problems of the old.

In such times the Church was fortunate in finding a pope who belonged to both ages. Leo XIII, the pope of *Rerum novarum*, came to the papacy in 1878, taking the name Leo because, as he said, the Church had need of a lion. His strength and flexibility seem remarkable when one remembers his age — seventy-eight when he came to power — and when one looks at a photograph of him surrounded by the papal court. The Pope is slim, erect, vigorous, smiling; not one of the martyr-popes but a ruler who enjoys ruling, who rides in a litter like an ancient Roman and keeps pet ostriches in the Vatican gardens.

Leo used encyclicals as Franklin Roosevelt used fireside chats, and his pontificate is studded with their beautiful names: *Humanum genus, Aeterni patris, Longinqua oceani.* I cannot agree with those who say that his great encyclical of 1891, *Rerum novarum,* is evidence of democratic feeling; to me it sounds more like the roar of a good prince who has just found out that his *contadini* are being cheated by the overseer. But whatever the motivation, it showed the concern of the Pope for the problems of the poor, a realization that "the needs of man continually recur" and that a banding together into labor unions was the modern working out of the Scriptural "A man helped by his brother is as a strong city." He knew what child labor could do to human development: "As bad weather blights spring buds, so does hard labor at a tender age harm a child's abilities, so that he can never be truly educated."

It was in Leo's time that the Church arranged a negotiated peace with science. It was probably the embarrassment of the Galileo episode that saved the Church from condemning the Darwinian theory. Many individuals were firmly opposed to it, and Pius IX decorated an antievolutionist writer with the strongest expressions of praise and gratitude, but there was no *ex cathedra* condemnation. The Church took the stand that it was concerned with the origin of the soul, not the soma, and the old official date of man's creation, 5199 B.C., was quietly discarded. In its place we have adopted a belief that is, when one thinks of it, equally improbable — that man, in his present form, took two hundred thousand years to reach the level of Jericho. Having watched great archives accumulate and disappear one feels inclined to agree with Thomas Mann that "very deep is the well of the past" — deep enough to hold several civilizations. The Sybilline books are stuck away and forgotten, the Library of Alexandria is destroyed by arson and neglect, great archival accumulations of the Church disappear in invasion and civil war.

Leo never made peace with the Italian government, but he realized that the secular power of the papacy was over; in 1881 the donations of Constantine and of Charlemagne were no longer political documents. And in this peace after battle, the peace of defeat, he shocked his Curia by opening the Secret Archives of the Vatican to scholars of all faiths and countries. "The Church's one desire is truth." However, access to the Archives was to be limited to the material originating before 1815, and to be subject to the rigid rules and limitations that are still in force. The Archives were not to be considered open in the usual sense of the word; they remained the private archives of a reigning sovereign. They were opened to scholars in the same way that family archives are sometimes opened by the generosity of their owners to investigators who have a particular reason for consulting them. In theory the Vatican Secret Archives can be consulted only by the permission of the pope himself; in practice this function of decision is delegated to the Prefect of the Archives. The prefect not only has wide powers in granting or refusing permits, but can limit their period of validity, grant or refuse access to particular material, and withdraw a permit at any time he wishes. There are also many minor regulations, and the last general ruling, in 1927, advises scholars not to make nuisances of themselves: "Whoever for his own convenience needlessly avoids carrying out normal research work in the indices and habitually troubles archivists, scriptors, and ushers will render himself unwelcome."

The Italian anticlerical party was disappointed in its hope of finding the Secret Archives a repository for records of usurpations, crimes, and sexual perversions. But the question still remains as to whether the Secret Archives exercises internal censorship over its materials. What action is taken by a scriptor, custodian, or prefect when, in the course of his work, he comes across material that is morally or theologically controversial? Has a closed (*chiuso*) *fondo* gradually accumulated, the much-talked-of *fondo* about which nothing is actually known, a closed *fondo* which is categorically denied by Archives authorities? This is a question which puzzled me during the long time I spent working in the Secret Archives, and to which I still have not found any answer. My own personal impression is that no such material is destroyed. The men of the Archives have too much sense of the past, too much reverence for scholarship, too much obligation to learning, for that. But such documents may be omitted from the inventories, bound in volumes containing other documents of a very different kind, and relegated to some *fondo* that is closed because of chronological limitations or very seldom consulted.

This happened with the personal letters of Pope Borgia to the little clan of his devoted women, and with the original summary of the process of Giordano Bruno, and may have happened many other times that we do not know about. Such documents may eventually reappear in the future, when time has imposed its Treaty of Westphalia on our conflicts.

The opening of the Vatican Archives in 1882 occurred at a time when Europe was intensely nationalistic. Just as American Negroes are now searching Africa's past for material to heighten their new racial consciousness, so the nations of Europe searched the Church's Archives for data relating to their own countries and peoples. Historical institutes were founded in Rome; research missions were sent by nearly all European, and some Oriental, nations. The Archives of the Universal Church are unique in their quality of cutting across international boundaries; each nation could find in them something of its own. The Vatican rapidly became the world's most important center of historical research.

At first the work had no coordinated plan. The French *Scuola* of Rome assumed the responsibility of editing the medieval registers, and has now reached the end of the thirteenth century. The Germans published, and are still publishing, the Acts of the Nunciatures; the Germans of the Görres-Gesellschaft concentrated on some of the financial records of the Camera. The English were interested chiefly in the material in the registers which dealt with England. The Scots and the Belgians followed the same policy with the Registers of Petitions. This work still continues, though at a slower pace.

To meet the new demands of research, the Secret Archives stepped up its program of cataloguing and arranging. One of the great needs of a researcher is to know what has already been done on his subject. Books and articles based on the Archives have been written in many languages and have appeared in many places; articles, in particular, are difficult to locate, since they appear in dozens of magazines and separately as academic papers. Some way was needed for coordinating the international research work being done in the Vatican Secret Archives. In 1930 a meeting of the Historical Institutes of Rome decided that, though full coordination was not feasible, it might be possible to produce an international bibliography covering all material based on documents in the Vatican Archives. Each historical institute was responsible for material published in its own country.

This work was interrupted by the war. Then one morning the harbor of Anzio was black with ships. Mussolini and his mistress died in a perfection of degradation, and Italy, like a man coming to his senses, went back to being a democracy.

The project was resumed again in 1955. It was now to be the responsibility of the Institutes of Archaeology, History, and the History of Art, all located in Rome. The editorial staff was to have its offices in the Vatican Secret Archives and to carry on the work itself, with the collaboration of qualified scholars. An extensive card index was constructed for the use of the public at the Archives. Later, at the request of scholars, several copies were made of this card index for use at important centers of historical research, and in 1962, on the advice of the major American libraries, the index was reproduced in book form.

The present plan is to collect, in five or six volumes, a bibliography of the studies that have come out since the opening of the Archives in 1881. Later volumes are planned to cover the publications that appeared between 1815 and 1881. If money can be found, the project will be extended backward to meet the work of the archivist Baronio, who died in 1607.

So far four volumes have been published. For the first volume alone over a thousand books and articles were examined, in languages ranging from Catalan to Hungarian. Approximately 12,200 analytical index cards were made, relating to one hundred thirty-five *fondi* of the Archives. It is difficult to locate all the material based on Archives documents, and these indices contain many lacunae. One can trust a positive finding, but not a negative one.

Meanwhile the ingathering of the Church's archives continued. In 1892, in accordance with the policy of concentrating documents at the Vatican, the archives of the Apostolic Datary, with the two important series of Lateran registers of pontifical letters and of petitions, were brought from the Lateran. Between 1904 and 1908 the Lateran *brevi*, the registers of the Secretariat of Briefs, were added to the Vatican Archives. Other *fondi* sent to the Vatican include some of the archives of the Sacred Rota, the archives of the Congregation of Rites, which deals with sanctification, and the archives of the Congregation of the Council, which are of great historical value since they contain the periodical reports made by bishops to inform the Holy See of the condition of their dioceses and touch on social, economic, and political as well as on theological and ecclesiastical matters.

Several archives of the minor or special Congregations have also been added to the Vatican Secret Archives, such as that on the building of St. Peter's, important for art history, and the *fondi* of the Apostolic Palace, which records the expenses of the papal court. The latter include such items as a note of some gifts sent in the seventeenth century by a pope to a Chinese emperor, a list of musical instruments and compositions, and Corelli's "Concerto Grosso." Many archives of the confraternities returned, including that of Santa Lucia del Confalone, with a beautiful volume of plans of ancient Rome, fragments of Romanesque plays, and documents on the miracle plays performed in the Colosseum. Also sent to the Vatican were archives of suppressed Roman convents and the archives of the Augustinian, Capuchin, Franciscan, and Jesuit orders from 1545 to 1807. Other *fondi* which were added include one on military correspondence, dealing with the recruiting, arming, and payment of the papal troops. There is also the geographical *fondo* of the plans and maps which have been found in the ancient *fondi* of the Secret Archives — of special importance for the history of exploration and cultural contacts. An inventory has now been made for this collection, but not all the plans and maps that belong to the *fondo* have been discovered. Locating them is difficult, as they are not listed in the indexes of the Archives. Most maps are still in the thin tubes or the folders in which they were found. They are not only labeled with the region they represent but bear the name of the author and engraver, which make it possible to date them and determine their place of origin. There are also plans and maps in the new *fondi* that have come to the Archives, but the indexes, if they exist, are still in the offices of the respective Congregations and cannot yet be consulted without the permission of the Congregation to which they belong.

The closing years of the nineteenth century saw the return of the private archives of the Borghese, Boncompagni, and Ruspoli families whose members, as cardinals and popes, had worked in their own palaces and whose families had retained the Church documents as part of their estate. These archives contain documents of such importance that they must be considered as rightfully a part of the Vatican Secret Archives. For centuries they remained in private hands. But by 1891 a branch of the Borghese family, fallen on such evil days that they even changed their custom of naming the head of the family Scipione in the hope that it might change their luck, offered the Borghese Archives for sale.

The Prussian government, contemplating their purchase, commissioned the Prussian Historical Institute of Rome to make a complete inventory of the Borghese *fondo,* but as soon as it was known that the Vatican hoped to acquire the collection, Prussia withdrew and chivalrously presented its inventory to the Vatican. This inventory is in two large, heavy albums. In the first is written: "After seven years of unceasing toil, the undersigned has, with the assistance of two collaborators, concluded the classification of many thousands of papers which were previously in utter confusion." But these thousands did not include all the documents of the Borghese archives; many folders are still unexplored. When Pope Leo purchased them along with three hundred additional manuscript works for the Holy See, he assigned the family archives to the Secret Archives and the manuscripts to the Vatican Library. The printed books, bought by a Roman bookseller, unfortunately were dispersed. The papacy paid very high prices to the families whose archives it took over; much of the material had originally been Church property, but long uncontested possession had established ownership. Today the situation is reversed. There is a voluntary backwash of documents to the Archives, as the great families seek to transfer the responsibility for their storage and care. The younger generation takes little interest in the past, and the space required by family documents can be profitably rented. Archivists, on the other hand, are reluctant to give storage space to this inflow of material that cannot be used without the permission of the head of the family.

The Archives suffered losses as well. In 1902 the entire Borgian *fondo*, with its valuable collection of codices, was transferred to the Archives of Propaganda Fide. And between 1920 and 1930, serious losses occurred through the action of a Prefect of the Archives, the brilliant historian Angelo Mercati. The range of Mercati's interests (as well as the range of materials in the Archives) is shown by the subjects of his monographs: sacred music, Peter the Sinner, Matilda of Canossa, Michelangelo, the private libraries of the popes, Montecassino, ancient art, Copernicus, letters of scientists found in the Secret Archives. Yet over a ten-year period he removed all those volumes, codices, and documents not strictly pertinent to the Secret Archives from the miscellaneous *fondo* in Cabinets (*Armadi*) I to XV (among them two ancient works on astrology), and handed them over to the Vatican Library — an extraordinary action for a Prefect of the Archives, in view of the subtle rivalry that prevails between the two institutions. Possibly the fact that he had written on the Library as well as on the Secret Archives had given him a feeling for that organization as well. The works concerned had belonged to the Archives since they were first established, in the days when a clear distinction had not yet been drawn as to the functions of the two institutions. His act is still referred to, unofficially, as the sack of Monsignor Mercati.

For the Vatican Library and Archives, as for many of us who, as the historians put it, flourished at that time, the Second World War, with all its horror and fear, was a high point of existence. When the cultural wealth of the peninsula was endangered, the Church that was now without secular power was able, by spiritual power, to protect its great libraries. Like the cities of refuge in ancient Hawaii, the Vatican was exempt from war. To it came library after library, sometimes only a few days or weeks before the place where it had been was bombed to rubble. The Roman public municipal libraries, sent to Benedict's old Subiaco for safekeeping, were moved to the Vatican before their shelter at Subiaco was destroyed, and the Chigi archives were removed from the palace at Ariccia shortly before it was damaged.

The Library of Frascati, founded by the Stuart Cardinal York, was bombed, but when the Prefect of the Vatican Library visited the site he found that the books themselves were unharmed, and had them taken to the Vatican. Henry Benedict Mary Clement Stuart had been a man of wide interests; the nucleus of his library was ecclesiastical but it also contained literary, artistic, and scientific material, along with stray works such as one on a new method of dressing horses.

The Library of Grottaferrata, founded by the Abbot Nilo when he fled from the Saracens, came to the Vatican with its irreplaceable collection

of materials for the study of ancient Byzantine music. At the same time
the bronzes from the Museum of the Ships of Nemi, Nero's pleasure
barges that Mussolini had raised from the lake depths, were brought to
safety; the ships themselves were burned by the Germans.

But of all these guests of the Vatican, the most important was the
Library of Monte Cassino. In October 1943, two German officials warned
the abbot that Monte Cassino would soon be in the battle zone. A time
of hurried activity followed; the monks hastily knocked together wooden
packing cases to hold the codices. Drawers containing documents and
parchments were removed from their cabinets and carried, with their
contents still in them, to the waiting trucks. Among the things so hastily
loaded were books that had been kings' gifts, classical works by Seneca,
Tacitus, Cicero, that had been rescued from oblivion, works of Jerome
and Augustine, illuminated Books of Hours. Of parchments alone there
were forty thousand. After short stays at the Rock of Spoleto and at
Castel Sant'Angelo they arrived at the Vatican, safe from the bombing
that destroyed Monte Cassino (except, miraculously, Benedict's cell and
tomb). Like the many human refugees who crowded its cellars and corridors, the great libraries of Italy found safety and shelter in the Vatican.

For the postwar years, the Secret Archives' outstanding event has been
the extension of the period for which documents may be consulted. Leo
XIII permitted research for the period before the Council of Vienna in
1815; Pius XI, pope from 1922 to 1939, extended the date to 1846. Recently Paul VI has again advanced it to 1878, to include the pontificate of
Pius IX. This was a historically important period that covered the war
between the United States and Mexico, the American Civil War, the
Franco-Prussian and Crimean wars, the *Risorgimento*, and the first Vatican Council with its dogma of papal infallibility.

The time limits for research have been strictly enforced. When a press
conference was held to announce the opening of these new and important *fondi*, the historian Anna Maria Ghisalberti related that once,
having come on an 1847 document, he asked the Prefect Mercati whether
he might read it. Mercati, a man of great courtesy and sympathetic
toward research, snatched it angrily from his hand.

Some exceptions have been and are being made to the chronological
rules, in cases where exceptions would be of benefit to the Church. The
correspondence between Pius IX and King Victor Emanuel II has been
edited, and unpublished documents have been used in a book on the
relations between the Vatican and Nazism. A team of scholars is now
editing all the Vatican documents of the Second World War. The Holy
See has already published the letters of Pius XII to the German bishops

in response to Hochhuth's accusation of papal negligence with regard to the slaughter of the Jews.

When I visited the Archives for the first time I was shown, but from a considerable distance, the heavy door behind which lay the documents from 1846 on. Everything from 1878 on is still behind a closed door (*sub clave*), along with the daily output from the departments and offices of the Roman Curia. While historians search the archives of the old Church, the modern Archives continue as an active, functioning organ of the contemporary Church, an uneasy Church facing a troubled time, and trying to find a safe path through the strange world of the future.

X X I X

Today and Tomorrow

I CAME back to Italy after two years in the United States to find the Church in the process of *aggiornamento*. I had thought myself a liberal, but as often happens my liberalism wavered when something of my own was concerned, and I was rather shocked to find that *aggiornamento* had struck my Secret Archives. For one thing, a good deal of remodeling had been done — though I should have remembered that building is always going on somewhere at the Vatican. The Archives now has an outer entrance of its own, separate from that of the Library; I missed Hippolytus. The new entrance is through a very modern, sparsely furnished room with floors of light marble and a large businesslike table to hold the sign-in book. There is an elevator now, modest but modern, with walls of blond wood, and it works. A Coke machine and a coffee machine, of the most recent design, are unobtrusively installed in the locker room.

A person consulting an archivist no longer has to hold a conspiratorial conversation in a corner; there is a large reception room furnished with fine antiques from the papal apartments that the present pope has replaced with austerity modern. On a low table is a tapestry of Saint Peter's bark among the onrushing waves, a gift of a northern convent. The photostating room, which had formerly occupied the chapel and given me uneasy thoughts about that Kiev cathedral where the dome has been made into a planetarium, now has large and airy quarters on the top floor, overlooking the Vatican gardens, the shadow of Saint Peter's dome, and the jungle of modern construction that is imprisoning Vatican City.

Since the Archives now has its own entrance, new employees are stationed there, rather young and casually dressed, without that Vatican patina that one sees on the employees at the entrance to the Library. I felt rather sad at all these changes; coming to the Archives had always given me the feeling of escaping the world, and I often thought that it must have been in a scroll-room of the Temple that Solomon wrote his lines about the ways of pleasantness.

But when I entered the study room I found that it was still the old Archives. Here were the big black desks with the convenient bookracks for volumes too heavy for the hands, the uncomfortable chairs that keep one awake even on a sleepy day, the great clock, the silent assistance, the ancient throne of the prefect, the windows opening on the patio where young men from all the continents sit talking in the sun.

There was no other change in the Library except for the modern dress of the nuns studying there. Not all nuns look well in modern dress, and one can understand that American order which, having abandoned the ecclesiastical tent-dresses for sweaters and skirts, sent a hurry call for help to a charm school for airline stewardesses. But some of the costumes here were lovely. I could hardly take my eyes away from a young nun in a beautifully cut white dress, deep-pleated, with a girdle of blue ribbon. On her white bonnet was a very thin black veil, draped in the back in exquisite undulations. A few of the old nuns were wearing a full black mantle over their new costumes, as if to obey but not to approve.

There was still discussion of the theft of the Petrarch manuscripts, thought to have been a last-minute substitution for the theft that was actually intended — that of the Archives' collection of golden seals. An attempt was made to force the door that once led from the Library to the oldest part of the Archives, but this door dates back to the time when looting by enemy troops was regarded as a normal hazard, and it was strong enough to hold. The Petrarch manuscripts were a target of opportunity.

The Library and the Archives still operate on a principle of Christian trustfulness. In the Library one sees documents of the second and third centuries, things physically beautiful in their strong and perfect lettering, so that people who could not be tempted by diamonds might be tempted by these, exposed in glass cases that could easily be broken into. And when I attended an exhibition at the Archives, given for the United Nations' Food and Agriculture personnel, I arrived early and found myself now and then alone in the room with the Archives' most precious possessions, those usually kept in the safes. The golden seals were laid out on the table like a tray of cookies, covered only with a sheet of plastic. Later, when I commented on some of them, the plastic was lifted so that I could handle them. There are few places left in the world where courtesy still ranks so high in the hierarchy of values.

Looking at these surviving treasures I thought of all that had flowed through the archives of the popes, for over the millennia one sees, even in this institution devoted to stability, the *panta rhei* of Lucretius. Documents come in and accumulate, they are swept away by fire and invasion, but always there is the inflowing. What will there be, I wondered, in the next century?

We can be sure that the Archives of the next decades will contain material on the questions discussed at the Vatican Council, and on controversial subjects not fully discussed there, such as the growing rebellion against the soul-and-body dichotomy. Early in our history Saint Augustine's philosophy prevailed — "The love of this world is fornication against Thee" — and Christian society was taught that its men should hate their manhood, and that of its women the best should be barren. One can almost see here the justice of history, the revenge of Carthage for its salted fields. And so the life-force went underground, to reappear in strange and sometimes wonderful ways; and so the great pillars in Saint Peter's have the form of a pregnant woman. But now the life-force is no longer willing to hide, and the guerrilla army of *Amor Mundi* is offering open combat.

There will be records of the controversy on population control, for even if we can avert the age of famines the demographers predict, we will still have to decide whether we have any responsibility to our planet and its biota — whether God who blessed the whales on the fifth day of Creation wants them to be exterminated. Our present instructions are definite: "The earth must be fully exploited." But when we have ground the dolphins into hamburger and made the desert to blossom as the soy bean . . . ?

There will be discussions of new psychological findings that affect theology. There will be records of assaults on the mind of man, as new methods of control by drugs and electronic devices and new methods of brainwashing are perfected.

And there is the question of space, of extraterrestrial life, of the inclusion of nonterrestrial beings in the Church's ethical and religious system, and whether to take literally Christ's order to "teach my Gospel unto every creature." (Was this nonrestrictive term intentional, or only an accident of translation?) Perhaps a new *fondo* will have to be opened — that of Secretary of State for the Stars. Probably our first missionaries will be military chaplains (not even *Propaganda Fide* can finance a spaceship), or the young medical aidmen with religious medals hanging next to their dogtags; perhaps we shall someday canonize one of them as Apostle to Aldebaran.

I wondered, too, whether our present Secret Archives will survive into that future, or whether there will be new "disasters of this night," in the time that Esdras foresaw when "salt waters shall be found in the sweet, and all friends shall destroy one another, when wit shall hide itself, and understanding withdraw into his secret chamber." Our last invaders, like the early barbarians, were at least nominally Christian; our next may not be. The Vatican Secret Archives and the Vatican Library would have to depend on world opinion for protection against deliberate destruction — the mindless, joyful destruction that is visited on the files of American embassies. Protection against bombing, in one of the world's great capitals, is very slight. There is none against a direct hit, little against a firestorm — nothing to compare with the caves where the banks of America's eastern seaboard store their microfilmed financial records. And nothing to compare with that place in the mountains of Utah where the Church of Jesus Christ of the Latter-Day Saints has built an archives in the living rock to hold its genealogical records, as the archives at Tara kept the bloodlines of the tribes. The Mormon archives must be the most beautiful in existence — great round arches set in a jagged mountain, looking out over a view that makes one think of the Biblical cities of the plain.

From the American civilization, three bodies of documents have a chance to reach the post-atomic future — the financial records of the east coast, the genealogical records of the Latter-Day Saints, and the military manuals from the NORAD Command's hollow mountain in Colorado. And I doubt if the first two will survive. The people of New England may think their own lives more important than financial files; and what choice will the Mormons make between their genealogical records and the living genes of Mormon schoolchildren? We can only hope that, somewhere in the barracks under the mountain where the United States has its NORAD Command headquarters, some lance-corporal may have had a paperback anthology of poetry, some officer may have been reading history.

Saving our archives and libraries may be a task for the United Nations. Napoleon planned to preserve the world's learning by concentrating it in France; we know too much now about the fortunes of war to think that any one country can offer security. Yet an internationally owned library-archives might be recognized as belonging to all of mankind, particularly if it were located on an island or in an area considered international territory. Such an institution might be a unifying cultural influence, as an international center for scholars.

Modern methods of documentary reproduction would make it unnecessary for such organizations as the Vatican Library and Secret Archives or the British Museum to part with their original documents; the international library-archives could consist of duplicate or duplicated copies. And we can hardly say that it would be too expensive, when one of the smaller religious sects has found the money and the determination to build a mountain-archives with three storage vaults six hundred feet long, under seven hundred feet of granite, lined with steel and concrete and closed with bank vaults.

Considerable microfilming has already been done at the Vatican, less to safeguard material than to make it easily available to scholars and research workers. A project financed by the Knights of Columbus has deposited at Saint Louis University microfilms that cover large sections of the Vatican Library, along with thousands of color slides of illuminated manuscripts. But the Library lends itself to microfilming more conveniently than the Archives, where the question would be what to microfilm in this largely uncatalogued depository of materials. Probably the Archives documents most in need of precautionary photographing are the enormous imperfect indexes. Their disappearance in a fire, war, or civil disturbance could undo the work of generations.

Even if our precarious peace continues, time is a danger to archives documents. They are written on organic materials, and organic materials share something of the impermanence of the living creatures that produce them. Fungus has attacked many of the parchments; paper disintegrates with time. Recent Archives are in particular danger, for they are typewritten on paper of weak consistency, with what one archivist scornfully calls evanescent inks. "They come into the world with a poor constitution, like delicate children whose survival is uncertain." Our modern archives and books may not even last for a century. If the Du Pont Corporation wanted to make a contribution to peace that would equal its contribution to war, it might try to develop a nonorganic, nonflammable, chemically inert writing material — something that could not possibly be used for fuel or for toilet paper. Otherwise our civilization may transmit little written material to the far future except for the inscriptions on our tombstones, so much less revealing than those of the Greek Anthology, and the names of bureaucrats on our public buildings.

Then there is the problem of excavating these buried layers of Augustine's interpenetrating cities of God and man. Unless there is aid from the foundations it seems unlikely that the present staff will be greatly increased. Archivists do not think that translating machines would be practical at present, though I heard some talk of acquiring a computer. The use of a calculating machine to test the single authorship of the *Iliad* suggests that such machines might help in determining the authenticity of documents and the proper attribution of documents of unknown authorship. The use of translating machines may eventually be necessary if the Secret Archives are ever to be completely catalogued. These devices are already able to put Russian scientific articles into an English intelligible enough so that a scientist can tell whether the article is worth having translated by a human translator. Efficiency of this level would make a rough sort of indexing possible.

Eventually the scanning devices now being developed to help the blind to read and post office departments to economize may make it possible for a machine to scan a document by itself, without the use of a human copyist. One wonders what a scanning machine will do with illuminated initials, but in general Archives material could be scanned more easily than, say, addresses on envelopes, because of the regularity of the lettering. The scribes were professionals, and some medieval manuscripts look like a very superior printing job. Another factor that should make Archives documents ideal material for a scanning machine is the existence of distinctive scripts; the device could be set for *Beneventana, cancellaresca,* or whatever calligraphy a scribe had used.

What could we hope to find if the Secret Archives were completely catalogued? Surprises for historians, single documents that upset old assumptions, letters that throw new light on great and puzzling personalities, data that changes the aspect of an era as study of the Avignon documents has changed our view of the Avignon popes, maps like the Vinland map that recently brought a flood of inquiries into the Archives, master documents like the lost notebooks of Leonardo, sequestered material of the past — works of literature and philosophy that could not be accepted in their own day. The Archives may have kept the writings of some long-ago Teilhard de Chardin as the monks of Bobbio kept Rutilius' protest against asceticism, as the Bavarian Benedictines preserved the songs of the *Carmina Burana.*

There may be accounts of incidents that meant little to the men of an earlier day but are significant to us. An example of the surprising material that sometimes appears in religious writing occurs in the medieval "Voyage of Saint Brendan," a sixth-century Irish monk of the Age of Saints, one of those who took a leather coracle out to sea, trusting in God. Then: "One day, when the masses were over, they noticed a column rising out of the sea. This column was covered with a most unusual canopy — so strange indeed that the coracle could pass through the openings in it but no one could tell what substance it was made of. It was the color of silver and seemed harder than marble. The column itself was of pure crystal. The canopy was so big that it extended a mile on either side of the column and went down into the sea." What was the canopy? The big dish of a radio telescope? — a sail to catch the solar wind?

There is still a possibility that very old documents may be discovered.

The beautiful parchments from the earliest centuries that are on view in the Vatican Library are evidence that documents from the ancient world do sometimes survive. But physical survival is not necessary; documents hitchhike. They are copied into letters, embedded in other documents, quoted to support points of view. The Archives contains many monastery archives that have not been examined; some of them are conglomerate archives that include archives, libraries, and files from older institutions that had gone out of existence.

Yet the real value of the Secret Archives is not in intellectual discovery but in the sense of the past that they give to us, the rich regretful wisdom of our long human experience. And with this sense of the past is the sense of fellowship with its people, with all the men and women who searched for God in so many ways and times and countries, and tried to tell us what they found — "a brilliance that space cannot contain, a sound that time cannot carry away, a perfume that no breeze disperses, an embrace without any satiety." Not all of them write as simply as Saint Augustine; sometimes I cannot understand what they are saying. But here in the Archives, like Saint Pelagia in the restaurants of Antioch, I have heard the talk of the Christians.

Chapter Notes

PRINCIPAL ABBREVIATIONS USED IN THE NOTES

AA	Archivum Arcis
AC	Camera Apostolica (Apostolic Chamber)
Arm.	Armaria, Armarii
Card.	Cardinale (Cardinal)
Cod.	Codice (Codex)
Collect.	Collectoriae
Cong.	Congregazione (Congregation)
Epist.	Epistola
Instr. misc.	Instrumenta miscellanea
Mansi	Giovanni Domenico Mansi, *Sacrorum Conciliorum nova et amplissima collectio*
MGH	Monumenta Germaniae Historica
Misc.	Miscellanea
Nunz.	Nunziatura (Nunciature)
PG	Migne, Patrologia Graeca
PL	Migne, Patrologia Latina
Reg.	Registro (Register)
SA	Archivio Segreto Vaticano (Vatican Secret Archives)
SA Rome	Archivio di Stato di Roma (State Archives of Rome)
SS	Segretario di Stato (Secretariat of State)
Trib.	Tribunale (Tribunal)
Urb. Lat.	Codice Urbinate Latino (Urbinate Latin codex)
Vat. Lat.	Codice Vaticano Latino (Vatican Latin codex)
VL	Biblioteca Vaticana (Vatican Library)
VR	Registro Vaticano (Vatican Register)

I. THE CAVES OF THE TIME-STREAM

8 . . . *against a golden plain.*
There is an excellent discussion of the Vatican seals in P. Sella, *Le Bolle d'Oro
dell' Archivo Vaticano* (Vatican City, 1934).
8 . . . *that made Napoleon . . .*
An Archives treasure is the Decree of Reunion between the Greek and Latin
churches, signed in 1439 in the Duomo of Florence by Pope Eugene IV and
the Emperor John VIII Paleologus, the splendid horseman of Gozzoli's *Journey
of the Magi.* This agreement, made in fear of the Turks and giving the Holy
See and the Roman pontifex "primacy over the whole universe," never went
into effect. Here also are letters from the Khan of Persia in 1247 on the
conversion of the Mongols to Christianity. Some of the documents are ten or
twelve feet long; when they are hung on the walls for exhibit they give the
impression of tapestry — or of colored laundry hung indoors to dry on a rainy
day.

II. L'ARCHIVIO SEGRETO VATICANO

13 . . . *to serve the Curia.*
Clear discussions of the nature of the Secret Archives and of their content can
be found in Leslie Macfarlane, "The Vatican Archives," in *Archives*, 4 (1959),
29–44, 84–101, and in Karl August Fink, *Das Vatikanische Archiv*, 2d ed.
(Rome, 1951).
13 . . . *the National Library of Paris . . .*
L'Enfer (the Hell) of the National Library of Paris was set up by order of
the First Consul Napoleon Bonaparte on the model of the closed section of the
Vatican Library, but chiefly as a repository for selected erotic works. Its volumes
were to be uniformly bound in marble paper, the sheets edged with deep rose
to bring to mind the flames of Hell. See Guillaume Apollinaire *et al., L'Enfer de
la Bibliothèque Nationale* (Paris, 1913).
14 . . . *signature of Pope Borgia.*
These letters had been first discovered in 1627 by the archivist Gonfalonieri,
among other old documents. Shocked by their content but unwilling to destroy
them because of their historical value, he bound them into eight small booklets
and misplaced them in the hope that they would never be found — or that
they would not be found in his lifetime.

III. BETWEEN LEGEND AND HISTORY

22 . . . *idea of God.*
Eusebius, *The History of the Church from Christ to Constantine*, p. 86. At
other times he represented her as the mother of all things, or as the Holy
Spirit. Ancient writers say that statues were erected on the Tiberine Island to
Simon the Magician as Jove and to Helena as Minerva.
24 . . . *those of Peter.*
"The Bones of the Fisherman," *Time*, 5 July 1968, p. 48. The dirt found with
the bones is said to have come from the traditional area of Peter's crucifixion.
28 ". . . *this is his duty . . .*"
Fremantle, *A Treasury of Early Christianity*, pp. 45–56.
29 ". . . *those who hope in You.*"
B. Botte, *La tradition apostolique de Ignace de Rome* (Paris, 1946).

page
30 ". . . *of the Master.*"
    Fremantle, *A Treasury of Early Christianity*, p. 30.
30 ". . . *very great or serious* . . ."
    Fremantle, *The Papal Encyclicals in Their Historical Context*, p. 40.
30 ". . . *gold richly wrought.*"
    Fremantle, *A Treasury of Early Christianity*, p. 178.
31 ". . . *incense or other balsams.*"
    Eusebius, *Historia Ecclesiastica*, PG XX. (Usually we have quoted the English
    translation by Williamson, but in this particular case the account of Polycarp's
    martyrdom has been translated directly from the Greek original.) See also
    F. X. Funk, "Martyrium Polycarpi" in *Patres Apostolici.*
33 ". . . *different from you?*"
    L. Fortunati, *Relazione generale degli scavi* (Rome, 1859).
34 ". . . *middle of the public square.*"
    Eusebius, *The History of the Church*, p. 329.
35 ". . . *most prudent in every way.*"
    Ibid., p. 368.
35 ". . . *and shining eyes.*"
    Ibid., p. 413.

IV. THE CHURCH OF THE FIRSTBORN

36 ". . . *with us unalterably forever.*"
    Eusebius, *The History of the Church*, p. 403.
38 ". . . *of any kind anywhere.*"
    Ibid., p. 405.
38 ". . . *would be considerably eased.*"
    Durant, *The Story of Civilization*, III, 659.
38 ". . . *decision already reached.*"
    Eusebius, p. 405.
38 ". . . *conceive of the Deity.*"
    Durant, III, 659.
39 ". . . *writing to the church here.*"
    Fremantle, *The Papal Encyclicals in Their Historical Context*, p. 42.
40 ". . . *through the centuries.*"
    Giovanni Battista De Rossi, "De origine historia indicibus scrinii et biblio-
    thecae Sedis Apostolicae commentatio," in *Codices Palatini latini Bibliothecae
    Vaticanae* (Rome, 1886), I, 135, 151.
40 . . . *the desert saints.*
    See Helen Waddell, *The Desert Fathers* (Ann Arbor, 1960).
41 ". . . *bilious and ill-tempered of saints.*"
    Guido De Ruggero, *La filosofia del Cristianesimo* (2 vols.; Bari, 1950), I, 66–68.
41 ". . . *as there are copies.*"
    Fremantle, *A Treasury of Early Christianity*, p. 90.
42 ". . . *changes or correction therein?*"
    Ibid., p. 89.
42 ". . . *you may be occasionally mistaken.*"
    Ibid., p. 98.
43 ". . . *which you did not write?*"
    Ibid., p. 101.
44 ". . . *thin with fasting.*"
    Durant, *The Story of Civilization*, IV, 54.
45 ". . . *the Amiatino Gospel.*"
    A. Mercati, "Per la storia del codice Amiatino," in *Biblica* 3 (1922), 324–328.

page

V. THE WHITE BARBARIANS

47 *". . . perished in one city."*
Quoted in *Select Letters of Saint Jerome,* trans. by F. A. Wright (New York, 1933), p. x.

49 *. . . by a Romanized Goth, . . .*
SA, AA Arm. I-XVIII, ii. 3058. See L. Bruzza, *Regesto della Chiesa di Tivoli,* and "La Charta Cornutiana," in L. Duchesne, *Le Liber Pontificalis,* I, CXLVI-CXLVII.

53 *". . . this grace of hospitality."*
Ildefonso Schuster has an excellent discussion of the *Liber Diurnus* in his *Storia di San Benedetto e di suoi tempi* (Abbazia di Viboldone [S. Giuliano Milanese], 1953).

VI. THE INFRASTRUCTURE

55 *". . . given to sleep."*
Fremantle, *A Treasury of Early Christianity,* p. 461.

57 *". . . shut in by ancient walls."*
Ibid., pp. 455–456.

59 *". . . men of the white language."*
Lady Wilde, *Ancient Legends, Mystic Charms, and Superstitions of Ireland,* 2 vols. (Boston, 1887), I, 125–127.

60 *". . . his innumerable books."*
Select Letters of Saint Jerome, p. 171.

62 *". . . minuscula cancellarescu."*
On the scriptoria of the monasteries, see F. Lesne, *Les livres: "scriptoria" et bibliothèques du commencement du VIIe à la fin du XIe siècle* (Lille, 1938). Until the twelfth century learning was largely the concern of the Church, and manuscripts were copied in the scriptoria of the monasteries and of important episcopal seats. But with the establishment of the great universities, culture and learning spread in the secular city. The major market for books was no longer in the Church, and the needs of a large number of readers determined the choice of texts to be copied. Workshops arose in the university cities, employing many workmen on a division-of-labor basis — preparers of parchment, copyists, miniature artists, proofreaders, binders of codices. Sale of the codices was handled by *librarii* under the supervision of the academic authorities. See G. Cencetti, *Lineamenti di storia della scrittura latina* (Bologna, 1954). Books had become an industrial product.

VII. GREGORY THE GREAT

65 *". . . announced itself openly."*
Gregory the Great, *Libri Dialogarum* III, 38, ed. by U. Moricca, in *Fonti per la storia d'Italia* (Rome, 1924).

67 *". . . presented by Your Excellency."*
These letters of Gregory the Great have been drawn from his *Registrum Epistolarum,* ed. by P. Ewald and L. M. Hartmann, in MGH Epistolae I-II (1891–1899).

68 *. . . authenticity of his tales.*
Gregory was dealing with the almost impossible problem of verification of non-repeatable phenomena. We encounter it in our own time in regard to flying saucers and sea monsters, and are reduced to doing just what Gregory did — trying to determine the reliability of the witnesses.

page
69 ". . . *well-proportioned whole*."
 Donald J. Grout, *History of Western Music* (New York, 1960), p. 29.
70 . . . *study of religious disciplines.*
 England was the first country, after Italy, to receive the Gregorian chant. Bede, in his *Ecclesiastical History of the English People,* tells of the work done by "*Johanne cantatore Sedis Apostolicae*" to teach liturgical singing in the English monasteries. The barbarians loved music and would walk miles to hear a performance. British boys were thought to have excellent voices, and when they were sent to the music schools they were taught other things as well, and were subjected to the controlled environment that all ages but our own have thought necessary for the civilization of the young.
70 ". . . *Book of Tears.*"
 Gildas sapiens: De excidio et conquesta Britanniae ac flebili castigatione in reges, principes et sacerdotes, ed. T. Mommsen, Chronica minora III (Berlin, 1898), pp. 25–90 (MGH Auctores Antiquissimi, 13).
74 ". . . *God, the All-Wielder . . .*"
 Charles W. Kennedy, *Early Christian Poetry* (New York, 1963), p. 94.
75 ". . . *stamped and sealed.*"
 The story of Saint Wilfrid, as quoted here, is from J. F. Webb, *Lives of the Saints* (Baltimore, 1965), pp. 167–192.

VIII. THE ARCHIVES AT THE TOMB

77 . . . *kisses of the faithful.*
 Copies of the imperial decree ordering destruction of the holy images in the churches were torn to pieces by angry crowds; there was insurrection against government officers. "We are compelled," Pope Gregory II wrote to the Emperor, "to write to you with rude and trivial words, because you yourself are rude and trivial. Lay down your arrogance and listen to us with humility. Go to the elementary schools and tell the children that you are the persecutor of images. They will throw their little tablets at your head, and what you would not learn from the scholars you will learn from the ignorant. If you dare to send anyone to overthrow our statue of Saint Peter, we wash our hands of the blood which will be shed; it will fall on your own head and neck" (PL LXXXIX).
81 . . . *received from the Holy See.*
 The letters from the Pope to Pepin quoted in this chapter were preserved through the Codex Carolinus. See W. Gundlach, *Epistolae Merowingici et Karolini aevi I* (Berlin, 1892) (MGH Epistolae, III).
82 ". . . *white as any flower of spring.*"
 Dorothy L. Sayers, ed., *The Song of Roland* (Baltimore, 1964), p. 184.

IX. DISASTERS OF THIS NIGHT

84 . . . *place of destination.*
 A. Lapôtre, *L'Europe et le Saint Siège a L'Epoque Carolingienne: Première Partie, Le Pape Jean VIII* (872–882) (Paris, 1895).
86 . . . *well worth examining.*
 See A. Lapôtre, "Le souper de Jean Diacre," in *Mélanges d'Archéologie et d'Histoire,* 21 (1901), and G. Arnaldi, "Giovanni Immonide e la cultura a Roma al tempo di Giovanni VIII" in *Bollettino Istituto Storico Italiano,* LXVIII (1956), 33–89. Lapôtre considers this play very important, commenting that to understand a century it is useful to know not only how it worked but how it amused itself.

page

88 "... *wild, sour, bitter wine?*"
This letter, like the other letters of Pope John VIII quoted in this chapter, is drawn from the VR I in the Secret Archives.

89 "... *back to its burial place.*"
Auxilius, "In defensionem sacrae ordinationis papae Formosae." See Ernst Dümmler, *Auxilius und Vulgarius* (Leipzig, 1866).

93 "... *the last of the monks.*"
P. Damiani, *Liber Gomorrhianus*, in PL CXLV. Damiani, a brilliant preaching friar who fought with great energy for the reformation of the Church, in this treatise analyzes the "sins against nature" coolly and with meticulous anatomical detail. He dealt not only with homosexuality, endemic in this part of the world from ancient times to our own, but with bestiality, a greater problem then than now, since medieval man lived in constant contact with animals, as we now live in constant contact with machines. Some parts of the treatise are rather amusing. The therapy recommended for a clergyman or monk guilty of attempting to corrupt the young was public beating, having the face spat upon, and imprisonment in heavy chains and in confined quarters for six months. During this period he was to be fed only three times a week, on barley bread. For an additional six months he was sent to an isolated country house to engage in prayer and manual labor, being at all times under the surveillance of an ancient spiritual father. If he was allowed to go for a walk, greater precautions were to be taken. he was to be accompanied by *two* ancient spiritual fathers.

94 "... *the infamy of calumniators.*"
L. Tosti, *La Contessa Matilde e i romani pontefici* (Florence, 1859). This study is based chiefly on Donizone's *Vita Mathildis a Donizone scripta*.

98 ... *reported having seen?*
Eusebius, *The History of the Church*, pp. 287, 301–302.

X. THE VIATORY ARCHIVES

99 "... *and the royal power.*"
Fremantle, *The Papal Encyclicals*, p. 70.

101 "... *the wife in thy bosom.*"
Durant, *The Story of Civilization*, I, 261–262.

103 "... *blessed apostles Peter and Paul.*"
SA, VR VIII, Epist. 261.

106 ... *windows and telephones.*
SA Rome, Camer. I, "Viaggi dei pontefici," b 1562. As far as I know, this is unpublished.

XI. THE ROAD TO EXILE

109 "... *held in private.*"
Giacomo (Stefaneschi), Card. di San Giorgio al Velabro, "Opus Metricum," ed. by F. X. Seppelt, in *Monumenta coelestiniana* (Paris, 1921), pp. 1–146.

111 "... *God has taken away.*"
This story is told in a letter written between September 21 and October 11, 1303, by a courtier of Boniface VIII to some friends in England. The original text is to be found in the Codex 14 C.I. of the British Museum. Cf. MGH *Scriptores*, XXVIII, 621.

112 "... *to another poor man.*"
MGH *Scriptores*, XXVIII, 621.

page

XII.   INTERLUDE AT AVIGNON

115 . . . *correspondence of the Holy See.*
Jean Gallotti, *Le Palais des Papes* (Paris, 1949), pp. 42–43, 45.
116 . . . *look like Chinese sages.*
There is a tradition, with some support from contemporary writings, that Giotto himself worked at Avignon and died there. Enrico Castelnuovo (*Un pittore italiano alla corte di Avignone*, p. 26) thinks that the legend may have arisen from the fact that Giotto sent some of his works to Avignon. It is certain, however, that Benedict XII invited Giotto to his court and that only the artist's death prevented his arrival.
118 ". . . *guise of a woman.*"
Langlois, in *Revue des deux mondes*, CIII (1891), 415, quoted by G. Mollat, *The Popes at Avignon, 1305–1378* (New York and Evanston, 1965), p. 244.
118 ". . . *couverture of sandal wood.*"
Much of the material on Joan of Naples is based on the work of her biographer, Emile J. Léonard, *Histoire de Jeanne Ire, reine de Naples* (Monaco, 1932).
120 ". . . *there is perfect freedom.*"
Cf. Mansi, XXV, 416.
121 . . . *regular series of registers.*
The regular registers, now called the Avignon Registers, were of paper. Into them the pope's documents were copied, in the order in which they were received by the copyists. From the time of Clement VI (1342–1352) the bulls were classified by subject matter, under such headings as "Final Absolution," and brief summaries of the documents contained were given at the beginning of the registers (Mollat, *The Popes at Avignon,* pp. 293–294).
122 . . . *to feed its central core.*
Much of the material on the finances, records, and organization of the Avignon Church has been summarized from Mollat's *The Popes at Avignon.*
123 ". . . *a blessing for my sick eyes.*"
SA Collect. 125.
123 . . . *in the Miscellanea series.*
Legal research based on the archives continued at Avignon. Clement V completed the *Corpus juris canonici,* a compilation of ecclesiastical law, with a seventh volume of the decretals known as the *Clementinae,* and John XXII added other constitutions, known as the *Extravagantes* (Mollat, *The Popes at Avignon,* pp. 7, 17).

XIII.   SON OF THE SUN AND MOON, POPE OF THE SEA

128 ". . . *the world into good shape.*"
J. Gallotti, *Le Palais des Papes,* p. 171.
129 ". . . *elect an authentic pope.*"
My chief source for the story of Benedict XIII is the work of his biographer, Georges Pillement (*Pedro de Luna, le dernier Pape d'Avignon*). I am indebted to him not only for the details of Benedict's papacy but for the correspondence between the Count d'Armagnac and Joan of Arc.
131 ". . . *instruments of war.*"
Concilio di Siena, *Ratifica della condanna di Benedetto XIII, Anti-papa* (1423); cf. Mansi, XXVIII, 1060.
132 ". . . *enter the House of God.*"
Christian Murciaux, *Pedro de Luna* (Paris, 1963), pp. 283–284.

page

XIV. THE ARCHIVES UNDER THE ANGEL

136 ". . . *bought for His Holiness.*"
Alberto de Zahn, "Notizie artistiche tratte dall'Archivio Segreto Vaticano," pp. 166–194.

137 ". . . *that we are to govern.*"
Pius II, *Memoirs of a Renaissance Pope* (New York, 1962), pp. 149–150.

139 . . . *by a royal fugitive, . . .*
The rescuer of this relic was Thomas, brother of the slain Emperor Constantine (ibid., pp. 241–242).

139 ". . . *filled the air.*"
Ibid., p. 253.

143 ". . . *of the Latin Speech.*"
Henry Osborn Taylor, *Thought and Expression in the Sixteenth Century* (New York, 1962), I, 67.

146 ". . . *greenest and grassiest.*"
Pius II, *Memoirs of a Renaissance Pope*, pp. 155, 162.

149 ". . . *sweeter than honey.*"
George B. Parker, *The English Traveller to Italy* (Palo Alto, Calif., n.d.), I, 603–604.

XV. GREATER THAN EUROPE AND AFRICA

154 . . . *to confirm the testimony.*
Samuel Eliot Morison, *Admiral of the Ocean Sea: A Life of Christopher Columbus* (Boston, 1942), pp. 135–137.

155 . . . *the Indus Valley in 2500 B.C.*
Carleton S. Coon, *The Story of Man: From the First Human to Primitive Culture and Beyond* (New York, 1954), pp. 354–359.

156 . . . *in two successive days.*
A copy of the first edition of Dati's poem is in the British Museum.

160 ". . . *and in good customs.*"
SA VR 879.

XVI. THE *AVVISI* AND THE MEN ILLICITLY CURIOUS

163 . . . *as to what was happening.*
The *avvisi* were also called *avisi, advisi, avvisi et ritorni* (for the *avvisi* which came, or came back from, other cities). They were also called *nove* (news), *novelle,* and *novelline* (short news). See Cesare D'Onofrio, "Gli avvisi di Roma dal 1554 al 1605 conservati in biblioteche ed archivi romani," in *Studi Romani,* 5 (1962), 529.

166 . . . *had actually been present.*
The examples of *avvisi* given come from Urb. Lat. 1038–1041 (VL).

167 . . . *England would again be Catholic.*
Nuovi Avvisi di Anversanel'anno 1554 (VL), pp. 14, 16.

169 . . . *published in 1621 . . .*
SA Arm. IV, 47.

169 . . . *had good reason to fear it.*
Many of the facts concerning the *avvisi* that are given in this chapter, as well as the story of Hannibal Cappello, are from D'Onofrio, "Gli avvisi di Roma . . ."

XVII.   CHALLENGE AND RESPONSE

172 ". . . *of delight shall be opened."*
Durant, *The Story of Civilization,* VI, 338.

174 ". . . *if anything happens to me."*
Roland H. Bainton, *Here I Stand: A Life of Martin Luther* (New York, 1964),
p. 136.

181 ". . . *dignity that they never deserved."*
SA Misc. Arm. III, 252.

181 ". . . *praying to the celestial bridegroom."*
Vat. Lat. 7933.

182 ". . . *we have behaved very strangely . . ."*
Ludwig von Pastor, *Storia dei Papi,* IV, 269.

183 ". . . *praise the children of the Lord."*
This pasquinade is attributed to Aretino.

183 ". . . *before the thrones of kings."*
Hubert Jedin, *Storia del Concilio di Trento* (2 vols.; Brescia, 1949), I, 347–348.

184 ". . . *the name of God."*
"Consilium delectorum Cardinalium ad reformandam Ecclesiam (1537)," Mansi,
Suppl. V, p. 539.

185 ". . . *to serious scandal."*
Jedin, *Storia del Concilio di Trento,* I, 455–456.

XVIII.   THE REBELS

188 ". . . *in a clear open way."*
Innocent VIII, "Processo sul libro delle novecento proposizioni di Pico della
Mirandola," 20 February 1487. Cf. *Bullarium Romanum* (Turin, 1860), V,
327 ff.

188 ". . . *within two days."*
Innocent VIII, "Condanna di molte proposizioni di Giovanni Pico," August
1487. Cf. *Bullarium Romanum,* V, 327.

193 ". . . *the heart of Savonarola."*
This account of Savonarola's preaching, imprisonment, and death is almost
entirely based on Secret Archives material.

194 ". . . *the whole terrestrial globe."*
Giorgio de Santillana, *The Age of Adventure: The Renaissance Philosophers,*
p. 256.

194 ". . . *that God is limited?"*
Ibid., pp. 264–265.

194 ". . . *an infinite image . . ."*
Ibid., p. 263.

199 . . . *held out to him.*
This report of the trial of Giordano Bruno is based on the original records in
the Secret Archives, published by Mercati in 1942.

199 . . . *the trial of Galileo.*
This not very large volume, of about two hundred folios, bound in white
parchment, contains the third interrogatory and bears the original signature of
Galileo himself (May 10, 1633).

201 . . . *nature of the nebulae.*
The quotations in this paragraph are from *Discoveries and Opinions of Galileo,*
trans. and ed. by Stillman Drake (Garden City, N.Y., 1957), pp. 21–28.

201 ". . . *clouds or crosswinds."*
Ibid., p. 144.

page

202 ". . . *abandon the said opinion.*"
Giorgio de Santillana, *The Crime of Galileo*, p. 122.

203 ". . . *no more about it* . . ."
Ibid., pp. 240–241.

203 ". . . *weak and not conclusive.*"
Ibid., p. 241.

203 ". . . *he does hold.*"
Ibid., pp. 245–246.

204 ". . . *conviction by their cogency.*"
Ibid., p. 255 (abbreviated).

204 . . . *his young child crying.*
Ibid., p. 223n.

XIX. BEATRICE CENCI

208 ". . . *Pontificate of Clement VIII.*"
SA Misc. Arm. XI, 210. The chapter is mainly based on this document.

210 ". . . *defense of her honor.*"
George Bowyer, *A Dissertation on the Statutes of the Cities of Italy; and a Translation of the Pleading of Prospero Farinacio in Defence of Beatrice Cenci and Her Relatives* (London, 1838), pp. 74–84.

211 ". . . *from the ordinary punishment.*"
Ibid., p. 92.

211 ". . . *to confess as he did.*"
Ibid., pp. 92–93.

211 ". . . *a custom, not a man.*"
From Shelley's "Beatrice Cenci."

XX   SCANDALOSA, IMPIA, CONTRA VERBUM DEI

214 ". . . *bears a child again.*"
Lady Wilde, *Ancient Legends, Mystic Charms, and Superstitions of Ireland*, II, 87.

216 ". . . *not as our hands.*"
M. Sanudo the Younger, *Diarii* (58 vols.; Venice, 1879–1902), vol. 25.

220 . . . *the abbess, and three others.*
This process is in SA Fondo Carpegna, 40.

XXI. THE TOWER OF THE WINDS

224 ". . . *with very white linen.*"
Vat. Lat. 3211.

229 . . . *much earlier for a soprano.*
"This World," San Francisco *Chronicle*, 21 Nov. 1965, pp. 28–29.

229 . . . *great political influence.*
Ibid., p. 29.

230 . . . *when the wind changes direction;*
The Tower of the Winds is said to have taken its name from the anemoscope which occupied so prominent a place in the Meridian Room. However, an observatory known as the Tower of the Winds had been built at Athens in the century before Christ; since it is still standing, it may have been known to the scientists of the Vatican. See Derek J. de Solla Price, "The Tower of the Winds," *National Geographic* (April 1967), pp. 587–596.

The decoration of the Loggia of the Winds was executed by Nicolò Circi-

page

gnani (Pomarancio), under the supervision of Father Danti. Details of the landscapes were done by the Flemish painter Matthew Brill of Antwerp.

A manuscript entitled "Anemographia F. Egnatii Dantis O.S.D.," originally the possession of the Secret Archives, is now in the Vatican Library as Vat. Lat. 5647. See John W. Stein, S.J., "The Meridian Room in the Vatican 'Tower of the Winds,'" also in the Vatican Library. This is an English translation of a description of the Meridian Room published in the *Illustrazione Vaticana*, IX (1938), 10.

XXII.   TOP SECRET

234 "... *that of our ministers.*"
SA Rome (Archivio Camerale), "Chirografo di Paolo V del 2 dic. 1614."
237 ... *are still in use.*
For the Lonigo episode, I have used, in addition to documents in SA Rome, L. Sandri's "Un prefetto dell'Archivio Vaticano, Michele Lonigo (1572–1639), ed il suo processo," in *Studi in onore di Riccardo Filangieri*, II.
242 ... *have not yet been published.*
Some of the material on the duties of the nuncio, especially with regard to the regular correspondence he was to carry on with the Holy See, has been drawn from Dominic Conway's "Guide to Documents of Irish and British Interest in the Fondo Borghese," in *Archivium Hibernicum*, ser. 1, 23 (1960), 1–147; 24 (1961), 31–102.
243 "... *in store for the offender.*"
Baldassare Castiglione, *The Book of the Courtier by Castiglione* (Garden City, N.Y., n.d.), p. 160.
244 "... *their temporal life together.*"
On the Bolognetti story, in addition to the SA documentation (his final report is in *Fondo Borghese*, ser. 1, I, 174), see Aldo Stella, *Chiesa e Stato nella relazioni dei Nunzi Pontifici a Venezia* (Vatican City, 1964).

XXIII.   THE QUEEN OF THE VANDALS

245 ... *expected no such results.*
This chapter is based chiefly on Archives documents.
249 ... *a deeply learned man.*
Until recently there were ninety-nine letters dealing with Christina, written by Holstenius and by the cardinal-historian Bentivoglio, in the Archives' old collection of Miscellanea. After many days of searching I found that they had been transferred to the archives of the Congregation of Propaganda Fide (a detached portion of the Secret Archives) as dealing with the phenomenon of conversion. Perhaps some future Fulton Sheen will find them useful.
250 "... *made all things vibrate.*"
SA Misc. Arm. XV, 89.
251 ... *cut through houses and palaces.*
Ibid. All this was financed by a method one hopes modern cities will not adopt: the buildings left standing were taxed *pro rata* to pay for the demolition and beautification of the areas near them. This was particularly unpopular with "families of small fortune," who felt they could have done with less *bellezza* and lower taxes.
252 ... *who had ever given her shelter.*
Decio Azzolini, one of the ablest and most attractive of the cardinals created by Alexander VII, had been put in charge of the queen's confused finances and, unofficially, in charge of the queen. A man whose interests ranged from

page

vernacular poetry to the problems of papal election, he was one of the politically independent group of eleven cardinals known as the Flying Squadron, often mentioned in the *avvisi*, which threw its bloc vote to whichever papal candidate it thought would best serve the Church. The queen regarded him with respect, and his patience and authority became stabilizing influences in her life. Sensing her need for occupation, he encouraged her to develop a salon, one of those continuous seminars that were once a part of urban social life, and Christina's palace in Trastevere at the foot of the Janiculum became a center of Rome's intellectual and artistic activity.

XXIV.   WHERE AFRIC'S SUNNY FOUNTAINS

258   ". . . *pray to our Lord.*"
SA Misc. Arm. VI, 39.
259   . . . *each with its own bazaar.*
This report (SA Misc. Arm. XV, 85), written in a rather pedestrian style, is interesting for its description of an absolute monarchy. The king never left his palace and cared nothing for his subjects; one night his jester avoided singing him to sleep, in the hope that he might hear the moans and cries of his people. But instead of hating him they worshiped him as a god; every scrap of his garments was kept as a relic, and water in which he had washed his hands was used against severe illness. He was believed to have prophetic gifts and power to resuscitate the dead. In moments of crisis people did not invoke the name of God but the name of the king — "You are our faith and we believe in you."
261   . . . *the Malabar Rites were forbidden.*
The thorny question of the Malabar Rites is heavily documented in the Secret Archives.
262   ". . . *the foreman belong you-me.*"
Harper's Magazine, 227 (July, 1963), 72.

XXV.   THE CONCLAVES

267   ". . . *fate of that day.*"
Pius II, *Memoirs of a Renaissance Pope,* p. 86.
269   . . . *one of the best cardinals . . . is elected . . .*
SA Arm. II, 122, and Arm. II, 29.

XXVI.   THE SAINTS

271   . . . *James the Deacon.*
The story of Pelagia as it is recounted here is from Helen Waddell's "The Life of Saint Pelagia the Harlot," in *The Desert Fathers,* pp. 173–188.
274   . . . *by the tenth century.*
Durant, *The Story of Civilization,* IV, 743.
274   . . . *is in a Sicilian cathedral.*
Thomas à Becket's canonization followed one of the first papal processes for the recognition of a saint already acclaimed by the people. Pope Alexander III, a learned jurist, heard the testimony of those who had seen miracles at Thomas's tomb, and with great solemnity proclaimed him as a saint. The decree of 1173 sent to the English episcopacy and the English people is a basic document in canon law (PL, Epist. 1279).
276   . . . *the first American saint.*
In the study of Mother Cabrini I have used, in addition to modern biographies, the original acts of the process: "Processus Beatificationis et Canoniza-

page

tionis Servae Dei Franciscae Xaverio Cabrini," 14 vols., kept in the Secret Archives and in the archives of the Congregation of Rites.

279 ". . . *Convent of the Sacred Heart"*
T. S. Eliot, "Sweeney Among the Nightingales" in *Poems 1909–1925* (London, 1942), p. 80.

279 ". . . *Sisters of the Sacred Heart."*
Pietro Di Donato, *Immigrant Saint: The Life of Mother Cabrini* (New York, Toronto, and London, 1960), p. 116.

XXVII. I AM CHARLEMAGNE

285 ". . . *for the papal chapel choirs."*
David Silvagni, *La Corte e la Società Romana nei secoli XVIII e XIX* (Naples, 1967), I, 37–39. This is a reprint of a three-volume edition published 1882–1885. Its interest lies in the fact that Silvagni used as a source the contemporary diary of Abbé Lucantonio Benedetti (d. 1837). This diary was based not only on the Abbé's own observations but on documents from the state archives and those of leading patrician families.

287 . . . *in the September massacre.*
SA SS *Francia* 583.

288 ". . . *But it was only candy."*
G. B. Tavanti, *I fasti di S. S. Pio VI,* in "Italia," III (1804), 352 ff.

290 ". . . *luck in all possible ways . . ."*
SS *Francia* 602.

291 ". . . *This plan succeeded everywhere."*
M. Guizot and Madame Guizot de Witt, *France,* trans. by Robert Black (New York, 1897), VII, 299.

292 . . . *memoirs of Marino Marini.*
Marino Marini, *Memorie storiche dell'occupazione e restituzione degli Archivi della S. Sede . . . ,* in *Regestum Clementis Papae V,* pp. 228 ff.

XXVIII. FONDI GAINED AND LOST

306 . . . *the Congregation to which they belong.*
SA, Introduction to the Inventory of the *Fondo Piante e Carte Geografiche.*

306 . . . *inventory to the Vatican.*
Dominic Conway, "Guide to Documents of Irish and British Interest in Fondo Borghese, in *Archivium Hibernicum,* ser. 1.

308 . . . *shelter in the Vatican.*
See A. M. Albareda, *Biblioteche ospiti della Vaticana nella seconda guerra mondiale* (Vatican City, 1945).

XXIX. TODAY AND TOMORROW

312 ". . . *fornication against Thee"*
Saint Augustine, *The Confessions of St. Augustine,* trans. by Rex Warner (New York, 1963), p. 31.

316 ". . . *went down into the sea."*
J. F. Webb, trans. and ed., *Lives of the Saints,* p. 59.

316 . . . *gone out of existence.*
One of the scholars of the Dead Sea Scrolls has even suggested that the greatest of Christian archives are still to be discovered; that the early Christians, so like the Essenes in other ways, probably resembled them in their concern for preserving their sacred writings. "Was there for the Christians, as

page

for the Essenes, a spiritual center in the desert . . . ? If this be so, then we may expect one day the archaeologists or Bedouin to bring in from the wilderness the remains of a Christian library earlier in date than any of the Gospels and a good deal nearer their source in language and thought Before such a find even the Essene scrolls from Qumran would pale into insignificance" (John Marco Allegro, *The Treasure of the Copper Scroll* [Garden City, N.Y., 1960], p. 127).

316 ". . . *an embrace without any satiety.*"
Saint Augustine, *The Confessions*, p. 215.

Selected Bibliography

Works on the Archives

BOOKS

Battelli, Giulio. *L'Archivio Segreto Vaticano: Archivio di Stato di Roma, Scuola di Paleografia, Diplomatica e Archivistica, Lezioni Speciali.* Rome, 1961–1962.

Bibliografia dell'Archivio Vaticano. 4 vols. Vatican City, 1962–1966.

Bordier, Henri. *Les Archives de la France.* Paris, 1855.

Brom, Gisbert. *Guide aux archives du Vatican.* Rome, 1911.

Casanova, Eugenio. *Archivistica.* Siena, 1928.

De Laborde, L. *Archives de la France, leur vicissitudes pendant la révolution, leur régénération sous l'empire.* Paris, 1866.

Fink, Karl August. *Das Vatikanische Archiv: Einführung in die Bestände und ihre Erforschung.* 2d ed. Rome, 1951.

Marini, Gaetano. *Memorie istoriche degli archivi della S. Sede.* Rome, 1825.

Marini, Marino. "Memorie storiche dell occupazione e restituzione degli Archivi della S. Sede e del riacquisto dei Codici e Museo Numismatico del Vaticano, e de' manoscritti . . . ," in *Regestum Clementis Papae V.* Rome, 1885.

MONOGRAPHS AND ARTICLES

Alcandri, Edvige Barletta. "Gli 'Archiva Ecclesiae.'" *Estratto dalla rassegna degli Archivi di Stato, Anno XXVI.* 1–2 (Jan.-Aug., 1966).

Amati, G. "Notizia di alcuni manoscritti dell'Archivio Segreto Vaticano," *Archivio Storico Italiano,* ser. 3, III (1866).

Ancel, R. "Etude critique sur quelques recueils d'Avvisi," in *Mélanges d'Archéologie et d'Histoire,* XXVIII (1908).

"Aperto L'Archivio Vaticano per i Documenti fino al 1878," in *Corriere della Sera,* 8 December 1966.

Battelli, Giulio. "Archivio Vaticano," *Enciclopedia Cattolica,* XII (Vatican City, 1955).

Berlière, N. "Aux Archives Vaticanes," *Revue Bénédictine,* 20 (1903), 132–173.

Cenci, P. "L'Archivio della cancellaria della Nunziatura Veneta," in *Miscellanea F. Ehrle* (Vatican City, 1924). "Studi e Testi," 41.

Conway, Dominic. "Guide to Documents of Irish and British Interest in Fondo Borghese," in *Archivium Hibernicum,* ser. 1, 23 (1960), 1–147; 24 (1961), 31–102.

De Angelis, Luigi. "Il Papa, la Chiesa e gli archivi ecclesiastici," in *L'Osservatore Romano,* 18 February 1962.

De Rossi, Giovanni Battista. "La Biblioteca della Sede Apostolica," in *Studi e documenti di storia e diritto,* 5 (1884).

————. "De origine historia indicibus scrinii et bibliothecae Sedis Apostolicae commentatio," in *Codices Palatini latini Bibliothecae Vaticanae* (Rome, 1866), I.
De Zahn, Alberto. "Notizie artistiche tratte dall'Archivio Segreto Vaticano," in *Archivio Storico Italiano*, ser. 3, vol. VI, pt. 1 (1867).
Ehrle, F. "Die Frangipani und der Untergang des Archives . . . ," in *Mélanges E. Châtelain* (Paris 1910).
Fabre, Paul. "Le Vatican de Sixte IV," in *Mélanges d'Archéologie et d'Histoire*, 15 (Paris, 1895), nos. IV and V.
Gachard, Louis Prosper. "Les Archives du Vatican," in *Bulletin de la Commission Royale d'Hist.*, Ser. IV, I (1874), 211–386.
Gasparolo, Francesco. "Costituzione dell'Archivio Vaticano e suo primo indice sotto il pontificato di Paolo V: manoscritto inedito di Michele Lonigo," in *Studi e documenti di storia e diritto*, 8 (1887), 3–64.
Gini, Corrado. "Gli Archivi e il progresso delle scienze sociali," in *Miscellanea Archivistica Angelo Mercati* (Vatican City, 1952). "Studi e Testi," 165, 15–19.
Giusti, Martino. "Estesa al pontificato di Pio IX la consultazione dei documenti dell'Archivio Vaticano," in *L'Osservatore Romano*, 8 December 1966.
————. "I registri vaticani e la loro continuazione," in *La Bibliofilia*, 60 (1958), 130–140.
————. "I registri vaticani e le loro provenienze originarie," in *Miscellanea archivistica Angelo Mercati* (Vatican City, 1952). "Studi e Testi," 165, 383–459.
————. "Note sui registri Lateranensi," in *Mélanges Eugène Tisserant* (Vatican City, 1964). "Studi e Testi," 234, 229–249.
————. *Studi sui registri di bolle papali* (Vatican City, 1968). "Collectanea Archivi Vaticani," 1.
Gnoli, Domenico. "Bramante ed il palazzo della Cancelleria," *Studi Romani* (Sept.-Oct. 1957).
Guerrieri, Augusto. "Giustizia per Pio XII," in *Corriere della Sera*, 9 March 1966.
Leccisotti, Tommaso. "La tradizione archivistica di Montecassino," in *Miscellanea Archivistica Angelo Mercati* (Vatican City, 1952). "Studi e Testi," 165, 227–261.
Macfarlane, Leslie. "The Vatican Archives; with special reference to sources for British medieval history," in *Archives*, 4 (1959), 29–44, 84–101.
Masetti Zannini, G. L. "Leone XIII: L'Archivio e la Biblioteca Vaticani," in *L'Osservatore Romano*, 4 March 1962.
Mercati, Angelo. "La Biblioteca Apostolica e l'Archivio Segreto Vaticano," in *Vaticano* (Florence, 1946), 471–493.
————. "Schema della disposizione dei fondi nell'Archivio Vaticano," *Bulletin of the International Committee of Historical Sciences*, 5 (1933), 909–912.
Moroni, Gaetano. *Dizionario di Erudizione Storico-Ecclesiastica*. Vols. II and V. Venice, 1840, 1861.
Renouard, Yves. "*Intérêt et importance des Archives Vaticanes pour l'histoire économique du moyen âge, spécialement du XIVe siècle*," in *Miscellanea Archivistica Angelo Mercati* (Vatican City, 1952). "Studi e Testi," 165, 21–41.
Reumont, Alfredo. Review of M. Gachard's *Les Archives du Vatican*, in *Archivio Storico Italiano*, ser. 3, vol. XX (1874).
Sabatini, Francesco. "La famiglia e le torri dei Frangipani in Roma," in *Monumenti e reliquie medioevali della città e provincia di Roma* (Rome, 1907).
Samaran, Charles. "Problèmes archivistiques d'aujourd'hui et de demain," in *Miscellanea Archivistica Angelo Mercati* (Vatican City, 1952). "Studi e Testi," 165, 1–13.

General Works

BOOKS

Ademollo, A. *L'opera edilizia di Sisto V*. Rome, 1870.

Allier, R. *Les frères du Libre Esprit*. Paris, 1905.

Apollinaire, Guillaume, Fernand Fleuret, and Louis Perceau. *L'Enfer de la Bibliothèque nationale*. Paris, 1913.

Bainton, Roland H. *Here I Stand: A Life of Martin Luther*. New York, 1964.

Balan, P. *Il Pontificato di Giovanni VIII*. Rome, 1880.

Bartholomeis, V. *Origini della poesia drammatica italiana*. Turin, 1952.

Berthelet, G. *L'elezione del papa, storia e documenti*. Rome, 1903.

Biaudet, H. *Les nonciatures apostoliques permanentes jusqu'au 1648*. Helsinki, 1910.

Botte, B. *La tradition apostolique de Ignace de Rome*. Paris, 1946.

Boyle, Leonard. *A Short Guide to St. Clement's*. Rome, 1963.

Bruzza, L. *Regesto della Chiesa di Tivoli*. Rome, 1880.

Cagna, F. *De processu canonizationis*. Rome, 1940.

Castagnoli, Ferdinando, Carlo Cecchelli, Gustavo Giovannoni, and Mario Zocca. *Topografia e urbanistica di Roma*. Bologna, 1958.

Castelnuovo, Enrico. *Un pittore italiano alla corte di Avignone: Matteo Giovannetti e la pittura in Provenza nel secolo XIV*. Turin, 1962.

Castiglione, Baldassare. *The Book of the Courtier by Castiglione*. Garden City, N.Y., n.d.

Cecchelli, C. *Monumenti cristiano-eretici di Roma*. Rome, 1944.

Concetti, G. *Lineamenti di storia della scrittura latina*. Bologna, 1954.

D'Abrantès, Duchesse. *Mémoires de la Duchesse d'Abrantès: souvenirs historiques sur Napoléon (Extraits)*. 2 vols. Paris, 1831–1835.

D'Elia, Pasquale. *Sunto storico dell'attività della Chiesa Cattolica in Cina*. Rome, 1951.

Delacroix, S. *Histoire universelle des missions catholiques*. 4 vols. Paris, 1956–1959.

De la Ferrière, Hector. *Deux drames d'amour: Anne Boleyn–Elizabeth*. Paris, 1894.

Delehaye, H. *A travers trois siècles: l'oeuvre des Bollandistes de 1615–1915*. Brussels, 1920.

——. *Dévotions et pratiques ascétiques du moyen âge*. Maredsous, 1929.

——. *Les origines du culte des martyrs*. Brussels, 1933.

De Luz, Pierre. *Histoire des Papes*. 2 vols. Paris, 1960.

De Santillana, Giorgio, ed., *The Age of Adventure: The Renaissance Philosophers. With introduction and interpretive commentary*. New York, 1956.

——. *The Crime of Galileo*. Chicago, 1955.

Duchesne, Léon. *Le Liber Pontificalis*. 2 vols. Paris, 1886, 1892.

Durant, Will. *The Story of Civilization*. Vols. I–VI. New York, 1935–1957.

—— and Ariel Durant. *The Story of Civilization*. Vols. VII–IX. New York, 1961–1965.

Escobar, Mario, and Andrea Lazzarini. *Vaticano e Chiesa cattolica*. Documentario originale di Leonard von Matt. Genoa, 1954.

Eusebius. *The History of the Church from Christ to Constantine*. Translated with an introduction by G. A. Williamson. Baltimore, 1965.

Féret, P. *Histoire diplomatique: La France et le Saint Siège sous le Premier Empire: La restauration et la monarchie de juillet, d'après les documents officiels et inédits*. Paris, 1911.

Ferrara, Orestes. *Alexander VI Borgia.* Zürich and Stuttgart, 1957.
———. *Il sec. XVI visto dagli Ambasciatori Veneziani.* Milan, 1960.
Finke, H. *Aus den Tagen Bonifaz VIII.* Münster, 1902.
Fortunati, L. *Relazione generale degli scavi.* Rome, 1859.
Fremantle, Anne. *The Papal Encyclicals in Their Historical Context. Introduction by Gustave Weigel, S.J.* New York, 1963.
———. *A Treasury of Early Christianity.* New York, 1960.
Frisi, Francesco, and Giuseppe Matrimonti. *Memorie storiche della città di Monza.* Monza, 1841.
Gallotti, Jean. *Le Palais des Papes.* Paris, 1949.
Gasquet, Francis Aidan. *A Life of Pope Gregory the Great.* A critical edition of the *Vitae Papae Gregorii* written about the year 773 by a Benedictine monk of Whitby. Westminster, 1904.
Giaquinto, G. *Ricerche sull'istituto giuridico della canonizzazione dalle origini alle decretali di Gregorio IX.* Rome, 1947.
Gregorovius, Ferdinando. *Storia della città di Roma nel medioevo.* "Storia della città di Roma dall'anno 1355 al 1420", Vol. 12. Città di Castello, 1943.
Grisar, Hartmann. *Roma alla fine del Mondo Antico.* 2 vols. Rome, 1930.
———. *San Gregorio Magno.* Rome, 1904.
Grout, Donald J. *History of Western Music.* New York, 1960.
Guarducci, Margherita. *Le relique di Pietro sotto la Confessione della basilica vaticana.* Vatican City, 1965.
———. *La tradizione di Pietro in Vaticano alla luce della storia e dell'archeologia.* Vatican City, 1963.
Guerrazzi, Francesco. *Beatrice Cenci.* Milan, 1864.
Hermas. *Il Pastore di Erma: Traduzione dal greco di Pietro Baldoncini.* Vatican City, 1920.
Jedin, Hubert. *Storia del Concilio di Trento.* 2 vols. Brescia, 1949.
Jerome, Saint. *Select Letters of Saint Jerome.* With an English translation by F. A. Wright. New York, 1933.
Joergensen, J. S. *Francesco d'Assisi.* Copenhagen, 1900.
Kennedy, Charles W. *Early Christian Poetry.* New York, 1963.
Klauser, T. H. *Doctrina Duodecim Apostolorum.* Bonn, 1940.
Labande, L. H. *Le Palais des Papes et les monuments d'Avignon au XIV siècle.* Marseilles, 1925.
Lapôtre, A. *L'Europe et le Saint Siège a l'Epoque Carolingienne: Première Partie, Le Pape Jean VIII (872–882).* Paris, 1895.
Latourette, Kenneth Scott. *A History of Christianity.* New York, 1953.
Lauer, P. H. *Le Palais de Lateran.* Paris, 1811.
Léonard, Emile J. *Histoire de Jeanne Ire, reine de Naples, comtesse de Provence (1348–1382).* Monaco, 1932.
Lesne, F. *Les livres: "scriptoria" et bibliothèques du commencement du VIIe a la fin du XIe siècle.* Lille, 1938.
Lizérand, G. *Le dossier de l'affaire des Templaires.* Paris, 1923.
Marchetti Longhi, Giuseppe. *I Papareschi e i Romani.* 2 vols. Rome, 1947.
Menen, Aubrey. *Rome for Ourselves.* New York, Toronto, and London, 1960.
Mollat, G. *The Popes at Avignon, 1305–1378.* New York and Evanston, 1965.
Morison, Samuel Eliot. *Admiral of the Ocean Sea: A Life of Christopher Columbus.* Boston, 1942.
———, trans. and ed. *Journals and Other Documents on the Life and Voyages of Christopher Columbus.* New York, 1963.
Murat, Princesse Lucien. *La Reine Christine de Suède.* n.p., 1930.
Muratori, Antonio. *Il Cristianesimo felice nelle Missioni de' Padri della Compagnia di Gesù nel Paraguai.* Venice, 1752.
Parker, George B. *The English Traveller to Italy.* Vol. I: *The Middle Ages (to 1525).* Palo Alto, Calif., n.d.

Pastor, Ludwig von. *Storia dei Papi.* 20 vols. Rome, 1908–1934.
Perels, E. *Papst Nikolaus I und Anastasius Bibliothecarius.* Berlin, 1920.
Petruccelli della Gattina, F. *Histoire diplomatique des conclaves.* 4 vols. Paris, 1864–1865.
Picavet, E. *Gerbert un Pape philosophe.* Paris, 1897.
Pillement, Georges. *Pedro de Luna, le dernier Pape d'Avignon.* Paris, 1955.
Pius II (Piccolomini, Aeneas Sylvius). *Memoirs of a Renaissance Pope: The Commentaries of Pius II, an Abridgment.* Translated by Florence A. Gragg. Edited, with an introduction, by Leona C. Gabel. New York, 1962.
Ratti, Achille. *La fine di una leggenda ed altre spigolature intorno al "Liber Diurnus Romanorum Pontificum."* Pavia, 1913.
Rohault de Fleury, Georges. *Le Lateran au moyen age.* Paris, 1877.
Saba, Agostino. *Storia della Chiesa.* Vol. I: *Dalle origini al secolo VIII.* Vol. II: *Dal potere temporale dei papi a Bonifacio VIII.* Turin, 1938, 1940.
Savage, Henry. *The Love Letters of Henry VIII.* London, n.d.
Sayers, Dorothy L., ed. *The Song of Roland.* Baltimore, 1964.
Schuster, Ildefonso. *Storia di San Benedetto e dei suoi tempi.* Abbazia di Viboldone [S. Giuliano Milanese], 1953.
Silvagni, David. *La Corte e la Società Romana nei secoli XVIII e XIX.* 3 vols. Naples, 1967.
Spearing, E. *The Patrimony of the Roman Church in the Time of Gregory the Great.* Cambridge, 1918.
Stella, Aldo. *Chiesa e Stato nelle relazioni dei Nunzi Pontefici a Venezia.* Vatican City, 1964.
Taylor, Henry Osborn. *Thought and Expression in the Sixteenth Century.* Bk. I: *The Humanism of Italy.* New York, 1962.
Volpe, Gioacchino. *Movimenti religiosi e sette ereticali nella società medioevale italiana: secoli XI–XIV.* Milan, 1961.
———. *Il Medio Evo.* Florence, 1958.
Waddell, Helen. *The Desert Fathers.* Translations from the Latin with an Introduction. Ann Arbor, Mich., 1960.
Webb, J. F., trans. and ed. *Lives of the Saints: The Voyage of Saint Brendan; Bede: Life of Cuthbert; Eddius Stephanus: Life of Wilfred.* Baltimore, 1965.
Wilde, Lady. *Ancient Legends, Mystic Charms, and Superstitions of Ireland. To Which is Appended a Chapter on "The Ancient Races of Ireland," by the late Sir William Wilde.* 2 vols. Boston, 1887.

MONOGRAPHS AND ARTICLES

André-Michel, R. "Le procès des Visconti," in *Mélanges d'Archéologie et d'Histoire,* 11 (Paris, 1906), no. 26.
Arnaldi, Girolamo. "Giovanni Immonide e la cultura a Roma al tempo di Giovanni VIII," *Bollettino Ist. Stor. It.,* LXVIII (1956), 33–89.
Bongi, S. "Le prime gazette in Italia," *Nuova Antologia,* XI (1869).
Callahan, Daniel. "America's Catholic Bishops," *Atlantic Monthly* (April, 1967).
Caspar, E. "Studien zum Register Gregors VII," *Neues Archiv,* XXXVIII (1913) 143–226.
Dati, G. *Ottave sulle isole che ha recentemente scoperte il Re di Spagna.* Rome, 1891.
Dobschütz, E. von. *Das Decretum Gelasianum: De libris recipiendis et non recipiendis.* Text and analysis. Leipzig, 1912.
D'Onofrio, Cesare. "Gli Avvisi di Roma dal 1554 al 1605 conservati in biblioteche ed archivi romani". *Studi Romani,* 5 (1962).
Florin, M. "Innocenz III als Schriftsteller und als Papst," *Zeitschrift für Kirchen Geschichten,* 45 (1926), 344–358.

Funk, F. X. "Didachê," and "Martyrium Polycarpi," in *Patres Apostolici* (Tübingen, 1901).

Hertling, L. "Materiale per la storia del processo di canonizzazione," *Gregorianum* 16 (1955).

Kuh, Katharine. "The Circuitous Odyssey of Irish Art," *Saturday Review*, 23 March 1968.

Lapôtre, A. "Le Souper de Jean Diacre," in *Mélanges d'Archéologie et d'Histoire*, XXI (1901).

Sandri, Leopoldo. "Un prefetto dell'Archivio Vaticano, Michele Lonigo (1572–1639), e il suo processo," in *Studi in onore di Riccardo Filangieri* (Naples, 1959), II.

Sepulcri, A. "I Papiri della Basilica di Monza e le reliquie inviate da Roma," in *Archivio Storico Lombardo*, III (1903), fasc. XXXVIII.

Viard, J. "La messe pour la peste," in *Bibliothèque de l'Ecole des Chartes*, 61 (1900).

Villiers, Alan. "Prince Henry, the Explorer Who Stayed Home," *National Geographic* (Nov., 1960).

Index